LEADERSHIP

Sara Miller McCune founded SAGE Publishing in 1965 to support the dissemination of usable knowledge and educate a global community. SAGE publishes more than 1000 journals and over 800 new books each year, spanning a wide range of subject areas. Our growing selection of library products includes archives, data, case studies and video. SAGE remains majority owned by our founder and after her lifetime will become owned by a charitable trust that secures the company's continued independence.

Los Angeles | London | New Delhi | Singapore | Washington DC | Melbourne

Naveena Prakasam

LEADERSHIP

A Diverse, Inclusive and Critical Approach

Los Angeles | London | New Delhi
Singapore | Washington DC | Melbourne

Los Angeles | London | New Delhi
Singapore | Washington DC | Melbourne

SAGE Publishing Ltd
1 Oliver's Yard
55 City Road
London EC1Y 1SP

SAGE Publishing Inc.
2455 Teller Road
Thousand Oaks, California 91320

SAGE Publishing India Pvt Ltd
B 1/I 1 Mohan Cooperative Industrial Area
Mathura Road
New Delhi 110 044

SAGE Publishing Asia-Pacific Pte Ltd
3 Church Street
#10-04 Samsung Hub
Singapore 049483

Editor: Ruth Stitt
Editorial Assistant: Charlotte Hegley
Production editor: Sarah Cooke
Marketing manager: Lucia Sweet
Cover design: Francis Kenney
Typeset by: C&M Digitals (P) Ltd, Chennai, India
Printed in the UK

Library of Congress Control Number: 2022944463

British Library Cataloguing in Publication data

A catalogue record for this book is available from the British Library

ISBN 978-1-5297-6908-1
ISBN 978-1-5297-6907-4 (pbk)

At SAGE we take sustainability seriously. Most of our products are printed in the UK using responsibly sourced papers and boards. When we print overseas we ensure sustainable papers are used as measured by the PREPS grading system. We undertake an annual audit to monitor our sustainability.

CONTENTS

DETAILED CONTENTS

LIST OF CASE STUDIES

Chapter 2

Chapter 3

Chapter 4

Chapter 5

Chapter 6

Chapter 7

Chapter 8

Chapter 9

Chapter 10

Chapter 11

ABOUT THE EDITOR AND CONTRIBUTORS

About the Editor

Naveena Prakasam is a lecturer in Organisational Behaviour (OB) and Human Resource Management (HRM) at the Department of HRM and OB at Southampton Business School, University of Southampton. Naveena's primary area of research interest is leadership studies with a particular focus on authentic leadership, as well as critical and diverse approaches to leadership. Naveena is also interested in inclusion/exclusion in organisations. Her areas of research extend to the digital context in which she has investigated populist responses to leadership and inclusion/exclusion in digital media platforms. Naveena completed her PhD at Durham University Business School. Her doctoral work investigated authentic leadership and the notion of 'authentic performances', examining two supposedly opposing constructs – authenticity and impression management – in conjunction. This project cemented her interest in leadership.

About the contributors

Desireé Joy Cranfield is a Senior Lecturer within the School of Management at Swansea University, Wales. She has a PhD in Knowledge Management, Southampton University, UK, and an MSc in Data Communication Systems, Brunel, UK. Dr. Cranfield has completed a PGCert for teaching within Higher Education and is a Senior fellow of the Higher Education Academy (HEA). Her academic experience spans more than 20 years' experience, both within the UK and in South Africa, and she has undertaken several management roles within the Higher Education context. She is an HEA mentor and assessor within the university. Her research interests lie within the context of public sector organisations, and she is keenly interested in the adoption and use of technology within this context to enhance learning and teaching, as well as improve processes and practices. She is also keenly interested in how knowledge sharing takes place as part of knowledge management more broadly, and how creating opportunities for 'informal conversations' can be used as a technique to enhance practice.

Geraint Harvey is DANCAP Private Equity Chair in Human Organization and Professor of HRM at Western University, Ontario. Harvey's research has focused on the changing nature of work. Harvey has been commissioned to undertake research by a variety of international organisations and his findings have been published in a range of media.

Louisa Huxtable-Thomas is an Associate Professor in the School of Management, Swansea University, and leads on engagement and impact, as well as coordinating the Executive Education provision. Combining theories and empirical knowledge gleaned from the fields of business, social science, education and psychology, Louisa's research interests relate to how people's behaviours, either as leaders, entrepreneurs or policy makers have an influence on societal and economic welfare. Louisa had a varied early career, encompassing work in environmental consultancy, policy making at regional and local government level as well as business support and incubation. Louisa's doctoral research brought this prior knowledge together and identified the ways in which businesses can successfully participate in environmental policy making. Since then, Louisa has played a key role in supporting businesses through projects such as incubation, innovation and commercialisation as well as early-stage R&D, most recently focusing on the intersection between entrepreneurship and leadership.

Russ Huxtable is Head of Advisory and Strategy lead for ISARR, a well-established technology company that specialises in risk and resilience. As a thought leader for ISARR, he has written many articles on leadership in relation to organisational resilience and crisis management. Russ has a broad portfolio of practical leadership experience across several sectors. In the commercial environment, he specialised in supply chain leadership for companies operating in austere post-conflict countries. With over 30 years' military experience, Russ held several senior leadership roles within the Royal Air Force. During this time, he was also the UK's liaison officer within the Joint Staff at the US Pentagon and was seconded to both the UN and US Federal Emergency Management Agency to provide specialist planning advice. In the Higher Education sector, he has worked closely with academic colleagues in managing risk and developing resilience at the strategic level.

Carl Rhodes is Dean and Professor of Organization Studies at the University of Technology, Sydney Business School. Carl writes about the ethical and democratic dimensions of business and work. This work endeavours to question and reformulate the role of business in society so prosperity can be shared by all. Carl's most recent books are *Woke Capitalism: How Corporate Morality is Sabotaging Democracy* (Bristol University Press, 2022), *Organizing Corporeal Ethics* (Routledge, 2022, with Alison Pullen) and *Disturbing Business Ethics* (Routledge, 2020).

Andrea Tick is an associate professor at Óbuda University, in the Keleti Faculty of Business and Management. She completed her MA in English Language and Literature, Mathematics and Computer Sciences at the University of Szeged, her BSc in Economics in Budapest, and her PhD in Military Sciences in 2009. She has over 28 years' experience in teaching in Higher Education where she teaches statistics, data analytics and the Business Intelligence in ERP system. Her research interests include eLearning, user behaviour in the field of digital learning, cyber awareness, and the human factor in cyber security. She is a developer of several digital courses and is author and co-author of several research papers and books. She has respectable experience and practice in the field of blended and digital learning. During her career, she has developed several new solutions to enhance knowledge delivery. She is regularly invited to give guest lectures in European Higher Educational institutions.

Isabella Venter is a South African citizen, who obtained her doctoral degree from the University of Pretoria. She has held positions at the Council for Scientific and Industrial Research (CSIR), the Faculty of Military Science, Stellenbosch University, and the Business School of Stellenbosch University, before joining the Computer Science department at the University of the Western Cape. Until April 2017, she acted as Chairperson of the department and is currently the Chair of the Management Committee of the OpenServe/Aria Technology for Africa Centre of Excellence. She is a National Research Foundation rated researcher. Her research interests are computer science education, information communication technologies for development (ICT4D) and human computer interaction (HCI).

James Wallace is a lecturer within the Management, Employment and Organisation subject group at Cardiff Business School, Cardiff University, UK. His research interests include critical management and organisation studies, particularly issues such as power and identity in the workplace.

ACKNOWLEDGEMENTS

I would like to thank all the contributors of this textbook. I would also like to express my gratitude to everyone at SAGE Publishing for their continued support throughout this process, and the reviewers for their valuable feedback.

Chapter objectives

The objectives of this chapter are:

To provide a review and critique of early approaches to leadership which were predominantly trait focused.
To provide a review of leadership skills.
To critically evaluate leadership traits and skills in relation to practice.

Learning Objectives Each chapter begins with a handy checklist highlighting the key aims and content covered in the chapter.

Mini case study 2.3

Audre Lorde: a singularly plural leader

Audre Lorde was an American writer, feminist and civil rights activist who described herself as a 'Black feminist lesbian poet warrior mother'. She can be viewed as an example of a leader who resisted the status quo which during the time of **second wave feminism** in an America still largely concerned white women and did not accurately represent the points of view of Black women's feminist struggles. Audre Lorde was one of the pioneers of intersectional feminism who led activism through her poetry. For Lorde, gender oppression was inseparable from other forms of oppression, and her feminism is grounded in intersectionality which means that multiple forms of oppression such as 'sexism, racism, classism, transphobia and heterosexism' should be viewed in conjunction (Lieberman, n.d.: para 3). Audre Lorde was one of the founders of the Combahee River Collective which provided an opportunity for social activism for women of colour, many of whom had been excluded from political movements that were only able to deal with one form of oppression. The name came from Harriet Tubman's 1863 military raid on the Combahee River in South Carolina through which 750 enslaved people were freed. These members of the Collective were described as refugees of other organisations such as labour unions and anti-war groups which did not fully represent or advance their interests (Pullen, Rhodes, McEwen and Liu, 2019). Drawing on Fletcher (2004) and Carroll, Ford, and Taylor (2019) Pullen et al. (2019) argue that the movement offered a way to disrupt how we think about leadership by undermining the individualistic and heroic views of leadership which were entrenched in the trait focused views of leadership. In the case of the Collective as well as Lorde's work, solidarity is highlighted as a key feature of leadership. Audre Lorde's leadership is best noted in her resistance to categorisation by society.

Questions

1. What traits do you think made Lorde a good leader?
2. To what extent is leadership about the individual versus the group?

Mini Case Studies Each chapter includes mini case studies to help you link theory with practice, including examples from non-Western contexts. Related questions will test your understanding of important topics.

Student Exercises Student exercises throughout include thought-provoking activities related to the chapter topic.

Reflective Questions A range of questions provide a starting point for further discussion of important issues.

Decolonising Leadership Feature
This feature highlights relevant journal articles from non-Western contexts and scholars, which move beyond dominant, Western-centric and/or masculine perspectives of leadership.

Key Summaries Each chapter concludes with a summary of the main issues covered to consolidate what you have learned.

Further Reading At the end of each chapter, you will find a suggested list of books and journal articles to help you explore topics further.

ONLINE RESOURCES

Leadership: A Diverse, Inclusive and Critical Approach is accompanied by a range of online resources designed to support teaching. Instructors can visit study.sagepub.com/prakasam to access:

Teaching Guide includes reflective questions and case study teaching notes for each chapter.

PowerPoint slides including figures and tables from the book, which can be downloaded and customised for use in your own presentations.

SAGE Business Cases provide you with additional case studies linking to key themes in the book that you can use in tutorials.

PART 1
SETTING THE SCENE

1
INTRODUCTION

Naveena Prakasam

The aim of this textbook is to offer readers a comprehensive account and critique of leadership by presenting an inclusive, diverse, and critical approach to the field of leadership studies. Such an approach to leadership is important because leadership discourse has been dominated by Westernised and masculine notions of the concept, focused mainly on Western contexts (Bolden and Kirk, 2009; Ospina and Foldy, 2009; Ford, 2010; Edwards, 2015; Liu and Baker, 2016).

Reflective question

1. Why study leadership?

I want you to think about why studying leadership matters.

2. Is it due to an increased business or organisational performance that can be achieved through certain types of leadership?
3. Is it to help us manage crises such as the Coronavirus pandemic?

Think of at least two reasons why studying leadership matters. Make a note of these and revisit your notes at the end of this chapter.

The global context

The current state of leadership from a practical standpoint is disconcerting. For some time, there have been concerns raised by scholars due to the increase in corporate scandals; the financial crisis of 2008 was cited as one of the main reasons for studying leadership a decade ago, and was used as a basis to argue for further emphasis on ethics, authenticity, and for a new way to 'do leadership' (Walumbwa et al., 2008; Liu, 2010). Since then, subsequent global political trends have indicated an altered situation. Global shifts such as **Brexit**, **Trumpism** and the election of right-wing leaders in various parts of the world, reveal a critical juncture (Nkomo et al., 2019), and have implications for how people perceive leadership. Related to this, in the business context, the Cambridge Analytica scandal unveils questions over data safety, and Facebook's potential role in influencing the outcomes of both the 2016 US elections and the Brexit vote – indicating the depletion of individual freedoms, and the intensified surveillance that confronts us – resulting in our controlled, subjugated state, with questions arising over the leadership that perpetuates this. A critical juncture emphasising the importance of an inclusive perspective of leadership is the killing of George Floyd due to police brutality, which intensified the Black Lives Matter movement in early 2020, resulting in protests in the United States, as well as globally. These protests are an example of resistance to structures, processes, and prevailing systemic inequalities.

More recently, we have been confronted with the crisis of COVID-19. Questions about leadership therefore seem crucial as politicians are faced with tough decisions such as determining whether to close schools and how to contain the virus. Decisions about nationwide lockdowns have been challenging as they often encounter criticisms. Such crisis situations push us to reconsider the ways in which governments and leaders act in the frame of societal problems (Grint, 2020).

Understanding leadership – a note from the editor

Before delving further, I would like to provide readers with an overview of how my own understandings of leadership have evolved. When I started researching leadership a decade ago, I was not so much interested in the traits that leaders possessed, but more in how leadership was viewed by other people or the audience members. I was interested in the performance of leadership and the behind-the-scenes preparation for such performances, which include aspects like examining how leaders rehearsed their speeches and worked on their body language to deliver an authentic performance (Prakasam, 2014). My early understandings of the world of organisations, and individuals who were referred to as 'leaders' were shaped largely by a field that is widely known as 'symbolic interactionism' which can be defined as:

> the study and analysis of the developmental course of action that occurs when two or more persons (or agents) with agency (reflexivity) join their individual lines of action together into joint action. (Denzin, 2004: 81)

This led me to focus on the eye of the beholder, as well as interactions between individuals that produced leadership.

Moving beyond symbolic interactionism, I now lean towards critical understandings of leadership. Critical theorising of leadership questions standard leader-centric definitions of leadership and views power relations as central to the understanding of leadership (see Ford and Harding, 2011, 2018; Alvesson and Spicer, 2012; Alvesson and Kärreman, 2016). This is explored in further detail in the following section where I discuss the approach taken by this leadership textbook and give an overview of what each of the chapters cover. I start off by looking at what inclusive, diverse and critical mean, as these terms are integral to the approach taken.

What do diverse, inclusive and critical mean?

'Diverse', 'inclusive' and 'critical' can mean several things. I define what each term means in the context of the textbook.

Diverse

This textbook is aimed at recognising diverse views of leadership. By 'diverse', this textbook refers to the numerous different and wide-ranging perspectives of leadership. Leadership as a field is vast and is made up of multiple, sometimes competing perspectives of viewing leadership.

By diverse, I also refer to diversity in terms of people possessing different biological and demographic characteristics as well as identities. Most leadership theorising within leadership studies occurred in Western contexts, which means that leadership is therefore dominated by Western notions of what leadership should be. Additionally, it has also been dominated by focusing on men as examples of great leaders, resulting in early theorising of leadership having a masculine focus.

To exemplify what diverse means, let us look at an example pertaining to race. Greedharry, Ahonen and Tienari (2020) provide a comprehensive overview and critique of the conceptualisation of race and identity in organisations. They argue that race continues to be under researched in the field of organisation and management studies, and that most of the studies of race in the field continue to be limited to the fields of cross-cultural management, diversity management and inclusion. Greedharry et al. (2020) call for the study of race as an organising principle which considers how structures and processes of organisations contribute to the construction of racialisation – what this means is that instead of seeing race simply as an identifier that affects certain groups of people, and studying the management of such racialised individuals, the study of race should look at organisational and management practices that contribute to such racialisation. Building on this point, in the context of this leadership textbook, diverse does not just mean diverse contexts, or perspectives, but a critical examining of such approaches in relation to leadership studies. The intention of this leadership textbook is, then, to use a diverse, inclusive and critical approach throughout, and not to just confine such approaches to diversity management.

Inclusive

It is worth noting that inclusive approaches to leadership are not new. Adapa and Sheridan (2018) in their edited collection offer inclusive leadership to challenge existing stereotypes of masculinity and agency. Their edited volume *Inclusive Leadership: Negotiating Gendered Spaces* consists of research contributions from various scholars. One of these contributions includes a study of a biracial Australian-Chinese woman CEO resisting the powers embedded in masculine and white notions of leadership. This chapter is written by Helena Liu, and this analysis is based on a framework from Black feminist thought offered by Patricia Hill Collins. Liu's (2018) chapter offers a contribution to inclusive leadership by shedding light on the experiences of how a non-white woman CEO 'does' leadership. Moreover, Liu utilises a framework from Black feminism, adopting inclusivity in the theorising of leadership, which departs from the normative theorising of leadership. Hence, her approach is inclusive both in terms of being about an individual who resists the stereotypical, **heteronormative** descriptions of a leader and in terms of its theorising, using a perspective that is not embedded in traditional and dominant perspectives of leadership – offering something different – resisting these descriptions.

An 'inclusive' perspective refers to the inclusion of individuals with diverse characteristics and how they might understand or engage with leadership. This book aims to recognise that leadership must not continue to be understood within the frame of reference of certain groups of people with certain demographic characteristics (Western, white, male). However, leadership is not just about individuals. By 'inclusive', this textbook refers to including approaches to leadership that promote inclusion, but also refers to theorising leadership in an inclusive way – this means not leaving out leadership perspectives that offer something different or non-mainstream – challenging our ideas about leadership.

Critical

This book adopts a critical view of leadership studies. By this, I mean that the book will offer a critique of mainstream theorising of leadership and engage with critical perspectives. Broadly speaking, critical assumptions of leadership focus on how power relations shape leadership (Alvesson and Spicer, 2012). A combination of both critical and diverse approaches can be understood through readings of critical diversity studies. In fact, as Nkomo et al. (2019) argue, a binary distinction can be made between mainstream approaches, and critical approaches to diversity in the workplace, and there is also a difference between individual and structural explanations for inequality. For instance, critical diversity scholars argue that the business case approach to diversity (the idea that diversity is good for business) would detract from a focus on inequality experienced by disadvantaged groups, which is caused by systemic exclusion in organisations (Linnehan and Konrad, 1999; Noon, 2007; Zanoni et al., 2010). From a critical diversity studies perspective, Ahonen et al. (2014) question the way diversity work is done by diversity researchers who create categories whilst doing so – such categorisation is critically examined and questioned; classifying and categorising based on biological characteristics are seen as being embedded in hidden power relations, and this is viewed as biopolitical and governmental. Biopolitics and **governmentality** are terms introduced by Michel Foucault, a French philosopher. Biopolitics refers to political practices and processes seeking to control entire populations through administration with the aim of putting life in order (Foucault, 1998). Governmentality broadly refers to activities intended on controlling the conduct of people. Both of these ideas of Foucault are ultimately about subtle forms of power. By examining such hidden power relations prevalent in doing diversity research, Ahonen et al. (2014) offer a critical approach to diversity.

Therefore, it is not only important to approach diversity in terms of standard, normative definitions, but to also take a critical approach to the mainstream theorising of diversity itself.

Paradigms

We all view the world differently – this is also the case for researchers. Before we begin tracing the development of leadership studies in this textbook, it is essential to view the different lenses through which leadership may be viewed. In order to understand this, it is important to explore the concept of a **paradigm**. There are diverse, and sometimes contradictory, views of paradigms. Paradigms may simply be referred to as approaches or a set of assumptions that researchers have. For instance, let us consider how we might want to investigate a particular research topic. If we were to examine 'happiness' amidst a group of factory workers, there are various ways in which we could go about researching this – how we would go about this would depend on the way the question was to be framed. If we were to use an existing definition of happiness and a corresponding standardised measure for it such as The Oxford Happiness Questionnaire, we could ask factory workers to fill this in, and we would then have insight into the happiness levels of these workers. This refers to a stable and fixed idea of happiness, with the questionnaire containing several statements for which respondents must pick from 'strongly agree' to 'strongly disagree'. On the other hand, if we wanted to know how people understand happiness, we might have open - ended questions about this, or talk to people about their ideas of happiness. These two ways of going about the study of happiness would fit within different sets of assumptions, and as a result, different paradigms. If we were to apply the same logic to understanding 'leadership', we would find that there are myriad definitions of leadership. The different paradigms are explained in further detail below.

Thomas Kuhn came up with the term *paradigm* to refer to a set of assumptions that scientists have about the natural world, and these assumptions are taken for granted to be correct (Kuhn, 1970). These paradigms then shape the research that is carried out (Chapman et al., 2005). Gibson Burrell and Gareth Morgan wrote a textbook titled *Sociological Paradigms and Organisational Analysis* in 1979 which is widely referenced by organisational theorists. Their classification of paradigms included: functionalism; interpretivism; radical structuralism; and radical humanism.

John Hassard's paper titled 'Multiple paradigms and organisational analysis' (1991) consisted of a case study which adopted Burrell and Morgan's (1979) four paradigms to provide a multiple paradigm study. Functionalism relates to scientific method, and research within this paradigm would use quantifiable measures such as questionnaires to research leadership. Alvesson and Spicer (2012) classify three main strands of leadership studies whilst offering a critical theorising of leadership: functionalist, interpretive and critical assumptions. These paradigms, or underlying assumptions, provide a useful classification system of leadership studies. Let us look at what each paradigm means.

Functionalism assumes that leadership is a 'fairly stable object that exists out there in the world' (Alvesson and Spicer, 2012: 370). Some of the approaches to leadership within functionalism include: trait-focused approaches which look to identify the traits that make up leadership (House and Aditya, 1997); task-centric and people- centric approaches (House and Aditya, 1997); contingency approaches, popularised by Fiedler (1967), which look at situations in which leadership takes place;

transformational style of leadership focused on visions (Bass, 1985; Bennis and Nanus, 1985; Sashkin, 2004; Hartnell and Walumbwa, 2011); and follower-centred approaches (Hollander, 1992; Bligh, 2011). Alvesson and Spicer point out that while these approaches differ in terms of the variables they focus on, they all share the same underlying assumptions of functionalism which view leadership as a measurable object that can be investigated and analysed using scientific analytical tools (2012: 370–371).

Interpretivism in the leadership context is concerned with viewing leadership as socially constructed. Researchers are interested in how the idea of leadership is constructed by various individuals through interactions. Within this paradigm, studies of leadership are based on qualitative methods such as interviews or observation. Within interpretive assumptions, Alvesson and Spicer (2012) outline four approaches. The first approach includes symbolic leadership where the framing of the reality of others is the focus. Smircich and Morgan's (1982) seminal work on leadership as a management of meaning exemplifies this approach where 'leadership is realised in the process whereby one or more individuals succeed in attempting to frame and define the reality of others' (Smircich and Morgan, 1982: 258). The second approach looks at the processes of social construction (Uhl-Bien, 2006; Fairhurst and Grant, 2010). The third approach focuses on the use of language and how and when the term 'leadership' may be used (Pondy, 1978; Kelly, 2008). The fourth approach focuses on clashes in terms of the construction and language used to understand and interpret leadership (Alvesson and Spicer, 2012). While interpretive assumptions explore meanings that individuals assign to leadership, Alvesson and Spicer point to three limitations of interpretive assumptions. First, the accounts of leadership by various respondents are taken for granted. Second, interpretive studies do not look into power and domination, and ignore the 'unequal' leadership dynamics that are prevalent in society and organisations (2012: 371–372). Third, social structures that create situations which lend themselves to some individuals being leaders, and others being followers, are not explored critically.

Critical assumptions move one further step beyond interpretive assumptions. Interpretive assumptions focus on meanings and the various interpretations of leadership. Critical scholars of leadership are also interested in interpretive assumptions. However, in addition to interpretive assumptions, critical scholars focus on how power relations and ideological assumptions underpinning institutions shape leadership understandings. Hassard and Wolfram Cox (2013) write about **post-structuralism** and **postmodernism**, which have begun to influence organisational research. Such approaches fall within critical assumptions. In the leadership context, critical scholars are interested in patterns of power and domination, as well as gendered notions of leadership using feminist perspectives (Alvesson and Spicer, 2012). Hence, within leadership research, functionalism, interpretivism and critical assumptions form a useful classification of the way in which leadership is approached.

Returning to the Burrell and Morgan classification, while we have examined functionalism and interpretivism – as Hassard and Wolfram Cox (2013) point out – organisation studies have changed significantly since that classification, and there has been a rise in post-structuralism influenced hugely by Michel Foucault. This falls within the critical assumptions that I have just discussed.

Overview of chapters

Beginning with the evolution of leadership approaches, this edited textbook explores the different facets and wide-ranging approaches to leadership.

Chapter 2 traces the development of leadership by reviewing early approaches to leadership that were predominantly trait focused and entrenched in this idea that leaders are born. The trait-focused approach to leadership studies is explored and critically reviewed. Charismatic leadership is explored given that charisma is viewed as a trait, and a critique of charismatic leadership is provided. The chapter then moves on to discussing leadership skills, embedded in the notion that leadership may be learnt. The second mini case study is a fictional account set in the context of Higher Education.

In Chapter 3, departing from the previous chapter, readers will be introduced to styles of leadership, starting with some early and mostly positivist conceptualisations. The styles of leadership such as charismatic, transformational and authentic will be reviewed and critically examined. Charismatic leadership will be revisited, as charisma is both a trait and a dominant style of leadership. The chapter also provides an overview of the leader versus management debate.

Chapter 4 focuses on the social construction of leadership and begins by defining social constructionism in the leadership context (see Fairhurst and Grant, 2010). The four dimensions within the social construction of leadership are discussed. Theories including the romance of leadership (Meindl, 1995) and implicit leadership theories (Eden and Leviatan, 1975; Rush et al., 1977) are discussed and critically reviewed. Authentic leadership is seen through a social constructionist lens and followership approaches are critically reviewed.

Chapter 5 focuses on relational leadership. The two perspectives within relational leadership, entity and relational, are reviewed. Theories reviewed include leader-member exchange, charismatic relationship, and network theories. A social constructionist approach to empathic leadership practice is reviewed. An indigenous

Māori perspective to relational leadership is explored, and dimensions of collective leadership are discussed.

In Chapter 6, entrepreneurial leadership is explored critically in the context of unpredictable global change and crisis. The chapter considers the context of 'crisis' from a critical contemporary perspective on entrepreneurship, and in considering the role of leadership in 'intrapreneurship'.

Chapter 7, 'Power and the dark side of leadership', begins by exploring the different understandings of power and reviews the field of critical leadership studies. We then discuss the dark side of leadership which includes normative perspectives, such as the toxic triangle.

Chapter 8, 'Leadership, ethics and strategic HRM', looks at the leadership of strategic human resource management (SHRM) and questions the ethics of such leadership. The chapter provides a critical take on the 'hard' versus 'soft' approaches to SHRM and offers an alternative perspective on ethical leadership in its relation to people management.

Chapter 9, 'Leadership and the digital age', explores leadership in the digital age which is more pressing than ever given that COVID-19 has forced workplaces to embrace digital ways of working. The role of the leader and the implications for leadership within an ever-increasing interconnected world, underpin the narrative.

In Chapter 10, 'Datafication, surveillance and leadership', the implications for leadership in the age of increased surveillance and datafication are explored. The anxieties and obscurities surrounding contemporary leadership are examined, followed by a consideration of the increased surveillance-laden context we inhabit. Leadership and power are scrutinised in relation to their potential implications.

In Chapter 11, the domination of Western, white, and masculine-centric approaches to leadership are critiqued while examining the gendering and racialisation of leadership and exploring issues pertaining to exclusion and inclusion in leadership. The chapter reviews feminist phenomenology, intersectionality and postcolonial and decolonial approaches to leadership.

The concluding remarks are presented in Chapter 12, which ties together all the chapters and contains personal reflections and lessons.

──Reflective question revisited──

At the start of this chapter, you were asked to make a note of at least two reasons why studying leadership matters.

1. Are your reasons still the same or have they changed? Think about why this might be the case.

2
EVOLUTION OF LEADERSHIP THEORIES 1: TRAITS AND SKILLS

Naveena Prakasam

Chapter objectives

The objectives of this chapter are:

- To provide a review and critique of early approaches to leadership which were predominantly trait focused.
- To provide a review of leadership skills.
- To critically evaluate leadership traits and skills in relation to practice.

Introduction

The goal of this chapter is to examine how understandings of leadership have evolved, ranging from largely trait-based approaches to further ways of understanding leadership which emphasise aspects that can be learnt, such as skills. While leadership styles can also be learnt, we focus on leadership styles in Chapter 3 of this textbook. We begin this chapter with an overview of early theories that were ingrained in the trait approach, which placed a strong emphasis on individuals being born with certain types of leadership abilities. This chapter then moves on to looking at leadership from a different philosophical perspective: **tabula rasa** – the idea that individuals are born with a blank state. This is based on Locke's

(2000) idea of 'epistemic innocence', using the metaphor of a child as a privileged vessel (Rekret, 2018: 26). We then arrive at skills-based perspectives on leadership, which are embedded in the notion that leadership may be 'learnt'.

The terms 'traits' and 'characteristics' are often used interchangeably in the leadership literature. According to *Dictionary.com*, a trait refers to 'a distinguishing characteristic or quality, especially of one's personal nature' and a characteristic is defined as 'a distinguishing feature or quality'. Given the similarity in definitions, for the purposes of this chapter, traits and characteristics are seen as being the same thing. Other terms used to refer to traits include 'attributes' and 'qualities' (Zaccaro, Kemp and Bader, 2004: 101–124), which you might come across in several leadership texts.

Great Man Theory and other early approaches

One of the earliest approaches to studying leadership was based on traits that 'great men' possessed. The '**Great Man Theory**' as it came to be known, refers to an understanding of leadership based on the traits and characteristics that a few great men possessed. These men had reached great positions of responsibility, and it was Carlyle who proposed this theory in 1866 (Schedlitzki and Edwards, 2014). Carlyle's 'fascination with great men of history effectively reduced the role of mere mortals to extras' (Grint, 2011: 8).

As Bratton (2020) points out, such an approach to studying great male leaders came from nineteenth-century Britain and was based on Anglo-Saxon values. Bratton describes such a view of leadership as 'elitist, sexist, misogynous, xenophobic, and racist' (2020: 23). Approaches that focused solely on the successes of White male leaders can be viewed as exclusionary. However, such exclusionary views went unquestioned in the past, particularly in the colonial era. Conquests of places, and the heroism demonstrated through those conquests, were seen in a positive light, and the individuals leading such conquests were seen as great leaders.

Winston Churchill appears in numerous texts, and popular culture references, and is frequently referred to as a great leader due to his achievements in World War Two. However, there have been indications of Churchill's racist beliefs. A BBC article by Tom Heydon refers to Churchill's problematic and racist views where he believed that white men were superior to non-white men (Heydon, 2015). Many have defended Churchill's views by suggesting that such views were common during Edwardian times. Despite this issue, Churchill continues to be glorified, which contributes not just to the perpetuation of 'Great Man Theory', but by implicitly suggesting that individuals are great leaders despite the evidence of their racist beliefs, this presents a danger that such prejudiced beliefs become less obvious. As a result, they may become tacitly accepted.

When a form of prejudiced belief is not seen as problematic, notions of what makes a good leader automatically become exclusionary.

The film *The Wolf of Wall Street* portrayed the rampant sexism and deplorable behaviour of male stockbrokers, presenting Wall Street as a perverse world. It portrays how darker traits, such as greed and narcissism, were associated with success in stockbroking. A culture rife with toxic masculinity was portrayed in the film, which presents an opportunity for us to think critically about leadership traits and their outcomes. For instance, it is interesting to think about whether negative traits may be linked to positive outcomes. Adopting a critical approach to trait perspectives is useful from a practice perspective, as unacknowledged assumptions about traits might limit their growth and practice as a leader. To that end, Judge, Piccolo and Kosalka (2009) examine both the brighter and darker sides of leadership traits, which we explore later.

A redeeming feature of the use of Great Man Theory from the perspective of diversity and inclusion is the theory's subsequent usage since Carlyle's initial proposal. Great Man Theory has been used to consider individuals who were not just male, white or predominantly European, but has been applied to men and women from different parts of the world. Exemplifying this point, Harrison highlights that 'The lives and achievements of political leaders such as Napoleon Bonaparte, Indira Gandhi, Martin Luther King, and others' (2018: 17) have been examined to differentiate leaders from non-leaders. The list of leaders mentioned in this example includes individuals from diverse countries and races, and includes both men and women. Hence, it is useful to consider whether such an approach to leadership may still be useful when it is not limited to leaders of a specific gender, nationality, or race, as was the case in Victorian times.

Drawing on Shamir et al. (2005), Taylor (2019) suggests that the essence of Great Man Theory's contribution lies in considering leaders' histories and biographies. Taylor (2019) argues that it may be possible to learn from the histories and biographies of these leaders which tell us about the various life events that may have shaped their leadership traits and skills (Taylor, 2019). Considering the limitations of Great Man Theory being exclusionary, and the value in understanding leaders' life histories further, the first mini case study in this chapter explores some aspects of the life of Audre Lorde, a renowned feminist.

Mini case study 2.1

Audre Lorde, biography and traits

Audre Lorde was an American writer, feminist and civil rights activist who described herself as a 'Black feminist lesbian poet warrior mother'. She can be viewed as an example of a leader who resisted the status quo which, during the time of **second wave feminism** in America, still largely concerned white women and did not accurately represent the points of view of Black women's feminist struggles. Audre Lorde was one of the pioneers of intersectional feminism who led activism through her poetry. For Lorde, gender oppression was inseparable from other forms of oppression, and her feminism is grounded in intersectionality which means that multiple forms of oppression such as 'sexism, racism, classism, transphobia and heterosexism' should be viewed in conjunction (Lieberman, n.d.: para 3). Audre Lorde was one of the founders of the Combahee River Collective which provided an opportunity for social activism for women of colour, many of whom had been excluded from political movements that were only able to deal with one form of oppression. The name came from Harriet Tubman's 1863 military raid on the Combahee River in South Carolina through which 750 enslaved people were freed. These members of the Collective were described as refugees of other organisations such as labour unions and anti-war groups which did not fully represent or advance their interests (Pullen, Rhodes, McEwen and Liu, 2019). Drawing on Fletcher (2004) and Carroll, Ford, and Taylor (2019), Pullen et al. (2019) argue that the movement offered a way to disrupt how we think about leadership by undermining the individualistic and heroic views of leadership which were entrenched in the trait-focused views of leadership. In the case of the Collective as well as Lorde's work, solidarity is highlighted as a key feature of leadership. Audre Lorde's leadership is best noted in her resistance to categorisation by society.

Questions

1. What traits do you think made Lorde a good leader?
2. To what extent is leadership about the individual versus the group?

Psychology-based studies on traits

There are several different definitions of traits that come from the discipline of psychology. Let us begin by considering a few definitions. According to Allport (1961), a trait is a 'neuropsychic structure having the capacity to render many stimuli functionally equivalent, and to initiate and guide equivalent (meaningfully consistent) forms of adaptive and expressive behaviour' (Allport, 1961: 347). This definition by Allport indicates that traits are immune to situational factors (Zaccaro et al., 2004). Therefore, it might be useful to consider what such an understanding of leadership would have on nurturing a team.

Zaccaro, Kemp and Bader define leader traits as 'relatively coherent and integrated patterns of personal characteristics, reflecting a range of individual differences, that foster consistent leadership effectiveness across a variety of group and organizational situations' (2004: 104).

Another definition of a trait by Buchanan and Huczynski includes 'a relatively stable quality or attribute of an individual's personality, influencing behaviour in a particular direction' (2017: 183).

Much of the leadership research on traits comes from the discipline of psychology. One of the earliest analyses of leadership comes from Galton's (1869) theory of hereditary genius which includes two main ideas that have shaped popular understandings of leadership. First, genius is seen as a 'unique property of extraordinary individuals' and, second, the 'unique attributes of such individuals in relation to their inherited genetic makeup' (Zaccaro, 2007: 6) are stressed. Galton (1869) emphasised the idea that traits were inherited, and even went as far as proposing 'eugenics', or selective mating to produce the best leaders. There are ethical issues with such an approach to looking for desirable traits in leaders as it implies that individuals who do not come from a lineage of a desirable genetic makeup will not be able to go on to be a leader. Lindebaum and Zundel's (2013) critique of a neuroscientific approach offers a pressing ethical issue for us to consider. The implications of a neuroscientific approach to leadership, which uses brain scans to screen potential individuals for jobs, might be that some people do not make it through the initial screenings during recruitment if they are deemed undesirable and unfit for the job. Therefore, such approaches are exclusionary and have ethical implications that need to be refuted, as done by Lindebaum and Zundel (2013).

Early writings on traits until the first half of the twentieth century investigated differentiating leaders from non-leaders. Such research in American psychology was embedded in functionalism, laying emphasis on 'typical operations of consciousness under actual conditions' (Angell, 1907: 61; Zaccaro et al., 2004: 104). As explained in Chapter 1, functionalism is a methodological paradigm which assumes that leadership is measurable.

Early reviews of the trait literature by Gibb (1947), Jenkins (1947) and Stogdill (1948) examined several studies in which leader effectiveness and traits were associated. However, the findings of these studies were rarely replicated in multiple studies, and as a result, scholars at the time thought that there were few universal traits that were associated with 'effective leadership', which led to an abandonment of the search for universal traits by some scholars. Stogdill however did not call for such an abandonment, but instead called for an investigation of the interactional effects of traits with various situational demands that leaders faced (House and Aditya, 1997: 410).

A review of the studies carried out by Stogdill (1948), Jenkins (1947) and Bird (1940) summarised the six primary approaches to studying traits which include: 'observation of behavior in group situations that afforded leader emergence; sociometric choices by peers; nominations by qualified observers and raters; selection of individuals into leadership positions; analysis of biographical data and case histories of leaders and non-leaders; and interviews with business executives and professionals to specify leader characteristics' (Stogdill, 1948: 36–38 in Zaccaro et al., 2004: 105).

Stogdill's (1948) study on leader traits, in which he analysed 124 studies on leader traits between 1904 and 1947, was a turning point for the field. He came up with eight traits that differentiated leaders from non-leaders, including: 'Intelligence; Alertness to the needs of others; Insight; Initiative; Responsibility; Persistence in dealing with problems; Self-confidence; Sociability' (Harrison, 2018: 19). Whilst putting forward the eight traits, he nevertheless emphasised the importance of considering situational variables. The early approaches to trait-based studies had methodological issues which included limited data, biases and errors. As a result of Stogdill's critique of trait approaches to leadership, researchers started to view leader trait models less favourably, and as unable to explain leadership emergence and effectiveness (Zaccaro et al., 2004). However, Carroll, Ford and Taylor (2019) argue that although the abandonment of the trait theory of leadership is credited to Stogdill's (1948) review, this is not the complete picture. According to archival research, Shartle, who was Stogdill's boss, had already started focusing on leader behaviours three years prior to the publication of Stogdill's critical review.

Before we explore the literature on leader traits further, let us examine the Big Five dimensions that laid the foundation of several trait-based studies on leadership, which was developed in the 1980s, coinciding with the resurgence of the trait approach to leadership (House and Aditya, 1997; Zaccaro, 2007).

Big Five dimensions

The Big Five are trait clusters that capture the main dimensions of personality (Buchanan and Huczynski, 2017). These clusters are extraversion, conscientiousness, neuroticism, openness and agreeableness. The first letters spell out OCEAN. The Big Five within personality research have become an organising structure, and a reasonable measurement approach within leadership (Judge, Piccolo and Kosalka, 2009).

According to Buchanan and Huczynski, openness to experience runs on a continuum from 'explorer' at one extreme to 'preserver' at the other, where explorers are suited to professions such as architects and entrepreneurs who may be open to new ideas and doing things differently. Preservers, on the other side of the spectrum, are associated with professions such as finance managers, stage performers and project managers (2017: 192).

Conscientiousness refers to the extent to which an individual is responsible, organised, dependable and persistent (Robbins and Judge, 2016). An individual in a leadership position who is conscientious would display behaviours that indicate higher levels of responsibility.

Extraversion refers to the extent to which individuals are sociable, assertive, and comfortable in relationships. A *Harvard Business Review* article by Gino (2015) highlights that extroverted leaders were more effective in teams whose team members were introverts but when team members are more proactive, and take matters into their own hands, it is introverted leaders that were seen as more effective. This study by Gino indicates that scoring high on extraversion does not automatically lead to better leadership, as factors such as the complexity of team dynamics and individual differences between teams would affect trait clusters, which leads us back to the issue prevalent in trait-focused studies of leadership, that they are predominantly individual centric.

Agreeableness encompasses traits such as trust, straightforwardness, altruism, compliance and modesty.

Neuroticism refers to 'negative emotionality' which encompasses 'worry, anger, discouragement, self-consciousness, impulsiveness, vulnerability' (Buchanan and Huczynski, 2017: 193). Those that score high on neuroticism are reactive or emotional, but this is seen as being useful for some professions such as social scientists, academics, or customer service professionals.

Shahzad, Raja and Hashmi (2020) found support for the trait theory of leadership in which they found that extraversion, conscientiousness, and openness to experience were positively related to authentic leadership, and neuroticism was negatively linked to it. This study, along with several others, has linked the Big Five dimensions to various leadership styles. Felfe and Schyns (2010) found that if people perceived you to be high in emotional stability, openness, agreeableness and extraversion, they would attribute you with transformational leadership. Therefore, it is interesting to note such empirically justified relationships between leader traits and styles.

Judge, Bono, Ilies and Gerhardt (2002) carried out a meta-analysis and found that the Big Five trait clusters together were related to **leader emergence** as well as **leader effectiveness**. 'Leader emergence' refers to the extent to which an individual is recognised as a leader in a group and 'leader effectiveness' is the extent to which one performs well in that role of a 'leader' (Judge, Piccolo and Kosalka, 2009: 856). In response to this meta-analysis, an important criticism of the five-factor model came from Kaiser, Hogan and Craig (2008) who argued that how leaders are regarded (or perceived) tells us little about leading effective teams or about how these traits lead to organisational outcomes. Supporting this, Morgeson, Campion, Dipboye, Hollenbeck, Murphy and Schmitt (2007) argue that a distinction needs to be made between perceived influence and organisational effectiveness. Perceived influence of leader traits on organisational effectiveness refers to the subjective evaluations of individuals and how well those individuals consider the leader traits to influence organi-sational outcomes. The distinction between perceived influence and actual organisational outcomes is an important one, especially in functionalist studies of leadership that rely on quantitative measures and largely view leadership as a stable object (Alvesson and Spicer, 2012).

Morgeson et al. (2007) provide a critique of personality measures and argue that the use of self-report personality measures should be reconsidered in organisational scenarios such as personnel selection, given the very low **validity** of personality tests for predicting job performance. Responding to the criticism, Ones, Dilchert, Viswesvaran and Judge (2007) point out that personality tests measured by self-reporting have substantial validities, and that faking does not ruin the validity. Colbert, Judge, Choi and Wang (2012) argued that self-ratings of personality may underestimate the relationship between leadership and personality, and carried out a study on all five personality variables and used both self and observer ratings. They found that extraversion was most strongly related to leadership through both self and observer ratings, and argue that the five-factor model reveals more consistent rela-tions between traits and various outcomes.

Critique and resurgence

Zaccaro (2007) puts forward four points in his critical review of the trait approach that models and theories of traits need to consider. First, Zaccaro points out the absence of a coherent and meaningful conceptual construction of leader attributes and traits. Frameworks of leadership traits need to be comprehensive, and not just focus on a small number of individual differences that predict leadership given the complexity of leadership. Second, trait studies do not examine the integration of leader attributes. Failure to do so leads to a limited understanding of the complex relationships between a combination of different attributes and outcomes. The third critical point involves considering the 'situation' as individuals with certain traits may be leaders in one situation but not all situations. The most prominent work carried out on considering situations is Fiedler's contingency model which considers the combination of leader styles and situations (see Fiedler, 1964). Fourth, 'trait perspectives of leadership need to consider how leader attributes may differ in their sensitivity to situational factors and their proximity, in cause, to leadership behavior' (Zaccaro, 2007: 7). This means that it is not sufficient to consider situations alone as factors that might affect leader behaviours, but one must also consider how situational factors may interact differently with leader traits due to certain attributes' sensitivity to factors. Dinh and Lord (2012) similarly argue for the importance of moving beyond stable traits and into more event-level analysis of traits which considers situational factors.

In their special issue editorial titled 'Leadership and individual differences: At the cusp of a renaissance', Antonakis, Day and Schyns (2012) emphasise the importance of the trait approach since its renewal. One of the papers in this special issue by Zaccaro (2012), 'Individual differences and leadership: Contributions to a third tipping point', highlights the tipping points in leadership research and individual differences. The first tipping point encompasses the early reviews of trait research by Stogdill (1948) mentioned earlier in this chapter. In the aftermath of Stogdill's (1948) review, there was a dearth of leadership research on individual differences, moving more towards studies on situational factors. This may even be explained by the shift towards behavioural approaches to leadership even prior to Stogdill's review (Taylor, 2019). However, scholars (see House and Baetz, 1979; Lord, De Vader and Alliger, 1986; Zaccaro et al., 2004; Day and Zaccaro, 2007) have suggested that this unpopularity of traits and individual differences was misguided and unwarranted. This resulted in most textbooks published after that period negating the importance of traits (e.g., Ghiselli and Brown, 1955; Blum and Naylor, 1956; Secord and Backman, 1974; Muchinsky, 1983; Baron and Byrne, 1987).

The second tipping point encompasses three aspects according to Zaccaro (2012). The first includes the publication of several meta-analyses that provided support to traits (e.g., Lord et al., 1986; Judge, Bono, Ilies and Gerhardt, 2002; Judge, Colbert and Ilies, 2004; Derue, Nahrgang, Wellman and Humphrey, 2011; Hoffman, Woehr, Maldagen-Youngjohn and Lyons, 2011). The second aspect concerns the focus on the inspirational influence of leaders, and focusing on the extraordinary qualities of leaders (e.g., House, 1977; Burns, 1978; Bass, 1985; Conger and Kanungo, 1987). A subsequent section in Zaccaro's paper examines charismatic leadership. The third aspect includes the focus on perceptions of leader traits that involved follower ratings, which includes leader categorisation theory, proposed by Robert Lord. Zaccaro (2012) points to the emergence of a third tipping point within the trait-based approaches to leadership and makes a strong case for such approaches. These include complex multivariate analyses of leader traits which is moving a step further from linear and bivariate analyses. An example of the multivariate approach includes a study by Foti, Bray, Thompson and Allgood (2012) which examined 'sensitivity, intelligence, and dedication, and one "anti-prototypic" trait of tyranny' (Zaccaro, 2012: 723).

In a subsequent comprehensive review of individual differences in leadership, Zaccaro, Green, Dubrow and Kolze (2018) point to a proliferation of studies on individual differences and underline the importance of considering the context and other situational characteristics in relation to leader traits.

Implicit leadership theory and leadership categorisation

Eden and Leviatan (1975) came up with leadership categorisation theory which laid emphasis on the perception of leader traits (by followers) as well as behavioural ratings of leaders. This was based on followers or viewers' ratings, as well as classifications between leaders and non-leaders. These categorisations are guided by **implicit leadership theories** (ILTs) which are unconscious mental representations of leaders that followers have which help them distinguish leaders from non-leaders (Shondrick and Lord, 2010; Shondrick, Dinh and Lord, 2010). The birth of leadership categorisation and implicit leadership theories marked a turn in leadership theorising, as the emphasis started to shift towards perceptions of the observer or follower, and laid emphasis on how followers viewed leaders. According to leadership categorisation theory, recognising someone as a leader depends on whether there is a match between the target individual's (leader's) features and the follower's mental representation of a leader. These mental representations are known as prototypes (Lord, Foti and De Vader, 1984; Shondrick and Lord, 2010).

Student exercise

This exercise is based on the use of a drawing exercise to teach students about implicit leadership theories proposed by Schyns, Kiefer, Kerschreiter and Tymon (2011). They point out that teaching ILTs raises awareness of the social context and one's own implicit leadership theories, and as a result develops leaders and leadership. First, take 10 minutes to think about what makes a good leader on your own. Second, in small groups, interview each other and discuss which points you agree and disagree on. Then, in your small groups, draw a leader. The third and final stage involves a presentation of each drawing to the class as well as examining the similarities and differences between the drawings.

Charismatic leadership

Charismatic leadership can be associated with trait-based research on leadership as well as research that focuses on follower perceptions (Conger and Kanungo, 1987, 1998; Meindl, 1990; Schyns and Sanders, 2007; Parry and Kempster, 2014). Relational perspectives of the charismatic relationship that look at leader-follower processes have also been studied (House, 1977; Gardner and Avolio, 1998) and there exist critical reviews of charismatic leadership (for e.g., Calàs, 1993; van Knippenberg and Sitkin, 2013; Spoelstra, 2019).

We focus on follower attributions in further detail in a subsequent chapter. However, given that charisma was perceived as a trait, and was the subject of focus of many trait-focused studies on leadership, we focus on this 'special quality' of leaders in this section, as well as on its critique.

The term charisma is used to refer to the special quality that leaders possess and has been researched extensively within the leadership literature. Literature on charismatic leadership dates to the 1970s. Berlew (1974) published elementary concepts of the construct. According to Zaccaro et al. (2004), House (1977) came up with the first piece of research on charismatic leadership, followed by Burns (1978), Bass (1985), Tichy and Devanna (1986), Conger and Kanungo (1987) and Sashkin (1988).

In her paper titled 'Deconstructing charismatic leadership: Re-reading Weber from the darker side', Marta Calàs provides a review and critique of the initial studies of charismatic leadership. She points out that using charismatic leadership for specific uses by 'cutting it to size' was what several studies had been doing. These include studies by Conger (1989), House, Spangler and Woycke (1991) and Nadler and Tushman (1990). For Conger (1989), charismatic leadership was viewed as being useful in enhancing leadership skills. For House et al. (1991), charismatic leadership was required mostly in situations that required a highly involved leader. For Nadler and Tushman (1990), charismatic leadership was 'necessary but not sufficient for effective organizational change' (Calàs, 1993: 306).

Before the psychology-based studies on charisma, it was originally Max Weber, a famous sociologist, who came up with the notion of charismatic authority. For Weber, 'a charismatic leader is an extraordinary individual guided by their dreams, visions and moral values that are not contaminated by social and economic conduct' (Spoelstra, 2019: 747). Weber makes a distinction between charisma and bureaucracy, and notes that the charismatic leader is guided by dreams and values. The bureaucrat, on the other hand, is fully part of the economy. Spoelstra (2019) writes that:

Weber (1978) himself, in one of his political writings called 'Parliament and government in a reconstructed Germany', suggested that bureaucrats ought to follow the rules and charismatic politicians ought to stick to their vision or their moral values. (1403–1404)

Drawing on Weberian understandings, Spoelstra (2019) argues that the charismatic leader is one that is placed in opposition to administrative tasks, organisational processes, and services. The charismatic leader is seen as larger than life, an extraordinary individual who is placed much higher than the office itself.

An important criticism of the trait-based approach to charisma within leadership studies was the lack of a complete consideration of Weber's notion of charisma. By adopting a Derridean deconstructionist approach, Calàs (1993) unpacks and unpicks the way organisational scholars have treated charisma in leadership, and in the process, bureaucratised their treatment of charisma by moving away from Weber's initial ideas. Derrida was a French philosopher who came up with a form of analysis known as 'deconstruction'. This form of analysis is used to examine texts. Marta Calàs adopted this technique to analyse texts about charismatic leadership. Calàs (1993) points out that organisational scholars have omitted aspects of Weberian conceptualisations of charisma and have created a 'suspicion of charisma' to maintain conventional notions of management based on bureaucratic authority. Therefore, an incomplete understanding of Weberian charisma may explain the problematical understandings of charismatic leadership in the leadership literature. While Bass (1990) draws on Weber's contributions in his review of charismatic leadership, most of his reviewed work attempted to reduce the phenomenon to a few psychological variables. Calàs argues that Bass's (1990) review does not consider one aspect of Weber's contribution of charismatic phenomenon which is known as 'routinization' (Calàs, 1993: 311).

There are two types of charisma, genuine and routinised charisma. Genuine charisma is antithetical to rules, routines and aspects that characterise bureaucracy, and refers to superhuman-like qualities. On the other hand, routinised charisma refers to the moment when social order is restored (Burrell and Morgan, 1979). Much of the literature focuses on genuine charisma without considering the routinisation of charisma.

Weber's notion of the charismatic leader evolved from a simply emotional force that existed beyond the reach of bureaucracy, to that of a mature responsibility which could exist in a 'utopic' space away from bureaucracy, as pointed out by Dow (1978). What this means is that the distinction between genuine and routinised charisma is important due to the maintenance of social order (Greenfeld, 1985; Burrell and Morgan, 1979), and that the excitement of genuine charisma takes place due to lost values. The charisma is routinised when social order is restored.

Much of the research on leader traits that drew on Weber (for example, Bass, 1990) was based on an incomplete consideration of Weber's ideas of charisma. This resulted in the absence of deliberation on the complexity of Weber's work. Calàs (1993) argued that researchers made researching an extraordinary quality like charisma as ordinary as possible due to the bureaucracy of their writings.

An important point to note about Calàs' ideas is her comment on race.

> The use of 'darker characters' such as Lenin, Hitler, Mussolini, Mao Zedung, Castro, Arafat, Qaddafi, and Khomeini, conflated with the 'dark good guys' – Ghandi (sic), King, and Jackson in conventional illustrations of problems with 'extraordinary' charismatic leadership extends strong racist images over who is fit to manage in ordinary organizations. (1993: 325)

The excerpt from her paper suggests that by using examples of 'dark good guys' as charismatic leaders, the organisational literature on charismatic leadership automatically appropriated the leadership and management of 'ordinary' organisations to the ordinary mainstream – that is 'American, white, heterosexual men' (Calàs, 1993: 325). In this way, those who did not fit into the mainstream (non-white men, women, and others) were left out as examples of individuals who could lead ordinary organisations. This is an example of exclusionary attitudes to normative, everyday understandings of who is capable of leading ordinary organisations.

Dark traits

In the personality literature, the three personality traits of **narcissism**, **Machiavellianism** and psychopathy are known as the **dark triad** (Paulhus and Williams, 2002). The concepts of narcissism and psychopathy came from the clinical literature and are both psychiatric disorders in the DSM-IV (now DSM-5) psychiatric classification. Machiavellianism, on the other hand, comes from the philosophy of 'Niccolò Machiavelli, a political advisor to the Medici family in the 1500s' (Furnham, Richards and Paulhus, 2013: 200).

As Landay, Harms and Credé (2019) point out, clinical practice has been based on the psychopathic features outlined in Cleckley's (1941) seminal text *The Mask of Sanity*. These psychopathic features include superficial charm, lack of anxiety, unwillingness to accept blame, lack of impulse control, and lack of empathy. In the organisational context, scholars have studied corporate or organisational psychopathy (e.g., Clarke, 2005; Babiak and Hare, 2006; Boddy, 2011). Psychopathy is viewed as being composed of three distinct elements, which results in producing a psychopathic personality.

These elements include boldness, disinhibition, and meanness. Through their meta-analysis of psychopathic features and their associations with leadership emergence, leadership effectiveness and transformational leadership, Landay et al. found that individuals with psychopathic tendencies were more likely to emerge as leaders, and these leaders were found to be less effective.

Interestingly, gender seems to have moderated these associations, suggesting that while women are penalised for displaying psychopathic tendencies, men are rewarded for similar behaviours. Landay et al. also found through their complex curvilinear analyses that moderate levels of psychopathic tendencies can be linked to increased ratings of leadership effectiveness. However, they conclude by suggesting that we still have a lot to learn about leadership, dark personality traits and gender (2019: 191). An important observation to be made here concerns prejudice in relation to gender. Gender is an important consideration in trait research given the penalties female leaders bear.

Narcissism refers to the extent to which individuals have exaggerated views of their own self-worth (Judge et al., 2009). As Braun (2017) points out, the term originated in Greek mythology when Narcissus fell in love with his own reflection in a pool of water. He then died in misery upon realising he would not be able to seduce his own image. According to DSM-5, some of the criteria for narcissism include a 'grandiose sense of self-importance; fantasies of unlimited success, power, brilliance, beauty, or ideal love; believes that one is "special" and unique; requiring excessive admiration; sense of entitlement, interpersonally exploitative behavior; lack of empathy; being envious of others' (2017: 3). While definitions within organisational psychology draw on these traits in the DSM-5, narcissism within this discipline is seen as a personality trait rather than a mental illness.

Providing an example of a leader portraying narcissism, Braun (2017) argues that research on the former president of the United States, Donald Trump (e.g., Ahmadian, Azarshahi and Paulhus, 2017; Visser, Book and Volk, 2017) shows that Trump's public personality profile is indicative of both psychopathy and narcissism due to perceptions of 'exceptionally low humility and agreeableness, very low emotionality, and low conscientiousness'. Moreover, Trump's strong self-promotional style accentuates his narcissistic grandiosity.

Braun (2017) calls for further research on narcissism and leadership effectiveness due to the inconclusive answer to whether narcissistic leaders are effective leaders. This is due to both positive (e.g., Galvin et al., 2010) and negative outcomes (Judge et al., 2006) found in existing studies. In addition, the answer to this question is dependent on what sort of ratings were used, and what level of analyses were carried out.

Judge et al. (2009) highlight that Machiavellian leaders are strategic in their thinking and can navigate power dynamics in complex environments. While descriptions of Machiavellianism portray a cunning, manipulative, immoral style of management, the original suggestions in *The Prince*, the work by Machiavelli from which Machiavellianism originates, are less extreme. This view is also echoed by Cunha, Clegg and Rego (2013) who argue that sometimes even virtuous leaders need to participate in power dynamics as certain situations inevitably call for this style of management.

Existing research (e.g., Drory and Gluskinos, 1980; Dingler-Duhon and Brown, 1987; Deluga, 2001) suggests that highly Machiavellian leaders show considerable flexibility in handling structured and unstructured tasks and are even described as charismatic. Furthermore, such leaders are viewed as successful at building political connections through strategic self-disclosure (Judge et al., 2009).

We have thus explored the dark triad of personality traits in this section in relation to leadership. It should be noted that dark traits extend beyond the triad. For instance, Chabrol, Van Leeuwen, Rodgers and Séjourné (2009) proposed the dark tetrad, which added sadism to the dark triad.

Contemporary research

There continues to be an increase in studies which examine traits and leadership. We will explore some of these contemporary studies on traits and leadership in this section.

We will look at a paper that explores how sex and gender interact to produce leadership outcomes. Before we do so, it is necessary to distinguish between sex and gender. Taylor (2019) explains that sex refers to a biological trait, and gender is socially constructed. Such a perspective on gender considers the complex ways in which gender can be researched from a trait approach, and this is a move away from a deterministic approach to leadership. To that end, Gartzia and Baniandrés (2019) consider trait theories from a gender perspective. **Communion** and **agency** represent two dimensions of gender traits where communion refers to femininity, and agency refers to masculinity. The femininity traits encompass being empathetic, sociable, understanding, or caring. Masculine traits or agency traits, on the other hand, include being independent, ambitious, or assertive and capture socially desirable traits for men. Gartzia and Baniandrés (2019) refer to the 'female advantage' which is the notion that feminine traits in leadership are advantageous for businesses (Desvaux et al., 2008), and claims that there is a female advantage in leadership have been popular (Helgesen, 1990). However, the business case that is made for female leadership is often too simplified because in diversity research the research literatures are much more wide-ranging than that adopted by advocates, which suits their position on policy with little regard for the generalisability and validity of the scientific findings (Eagly, 2016). By carrying out three quantitative studies, Gartzia and Baniandrés (2019) explored the extent to which stereotypically feminine/masculine leadership traits move beyond leaders' sex in relation to leadership effects. This study shows that communion and agency (femininity and masculinity) were better predictors of leadership outcomes than biological sex. These findings highlight that men with communal (feminine) traits have a feminine advantage too which produces more positive responses from employees. The notion of a 'feminine advantage' comes from role congruity theory that argues that there are 'stereotypes about women and stereotypes about men developed from the observance of women and men in separate and distinct social roles' (Eagly and Karau, 2002 in Bauer, 2020: 664). In leadership studies, the emphasis on communal dimensions of leadership focusing on relational and emotional aspects constitutes the feminine advantage. This study therefore emphasises the distinction between gender and biological sex, and sheds light on the intricacies of traits from a gender perspective. Badura, Grijalva, Newman, Yan and Jeon (2018), through their meta-analysis of gender and leadership emergence, found that the gender gap in leader emergence has been shrinking but has not completely disappeared. In their meta-analysis, they examined communion and agency traits in relation to leadership emergence.

A relevant study to consider about leader traits is a study on 'trait affect' by Joseph, Dhanani, Shen, McHugh and McCord (2015) which sheds light on the relationship between emotions and leader traits. Joseph et al. (2015) looked at the idea 'if happy leaders were good leaders' through their meta-analysis of various research studies that had looked into affect. Before we investigate the definition of trait affect, let us first explore what 'affect' means. According to the *Oxford English Dictionary*, and in the context of Psychology and Psychiatry disciplines, affect is 'a feeling or subjective experience accompanying a thought or action or occurring in response to a stimulus; an emotion, a mood' (*Oxford English Dictionary*, OUP, 2000). Trait affect then is defined as an individual's 'affective lens on the world' (Barsade and Gibson, 2007: 38). This refers to how individuals feel about the world and is about emotions.

Affective processes are more commonly known as emotions (Barsade and Gibson, 2007). Affect encompasses both short-term and long-term stable tendencies to feel and act in certain ways. *Feeling states* are the short-term affective experiences, whilst *feeling traits* are the more stable tendencies to act in certain ways (Watson and Clark,

1984; Barsade and Gibson, 2007). In this context, trait affect then refers to the more stable tendencies of how individuals would act. There are both positive and negative types of affects. Positive affect refers to the positive dispositions. More specifically in relation to traits, trait positive affectivity is used to refer to 'individuals who tend to be cheerful and energetic, and who experience positive moods, such as pleasure or well-being across a variety of situations as compared to people who tend to be low energy' and trait negative affectivity is used to refer to 'individuals who tend to be distressed and upset and have a negative view of self over time and across situations, as compared to people who are more calm, serene and relaxed' (Barsade and Gibson, 2007: 38).

By conducting a meta-analysis with the aim of providing a quantitative summary, Joseph et al. (2015) found that leader trait affects predicted leadership criteria. 'Leadership criteria' in this study broadly included leadership styles, behaviours, emergence and effectiveness, and narrower leadership criteria such as transformational and transactional leadership behaviours. Interestingly, leader trait affect was seen as predicting leadership criteria above and beyond two of the Big Five personality traits: extraversion and neuroticism. This meta-analytic study highlights the role of emotions in understanding leadership effectiveness, as well as how emotions are linked to leader traits.

It is important to examine the above study critically. We explored a few philosophical paradigms in Chapter 1, and the study by Joseph et al. is clearly entrenched in functionalism as it deals with 'numbers' and provides a quantitative summary of various existing studies. While quantitative studies have dominated the study of leader traits, one of the downsides of such studies relates to the use of ratings in questionnaires which would be based on an individual's perception of themselves.

Another study that contributes to the literature on both traits and emotions is one by Walter and Scheibe (2013) who put forward a model that links leaders' age to outcomes and leader effectiveness by considering emotions, and emotional aging. Their conceptual study points to various inconsistencies in the existing literature on leader age and leader effectiveness, but nonetheless sheds light on areas to consider concerning leaders' emotional stability.

Reflective question

1. What can we learn about leader traits and emotions through observing interactions?

Tabula rasa and leadership skills

In the previous sections, we focused on leader traits, which continue to be studied in leadership research. However, as we have seen, the past decade has seen more complex forms of analysis of leader traits. Before we move on to leadership skills, let us examine the notion of tabula rasa put forward by the philosopher John Locke. Tabula rasa essentially refers to a 'blank slate'. It refers to the idea that we are all born with a mind as a blank slate, and that individuals are then shaped by knowledge and experiences. Rekret suggests:

> The notion of the mind as a blank slate served an early modern desire for independence from the entrenched norms and values of feudal society. (2018: 26)

Adopting this view is a departure from a trait-based understanding of leadership, which is embedded in the notion that leaders are born, and not made. Locke's concept presents itself as an opportunity to free oneself from norms and attachments to lineages. When we look at a skills-based understanding of leadership, which is the remaining topic of focus in this chapter, this aligns with a 'blank slate' view.

According to the *Oxford English Dictionary*, a skill refers to the

> capability of accomplishing something with precision and certainty; practical knowledge in combination with ability; cleverness, expertness. Also, an ability to perform a function, acquired or learnt with practice (usually plural). (*Oxford English Dictionary*, OUP, 2000)

In comparison to traits and other approaches to leadership, leadership skills have received limited attention (Mumford, Campion and Morgeson, 2007). This is still the case over a decade and a half later, as database searches on leadership skills return a lower number of search results as compared to that of leader traits. Mumford et al. (2007) argue that there are two reasons for focusing on leadership skills: first, skills mean that people can become better leaders, and the second reason involves the fact that the focus is more on the job as opposed to the individual leader. Such an approach to leadership is inclusive as it provides an opportunity for everyone to become better leaders. Mumford et al. (2007) provide a comprehensive overview of the various skills-based models and approaches of leadership. They examine four levels of leadership skill requirements across three organisational levels. Through a review of literature, four broad categories of leadership skills were identified: cognitive skills, interpersonal skills, business skills and strategic skills. We define each of the four sets of skill requirements here.

Cognitive skills

Cognitive simply refers to thinking, and cognitive skills encompass basic cognitive capacities such as: collecting, processing and disseminating information. They include communication skills such as speaking, active listening, and writing, as well as reading comprehension skills. Active learning skills are also seen as being part of cognitive skills (Mumford et al., 2007).

Mumford, Todd, Higgs and McIntosh (2017) identified nine key cognitive skills that leaders need for increased performance. These skills are independent but interact during problem solving. They are problem definition; cause/goal analysis; constraint analysis; planning; forecasting; creative thinking; idea evaluation; wisdom; and sense-making/visions.

Let us explore further what each of these cognitive skills means. Information gathering from the firm's internal as well as external environment by focusing on factual as well as inconsistent information should form the basis for *problem definition*. Problem definition would involve important restrictions being imposed whilst determining which goals to keep.

Goal analysis can be understood as identifying viable goals to be pursued from a large set of potential objectives by the leader. *Causal analysis* involves looking into actions that lead to large, direct and synergistic effects. *Constraint analysis* involves analysing the constraints to the solutions of problems. Given that most problems and solutions are often devised in complex systems, it is inevitable that some proposed solutions may have constraints that need to be dealt with. As a result, constraint analysis is presented as one of nine cognitive skills that leaders must possess.

Planning involves a 'mental simulation of future actions' (Mumford et al., 2017: 31). This means that actions need to be visualised before they are undertaken. Planning is hence a critical skill that leaders need to enhance leader performance. *Forecasting* is essentially a prediction of what will happen. Forecasting is a skill that involves predicting outcomes for the plans that are to be executed. A study by Byrne, Shipman and Mumford (2010) found that forecasting was a powerful predictor of leader performance.

Creative thinking involves coming up with novel and non-traditional solutions to problems that emerge. Studies have shown that creative thinking skills can be developed, and that these skills are useful and contribute to leader performance (e.g., Mumford, Marks, Connelly, Zaccaro and Reitor-Palmon, 2000a). *Idea evaluation* involves the assessment of ideas that emerge through creative thinking, as creative thinking would lead to multiple ideas, and these ideas will need to be assessed before proceeding further with the most feasible ideas. *Wisdom* can be understood as a set of skills related to social judgement that include self-objectivity, self-reflection, systems perception, awareness of solution fit, judgement under uncertainty, and systems commitment. These skills are found to increase with experience (e.g., Mumford et al., 2000a) and can be shared with other members (e.g., Silver, Benitez, Armstrong and Tussey, 2018).

Sensemaking/visioning is about crafting visions that are appropriate for followers. A qualitative study by Foldy, Goldman and Ospina (2008) found that leaders framed their visions in accordance with the impact that they would have on their followers which communicated an image of how significant problems must be addressed by a leader and their followers. Marcy (2015) found that leaders craft visions to help understand situations as well as undermine existing systems through which followers view problems. Therefore, sensemaking/visioning is an important cognitive skill that is seen as having a direct impact on followers. We critically explore leader-follower relations later in this textbook (see Chapter 4). These nine critical cognitive skills are hence viewed as being helpful in problem solving (Mumford et al., 2017).

Interpersonal skills

These involve interacting with people and influencing others. Interpersonal skills are an amalgamation of social capacities (Zaccaro, 2017); social judgement (Mumford et al., 2000a); social complexity and differentiation (Hooijberg et al., 1997); and human relation skills (Katz and Kahn, 1978). Mumford, Zacarro, Harding, Jacobs and Fleishman (2000b) proposed that social judgement skills include: perspective taking; social perceptiveness; behavioural flexibility; and social performance. Perspective taking refers to the understanding of attitudes others have toward a particular problem or solution. Social perceptiveness refers to having insight and awareness into how others within an organisation function. Behavioural flexibility refers to the ability to change and adapt one's behaviour to understand others' perspectives within an organisation. Social performance is the capacity to effectively communicate the leader's vision to others based on the leader's understanding of others' perspectives.

Business skills

Business skills encompass skills that are about specific functional areas. Examples of such functions include 'management of material resources (Katz, 1974), operations analysis (Huffman and Hegarty, 1993) and management of personnel resources as well as financial resources' (Mumford et al., 2007: 157). These function-related skills would vary depending on the industry/sector or the type of organisation. For instance, specialist project management skills have been in demand in organisations such as construction firms, where a project manager would work with various members from different parts of the organisation, with their expertise ranging from structural engineering to architecture, civil engineering and electrical engineering, among others. The role of the project manager would then be to work with all the different individuals to ensure that the clients' needs are met.

Strategic skills

Strategic skill requirements require a systems perspective to deal with a particular problem. A systems approach essentially refers to the consideration of the fact that everything is interrelated, so a decision affecting one unit may have consequences for other parts of the organisation. Adopting a systems approach would then involve careful planning whilst making important decisions. Schoemaker, Krupp and Howland (2013) propose six skills that are needed for a strategic leader and they have designed an assessment that can be taken to determine to what extent an individual has each skill.

These strategic skills include the ability to anticipate; challenge; interpret; decide; align; and learn.

'Anticipate' refers to scanning the environment for any signals for change. 'Challenge' is about questioning the status quo and possessing divergent views. 'Interpret' is about getting diverse stakeholders to interpret data or information that might seem ambiguous. 'Decide' is about making decisions quickly, as leaders do not tend to have much time to think about doing things. 'Align' is about finding common ground with people. It is useful to know the right people and to find common ground with them in order to get things done. The ability to 'learn' is an important strategic skill as well as a cognitive skill that Mumford et al. (2007) suggest. We often learn more from our failures than our successes, and sometimes individuals in leadership positions are not good at learning as they think that they know everything.

Mini case study 2.2

Higher Education

This is a fictional mini case study set in the context of Higher Education.

May is an early career academic in a university and her responsibilities include meeting both teaching and research objectives. May is an ambitious and determined individual who has numerous administrative responsibilities in addition to her core research and teaching duties. She has been appointed to a role that involves leading on an Equality, Diversity and Inclusion (EDI) programme. This leadership

(Continued)

role involves the management and leadership of four sub-groups within the pro-gramme. These sub-groups have their own leaders. The leadership role is an enor-mous responsibility for someone early in their academic career, and requires meet-ing the strategic objectives of the programme, as well as having to lead four different sub-groups with different functions and ensuring that these sub-groups are meeting their aims. Interpersonal skills seemed to be crucial due to the presence of two members of the programme that were particularly perceived as uncooperative. They frequently voiced concerns or undermined the team's and May's efforts through their unconstructive comments. May had finally had enough when she received an email from one member that questioned the direction and the tireless efforts of May and the rest of the team. May found it particularly problematic due to the member's questioning of the focus on equality initiatives. May decided that the member did not have the values that were needed to be part of the programme. However, instead of escalating the issue, May thought that she needed to think carefully about the com-plex team dynamics she found herself in. The EDI programme was something she was leading on top of her existing teaching and research commitments, and she had not been given enough hours to work on this additional task. The situation in which May had to lead was therefore complicated by several factors.

Questions

1. What leadership skills would be useful for May in this situation?
2. What do you think could be some of the complicating factors in this situation?

Conclusion

The objective of this chapter was to provide an inclusive overview of early approaches of leadership which were predominantly trait focused. We have reviewed and critiqued early approaches to the trait-based view of leadership studies such as the Great Man Theory, and examined psychology-based perspectives on traits including the Big Five dimensions. Dark traits, as well as charismatic leadership, were reviewed including a discussion of implicit leadership theories (ILTs) which focus on followers' perceptions of traits. ILTs will be explored further in Chapter 4 in which we explore the eye of the beholder view of leadership in further detail. Relevant contemporary research on traits was reviewed before moving on to leader-ship skills which are based on the notion that leaders are made, and we explored Mumford et al.'s (2007, 2017) overview of leadership skills. Chapter 3 focuses on a review and critique of leadership styles.

Key summary

- Early ideas of trait-based studies on leadership based on Great Man Theory were exclusionary as they seemed to portray only certain individuals with certain biological characteristics as leaders.
- Despite several criticisms of the trait approach, there has been a resurgence of the trait approach evidenced by the increase in contemporary research.
- Implicit leader theories are the lay images people have about leaders and focus on follower perceptions of leaders.
- Charisma is a trait, but the studies of charismatic leadership extend beyond a trait-based approach.
- A leadership skills approach is based on the idea that leadership can be learnt, and the emphasis is on the job rather than the individual leader.

Further reading

Asad and Sadler-Smith's (2020) paper examines two dark traits, hubris and narcissism, in relation to power and argue that hubris and narcissism are behaviourally distinct. This paper sheds light on the usefulness of studying the darker aspects of leader traits and contributes to a different perspective that does not focus on characteristics or attributes, but power.

Asad, S. and Sadler-Smith, E. (2020) 'Differentiating leader hubris and narcissism on the basis of power'. *Leadership*, 16(1): 39–61.

Jansson, Doving and Elstad (2020) conducted an empirical study of individuals within the music domain to understand how they made sense of their leader competencies. This paper sheds light on leader competencies and how these contribute to practice.

Jansson, D., Døving, E. and Elstad, B. (2021) 'The construction of leadership practice: Making sense of leader competencies'. *Leadership*, https://doi.org/10.1177/1742715021996497 (accessed 9 September 2022).

Rehbock, Verdorfer and Knipfer (2019) apply implicit leadership theories to academia by asking pre- and post-doctoral researchers to specify the characteristics of a professorial leader. The results showed that the ILTs in an academic context are different to a business context and therefore the academic context deserves attention.

Rehbock, S. K., Pircher Verdorfer, A. and Knipfer, K. (2019) 'Rate my professor: Implicit leadership theories in academia', *Studies in Higher Education*, 28: 1–13.

3

EVOLUTION OF LEADERSHIP THEORIES 2: LEADERSHIP STYLES, LEADER VERSUS MANAGER DEBATE

Naveena Prakasam

Chapter objectives

The objectives of this chapter are:

- To examine the importance of context in leadership.
- To explore and provide a critical overview of leadership styles and their importance in organisational and wider societal contexts.
- To critically review the leader versus manager debate.

Introduction

In this chapter, we explore a few leadership styles that have dominated the leadership scholarship. We begin with an overview of the role of context in leadership. We examine leadership styles, which include charismatic-transformational, transactional and authentic leadership styles. We then discuss the leader versus manager debate, and the different perspectives around this debate.

It is important to define leadership style before delving further into this area. A **leadership style** refers to manifestations or constructions of leader behaviour patterns and characteristics. It can be understood as a way certain behaviours or actions of leaders are executed. There are different types of leadership styles that are used as signifiers to refer to ways in which behaviours are enacted by leaders. For further clarity, it is important to distinguish between leadership traits and leadership styles. We have seen in Chapter 2 that leadership traits refer to the distinguishing features or characteristics of individuals that make them leaders, and leaders are known to be born with these traits. Leadership styles, on the other hand, can be learnt and developed.

Leadership styles have been studied and captured in ways that include using leadership measures in the form of quantitative questionnaires. For this reason, leadership styles are also referred to as leadership constructs. Leadership constructs have been referred to as 'theoretical abstractions' (Spoelstra, 2019: 744), intended as a means to explain empirical phenomena through leadership measures. Adopting a critical take, Spoelstra (2019) argues that those constructs have become something that explains other things once such a leadership construct is established. This means that leadership constructs are equated to the 'real' leadership, which are then used to explain other phenomena. For example, if you say that leadership is equal to measure X, then leadership from there onwards is equated to measure X. This measure X can then be related to other phenomena, leading to conclusions being made about leadership and various other phenomena. In other words, leadership constructs have become signifiers for leadership itself. When a construct is established, its artificial nature is forgotten. Spoelstra's argument points to the importance of recognising that the adjectives or styles that are used to signify the different types of leadership are socially constructed, and that they become more accepted once they are established. Here, it is useful to consider Sandberg and Alvesson's (2021) critique of dominant forms of theory. They argue that the most dominant types of theory are the ones that have explanatory power, that is, theory that explains phenomena. However, such explanatory knowledge pursuits might lead researchers to force a fit into explanatory moulds when such knowledges do not fit into the explanation-prediction form of theory. Sandberg and Alvesson's critique could be applied to Spoelstra's point about the limitations of the artificially constructed nature of leadership constructs. It could be argued that in the pursuit of seeking explanatory power, researchers have constructed many types of leadership styles.

Context and leadership

This section discusses the importance of considering context in relation to leadership. We begin by exploring some early perspectives that shed light on considering situational factors.

In response to the criticism that trait perspectives of leadership did not consider context, some context-based models of leadership were developed. Fiedler's (1978) model investigated the extent to which the Least Preferred Coworker (LPC) interacted with situational favourableness. The LPC is calculated by the quality of leader–member relations, the leader's positional power and the extent to which group tasks are structured clearly. Therefore, this perspective of leadership does not focus on traits alone, but also on various other factors that might predict performance.

A context-based model that explicitly relates to leadership styles is the path-goal theory of leadership developed by House (1971), which explored the interaction between various leadership styles, follower characteristics, and situational factors. The leadership styles include directive, supportive, participative and achievement oriented. The follower characteristics include the locus of control, task ability, and preference for structure. The situational factors in this theory encompass task structure, the leader's formal authority and the work group norms. The theory suggests that these factors predict whether such leader behaviours can enhance followers' motivation, satisfaction and performance. Both these theoretical models, Fiedler's theory and path-goal theory, include situational factors that together create a context which prescribes a particular leadership style for that situation (Oc, 2018). Therefore, context becomes important whilst thinking of which leadership style would be most useful.

Based on a review of context-related research on leadership, Oc (2018) offers an omnibus for context which includes where, who and when. The where dimension is the most studied and factors within this omnibus include national culture, institutions/markets and organisations. However, this classification is caveated by the fact that various theoretical frameworks and methodologies are adopted in each of these categories. For example, leader humility and leader integrity are perceived differently in different countries (see Oc, Bashshur, Daniels, Greguras and Diefendorff, 2015).

There is evidence of how market elements contribute to leaders' decision making as they affect how leaders construe a particular situation. This includes findings from Desmet, Hoogervorst and Van Dijke (2015), which demonstrate that leaders are likely to judge others' unethical behaviour from an instrumental as opposed to unethical perspective where there is increased market competition.

The who dimension refers to characteristics of the whole group, team, individuals being led and those leading. This dimension includes all relevant actors in the process of leadership that constitute the context. Examples of studies within this include those related to demographic diversity. For instance, demographic diversity is found to result in 'greater team creativity, stronger team performance, and lower turnover when leaders demonstrate transformational or participative leadership qualities' (Somech, 2006; Shin and Zhou, 2007; Kearney and Gebert, 2009; Oc, 2018: 225).

The when dimension includes the time at which research takes place, as well as events in time that subsequently shape leadership processes. For example, Schepker, Kim, Patel, Thatcher and Campion (2017) found that CEO succession has a negative effect on organisations' short-term performance but does not influence firms' long-term performance. Moreover, internally promoted CEOs make fewer strategic changes and boost long-term performance, but those hired externally deal with strategic change resulting in poorer long-term performance. In addition to the omnibus dimensions of where, who and when, discrete-level contextual factors such as task characteristics, team, organisation, social network, physical distance and time pressure seem to influence leadership outcomes. Therefore, it is also important to recognise how the omnibus and discreet contextual factors interact, and the impact they have on leadership outcomes.

Overall, we have seen that context plays an important role in leadership outcomes. However, going back to Spoelstra's (2019) point about leadership styles being signifiers and artificially constructed, we remember that many studies reviewed above in relation to context have used quantitative measures, and their limitations must be acknowledged. As Sandberg and Alvesson (2021) have noted, it is also important to be cautious of certain predictions and explanations. As we explore in more detail later in this chapter, we consider how the context itself can be socially constructed (Grint, 2005). This means that using fixed and stable measures to measure context may not take into consideration factors that influence the construction of the context.

In the following sections, we examine styles of leadership that have dominated the leadership discourse. We begin by examining **charismatic-transformational leadership**.

Reflective questions

1. Can you think of some examples of charismatic leaders?
2. Why do you think they are charismatic? Jot down some notes. Refer to them at the end of the following section.
3. Once you've read the following section, see if your perceptions have changed.

Charismatic-transformational leadership

Charismatic-transformational leadership style is the most researched leadership style in the leadership literature (Anderson and Sun, 2017). Charismatic and transformational leadership styles are often mentioned in conjunction, or even interchangeably, due to the similarities between the two styles (van Knippenberg and Sitkin, 2013; Anderson and Sun, 2017).

Although we explored charismatic leadership in Chapter 2 whilst focusing on leadership traits, and critiqued its use as a theory based on psychological variables, we revisit charismatic leadership given its dominance as a leadership style (Anderson and Sun, 2017). Another reason for this is its overlap and similarities to another dominant style of leadership known as transformational leadership. Therefore, we explore charismatic and transformational leadership in conjunction. These similarities have been discussed by several scholars (see Bryman, 1992; Conger, 1999; van Knippenberg and Sitkin, 2013; Anderson and Sun, 2017). Ronald Riggio provides an overview of the overlap as well as differences between charismatic and transformational leadership in this short YouTube video clip: www.youtube.com/watch?v=ZvezV2Zhihg (accessed 10 September 2022).

Leaders with exceptional qualities that affect followers as well as social systems are defined as charismatic leaders. The notion of charisma dates back to Max Weber (see Chapter 2 for details on Weberian theorising of charismatic leadership). Leadership researchers explored this further in the 1970s (van Knippenberg and Sitkin, 2013), including Berlew (1974) and House (1977) who published elementary concepts of charismatic leadership in organisational settings. However, Banks, Engemann, Williams, Gooty, McCauley and Medaugh (2017) argue that charisma has not been defined consistently in six decades while pointing to two overarching themes found in most definitions of charismatic leadership. These are antecedents/outcomes and an exceptional and miraculous ability.

The late 1980s and 1990s saw an increase in more comprehensive theorising and empirical research on charismatic leadership and its effects on outcomes within the organisational literature (Conger, 1999). Charismatic leadership encompasses leaders who articulate an inspirational vision for a desirable future. This inspiring vision is then seen as motivating followers who are willing to strive towards causes advocated for by the charismatic leader (Anderson and Sun, 2017). This is because followers perceive charismatic leaders as having extraordinary abilities and qualities. The personal magnetism that charismatic leaders exude enables followers to identify with such leaders (House, 1977; Anderson and Sun, 2017).

An important consideration of charismatic leadership relates to morality. Charismatic leaders are not necessarily moral. Even though morality itself is subjective with varying perspectives, even the evilest dictators such has Hitler are viewed as charismatic (Rees, 2012). The morality issue has therefore been articulated by several scholars (see Conger, 1999; Howell and Shamir, 2005; Tourish and Vatcha, 2005; Padilla, Hogan and Kaiser, 2007). Perinbanayagam (1971), a sociologist, carried out a **dialectical analysis** of the charismatic leadership of Hitler and Gandhi, where two individuals on opposing ends of the ethical spectrum were both considered charismatic leaders. Hitler and Gandhi provided ludicrous points of contrast for such an analysis: the lack of scepticism and followers who would seek to gain self-serving advantage by using compliments within Hitler's inner circle led to his own megalomania, whereas Gandhi's humility, and his acceptance and projection of his own weaknesses, meant that he did not develop any illusions of grandeur (Perinbanayagam, 1971).

Conger (1999) made a distinction between socialised and personalised charismatic leaders. Socialised charismatic leaders transcend their own self-interests to empower and develop followers by articulating visions that serve the collective interest. On the other hand, personalised charismatic leaders are viewed as narcissistic and manipulate followers into serving their own interests. Based on this distinction, it can be argued that Hitler had a personalised charismatic leadership style, whereas Gandhi embodied socialised charismatic leadership.

As mentioned previously, the charismatic and transformational leadership styles are similar. It is therefore important to examine the transformational leadership style before exploring the similarities between the two. It was initially Burns (1978) who described the notion of transforming leadership. Later, Bass (1985) built on this idea to come up with four components that constitute transformational leadership. The four components are *idealised influence, inspirational motivation, intellectual stimulation* and *individualised consideration. Idealised influence*, a term Bass (1985) used to describe charisma, refers to the extent to which a leader behaves in (admirable) ways which cause followers to identify with the leader, which involves the leader conveying a strong collective sense of purpose and collective mission. For example, when an individual idealises or portrays certain values by behaving in a particular manner, this may lead to followers identifying with the individual (leader). There are two aspects that must be noted here which include the leader behaviours as well as follower attributions of those behaviours (Antonakis, Simonton and House, 2016). This means that if a leader behaves in a way that makes the message clear as well as embodying desirable goals, then followers may attribute certain qualities to that leader. Van Knippenberg and Sitkin (2013) point out that idealised influence amalgamates actual leader behaviours, attributed behaviours and their effects on followers.

Inspirational motivation is about articulating a vision which inspires followers and communicating optimism about future goal attainment. Given the overlap between vision, mission and a collective sense of purpose, there are high correlations between idealised influence and inspirational motivation in existing empirical research. The combination of idealised influence and inspirational motivation results in charisma (van Knippenberg and Sitkin, 2013). It is also about providing meaning to tasks to motivate followers. *Intellectual stimulation* refers to the degree to which a leader challenges the existing assumptions of followers. It is about encouraging creativity amidst followers, which would enable them to solve complex problems. *Individualised consideration* relates to attending to follower needs. It refers to the extent to which a leader would attend to the needs of each of their followers, listen to their concerns, and provide coaching (Judge and Piccolo, 2004; van Knippenberg and Sitkin, 2013; Anderson and Sun, 2017).

Idealised influence and inspirational motivation are two of the components that are said to overlap between charismatic and transformational leadership styles (see Antonakis et al., 2016), which is one of the reasons for both styles to frequently be viewed in conjunction. For instance, van Knippenberg and Sitkin (2013) use 'charismatic-transformational leadership' as a label in their review and argue that there is no substantive difference between the two styles. They point out that the four components together can be viewed as constituting charismatic-transformational leadership. The confusion around this issue is attributed to the idealised influence and inspirational motivation encompassing charisma. This has led to transformational leadership being viewed as a more all-encompassing concept. Similarly, others including Judge and Piccolo (2004) and Walter and Bruch (2009) have combined charismatic and transformational leadership and argue that the findings from charismatic leadership and transformational leadership converge. Quantitative measures used to measure the two styles, which include the Multi-Leadership Questionnaire and the Conger-Kanungo scale for transformational and charismatic leadership respectively, also found the styles to be significantly correlated. Therefore, Anderson and Sun (2017) call for an abandonment of the distinction between the two styles.

Several contemporary studies of charismatic-transformational leadership have been conducted using various measures. Koo and Lee (2022) examine how employees found to be measuring high in Machiavellianism may be managed through transformational leadership in South Korea. A survey with 184 employees was carried out and the 34-item scale on transformational leadership developed by Wang and Howell (2010) was used. Interestingly, they found that individual-focused transformational leadership fails to reduce the negative relations between highly Machiavellian employees and pro-organisational behaviours. On the other hand, transformational leadership strengthens the negative relations between the two. The implication of this finding is that individual-focused transformational leadership (TL) should be negligibly adopted whilst dealing with highly Machiavellian employees.

Group-focused TL has a different impact on highly-rating Machiavellian employees. As group-focused TL involves looking at aspects beyond one's own self-interests in order to focus on the collective interest of the organisation, it diminishes the negative relations between Machiavellianism and pro-organisational behaviours. Therefore, Koo and Lee (2021) suggest that group-focused TL should be maximally employed on highly Machiavellian individuals. This study has important practical implications for managers who should be cautious with TL. The study emphasises the importance of recognising that transformational leadership is multi-faceted, with differing outcomes based on how it is exhibited. Managers need to consider minimising individual-focused TL when they observe signs of a Machiavellian personality in employees.

Pseudo-transformational leadership and the dark side of charisma

Bass and Steidlmeir (1999) distinguished between authentic transformational leadership (ATL) and pseudo transformational leadership (PTL); this distinction was made in response to concerns about the dark side of transformational leadership. ATL leaders are those who are heroic and display altruistic behaviours. Such leaders' focus is always seen as being on the greater good, and the well-being of their employees. They define pseudo-transformational leaders as those 'who fail to uphold ethical values and moral principles which is essential for transformational leadership' (Syed, Naseer, Nawaz and Shah, 2021: 236). A study of PTL in a non-Western context (Pakistan) carried out by Syed et al. (2021) provides some useful insights. The researchers used surveys to study bank managers in Pakistan. Pakistan's scores on several of **Hofstede's cultural dimensions** make the study more interesting. Hofstede's cultural dimensions, based on the national cultures of various countries, were born out of a worldwide survey of IBM employees. This large-scale study led to the development of dimensions such as power distance, uncertainty avoidance, individualism, masculinity, and time orientation. Pakistan scored high in power distance, collectivism (low on individualism) and uncertainty avoidance as well as masculinity and short-term orientations (Hofstede, 1991).

Syed et al. (2021) use the lens of affect and emotions to examine whether contempt intervenes in the relationship between PTL and outcomes. Drawing on Kruglanski, Piero, Manneti and De Grada (2006), they explore the boundary condition of 'epistemic motivation' which is defined 'as an individual's inclination to gain a thorough, systematic and rich understanding of the world around' (Syed et al., 2021: 236). In addition, they integrate affective events theory (AET) into their study. In Chapter 2, we explored the meaning of affect, which relates to emotions: 'AET is a theoretical framework [that] encompasses affective experiences with their causes and consequences, asserting the importance of emotions in shaping attitudes and behaviours' (Syed et al., 2021: 238). AET encompasses the notion that certain workplace events are perceived to support or suppress an individual's advancement towards goals through positive and negative affective responses. In the context of Syed et al.'s (2021) study, PTL behaviours represent these events. Moreover, they move beyond leader-centred perspectives to focus on follower-centric orientations. Their findings show that leaders' exploitative behaviours result in interaction avoidance and indirect aggression in followers. Such exploitative behaviours serve as negative events, which activate contempt, a negative emotion.

Syed et al. (2021) found contempt to be a unique emotional response to pseudo-transformational leaders that leads to followers' avoidance and indirect aggression. They provide further insight into the role of followers by investigating the role of followers' emotions, and passive behavioural responses to PTL. An important contribution of the study is that it was set in a non-Western cultural context, Pakistan, where power distance and uncertainty avoidance, two of Hofstede's cultural dimensions, are high, making it more suitable for revealing the negative effects of PTL. There are some limitations of the measure of PTL used in the study. Syed et al. (2021) combined and reversed idealised influence and inspirational motivation, which are two measures of the Multi-Leader Questionnaire (MLQ). However, this may not capture the true essence of PTL, and instead may indicate an absence of TL as opposed to PTL. Several criticisms of the MLQ exist (see Tourish and Pinnington, 2002; van Knippenberg and Sitkin, 2013; Alvesson and Karreman, 2016) which are discussed in a subsequent section. Qualitative approaches to studying such leadership styles are useful as they allow for rich detail to be captured.

Another study of transformational leadership that taps into the dark side of the leadership construct, and which is also set in the non-Western cultural context of Turkey, is that of Karakitapoğlu-Aygün and Gumusluoglu (2013). They refer to this dark side as non-transformational leadership, and not pseudo-transformational leadership. This is a qualitative study which alleviates the problems encountered by using quantitative measures. The authors carried out 31 semi-structured interviews with knowledge workers in Turkey. The bright and dark sides of TL in an organisational change context were explored, and the researchers were also interested in understanding the abuses of power in leadership that may occur. Hence, they set out to explore non-transformational leadership, which is viewed as a negative leadership construct, and represents a dark style of leadership. Non-transformational leadership in their study is used as an umbrella term encompassing several dark leadership styles. Turkey, despite being relatively collectivist and rating high on power distance, appears to be unique given the rapid social and economic change since the 1980s. Paternalism is a prevalent management as well as leadership style in the traditional business context of Turkey. Paternalistic leadership is seen as encompassing 'discipline, authority and power with fatherly benevolence' (Karakitapoğlu-Aygün and Gumusluoglu, 2013: 109). Hence, employees form close bonds with their leaders and avoid conflict, and leaders are expected to support and care for followers. Followers in return are expected to be compliant.

Karakitapoğlu-Aygün and Gumusluoglu (2013) found emerging categories of TL through their study. These included benevolent paternalism which refers to transformational leaders being perceived as behaving respectfully but firmly. This paternalistic category within TL relates to exhibiting fatherly qualities. Benevolent paternalism was found to be in line with the high power-distance orientation in Turkey. Other emergent categories included participative and collaborative orientation, which instils teamwork and cooperation and being proactive, where TL was expected to be assertive. The most frequently mentioned non-TL emergent category was destructive leadership which encompasses authoritarian behaviours. Destructive leaders display hostility towards their followers and portray coercive behaviours. Other emergent non-TL categories include being closed to new ideas and change, and active-failed leadership which involves focusing too much on bureaucratic procedures and following rules, as opposed to the big picture. Hence, these emergent categories can be attributed to the influence of culture on leadership. The studies by Syed et al. (2021) and Karakitapoğlu-Aygün and Gumusluoglu (2013) shed light on the dark sides of transformational leadership and point to the different signifiers used to refer to the dark side of the construct. For instance, Syed et al. (2021) used the term pseudo-transformational leadership which was developed by Bass and Steidelmeier (1999), whereas Karakitapoğlu-Aygün and Gumusluoglu (2013) used the label of non-transformational leadership as an all-encompassing umbrella term which included various different negative styles of leadership.

—Mini case study 3.1—

Kwame Nkrumah

Kwame Nkrumah was the first black political leader of Ghana, the first African nation to dispense with colonial rule, in 1957. Nkrumah was widely regarded as a charismatic leader (Tiger, 1963; Rooney, 2007). He was the prime minister and president of Ghana and was regarded as a revolutionary. Nkrumah was a significant part of the movement of independence from Britain's colonial rule which included his contribution along with the Convention People's Party (CPP) that secured Ghana's independence. In one of his books titled *Neo-colonialism: The Last Stage of Imperialism*, Nkrumah referred to **neo-colonialism** as the final and most dangerous stage of imperialism. At the heart of neo-colonialism is the idea that the State, in theory, may be independent but such a State's economic system and political policies are still affected by outside interests. The concept most associated with Nkrumah is neo-colonialism (Nimako, 2010).

Ghana's independence provided hope to several leaders of such independence movements all over Africa and extended as providing inspiration to civil rights leaders in the United States. Nkrumah's vision consisted of a united Africa. Nkrumah was critical of Western powers that constituted multinational companies and their threat to the economic prosperity of Third World countries that were moving towards independence at the time. This led to Ghana's government taking over the means of production and distribution. However, no profits were produced by these government enterprises, which subsequently led to a drain on Ghana's revenues. Nkrumah's vision of a united Africa also failed as it alienated other African leaders. Nkrumah's greatest weakness was to do with the fact that while he preached about the evils and exploitation of neo-colonialism, he presided over corrupt individuals who sold Ghana's future to greedy entrepreneurs. However, Nkrumah continued to be revered due to his revolutionary vision and action (Rooney, 2007). Nkrumah will be remembered due to his vision of a united Africa, despite the fact that his vision was not accomplished. His goal was for Africa's natural resources to be used to bring nations out of poverty and keep Western financiers away from their exploitation. While he stood on the world stage, and though Ghana's independence in 1957

(Continued)

inspired civil rights activists in the United States, he neglected to secure his home base. This resulted in a military coup in 1966 after which Nkrumah spent the remainder of his time in exile in Guinea.

Using Weber's charismatic authority, Tiger (1962) argues that charisma cannot remain stable and only exists in the process of originating. Over time, charisma becomes traditionalised. It was Nkrumah's extraordinary, larger-than-life qualities that brought him to the world stage at the start. Despite such charisma, and worldwide adulation for his role in the independence of Ghana and his ambitions for Africa, Nkrumah managed to alienate several people/groups through numerous plans that included both domestic and foreign policies. With his passionate ideology, he was in a rush to achieve huge ambitions for Ghana and used significant funds from the colonial-style Cocoa Marketing Board on several development programmes and initiatives. His refusal to accept financial restraints played into the hands of corrupt CPP members. Such corruption resulted in cocoa farmers receiving less and less for their crops, and eventually Nkrumah had alienated the abler peasant farmer group on which the future of Ghana's economic success depended. Nkrumah undermined peasant farmers (from the cocoa industry) and supported state farm agricultural policies instead. Nkrumah's policy towards cocoa farmers proved to be disastrous, which resulted in Ghana's prosperity in the cocoa industry being lost to the Ivory Coast and Togoland. Nkrumah's state farm policies contributed substantially to the failure of his regime.

Nkrumah's ideal 'was to create an African socialism and to construct a Ghanaian socialist state – a state backed by Western capitalism and by Eastern socialism, which would bring the benefits of both to the Ghanaian people and help them in their struggle to lift themselves from poverty and exploitation' (Rooney, 2007: 362).

As his vision so nearly succeeded, it continues to inspire people in Africa today.

Questions

1.   Based on this case study, to what extent is charismatic leadership important in world leaders?
2.   What are the downsides of charismatic leadership?
3.   What factors beyond Nkrumah's leadership style were responsible for specific outcomes?

Transactional versus transformational leadership

Burns (1978) originally viewed the transactional and transformational leadership styles as being on opposing ends of the same continuum. However, the transactional and transformational leadership styles have subsequently been contrasted in the literature as distinct dimensions (Bass, 1985, 1998). Referring to Bass (1998), Schedlitzki and Edwards point out that transactional leadership constitutes contingent reward, and management-by-exception. Contingent reward refers to an exchange relationship where the leader rewards others in exchange for whatever the leader assigns the others to do. Management-by-exception refers to the leader monitoring the performance of others and taking corrective action if there are any deviations from the expected standards, or any errors. This can be either 'active' or 'passive' which means that the leader either takes corrective action when necessary, or passively waits for any errors to occur to then go on and take action (2018: 77).

Kark, Van Dijk and Vashdi (2018) point out that the motivation that the transactional leadership style elicits from others is to do what is expected in order to avoid punishment, also referred to as management-by-exception passive or transactional passive, to receive rewards, that is, contingent rewards, or to prevent corrective action indicating a mistake is about to be made, which is referred to as management-by-exception active or transactional active. Kark et al. (2018) found that the transactional active leadership style, which refers to leaders monitoring others' mistakes, deviations and losses, may undermine followers' creativity because it relates to employees' situational prevention focus. What this means is that it is easier to discourage creativity than to encourage it, because the focus of a prevention system is on safety and security instead of development. The focus on prevention results in fewer resources being allocated to other ongoing goals such as development goals (Van Dijk, Seger-Guttmann and Heller, 2013; Schodl and Van Dijk, 2014).

The advantages of a transactional leadership style in relation to corporate social responsibility (CSR) are highlighted by Du, Swaen, Lindgreen and Sen (2013). For instance, transactional leaders set clear CSR-related goals and articulate explicitly the rewards to the relevant organisational members. Interestingly, Du et al.'s (2013) study found that transactional leadership enhances, whereas transformational leadership diminishes the positive relationship between institutional CSR practices and organisational outcomes. However, managers with greater transformational leadership were more likely to engage in institutional CSR practices.

Kang, Solomon and Choi (2015) in their study of 39 CEOs and 105 managers, found that both transactional and transformational leadership styles had a positive impact on followers' innovative behaviours. **Vroom's expectancy theory** is used to understand the effects of both perceived styles. While the transformational leadership style uses expectancy, a motivational force, to intrinsically motivate followers, transactional leaders, on the other hand, use instrumentality to extrinsically motivate their followers. Hence, empirical research indicates that both the transformational and transactional leadership styles can be beneficial to organisations.

Several scholars (see Bryman, 1992; Sadler, 1997; Antonakis and House, 2002; Gill, 2006; Edwards, Schyns, Gill and Higgs, 2012) have argued that transactional leadership is akin to management (Schedlitzki and Edwards, 2018). We discuss the leadership versus management debate later in this chapter.

Critique of charismatic-transformational leadership

Several criticisms of charismatic-transformational leadership have been provided by leadership scholars over the years. We review some of these criticisms in this section.

In their in-depth critique of charismatic-transformational leadership (CTL), van Knippenberg and Sitkin (2013) highlight four problems. It is important to note that these problems are interrelated. First, they argue that a clear definition of the construct seems to be lacking. There is an over-emphasis on exceptional leadership being out there and naturally occurring, stemming from ideas about CTL that have been inductively derived. Drawing on Yukl (1999), van Knippenberg and Sitkin (2013) argue that multi-dimensional models should clearly explain all the criteria for the exclusion and inclusion of dimensions. For example, it is unclear how individualised consideration, which is one of the components of the construct, is different from consideration (Judge, Piccolo and Ilies, 2004), empowering leadership (Arnold, Arad, Rhoades and Drasgow, 2000) or leader–member exchange (LMX) theory, as all these variables seem to focus on coaching and attending to followers' needs. The similarities and differences between these dimensions and other dimensions of leadership need to be explored further, as some of these aspects of leadership are considered charismatic-transformational, whereas others are not. To that end, van Knippenberg and Sitkin question why idealised influence, inspirational motivation, individualised consideration and intellectual stimulation are classified as charismatic-transformational (van Knippenberg and Sitkin, 2013).

Second, it is unclear how the different elements of CTL unite, and how they all combine with each other to form higher-order constructs. The justification for this additive model of CTL is questioned as they only seem to be proposed dimensions. Moreover, these dimensions are highly intercorrelated and therefore cannot be treated as separate dimensions. Van Knippenberg and Sitkin argue that 'what is currently missing is a configurational theory that is capable of explaining how and why different dimensions combine to affect outcomes' (2013: 13), which results in a lack of conceptual justification in research. Such measurement issues have been critiqued by others (see Tourish and Pinnington, 2002; Alvesson and Spicer, 2012; Alvesson and Kärreman, 2016).

The third issue is to do with the distinction between the cause and effect of the various dimensions of CTL. It is not clear how these dimensions are independent of the effectiveness of these elements. This is explained further by Alvesson and Kärreman (2016). In their critique of transformational leadership, they highlight the tautological issue inherent in the construct. This means that the behaviour is explained by its effects. It is not clear which elements of the construct lead to which outcomes; the outcomes and causes are conflated. The tautological problem with charismatic-transformational leadership, that is, the behaviours and their effects being combined, is highlighted as a primary limitation. An important aspect to consider in relation to the cause-effect problem with CTL is to do with attributions of charisma. Research studies that incorporate models of CTL do not consider attributions of charisma as outcomes. Instead, these attributions are seen as being equivalent to the charismatic-transformational leadership behaviours that are identified. The outcomes that are often studied include performance, creativity and motivation, to name a few. It is essential to distinguish between perceptions/attributions of leadership and leadership itself (van Knippenberg and Sitkin, 2013). The distinction between transactional and transformational leadership styles is also questioned, as the focus of extrinsic motivation, and rewards in transactional leadership would imply that any leadership style that focuses on intrinsic motivation would be charismatic and transformational, which indicates that the dimensions should be limited.

The fourth issue highlighted by van Knippenberg and Sitkin (2013) is to do with the invalidity of the empirical evidence gathered by a large number of studies due to the problems in the measurement model. They call for the abandonment of measures such as the MLQ (developed by Bass) because the measure does not capture the multidimensional nature of CTL. Idealised influence and inspirational motivation consist of overlapping content and are hence inseparable. Moreover, the highly correlated dimensions are collapsed into one (CTL) measure. The resulting additive unitary measure does not capture what it is intended to measure due to the disconnectedness between the conceptual and measurement model. This presents a problem with validity. There is also the issue of empirical distinctiveness from other measures (measures that are not CTL). These are to do with dimensions such as contingent reward and consideration. Contingent reward is a characteristic of a transactional style of leadership, which means that it should represent what charismatic-transformational leadership is not. However, empirical studies have found strong correlations between contingent reward and CTL (see Garman, Davis-Lenane, and Corrigan, 2003; Berson and Avolio, 2004; O'Shea, Foti, Hauenstein and Bycio, 2009).

Other criticisms of the construct include the ideological approach to transformational leadership, as articulated by Alvesson and Kärreman (2016). Ideology in this
context is referred to as painting a positive picture of leadership. The authors point to
several problems with transformational leadership. Leader-centricism refers to a
leader-centred approach to transformational leadership in which an individual is the
centre of the organisational universe. The over-emphasis on the individual leader
would result in other factors not being considered. Other problems of the construct
include the denial/minimisation of social setting, tautological issues, arbitrary exclusion of certain behaviours, disregard for social dynamics, incoherent constructs, and
do-goodism. We have already discussed the tautological, construct and measurement-
related issues in relation to van Knippenberg and Sitkin's (2013) critique. Denial/
minimisation of social setting and do-goodism are explained below.

The denial/minimisation of social setting, or regularly neglecting the context (see
Fairhurst, 2001), does not allow for a complete understanding of transformational
leadership. Moreover, the context itself can be complex, as Grint (2005) argues, as the
situations in which we need leaders are themselves socially constructed. The excessive
focus on the individual leader, and the skills they possess, would therefore result in an
insufficient understanding of leadership. The disregard for social dynamics involves a
lack of emphasis on the communication and influence processes within organisations.
Researchers have not sufficiently looked into how these influence processes would
affect managers. These social dynamics would inevitably impact leadership.

'Do-goodism' involves the association of leadership with good outcomes. Alvesson
and Kärreman (2016) critique the framing of leadership in terms of its good outcomes.
TL is associated with positive outcomes despite a number of flaws resulting in the domination of the ideological discourse of leadership. What this means is that the field of
leadership is successful due to the dominance of certain styles of leadership including
TL. Alternative views of leadership such as relational theory (Uhl-Bien, 2006), follower-
centred approaches (Meindl, 1995) and critical perspectives (Grint, 2005; Alvesson and
Spicer, 2012; Collinson, 2012) also reinforce the view that 'the alternative to leadership
is leadership, not peer relations, professionalism, autonomy, co-workership, organising
processes or mutual adjustment offering alternative framings and understanding than
what the leadership vocabulary invites' (Alvesson and Kärreman, 2016: 142). Therefore,
anything and everything is seen as leadership, and this phenomenon is attributed to the
dominance of studies on transformational leadership.

Authentic leadership

Authentic leadership (AL) is a style of leadership that has gained prominence in the
past two decades. The increase in corporate scandals resulting in heightened public

concerns about firms' leadership were cited as the main reason to develop this new form of leadership (Cooper, Scandura and Schriesheim, 2005; Gardner, Avolio, Luthans, May and Walumbwa, 2005; Avolio and Luthans, 2006; Liu, 2011). The definition of AL used in most (positivist) studies is the one developed by Walumbwa, Avolio, Gardner, Wernsing and Peterson (2008). AL is defined as 'a pattern of leader behaviour that draws upon and promotes both positive psychological capacities and a positive ethical climate, to foster greater self-awareness, an internalised moral perspective, balanced processing of information, and relational transparency on the part of leaders working with followers, fostering positive self-development' (Walumbwa et al., 2008: 94).

Walumbwa et al. (2008) developed a measure called the Authentic Leadership Questionnaire (ALQ) which is a 16-item measure intended to measure AL. These items were specifically designed to develop the four main components that were seen as constituting AL: self-awareness, relational transparency, balanced processing and internalised moral perspective. *Self-awareness* refers to showing an understanding of one's strengths and weaknesses and gaining an understanding of the self through exposure to others. *Relational transparency* is defined as presenting one's authentic self as opposed to one's fake self which involves openly sharing information with others. *Balanced processing* relates to leaders objectively analysing all relevant data before making decisions, and also challenging their deeply held views. Finally, *internalised moral perspective* refers to an integrated form of **self-regulation** (Deci and Ryan, 2003; Kernis, 2003; Gardner et al., 2005; Walumbwa et al., 2008 in Prakasam, 2014). Self-regulation is a process through which authentic leaders can align their values with their intentions and actions.

Hoch, Bommer, Dulebohn and Wu (2016) compare forms of positive leadership that emphasise moral behaviour, which include authentic leadership, ethical leadership and servant leadership, with transformational leadership. We discuss ethical leadership in Chapter 8. Hoch et al. (2016) adopt a meta-analysis of authentic and servant leadership and expand on prior meta-analyses of ethical leadership. The differences between authentic and transformational leaders revolve around the fact that leaders may be authentic and not transformational by simply displaying the ethical characteristics of authentic leadership. According to Avolio and Gardner (2005), genuine transformational leaders must be authentic. We have looked at both pseudo-transformational leadership and transformational leadership, where the main point of difference is to do with ethics. Even though the ethical aspects of authentic leadership have been added to the components of TL conceptualised by Bass (1985, 1998), there seems to be a significant conceptual overlap between authentic and transformational leadership (Hoch et al., 2016).

The meta-analyses by Hoch et al. (2016) reveal that authentic leadership shows high correlations with transformational leadership and therefore appears to be problematic.

Authentic leadership was found to explain very little incremental variance from transformational leadership in job performance. Authentic leadership was less important in explaining incremental variance in overall commitment, job satisfaction and employee engagement. Le, Schmidt, Harter and Lauver (2010) point out that a high proliferation of constructs results in construct redundancy, that is, the new constructs may not add anything new and useful. To that end, two criteria were proposed for construct distinctiveness – conceptual and empirical non-redundancy. Conceptual non-redundancy refers to whether two constructs have logically different conceptualisations. Empirical non-redundancy refers to 'constructs not being highly correlated and not having the same pattern of relationships with other variables' (Hoch et al., 2016: 520). In the case of authentic leadership, although TL and AL are conceptualised differently, the correlations between AL and TL in empirical studies were high. Consequently, the meta-analytic study by Hoch et al. (2016) questions the need for authentic leadership as a distinct construct. It is also essential to note that authentic leadership has been largely constructed by researchers, and determined through researchers' choice of inclusion of components such as self-awareness, relational transparency, balanced processing and internalised moral perspective (Nyberg and Sveningsson, 2014; Alvesson and Einola, 2019; Sandberg and Alvesson, 2021).

In the aftermath of the development of the ALQ, several studies were carried out that adopted this tool to measure AL. For instance, Shannon, Buford, Winston and Wood (2020) examined the impact of trigger events and crucibles on authentic leaders' development using a mixed-method study. First, they used the ALQ to measure the participants' authentic leadership. Qualifying participants were then interviewed using a Critical Incident Technique. The findings of the study demonstrated that both trigger events and crucibles affect authentic leaders' development. Additionally, spirituality was found to be a theme in the study.

Criticisms of authentic leadership

The construct of authentic leadership has garnered several criticisms. Many of these criticisms relate to the use of positivist measures such as the ALQ and others have to do more broadly with the overall concept of authenticity.

Given that the formal objectivist conceptualisation of AL stems from Positive Organisational Psychology, there appears to be excessive positivity associated with the construct, which has been critiqued (Alvesson and Einola, 2019). The criticisms for associating excessive positivity with leaders and the wider field of leadership studies have been echoed earlier by Collinson (2012), who uses the metaphor of 'Prozac' to highlight how leaders' excessive positivity leads to a reluctance to engage with alternative conceptualisations, which might lead to organisations and wider society being ill-prepared to deal with unforeseen events. Others have pointed to issues with the overly strength-based view of AL (Diddams and Chang, 2012) and the lack of consideration for weaknesses and imperfections in the conceptualisation of AL (Ford and Harding, 2011).

One of the criticisms of the construct is to do with the component of self-awareness. The over-emphasis on the self in self-awareness is seen as problematic. Sparrowe (2005) argues that the emphasis on the 'self' in self-awareness implies that authenticity lies on the inside (Sparrowe, 2005: 420). Therefore, other individuals, groups and organisations are viewed as sources of inauthenticity. Contemporary perspectives on authenticity such as the AL theory (for example, see Walumbwa et al., 2008) set the self over others. However, in doing so they fail to recognise the significant ways in which the self is constituted in relation to others. Nevertheless, saying that the self is constituted in relation to others does not dissolve the self into the other; the experience of the individual would remain solely their own (Sparrowe, 2005).

The inclusion of a moral component, an internalised moral perspective, has come into criticism. This is because authentic leaders may not necessarily always be moral, and whilst being true to their values, they might have immoral values. Claiming that a particular form of leadership is intrinsically moral is not only difficult to falsify empirically but also exceptionally difficult to argue logically. Sparrowe (2005) argues that leading from one's purpose can only be moral if one's purposes are moral. In fact, leaders might behave immorally because of the very fact that they are blinded by their own values. This is because values do not necessarily lead to one action, and positive values can in fact be in conflict (Price, 2003).

The self-report nature of survey questionnaires (such as the ALQ) may be problematic as leaders may hold inflated views of themselves. It has been highlighted that impression management may be an issue in self-report surveys (Gray and Densten, 2007; Randolph-Seng and Gardner, 2013). Asking subordinates of leaders to rate the authenticity of the leader might also be challenging, as leaders may be good at creating the impression that they are authentic (Gardner, Fischer and Hunt, 2009). Moreover, the quantification of authentic leadership through the obsession of measuring, modelling and conducting correlations can be seen as diverting our attention away from a genuine understanding of the world (Alvesson and Einola, 2021).

Overall, the notion of authenticity is far too complex, with rich existential underpinnings that have not been considered in leadership theorising, barring a few exceptions (see Algera and Lips-Wiersma, 2012). While recognising the importance of authenticity, critical scholars (Alvesson and Einola, 2019, 2021) have questioned the usefulness of the AL construct in organisational settings.

Modifying your leadership style

It can be incredibly frustrating for talented individuals to not be able to move ahead in their careers because they lack an appropriate leadership style (Peterson, Abramson and Stutman, 2020). People can appear more competent than they really are through a great leadership style. Actions and behaviours are crucial, and Peterson et al. (2020) argue that power and attractiveness are assessed based on what individuals display. For instance, when nervous whilst going into a big presentation, power markers would help project confidence and in turn be viewed favourably by audience members. Peterson et al. (2020) share an example of an executive they worked with, Martin, who was experiencing issues with his leadership style as he was constantly being given feedback that he was intimidating, domineering and coercive. Martin seemed to exhibit a much more powerful style in professional settings than in other social contexts. In order to help him soften his style, he was asked to adopt four specific markers. First, he was asked to reduce talking over others as he did that often. Second, he was to use questions to accompany his opinions, instead of using declarations. Third, he was asked to adopt 'partnership language' by using fewer 'I' references, and instead referring more to 'we' and 'our'. Finally, he was asked to slow down and restate what he had heard to demonstrate empathetic listening. These changes worked for Martin and he started to receive more favourable evaluations.

Questions

1. Should women, ethnic minorities and LGBTQ individuals have to carefully manage their leadership style in order to not suffer penalties in their career progression?
2. To what extent is it important to project authentic leadership?

Leader versus manager debate

There are various perspectives on the distinction between leadership and management. While Bennis and Nanus (1985) argued that 'managers do things right whereas leaders do the right things' (Buchanan and Huczynski, 2017: 600), Mintzberg (2009) suggests that we should not be trying to make this distinction as this is not useful to practice. As Edwards, Schedlitzki, Turnbull and Gill (2015) point out, leadership and management were viewed as the same by some (see Drucker, 1988), and as connected by others (see Mintzberg, 1980; Kotter, 1988, 1990; Bass, 1990; Hickman, 1990; Rost, 1991).

Edwards et al. (2015) came up with a conceptual framework with four quadrants that shed light on the leader versus manager debate. This conceptual framework considers the underlying assumptions of power and uses this as a basis for the four-part model. In the first quadrant, *managers doing leadership*, management is viewed as a position of responsibility within an organisational structure, and leadership is viewed through a traditional lens as a set of behaviours needed for managers to be effective and hence known as managers doing leadership (Alvesson and Sveningsson, 2003).

The second quadrant is *managers becoming leaders* where both management and leadership are viewed as positions of responsibility. This quadrant takes a figure-head perspective of leadership, where leadership is viewed as being higher on the hierarchical order. Bedeian and Hunt (2006) highlight that this assumption that leaders are top-level organisational members is limiting as it focuses solely on leadership as a position as opposed to an influence process.

The third quadrant is *'being' managers and leaders*. Here, management is seen as coping or getting by (Mangham, 1986; Watson, 1994) and is about uncertainty reduction. Here, both leadership and management are seen as emergent, self-focused, devoid of any influences by organisational authority, and are both viewed in relation to identity.

The fourth quadrant is *leaders 'doing' management* where leadership is viewed as the position of responsibility and management is the personal ability to cope or get by. In this quadrant, leadership is viewed from an assigned perspective, and management is viewed from an emergent perspective. Examples of this quadrant include biographies of charismatic business leaders' ability to lead large organisations successfully (Salaman, 2004) as well as biographies of political leaders (see Mandela, 1994; Mowlam, 2002; Obama, 2007). The case study about Nkrumah earlier in the chapter serves as a good example.

Grint (2005), through his analysis of three cases: Brent Spar; the Cuban Missile Crisis; and the war on Iraq, highlighted that situations requiring leadership themselves tend to be socially constructed, wherein a particular (leadership) approach is used to address the resulting socially constructed situation. Grint (2005) distinguishes between the situations as tame, wicked and critical, where tame problems have unilinear or straightforward solutions addressed through management. When faced with tame problems, managers would provide appropriate processes to solve problems. Wicked problems deal with uncertainty, requiring some form of collaboration and leadership. Finally, critical situations are those pertaining to crises where an authoritarian response labelled as 'command' is required.

Over a decade later, as Grint (2020) points out, the COVID-19 pandemic can be viewed through this classification where COVID-19 testing could be seen as a tame problem which gets the processes in order. Wicked problems in relation to COVID-19 would be those that aren't solvable but can be dealt with through a collective response which requires 'leadership' (p. 315). Examples of such leadership would include asking individuals and communities to help each other and asking them to self-iso-late. Given the complexity of wicked problems, no one quite knows what to do. Critical problems or crises require 'command' to 'coerce her or his followers into line to avoid a catastrophe' (Grint, 2020: 315). Examples of command include the closure of schools and businesses to prevent the spread. The pandemic is a wicked problem that seems to have no end in sight and no clear-cut solutions (Grint, 2020).

Another perspective of the idea of a manager and management comes from Sturdy, Wright and Wylie (2016) who view management as consulting. This view stems from the idea that because of managers becoming increasingly professionalised, we have ended up with consultant managers, which means that consultancy has become internalised within organisations. Examples include the transformation of HRM and internal auditing. For instance, there are roles such as HR business partners in several organisations. Sturdy et al. (2016) situate this within a **neo-bureaucratic organisation**. Before we explore what this means, it is essential to distinguish between a bureaucratic and a post-bureaucratic organisation. A bureaucratic organisation is made up of specialisation, standardisation, formalisation, centralisation, depersonalisation and collectivisation.

A post-bureaucratic organisation includes collaboration, flexibility, negotiation, dispersal (decentralisation), personalisation and individualisation. In essence, a post-bureaucratic organisation is opposite to a traditional bureaucratic organisation. The post-bureaucratic manager is portrayed like a consultant, as a partner and catalyst of organisational change and/or an expert dispensing advice through project-based working 'inspiration, expert advice … and proactive instigation of change' (Hales, 2002: 55; see also Tengblad, 2006 quoted in Sturdy et al., 2016: 185). 'Neo-bureaucracy is a hybrid that combines market and bureaucracy, centralised and decentralised control' (Sturdy et al., 2016: 187) or 'new and more distributed modes of organisation juxtaposed with bureaucratic modes of co-ordination and control' (Farrell and Morris, 2013: 1389 quoted in Sturdy et al., 2016: 187). Management as consultancy reflects this type of neo-bureaucratic hybrid. Hence, it is useful to consider the impact of such professionalisation of managers on the leader versus manager debate.

Conclusion

In this chapter, we began by defining leadership styles, and explored how they differ from leadership traits. The importance of context-based perspectives of leadership were explored early on given their impact on leadership and leadership outcomes. Dominant styles of leadership such as charismatic-transformational leadership and authentic leadership were explored and critiqued. We have seen that both leadership constructs, especially when explored through a positivist paradigm, have numerous issues. Finally, we reviewed various perspectives of the leader versus manager debate which presents a complex terrain. Chapter 4 explores the social constructionist lens and the eye of the beholder perspective in detail where we return to examining authentic leadership.

Decolonising leadership

Girei, E. (2017) 'Decolonising management knowledge: A reflexive journey as practitioner and researcher in Uganda', *Management Learning*, 48(4): 453–470.

Through an empirical study, Girei (2017) provides a reflexive account of a researcher in Uganda and her search for methodologies and research practices sensitive to the critiques of a Western-centric focus on management knowledges. The article addresses the challenges of the scholar, and her efforts to decolonise her methodological approach.

Key summary

- Leadership styles can be learnt and developed as opposed to leadership traits that individuals are born with.
- Context plays an important role in leadership outcomes.
- There has been a proliferation of leadership styles over the past two decades. Charismatic-transformational leadership (CTL) is one of the most researched constructs. Charismatic and transformational leadership styles have several overlapping dimensions, and are therefore referred to as a single construct by some scholars.
- CTL has garnered several criticisms which relate to construct development, the overlap between some of the dimensions that are said to make up the construct such as idealised influence and inspirational motivation, making it difficult to draw a distinction between them. The ideological approach to the construct has been seen as problematic.
- Pseudo-transformational leadership (PTL) was developed as a response to the criticism that the dark side of transformational leadership was overlooked.
- Contemporary research related to CTL and PTL in non-Western contexts reveals the importance of considering culture in the investigation of CTL and PTL.
- Authentic leadership (AL) was developed as a response to an increase in concerns over corporate scandals.

- The Authentic Leadership Questionnaire (ALQ) is a 16-item measure that measures the four components of AL which are self-awareness, balanced processing, internalised moral perspective and relational transparency.
- Criticisms of AL include measurement issues as well as the complexity of the notion of authenticity.
- The leadership versus management debate is complex, with varying perspectives on the relationship between the two. Underlying assumptions of power play an important role while theorising both.

Further reading

Davis, A. P. and Vila-Henninger, L. (2021) 'Charismatic authority and fractured polities: A cross-national analysis'. *The British Journal of Sociology*. DOI: 10.1111/1468-4446.12841

Gardner, W. L., Karam, E. P., Alvesson, M. and Einola, K. (2021) 'Authentic leadership theory: The case for and against', *The Leadership Quarterly*, 23(6).

Spiller, C. (2021) '"I AM": Indigenous consciousness for authenticity and leadership', *Leadership*. DOI: 10.1177/1742715021999590

4

THE SOCIAL CONSTRUCTION OF LEADERSHIP

Naveena Prakasam

Chapter objectives

The objectives of this chapter are:

- To review the social construction of leadership.
- To critically analyse the importance of followers and followership.
- To examine the social construction of leadership and followership in relation to practice.

Reflective questions

1. Why do you consider someone a leader?
2. Why do you consider someone a follower?
3. What factors contribute to the construction of leadership?

Introduction

The objective of this chapter is to explore the social construction of leadership, as well as consider the importance of followers. We explored implicit leadership theories (ILTs) in Chapter 2, which focuses on followers' perceptions of leader traits. ILTs focus on the eye of the beholder by analysing individual (follower) lay images of leaders. In this chapter, we focus entirely on the social construction of leadership and follower/followership approaches to leadership and examine the diverse approaches that fall within the social construction of leadership, as well as follower/followership. It is useful to revisit Smircich and Morgan's (1982) definition of leadership in which they argue that 'leadership is realised in the process whereby one or more individuals succeed in attempting to frame and define the reality of others' (Smircich and Morgan, 1982: 258). This definition points to the notion that leadership is co-constructed by several actors and processes. To this end, we will explore the meaning of **social constructionism** before proceeding further. We begin by examining the philosophical origins of social constructionism to understand the main assumptions of the paradigm and then we will look at the social construction of leadership to explore the different ways in which leadership has been approached that are subsumed in this approach. We then move on to a detailed discussion of followers and followership.

Social construction of reality

Social constructionism problematises the claim that knowledge can be derived from the unbiased observation of events (Burr, 2015). Hence, this emphasises the importance of the processes through which knowledge can be derived.

The birth of social constructionism can be largely attributed to Berger and Luckmann's (1966) *The Social Construction of Reality: A Treatise in the Sociology of Knowledge*. Before we explore the social constructionist view of leadership, it is useful to understand some of the arguments made by them, who based their view of reality as a social construction on Schutz's ideas. Alfred Schutz was an Austrian philosopher who made a significant contribution to **phenomenology**. Berger and Luckmann's work consists of three major parts: the reality of everyday life, society as objective reality and society as subjective reality. According to them, reality is a quality, something that belongs to phenomena that we see as being independent of our own choice. The other important term is knowledge, which is widely used in everyday language. This is the target of deep philosophical scrutiny which disputes the ultimate status of both 'reality' and 'knowledge' (Strati, 2000: 65).

According to Berger and Luckmann, our social world can be understood as a 'dialectical process of externalization, objectivation and internalization' (Cunliffe, 2008: 125). Externalisation refers to the idea that the social world constitutes ongoing activity and routines that are humanly produced. Berger and Luckmann (1966: 49) use the term objectivation to refer to 'products of human activity that are available both to their producers and to other men as elements of a common world'. Objectivation means that even though the social world is humanly produced, it is experienced as being objective because it affects our lives on an ongoing basis and is 'thing-like' (Steets, 2016: 94). For instance, although linguistic expressions can't be touched, they are real and are commonly recognised. We need to learn about them to be understood. The same can be applied to institutions (Steets, 2016). Internalisation refers to the notion that we take on our own identity and place by being socialised in the world through the interpretation of meanings (Cunliffe, 2008). Therefore, a dialectical process refers to considering the relationships between these varied ideas.

It can be argued that it is only through understanding how reality has been institutionalised that it is even possible to distinguish between objective and subjective reality. Institutionalisation refers to the way beliefs, norms and values become embedded within institutions. Objective reality refers to something that is independent of our minds. Subjective reality refers to something which is dependent on our minds. As Simpson (1967) argues, Berger and Luckmann (1966) understand knowledge to not purely mean ideology, like Marx, Engels, Nietzche and Mannheim, but rather everything that passes for knowledge in society. Here, knowledge means what everyone recognises it to be, and not only what the learned take it to be. It is helpful to think about leadership in this way as it helps us recognise that there are numerous definitions of leadership and therefore all those definitions of leadership can pass for what leadership is.

According to Berger and Luckmann (1966), new meanings emerge as objects are attributed new meanings to solve problems. By discovering and constructing new meanings, we are inclined to become aware of our own subjective role in making sense of the world. However, subjective reality turns into an objective one when a meaning attributed to something becomes part of the everyday shared routines of many (Light, 1967), which happens through institutionalisation. We are therefore constantly socially constructing meanings. However, teachers or pupils hardly think of themselves as rendering socially constructed meanings to objects. In fact, they see it as spreading the 'true' meaning. What was once a 'nominalistic' situation has become a 'realistic' one, and what was once given subjective meaning has become objective fact (Berger and Luckmann, 1966: 89 in Light, 1967).

Consequently, this transformation of subjective meaning into objective reality leads to 'social institutions' which seek to control and represent this objective reality as opposed to an individual's subjective one. This leads to the legitimation of institutionalised behaviour. Legitimation refers to the process of validating that all activities are justifiable. Institutional legitimation refers to everything in a universe constituting a symbolic universe, which encompasses all 'socially objectivated and subjectively real meanings, the entire historic society and the entire biography of the individual ... seen as events taking place within this universe' (Berger and Luckmann, 1966: 96; Light, 1967). The social construction of reality can only be maintained if the social order can be justified so that members can accept its legitimacy.

Common-sense knowledge does not always satisfy individuals' quest for knowing and, therefore, theoretical legitimation is needed to defend common-sense reality. Berger and Luckmann (1966) were therefore interested in the conscious process whereby knowledge is created, acquired, taken for granted, doubted, and finally, rejected.

Therefore, in these complex ways, society is socially constructed.

Social construction of leadership

It is useful to look at Fairhurst and Grant's (2010) work where they dissect the various approaches which fall within the realm of social construction in leadership studies by offering a sailing guide for the 'social construction of leadership' (Fairhurst and Grant, 2010: 171). They adopt Barnette Pearce's approach to social constructionism in their discussion of leadership studies. Earlier psychology-based studies of leadership are challenged, and a more social and cultural approach to leadership studies is introduced in which leadership is seen as co-constructed. Such a view of leadership privileges lay persons' constructions of leadership instead of imposing researchers' views on the topic, which was largely the case with the psychology-based studies. Leadership is therefore seen because of collective meaning making that embodies 'a complex interplay among leadership actors, be they designated or emergent leaders, managers and/or followers' (Meindl, 1995; Grint, 2000; Gronn, 2000, 2002; Collinson, 2006; Vine, Holmes, Marra, Pfeifer and Jackson, 2008 in Fairhurst and Grant, 2010: 172). As we have learnt in the preceding section, social constructionism recognises that there are multiple realities simultaneously competing for truth and legitimacy. Meanings are constantly produced and reproduced, creating structures that are stable yet constantly evolving through the unfolding of interactions (Giddens, 1979, 1984). Drawing on Gioia (2003), Fairhurst and Grant (2010) refer to 'intersubjectively produced enterprises' which suggest that such structures are not real (Gioia, 2003: 189; Fairhurst and Grant, 2010: 174).

The constructionist stance on leadership encompasses the idea that leadership is not determined by the nature of things. It may even go further to suggest that we would be better off without leadership (see Clegg and Hardy, 1996). An important point to remember here is that while a discursive approach which embraces critical theory is social constructionist, a constructionist stance does not automatically presume a critical one. Therefore, the realm of social constructionist approaches to leadership is quite broad.

There are four dimensions within social construction of leadership studies put forth by Fairhurst and Grant (2010). The first dimension is to do with the difference between the construction of social reality and the social construction of reality. The construction of social reality is about categories such as implicit theories and follower attributions. We discussed implicit leadership theories in Chapter 3. Followership and Meindl et al.'s (1985) romance of leadership, which looks at follower attributions, will be discussed in detail in the subsequent sections of this chapter. The social construction of reality is about the social aspects of the interactions themselves, instead of the cognitive processes amidst followers and audiences. Both poles within the dimension and construction of social reality, as well as the social construction of reality, consider the eye of the beholder view of leadership, but the latter considers the processual aspects and the emergent meanings resulting from interactions in addition to the interactions themselves. The second dimension is about theory versus praxis where theoretical knowledge is seen as an end in itself. This is on one pole of the dimension, and the practical use of theory is on the other. For instance, Liu's (2010) study on failure-framing strategies by leaders through the analysis of media texts can be seen as being about theory as the focus is on using media texts to comprehend what encompasses leadership failure. Praxis, on the other hand, is about viewing theory and practice in conjunction. For instance, Smolović Jones, Smolović Jones, Winchester and Grint (2016) discuss the praxis of democratic leadership development where they argue that their theoretical framework can only be understood in relation to the contextual experiences of both academics and practitioners.

The third dimension is the critical/emancipatory versus pragmatic intervention where the former is concerned with issues of power and domination and has emancipatory aims, whereas the latter is less to do with power. The critical pole encompasses critical management studies (CMS) within which Cunliffe (2009) points out that there are two schools of thought. These are poststructuralist, where realities are seen as being constructed by both discursive practices, and institutional structures and techniques; and **Marxist** and **Neo-Marxist**, where the politics of capitalism are examined. The fourth dimension is the monomodal versus multimodal. Monomodal studies focus on leadership actors' language whereas multimodal considers language use as just one way of understanding leadership and also looks at other aspects such as space, body, technology, and so on.

Fairhurst and Grant's (2010) four-dimensional classification within the social construction of leadership helps us delve further into the different approaches through which leadership can be explored that fall within the umbrella of social construction of leadership.

It would be useful to examine **discursive leadership** which sits within the social constructionist approach to leadership. The development of a discursive approach to leadership can be attributed to a linguistic turn within organisation studies (Alvesson and Kärreman, 2000). According to Fairhurst (2008), discursive leadership attempts to answer two questions. These encompass, first, what we can see, think and talk about with a discursive lens, and second, what leadership knowledge can be gained through the interplay of both discursive and psychological lenses. Fairhurst (2008) views the discursive leadership approach as a contrast to leadership psychology. She provides a distinction between 'little d' discourse and 'big D' Discourse. Discourse, based on Foucault's (1972, 1980) approach, is a system of thought that provides a resource to actors as they communicate; 'little d' discourse is talk in interaction (Fairhurst and Grant, 2010: 179).

Fairhurst (2008) provides some useful distinctions between discursive leadership and leadership psychology. These are very useful distinctions given that many of the leadership studies are psychology based (as we explored in Chapter 2). There are six differences outlined between the two. The first difference is to do with the object of the study. While leadership psychologists study causal models, and the interrelationships between the variables, such as dependent, independent and moderating variables, Fairhurst (2008) argues that the interaction that is studied is purely statistical. On the other hand, discourse analyses study discourse/Discourse which involves talk in interaction, interview discourse and other communicative practices that are dialogical. Hence, there is a focus on the interaction process itself.

The second difference is to do with ontology which is about the nature of reality. Leadership psychology essentialises leadership by focusing on trait theories, situational theories, or a combination of these that we explored in previous chapters. What essentialising means in this context is that an object, or in this case leadership, has a set of attributes that can be identified and measured. Discursive approaches, on the other hand, focus on socially constructed views, which move away from a fixed or stable view of leadership (see Alvesson and Spicer, 2012).

The third difference relates to power, where power is treated negatively by leadership psychologists, seen as exercised in a top-down fashion, while influence is viewed as a positive process (Collinson, 2006). Discursive scholars, on the other hand, see power as encompassing both positive and negative terms which might include Foucauldian relational views of power. Fourth, while discursive approaches emphasise the reflexive agency of leadership actors, there is an emphasis on language and human agency. The fifth difference is to do with the fact that discourse scholars do not primarily focus on building generalisable theory, but instead consider the context that encompasses cultural and political factors that would play a role in constructing leadership, and also look at how leadership may be constructed through interaction. The leadership psychology approach, on the other hand, examines cause and effect and looks at 'why' questions in relation to leadership.

The final and sixth difference that Fairhurst (2008) articulates is that while leadership psychology only has a secondary interest in social and communicative aspects pertaining to individual cognitions, discursive leadership scholars are primarily interested in complication and human interaction.

Adopting a discursive approach, Clifton and Mueni (2020) carry out a discourse analysis of how followers discursively construct transformational leadership, drawing on romance of leadership theory (which will be discussed in further detail in a subsequent section in this chapter). Their findings emphasise the role of 'things that matter' (Clifton and Mueni, 2020: 14), which form part of a socio-material perspective of leadership. A socio-material perspective looks at both humans and other material aspects in the construction of leadership. Socio-materiality focuses on this entanglement between the social and the material. For instance, Cooren (2020) proposes that materiality is a property of all organisational phenomena and that studying this phenomenon leads to processes of materialisation. Within an organisational context, this materialisation may involve thinking about a (strategic) plan, discussing it with colleagues and then implementing it. The context and focus of Clifton and Mueni's (2020) study were on Wangari Maathai, the first African woman to win the Nobel prize for sustainable development. Clifton and Mueni (2020) carried out interviews with four individuals who were winners of the Wangari Maathai prize. The death of Maathai inspired followers to start an environmental club and continue her work of planting trees. It is not only living leaders but also things that inspire followers; in this case, the autobiography of Maathai was a source of inspiration highlighting the importance of considering the socio-material aspects of leadership. Importantly, this study sheds light on an African aspect to the romance of leadership, transformational leadership as well as discursive leadership.

We looked at Grint's (2005, 2020) approach to social construction in Chapter 3 in relation to context, where the emphasis was on the situation itself being socially constructed, which subsequently required differing solutions depending on the nature of the situation/problem; for instance, tame problems requiring management solutions, wicked problems requiring leadership solutions and critical problems requiring command. These situations/contexts have implications for the social construction of leadership. Mini case study 4.1 looks at the context of COVID-19 in relation to the social construction of leadership.

Coronavirus, social construction and leadership

The year 2020 saw an unprecedented crisis affecting the whole world in the form of the COVID-19 pandemic.

While businesses/organisations were able to cope rapidly and adapt to the changes imposed by the pandemic, which included remote working, online education and ghost kitchens in the restaurant industry, political leadership and the public sector seemed to lag behind (Uhl-Bien, 2021). Uhl-Bien (2021) emphasises the importance of leadership by arguing that leadership can literally be the difference between life and death. One of the reasons why the pandemic and its leadership are relevant to the social construction of leadership is due to the interaction of the various elements that co-construct leadership in the complex world. For instance, media is a powerful modern control system (see Giddens, 1991) that can shift narratives about leadership effectiveness. Failed leadership also reflects failed followership where followers might turn a blind eye to leaders' misdirection (Uhl-Bien, 2021). However, protests erupted in Brazil against the response of Jair Bolsonaro's handling of the pandemic in which the death toll passed 500,000. Critics have accused Bolsonaro of choosing the economy over lives (Londono and Milhorance, 2021).

Elsewhere in the Global South, India saw an enormous rise in COVID-19 cases as well as deaths during its second wave due to a new (Delta) variant which has also been attributed to the failure of leadership. However, neo-colonial dynamics can be observed where the newly elected Biden administration in the United States (US) stopped the supply of raw materials needed for the manufacturing of vaccines in India during its second wave. Neocolonialism is the modern-day equivalent of colonialism where powerful nations, whilst advocating for freedom and equality, continue to exploit developing nations for economic imperatives (Sayed and Agndal, 2020). Here, the indirect form was the reasoning given by the US that they had to prioritise American people first, despite the increasing death rates in other parts of the world. While the ban was later lifted after much negotiation, the actions of the US did not only delay the manufacturing process of vaccines in India, the second largest manufacturer of COVID-19 vaccines globally, but also indirectly affected less developed countries in Africa and South Asia impacted by the pandemic, to which India was supplying vaccines. Despite this, most media articles continue to primarily focus on the mismanagement of the pandemic in the Global South, with only a few taking a critical view of the individualist, neo-colonial actions of Western nations such as the US, and their responsibility in the worsening situation caused by the pandemic. The media narrative continues to selectively focus on the assistance provided by the more powerful nations and their role in solving the COVID-19 crisis for the world, despite their exploitative actions.

1. What are the different factors that you can identify which co-construct leadership?
2. What is the role of followers during the COVID-19 crisis?
3. What is the role of media in co-constructing leadership?

The social construction of authentic leadership

In Chapter 3, we explored authentic leadership and reviewed some of the criticisms of the functionalist approach to authentic leadership. In this section, we review constructionist approaches to authentic leadership that encompass discursive and critical approaches.

Liu, Cutcher and Grant (2015) examine media analysis of a gendered construction of authentic leadership. Liu et al. (2015) carried out a multi-modal discourse analysis of the media representations of two banking CEOs, one male and one female, during the global financial crisis. 'Multi-modal analysis focuses on not just words as texts, but also visuals, and this enables us to explore the way in which the leaders perform their authenticity for the media as well as the way in which the media draws on gendered stereotypes and norms to construct the leaders as authentic or inauthentic' (Liu et al., 2015: 240). Liu et al. (2015) argue that being constructed as authentic depends on these leaders performing authenticity in line with gender norms. **Authenticity** is not something that individuals possess but is something that is attributed to them (Lawler and Ashman, 2012; Sinclair, 2013). This attribution of authenticity is not stable but is continually constituted through the enactment of embodied gendered leadership (Butler, 1988, 1999) entrenched in a context that itself is discursively constructed. The study by Liu et al. (2015) highlights the social constructionist nature of authentic leadership, and points to the role of media as a powerful entity that co-constructs leaders' authenticity.

Iszatt-White, Stead and Elliot (2021) use the lens of emotional labour to analyse one of the four components of authentic leadership, 'relational transparency', through interviews and diary studies with individuals in leadership positions. Their study is entrenched in the assumption that leadership is socially constructed. Their findings shed light on the complexity of authenticity, revealed when leaders disclose that they feel authentic even as they manage their emotions as a routine tool of accomplishing their leadership role. The paradoxical existence of inauthenticity seems inevitable. Iszatt-White et al. (2021) argue that participants' acceptance of emotional labour as routine in leadership practice leads to participants constructing authentic leadership as requiring inauthenticity.

The paradox of authenticity is well articulated by Guthey and Jackson (2005) who examine CEO portraits. CEO portraits seem to help represent the sense of visual identity and authentic presence that corporations lack. They argue that photographs of top management figures constitute an important aspect of the various symbolic activities of an organisation. They point out that the authentication of corporate identity through CEO portraits is akin to reinforcing individual identities through photographs and portraits. Photographs play a role in the production of individual identities as well as the modern institution of individual identity. Gurthey and Jackson (2005) demonstrate through the analysis of Per Morten Abrahamson's work (a renowned Danish photographer) as well as conversations with him, that at first glance, CEO portraits seem to convey an authentic presence, but on closer examination, they seem to expose the corporations' lack of authenticity due to the corporations' reliance on portraits to smooth over authenticity issues. 'In this paradoxical manner the CEO portrait smooths over the corporation's authenticity problems on one level but perpetuates or even intensifies them on several other levels at the same time' (Guthey and Jackson, 2005: 1077–1078), indicating an authenticity paradox. Hence, the preceding perspectives offer a different approach to authentic leadership, as reviewed in Chapter 3. The social constructionist view of authentic leadership sees both authenticity and leadership not as fixed constructs, but as continually evolving constructs based on various factors, including but not limited to follower views, leaders' performance and images as well as media narratives.

Romance of leadership

Meindl, Ehlrich and Dukerich (1985) define **romance of leadership** (ROL) as a tendency in academic research towards exaggerating leaders' contributions and treating leadership as causal and explanatory. They viewed leadership as socially constructed and further argued that leadership was in fact a perception playing a part in the way people attempt to make sense of the phenomena pertaining to organisations. Due to this, leadership has assumed 'a larger-than-life, romanticised role' (Meindl et al., 1985: 79). This would mean that followers did not only over-attribute organisational successes to leaders; corporate failures may also be largely attributed to individual leaders due to romanticised notions associated with leadership.

Meindl et al. (1985) hypothesised that any peak in performance, either low or high, tended to be linked to leadership. They carried out a series of studies, in order to investigate how many articles were relating performance to leadership in the *Wall*

Street Journal. The same process was carried out with doctoral dissertations to examine the interest in leadership and performance. These archival studies concluded that there had been considerable interest in attributing high or low performance to leadership. Experiments were also conducted using undergraduates as a sample where they were asked to answer vignette questions which related leadership and several other factors to the high/moderate/low performance of an organisation. Overall, the series of experiments indicated that extreme performances did lead to a proportional increase in the preference to use the leader as a causal explanation. Drawing on Pfeffer (1977) and Pfeffer and Salancik (1978), Meindl et al. (1985) argued that the propensity to assign high levels of control and influence to leaders arises from private needs to find causes among human actors.

The findings from Meindl et al.'s (1985) study indicate that the dependence on leadership is likely to exceed the reality of control and will be used to explain discrepancies which are actually uncontrollable. Meindl (1985) draws on evidence presented by Salancik and Meindl (1984) demonstrating that top management tries to produce an illusion of control by manipulating causal reasoning around performance issues. This pattern is realised in organisations which seem to show unpredictable performance histories that might indicate little or no control. Meindl et al. (1985) point out that the greater significance of leadership lies in the ability to manage the meanings and interpretations that relevant parties give to whatever events are deemed as important for the functioning of the organisation (Pondy, 1978; Daft and Weick, 1984). It may be that the symbolic gestures exhibited by leaders lead to the romanticised conception of leadership among followers.

Collinson, Smolović Jones and Grint (2018) offer a new way to think about romance of leadership by extending Meindl et al.'s thesis. Meindl et al. (1985) argue that 'leadership should be understood as intimately entangled in organizational symbolism and by extension wider social symbolism' (Collinson et al., 2018: 1627). It is in this way that their view was entrenched in social constructionism as their view was focused on language and other social processes managed by leaders, resulting in 'leadership' assuming a status of mystery and near mysticism. Collinson et al. (2018) argue that ROL was misrepresented/neglected in subsequent studies following Meindl et al.'s original proposition.

'Romanticism' is a broad and historically rich term and is not just about leader attribution. Collinson et al. also point out that the romanticism critique is useful to understand other influential theories such as authentic leadership, spiritual leadership and collective leadership (Collinson et al., 2018: 1625). While ROL has been extremely influential and highly cited in the field of leadership studies (for example, see Shamir, 1992; Gray and Densten, 2007; Felfe and Schyns, 2014), the central critique of Meindl et al. has been largely ignored in several subsequent studies (Collinson et al., 2018). Sergi, Lusiani and Langley (2021) have pointed to the visibility of ROL in the first few months of the COVID-19 pandemic where images of heroic leadership are prevalent. However, they point to the plural and relational forms of leadership that are less highlighted. They further argue that there is a paradox where there is a need to acknowledge that the social process of leading also involves the romance of the heroic individual despite collective work. Sergi et al. (2021) acknowledge the importance of approaching leadership more critically. For instance, leadership has been seen as:

> a social myth… , a fantasy…, a mystique…, leaderism… (and deemed a quest for saviours…, among others. Some have even gone so far as to suggest that leadership is an empty signifier… or that the entire concept rests on emptiness. (Sergi et al., 2021: 166)

However, Sergi et al. (2021) argue that several critical perspectives of management and organisation studies lead researchers and practitioners to be disillusioned, and therefore offer alternatives such as plural perspectives of leadership which offer a way beyond the individual focus of leadership.

Existing work on romanticism in relation to leadership studies sees romanticism as 'hope' for the future and is seen less critically by Kempster and Carroll (2016). They have not engaged with Meindl et al.'s original work. Kempster and Carroll's (2016) uncritical take on romanticism uses taken-for-granted and universally accepted meanings of 'ethical leadership, doing good and growing well' (Collinson et al., 2018: 1628). This is seen as problematic because there are varied perspectives on what constitutes ethics. To address these issues, Collinson et al. (2018) draw on Walter Benjamin's critique of romantic criticism which they argue helps extend Meindl et al.'s (1985) original ROL thesis. Romantic criticism, with its roots in the appreciation of art, may further perpetuate an uncritical and unitarist interpretation of art. Benjamin (1996) found the romantic account of criticism to be problematic because romanticism asks to appreciate art in and of itself which did support 'points of rupture' (Collinson et al., 2018: 1630).

Using Benjamin's critique of romanticism, Collinson et al. (2018) extend Meindl et al.'s ROL by putting forth three ways in which romanticism describes the distinct nature of contemporary leadership theories. The first way includes the romanticised assumptions of a natural leader, an approach that argues that leadership is a natural phenomenon and fails to recognise the social construction of leadership. Such 'natural' assumptions about leadership include the trait perspective of leadership (see Chapter 2 for a review and critique).

The second way which is a consequence of seeing leadership as a natural phenomenon is the overemphasis on the collective. Collinson et al. discuss the notion of **'expressive harmonious collectives'** which refers to the 'romantic notion of expression' located within 'harmonious collectives' (2018: 1630, 1634). What this means is that there is a tendency within leadership studies which favours collective work over rupturing power where leadership is portrayed as seeking dialogue and harmony. Moreover, **'expressive leadering'** refers to the commitment to collective work in the self-expression of leadership which emphasises an overly positive view of leadership.

The third way in which romanticism characterises contemporary leadership studies is through the romanticising of followers. Here, Meindl is critiqued for falling in his own trap of romanticism where he creates a dichotomy between leaders and followers. Even though Meindl claims to move away from a dominant focus on leadership, the individual leader remains the core focus of Meindl's (1995) view on followership. There are also not enough considerations of follower agency (Collinson et al., 2018). This critical view about followership agency is reverberated by Ford and Harding (2018). We discuss the followership perspective in much more detail in the next section in this chapter.

Followers and followership

Even though it has been stated that without followers there can be no leaders (Collinson, 2006; Uhl-Bien, 2021), the leadership literature has been more leadership focused. A **followership approach** is different to a follower-centric approach to leadership. In the previous section, we looked at Meindl et al.'s (1985) romance of leadership which is a follower-centric perspective which examines followers' views of leaders. A followership approach, on the other hand, looks at how followers view their own behaviour (Uhl-Bien and Pillai, 2007; Carsten, Uhl-Bien, West, Patera and McGregor, 2010). Carsten et al. (2010) conducted a qualitative study using interviews to explore how followers socially constructed their own roles as followers in different industries. Similar to the notion of the social construction of leadership, where leadership can be seen as encompassing a range of different meanings, and viewed through multiple frames of reference (Smircich and Morgan, 1982; Meindl et al., 1985; Fairhurst and Grant, 2010), Carsten et al. (2010) explored whether social constructions of followership would yield different meanings because of individual assumptions of being a follower.

We have seen earlier in this chapter that according to the social constructionist perspective, individuals interpret reality in relation to institutionalised norms (Berger and Luckmann, 1966). Carsten et al. (2010) investigate followership schema and contextual variables related to social constructions of followership. Followership schema can be defined as 'generalized knowledge structures that develop over time through socialization and interaction with stimuli relative to leadership and followership' (Fiske and Taylor, 1991; Carsten et al., 2010: 546). What this means is that the various institutional norms specific to organisations may influence these schemas by reinforcing certain standards of behaviour amidst individuals in various hierarchical roles. Earlier in the chapter, we looked at Berger and Luckmann's (1966) argument that subjective reality turns into objective reality when a meaning attributed to something becomes a part of shared routines (Light, 1967). This can be said for assumptions about leadership as well as followership in relation to power differentials between hierarchies, as well as a romanticised notion of leadership.

Drawing on several studies, Carsten et al. (2010) argued that followers would hold different types of schemas of followership that range from hierarchical views of followership as subordination and obedience (see Morrison and Milliken, 2000; Konst and Van Breukelen, 2005; Tynan, 2005) to followers as co-producers of leadership outcomes (see Graen and Uhl-Bien, 1995; Shamir, 2007). The other variable explored by Carsten et al. (2010) is organisational context. For instance, organisational climate, where it is overly bureaucratic, or empowering, would influence followers' schema. Leader styles would also influence the social constructions of followers. The finding from the 31 semi-structured interviews conducted in North America with individuals is that various industries demonstrated that while some individuals constructively question and challenge their leaders, others construct ideas of followers around passivity, obedience and deference (Carsten et al., 2010).

Implicit followership theories

Similar to implicit leadership theories that are about lay theories and assumptions people have about leaders (see Rosenberg and Jones, 1972), **implicit followership theories** (IFTs) can be defined as the individual assumptions people have about the traits and behaviours of followers. IFTs are made up of prototypes that are representative of the most commonly shared attributes of specific categories. These include categories of how followers are, as well as goal-derived/ideal followers, that is, how followers should be (Schyns and Meindl, 2005; Sy, 2010).

Sy's (2010) research into IFTs included a sample of 1362 participants across five separate studies where the content and structure of IFTs were identified, the relationship between IFTs and existing implicit leadership theories were examined and 'a pre-liminary nomological network of leaders' implicit followership theories' (Sy, 2010: 73) was established by investigating the consequences for leader–follower out-comes. The first sample included dyadic pairs of leaders and followers which enabled capturing views from both subordinates and managers. The findings indi-cated that the first-order structure of IFTs included industry, enthusiasm, good citizen, conformity, insubordination and incompetence. The second-order struc-ture encompassed follower prototype and antiprototype. These leaders' IFTs predicted interpersonal outcomes such as liking, relationship quality, trust and job satisfaction.

Both Carsten et al.'s (2010) study and Sy's (2010) study offer different approaches to the understanding of the social construction of leadership by focusing on notions of followership. One thing to bear in mind would be that the sample came from North America in both Carsten et al. (2010) and Sy's (2010) study. The ideas of fol-lowership would vary across cultures and geographic locations and it is therefore important to consider how the ideas of the ideal follower might vary across the globe. Schedlitzki, Ahonen, Wankhade, Edwards and Gaggiotti (2017) point out that what we know about leadership is only a fraction of what we could know, as most leader-ship understandings are Anglo-American. This is inevitably also true for followership studies. Urbach, Den Hartog, Fay, Parker and Strausse (2021) address this issue by arguing that the societal (national) culture of power distance, individualism–collectivism, future orientation and uncertainty avoidance shape implicit followership theories which in turn affect **proactive work behaviours** (PWBs). Proactive work behav-iours can be defined as individuals' proactive efforts in order to improve their work and organisation.

While Urbach et al.'s (2021) propositions in their conceptual article contribute towards thinking about the interrelationships between the various elements (IFTs, PWBs and culture dimensions), empirical research including qualitative and quantita-tive research is needed to understand followership in relation to contextual factors such as culture. While Hofstede's culture dimensions offer a useful categorisation in the understanding of national cultures, competing perspectives on culture also pre-vail. For instance, critical cross-cultural management research examines how power enters intercultural situations and how corporates such as large multinationals man-age them (Romani, Boussebaa and Jackson, 2020). Boussebaa (2020) discusses the importance of considering **corporate-led cultural globalisation**, which looks at how multinational corporates influence culture. Such critical perspectives of culture differ from merely looking at culture dimensions. Exploring such perspectives in rela-tion to followership and leadership in multinational corporate settings would yield valuable insights.

Categories of follower-centred and followership approaches

A systematic review by Uhl-Bien, Riggio, Lowe and Carsten (2014) offers a review and research agenda for followership theory where they examine the numerous approaches and studies to followership. The review by Uhl-Bien et al. (2014) categorises follower and followership approaches into five broad categories: leader-centric; follower-centric; relational view; role-based followership; and constructionist followership. The leader-centric approach views followers as recipients or moderators in producing outcomes. The trait approach and other leader-centred perspectives, including charismatic-transformational leadership that we examined in Chapters 2 and 3, fall within the leader-centric approach. The follower-centric approach is about how followers construct leaders and leadership. A couple of examples that fall within this category include Meindl et al.'s romance of leadership, and implicit leadership theories that we have looked at earlier in this chapter, as well as in Chapter 3.

The relational view of followers and followership interrogates how followers and leaders engage with each other in a mutual influence process. Some examples of this include leader-member exchange theory, and the toxic triangle. These theories will be explored in Chapters 5 and 7. The role-based followership category encompasses Sy's (2010) implicit followership theories, and Carsten et al.'s (2010) followership role orientations. Finally, the constructionist followership, as categorised by Uhl-Bien et al. (2014), views followers as co-creators, with leaders, of leadership. Earlier in this chapter, we looked at Fairhurst and Grant's (2010) analysis of the social construction of leadership, where social construction appears to represent a broad category with four dimensions subsumed within social construction (social construction of reality versus construction of social reality; theory versus praxis; critical/emancipatory versus pragmatic intervention; and monomodal versus multimodal). In relation to constructionist followership, Collinson's (2006) post-structuralist view in relation to identity falls within this category, but so does Shamir's (2007) view that leadership is jointly produced.

Collinson's (2006) post-structuralist perspective on follower identity emphasises the importance of viewing identity not from a unitarist perspective where identities remain fixed, but of recognising the state of flux of identity processes. Post-structuralist perspectives of power reject the notion of power being inherently negative and coercive. Instead, power is also seen as being productive, positive and creative in relation to the production of identity. More importantly, the voluntary followership that informs the thinking on follower identity is critiqued. Drawing on Foucault's **normalisation**, Collinson (2006) explains that organisational practices can regulate identity by producing 'disciplined and obedient selves' (Rose, 1989; Collinson, 2006: 182). Normalisation is a process by which identities are constructed through 'comparing, differentiating, hierarchizing, homogenizing and excluding' (Collinson, 2006: 182). By doing so, normalisation attempts to absorb others into the strategic aims and logic of the organisation. Normalisation operates in a top-down manner, and it is difficult to reverse (Krzyżanowski, 2020).

Collinson (2006) puts forth three identities that have re-occurred in leader-follower dynamics in the existing literature: conformist selves, resistant selves and dramaturgical selves. Several studies of followership promote the idea of a perfect follower which creates conformist selves. Collinson (2006) draws comparisons to Milgram's (1963) obedience experiments which highlighted the dangers of people's willingness to obey authority. Milgram's controversial experiments explain the Nazi extermination of six million Jews, where the explanation given was that of 'obeying orders' (184). Padilla, Hogan and Kaiser (2007) highlight the role of susceptible followers in the formation of the toxic triangle. Post-structuralist studies emphasise the importance of resistant selves. The focus on followers' opposition demonstrates the significance of differentiation in shaping identity construction as much as identification. This means that leaders cannot always control followers' perceptions, identities and practices.

The notion of dramaturgical selves comes from Erving Goffman's (1959) impression management, in which he used theatre as a metaphor to analyse everyday life. Goffman, a sociologist, argued that individuals strategically disclose or deliberately neglect information. Collinson (2006) argues that dramaturgical selves may be conformist, resistant or a mixture of both. The increased surveillance in workplaces leads to followers having to use impression management.

Other critical perspectives on followership include Ford and Harding's (2018) critique of follower/ship through an analysis of three seminal texts pertaining to leadership including distributed leadership, transformational leadership and servant leadership theories. Based on their analysis, Ford and Harding (2018) argue that leadership studies are underpinned by the desire for power and control over 'potentially dangerous masses labelled as followers' (Ford and Harding, 2018: 18), and critique the notion of followers being empty vessels waiting to be led. The asymmetric power relations between leaders and followers are highlighted by Ford and Harding (2018) who conclude that follower/ship, which remains an unexamined core of leadership, undoes leadership theory, and for this reason they recommend leaving follower/ship unexplored.

Kempster, Schedlitzki and Edwards (2021) offer a reflection of conversations with managers in the context of management education programmes about followership.

Based on these conversations, Kempster et al. (2021) problematise the 'axiomatic assumption of follower in the field of leadership studies' (p. 118). **Axioms** are statements accepted as true, so in this case, an axiomatic assumption of followers would mean that followers/follower identities exist. Based on their reflection of conversations, they question the existence of follower identifications with leaders and/or the organisational contexts they find themselves in and wonder if the appraisal of leader–follower dynamics would fundamentally change. Kempster et al. (2021) argue that follower identifications are rare in organisational contexts and question the notion that there can't be any leaders without followers. They point to the advent of social media, where being a follower means something completely different, and such social media followership would present itself as a redefined followership. For instance, Prakasam and Huxtable-Thomas (2021) examine an online community (subreddit) on *Reddit*, a digital media platform, which used to be dedicated to the followers of Donald Trump. Reddit offers a different kind of platform for organising, and a follower identity on such a platform would offer new insights to that of an organisation. What it means to be a follower of a famous figure would on a digital media platform differ from organisational contexts.

Mini case study 4.2

Steve Jobs

Steve Jobs was a co-founder and CEO of Apple Inc. and widely regarded as a charismatic leader. While Jobs gained prominence due to his exceptional presentation skills, stories of his narcissism and bad behaviour were also well known. Sharma and Grant (2011) carried out a **dramaturgical analysis** of Jobs' public performances in 1997–2007. This analysis consisted of three of Jobs' performances: the Microsoft deal, the MAC OS 9 eulogy and the iPhone introduction. The study highlights three main insights about the construction of Steve Jobs as a charismatic leader. Jobs uses narrative and storytelling in his public performances which contain an 'original state of affairs', 'a catalyst' and a 'consequent state of affairs' (p. 18), constituting a narrative identified in the 'Microsoft deal' and 'iPhone introduction' performances. The second key insight from the study relates to the construction of Jobs' charismatic relationship with followers through stage management. For instance, the Microsoft deal and Mac OS 9 eulogy were situations that were diffused by Jobs through his effective stage performances to win over audiences. The third important insight is to do with Jobs himself as the narrative which emphasises his individual heroic as well as tumultuous story of learning, growth and redemption (Sharma and Grant, 2011).

Steve Jobs' charismatic authority was present even after his death, demonstrated by unprecedented global mourning. Bell and Taylor (2016) examine the **framing** and memorialising of Jobs' death by examining temporary shrines and visual imagery. The followers (consumers) of Steve Jobs maintained Jobs as an ongoing presence through temporary sacred spaces with shrines and visual imagery. The three themes identified in the mourning practices were the construction of shrines as temporary organisational memorials, the distribution of photographs as a symbolic reminder of the inevitability of death, and finally the role of corporate memorialisation that disciplined mourners into letting go. This highlights the construction of leadership through socio-material practices, as well as the power relations present in the organisations attempting to control the mourning practices. Moreover, Bell and Taylor (2016) highlight the power of corporations such as Apple.

Questions

1. To what extent are effective stage performances important in the construction of leadership?
2. What role did followers play in the construction of Steve Jobs as an effective and charismatic leader?
3. How do socio-material practices contribute to Jobs' construction as a charismatic and effective leader?

Conclusion

We have examined the social construction of leadership as well as considering approaches to followers and followership approaches. We began by understanding the philosophical and sociological origins of social constructionism and then considered the broad category of the social construction of leadership and the various dimensions within this approach (Fairhurst and Grant, 2010). The importance of discourse to leadership was reviewed. The romance of leadership perspective was analysed, where we reviewed Meindl et al.'s (1985) original thesis, as well as recent critical insights into romance of leadership (Collinson, 2018; Kempster et al., 2021). A review of various approaches to followers and followership was provided and critically reviewed in which the existence of followers was constituted. The first mini case study investigated the COVID-19 pandemic in relation to leadership, as well as power relations and neo-colonial dynamics between the Global North versus South and the role of the media. This case study exemplifies the complexity in the social construction of leadership in crisis situations. The second mini case study examined the construction of Steve Jobs' leadership while he was alive, and also how his ongoing presence was maintained after his death through socio-material practices.

Decolonising leadership

Jimenez-Luque A (2021) Decolonial leadership for cultural resistance and social change: Challenging the social order through the struggle of identity, *Leadership* 17(2): 154–172.

This paper explains decolonial leadership through an empirical study conducted in a Native American organisation based in the United States.

Key summary

- Social construction of leadership is a large umbrella term encompassing various different approaches to leadership within this paradigm. Fairhurst and Grant (2010) offer four dimensions within which such approaches can be located. These dimensions include the construction of social reality versus the social construction of reality, theory versus praxis, critical/emancipatory versus pragmatic intervention, and monomodal versus multimodal.
- Romance of leadership emphasises the role of follower attributions in the social construction of leadership by attributing organisational successes and failures to individual leaders.
- Romance of leadership is critiqued and extended by looking at Walter Benjamin's critique of romanticism.
- There is a difference between follower-centred approaches versus followership approaches to leadership. Followership approaches focus on how followers view their own behaviour.
- Studies on followers and followership can be classified into leader-centric; follower-centric; relational view; role-based followership; and constructionist followership.
- Implicit followership theories are lay images individuals have about followers.
- The existence of followers has been questioned and critiqued and it is argued that followers' identities are in a state of flux. Most positivist/psychology-based approaches to followers assume a fixed identity of followers.

Further reading

Case, P., Evans, L. S., Fabinyi, M., Cohen, P. J., Hicks, C. C., Prideaux, M. and Mills, D. J. (2015) 'Rethinking environmental leadership: The social construction of leaders and leadership in discourses of ecological crisis, development, and conservation'. *Leadership*, 11(4): 396–423.

Hafner, C. A. and Sun, T. (2021) 'The "team of 5 million": The joint construction of leadership discourse during the Covid-19 pandemic in New Zealand'. *Discourse, Context & Media*, 100523.

Matthews, S. H., Kelemen, T. K. and Bolino, M. C. (2021) 'How follower traits and cultural values influence the effects of leadership'. *The Leadership Quarterly*, 101497.

PART 2
CONNECTEDNESS AND CONTEXT

5
RELATIONAL LEADERSHIP

Naveena Prakasam

Chapter objectives

The objectives of this chapter are:

- To review and critique approaches to relational leadership.
- To investigate the entity versus relational orientations within relational leadership.
- To explore non-Western theoretical approaches to relational leadership.

Introduction

Following on from exploring the social constructionist paradigm of leadership, this chapter explores relational leadership. The field of relational leadership is vast, and topics such as leader-member exchange (LMX) theory and collective leadership fall within the umbrella of or relate to relational leadership. In fact, the charismatic and authentic leadership constructs covered in the preceding chapters of this book can also be approached from a relational perspective (see Eagly, 2005 and Uhl-bien, 2006). In this chapter, we will cover these topics. In addition, we will be considering gender and relational leadership (Eagly, 2005; Uhl-Bien, 2011), and alternative, non-Western approaches to relational leadership, such as indigenous Māori leadership, will be reviewed. We begin by reviewing the two perspectives that fall within relational leadership: entity and relational perspectives.

Relational leadership is not a particular type or style of leadership (Crevani, 2019). Relational leadership encompasses several leadership theories and models which emphasise relational aspects of leadership. In a nutshell, relational leadership always views leaders as existing in relation with others. The dictionary definition of 'relational' is characterised by a relationship (*Oxford English Dictionary*, n.d.). To that end, it is necessary to look at 'leadership as a relationship' (Rost, 1993: 5) and move beyond essentialist understandings of leadership. For instance, in Chapter 2 we explored those early understandings of leadership that saw leaders as extraordinary great men with extraordinary characteristics that made them leaders. This way of thinking about leadership can be categorised as essentialist. Rost (1993) argues that focusing on traits, contingencies and knowledge about human behaviour does not lead to an understanding of 'leadership as a relationship' (Cunliffe and Eriksen, 2011: 1429).

While relational leadership moves beyond such approaches to leadership, some schools of thought emphasise individual leaders and their characteristics in approaching relational leadership – this is known as the entity perspective, which is explained in further detail in the following paragraphs.

What is relational leadership?

There are several definitions of relational leadership. According to Uhl-Bien:

> **Relational leadership theory** (RLT) is as an overarching framework for the study of leadership as a social influence process through which emergent coordination (e.g., evolving social order) and change (e.g., new approaches, values, attitudes, behaviors, ideologies) are constructed and produced. (Uhl-Bien, 2006: 654)

Crevani, Lindgren and Packendorff (2010) define relational leadership as:

> a perspective on leadership as social processes of relating, processes that are co-constructed by several interactors. Such processes are not mechanically reversible and controllable: instead, they are characterized by a social flow of interacting and connecting whereby organizations, groups, leaders, leadership and so forth are constantly under construction and reconstruction. (Crevani et al., 2010: 79)

Both definitions emphasise leadership as a process being constructed and repro-duced. The focus is not on individuals as leaders or followers but on social interactions and processes. This is a move away from viewing individuals or organisations as stable and fixed entities, and instead the emphasis is on the pro-cess of continual construction of organisations, and individual leaders. Before we delve further into a social constructionist or relational orientation of relational leadership, it is important that we understand the differences between the two broad approaches within relational leadership.

Classification within relational leadership: Entity perspective and relational perspective

There are two perspectives within relational leadership: **entity** and **relational per-spectives**. The term entity literally refers to being and existence, as opposed to non-existence, and this is an easy way to remember what the entity perspective within relational leadership entails. The entity perspective focuses on individual cognitions and perceptions as they engage in relationships. The relational view, on the other hand, sees organisations as ongoing multiple constructions made in the processes themselves. The two are, as a result, different ontologies.

In the entity perspective, the individual (leader or follower) is seen as a stable entity being able to control the relationship. From this perspective, organisations too are seen as stable and fixed entities. The focus here is on leaders and followers, as well as their perceptions and behaviours. Therefore, this views individuals as being able to control the internal and external order. The entity perspective can be viewed as a subject–object understanding of relationships in which social relations are enacted by individuals to influence other people and groups and acquire knowledge about them. The entity view takes an objectivist epistemological view of relational leadership, which means that there is a separation between mind and nature, and there exist objective truths. There is a clear separation between people and the contents of their mind (Uhl-Bien, 2006).

An entity perspective focuses on interpersonal relationships whereas a relational perspective focuses on 'relating to'; being in relation to the larger social system. With the latter, leadership is seen as a process of organising (Uhl-Bien, 2006: 604). Table 5.1 contains words that are associated with the entity and relational/social construction-ist approaches to relational leadership.

Table 5.1 Entity versus relational/social constructionist perspectives

Entity	Relational/social constructionist
Individuals, leaders, followers, organisations, behaviours, perceptions, cognitions, behaviours, relationships as fixed, one reality	Processes, leadership, construction, interactions, everyday conversations, framing, relationships as continually evolving, multiple realities

Examples of relational leadership models/theories within the entity perspective

Uhl-Bien (2006) provides a detailed review of the types of leadership theories and models that fit within the entity perspective.

Leader-member exchange (LMX) theory

LMX theory falls within the entity perspective of relational leadership as it focuses on the behaviour of the individual. LMX is about the dyadic relationship between two people (the leader and follower) as they interact with one another. There were several versions of the LMX theory, such as the vertical dyad linkage theory (see Dansereau, Cashman and Graen, 1973). The most widely understood definition was developed by Dienesch and Liden (1986), who define LMX theory as an informal exchange process between leaders and followers, which is personal and unstructured in the context of the workplace. Through this exchange process, followers come to define the role that they would play within that context, which could be a department, for example. Through this exchange process, leaders would develop close relationships with some followers; what could be known as the 'in-group' (Gottfredson, Wright and Heaphy, 2020).

There are three things that this relationship between leaders and followers is dependent on. These include, firstly, the personal physical or psychological characteristics individuals may bring to the relationship. These act as predispositions to interpersonal situations (Phillips and Bedeian, 1994). Secondly, the relationship is dependent on the expectations that the individuals have about the exchange. These expectations are developed based on past experience, and ILTs (see Chapter 2) (Lord and Maher, 1991). Thirdly, the nature of the interactions is dependent on how everyone assesses and reacts to the exchange whilst it is occurring as well as later (Homans, 1961; Blau, 1964; Jacobs, 1971; Uhl-bien et al., 2000).

Despite the popularity of LMX, concerns have been raised about the construct. Broadly, these concerns encompass conceptualisation issues, measurement and modelling. Gottfredson et al. (2020) reviewed several papers in top journals in which LMX was used as a variable in the study of leader–follower relations. They found upon examination of the definitions of LMX that there was substantial diversity in the definitions used. Specifically, four different foci in the definitions were found: a differentiation of relationships, differentiation of exchanges, relationship quality and exchange quality. Other identified issues included measurement issues as the measures did not capture LMX. These measures were all quantitative measures using questionnaires (for example, Scandura and Graen, 1984; Liden and Maslyn, 1998), and inconsistencies were found between the measures and conceptualisation. Due to these issues, Gottfredson et al. (2020) argue that LMX findings cannot be relied upon.

However, there are qualitative studies on LMX that address these issues, as qualitative methods allow for richer detail, and newer insights. For example, Kandade, Samara, Parada and Dawson (2021) examined how high-quality relationships developed within the context of family businesses using a multiple case study approach involving interviews. They found that a network of relationships between family and non-family stakeholders is important in fostering high-quality relationships.

Hollander's relational theory

Hollander and Julian's relational approach to leadership is an early approach to relational leadership that takes an entity perspective. Here the focus is on the social exchange between leaders and followers. Leadership is seen as a process that contains an influence relationship in which the leader is one among others in this relationship. This is a transactional relationship in which rewards would be achieved in return (Hollander and Julian, 1969).

Charismatic relationship

Another example of an entity perspective of relational leadership is charismatic relationships (Uhl-Bien, 2006). See Chapters 2 and 3 for a detailed description of charismatic leadership and its critique. A charismatic relationship develops when followers identify and respond to leaders that they view as charismatic. The charismatic relationship is then influenced by several factors including follower characteristics, such as their susceptibility to charismatic leadership.

Relational and collective self

There are two distinct concepts within the social self-concept (Uhl-Bien, 2006). These include the **relational self** and the **collective self**. The relational self develops from the role of the self in relationship with significant others. Hence, the self is entangled in relationships, as self-worth comes from the satisfaction of the other person in the relationship. Andersen and Chen (2002) argue that 'this has implications for self-definition, self-evaluation, self-regulation as well as personality functioning' (p. 619). The relational self can be observed in dyadic relationships such as explained by LMX. A study by Robert and Vandenberghe (2021) found that relational self-concept was associated negatively with laissez-faire leadership. This is because employees who define themselves based on dyadic relationships would respond negatively to laissez faire leadership due to the association of this leadership style with avoidance and inaction (Bass and Bass, 2008; Hinkin and Schriesheim, 2008; Avolio, 2011; Skogstad, Hetland, Glasø and Einarsen, 2014).

The collective self emerges from being part of a group, such as an organisation, or any other social category. Here, identifying with the collective is more prominent and the individual sees themselves as like other individuals within the collective. This consequently leads to depersonalisation of the self, and collective interest becomes more important here. In this context, the social identity theory of leadership developed by Hogg (2001) is important, as leaders and followers are seen within the context of being embedded in a social system where they share a group membership. For leaders to be effective, they must display characteristics that are archetypal of the normative characteristics within the group (Uhl-Bien, 2006) (see Chapters 2 and 3 for ILT).

Network theories

Network theories still emphasise heroic and individualised perspectives of leadership by highlighting the need for leaders to manage relationships and processes. Examples of network perspectives include social network theories, actor network theories (ANT) and social exchange theory. Social network theories highlight the individual leader's role in managing 'relationships between environmental, social and organisational network elements'. From an ANT perspective, the emphasis on leaders is less, as they are considered no more important than other elements in the network. Social exchange theory focuses on an exchange relationship between leaders and followers (Cunliffe and Ericksen, 2011).

Relational perspective

The relational perspective within the larger framework of relational leadership theory assumes that there are multiple realities (Uhl-Bien, 2006). The relational perspective takes a social constructionist view of reality. Within the relational perspective, organisations are not seen as entities, but as elaborate relational networks consisting of a complex interplay of outcomes between different individuals and the system that they become part of (Uhl-Bien, 2006). Here, power is seen as being distributed throughout the social arena, as opposed to being concentrated in certain individuals (Foucault, 1977). The emphasis here is on the collaborative dynamics as opposed to individuals.

The contributions to the relational perspective can be attributed to several scholars including Hosking, Dachler and colleagues (Uhl-Bien, 2006). As Hosking (1988) pointed out, it was important to understand leadership as a process as opposed to focusing on leaders as persons. Hosking (1988) urged that it was not enough to understand what leaders did, but that we needed to focus on processes. These processes include the way the interests and definitions of the social order are 'negotiated, found acceptable, implemented and renegotiated' (Hosking, 1988 in Uhl-Bien, 2006: 662).

In a similar vein to Hosking, Dachler (1992) argued that rather than focusing on content issues like leader behaviours, and elements such as what constituted employee motivation, it was important for organisational and management research to direct their attention to social processes. This is because issues such as behaviours cannot be seen as the facts of an objective organisational reality, but rather, a reflection of realities that are socially constructed and are constantly changing. Not focusing on the facts of an objective organisational reality is at the epicentre of the relational ontology that such a perspective on relational leadership takes (Rost, 1991; Dachler, 1992; Uhl-Bien, 2006).

Cunliffe and Ericksen (2011) argue that **relational ontology** is needed for relational leadership. Relational ontology refers to understanding social experience as intersubjective at the philosophical level. Ontology refers to the nature of reality. Hence, relational ontology emphasises the intersubjectivity of social experience. For example, this could refer to the complexity of mundane everyday relationships in an organisation. From a relational ontological perspective, organisations can be seen as communities of people and conversations. A relational ontology emphasises intersubjective experiences and a relational leader sees people as 'human beings-in-relation with themselves' (Cunliffe and Ericksen, 2011: 1431).

A relational ontology asks different questions, and does not focus on traits, behaviours, and types of people management techniques, like the entity perspective does. Drawing on Dachler (1992), Uhl-Bien argues that, instead, a relational ontology seeks to understand the way realities of leadership are understood within a 'network of relations and how organisations are designed, directed, controlled and developed on the bases of collectively generated knowledge about organisational realities' (Uhl-Bien, 2006: 662). Relational ontology is also about understanding how actions are 'embedded in collective sense-making and attribution processes from which structures of social interdependence emerge and in turn reframe the collectively generated organizational realities' (Dachler, 1992; Uhl-Bien, 2006: 662).

Using such an ontological approach, Cunliffe and Eriksen (2011) offer relational leadership as a way of 'theorising and doing leadership differently' (p. 1428). They lay emphasis on the everyday relational practices of leaders such as everyday interactions. They view relational leadership as an inherently moral and dialogical practice and draw on Ricoeur's work on ethical selfhood and Bakhtin's work on dialogism in their empirical research on relational leadership. Ethical selfhood is about recognising that we have an ethical responsibility towards how we treat others because we are always speaking and acting in relation to others. Dialogism refers to responsive conversations; it is about talking with others, and not to them. As opposed to being a model of leadership, relational leadership takes an intersubjective view of the world which offers insight into leaders in relation to others 'within the complexity of experience' (Cunliffe and Eriksen, 2011: 1434). For instance, a manager providing support for an employee whilst they are undertaking a difficult task through regular conversations can be seen as an example of relational leadership.

An ethnographic approach was used as a method to explore the relational leadership of Federal Security Directors, which were new positions set up after the establishment of the Transport Security Authority (TSA) in United States' airports in the aftermath of 9/11. They found that there was an emphasis on collaborative relationships. The absence of structures, systems, and expectations about what they should be doing allowed relational leadership to emerge in the case of the Federal Security Directors. Based on this argument, it is worth pondering over whether structures might then inhibit relational leadership from emerging – given that collaborative relationships shaped by everyday ongoing interactions are what shape relational leadership.

Based on their ethnographic study, Cunliffe and Ericksen (2011) suggest that 'relational leadership is a way of being-in-the-world that embraces an intersubjective and relationally-responsive way of thinking and acting' (Cunliffe and Ericksen, 2011: 1445). Thus, this definition, similar to Hosking and Dachler, moves away from entitative approaches (for example, emphasis on structures, and two-way influence processes).

In addition to Hosking, Dachler, Cunliffe and Eriksen, other approaches that fit within the relational orientation as opposed to entity perspective of relational leadership, include Sayles (1964), Drath (2001) and Murrell's (1997) perspectives (Uhl-Bien, 2006).

For Sayles (1964), organisations are systems in which managers' actions are embedded within the dynamic interpersonal relationships in addition to the organisational and environmental contexts. Activities such as planning and decision-making are seen as messy, interpersonal social processes instead of distinct managerial activities, because they are shaped by interactions with others. If we think of an organisation in this way, an organisation is not only made up of policies, rules and procedures, but it is also constituted by interpersonal relationships that are built by ongoing interactions.

Similarly, Drath's (2001) approach to relational leadership is not about leader-centric models such as that of personal dominance, or an interpersonal influence process. For Drath, relational leadership is a process of relational dialogue through which members of the organisation construct 'knowledge systems' (Uhl-Bien, 2006: 663) together. These knowledge systems produce complex knowledge principles, and in this way, leadership is constructed. For Murrell (1997), leadership is seen as shared and involving more parties to the process than just the exchange relationship between the leadership and follower.

Empathy

Empathy can be understood as the ability to be able to understand another person's experiences of feelings (*Oxford English Dictionary*, n.d.). Therefore, it is an important construct to investigate within relational leadership.

In this section, an overview of **empathic leadership** practice is provided, primarily drawing on the work of Jian (2022) who approaches empathy from a relational onto-logical perspective to offer a social constructionist view of empathy in leadership. Jian (2022) argues that empathic leadership practice must be grounded in ethics. This includes the ethics of generosity (Diprose, 2002), care (Nodding, 2013) and responsibil-ity (Levinas, 1969, 1998), which are examples of different types of foundational ethics.

Generosity as openness to others, caring for others as well as responsibility towards others, motivates empathy (Jian, 2022).

Jian's (2022) social constructionist interpretation of empathic leadership is different to how empathy has been approached through the entitative, mind-based approach. As we have seen with relational leadership, empathy too can be examined from both entitative and relational perspectives. For instance, in the context of leadership, the entity perspective would focus on empathy as a trait of a leader. In this context, the focus would be on how the individual empathic leader would influence the context. However, from a relational and social constructionist perspective, empathic leadership practice can be viewed as being constructed through communicative practices which relate to leader relations. In this context, such empathy construction taking place through communicative practice is 'foundational to being and relating in leadership relations'. What this means is that the focus is not just on the individual leader or the individual follower, but on the practice. In this way, empathy is constructed through a reciprocal way the leader can be both 'empathiser' and 'empathised' (Jian, 2022: 934).

Let us review the entity versus constructionist approaches to empathy further. The primary understanding of empathy comes from what is known as the 'theory of the mind' (Zahavi, 2010, cited in Jian, 2022: 933), which is the entity perspective. Within this approach, there are two different types of empathy: cognitive versus affective or emotional empathy. Knowing another person's state of mind through projection or simulation is known as cognitive empathy. Feeling how others feel emotionally is affective empathy. Both cognitive and emotional empathy fall within the mind-based approach and can be seen as adopting an entity perspective where cognitions and emotions are seen as being hidden, and located inside the minds of individuals (Zahavi, 2010, 2011; Walsh, 2014, cited in Jian, 2022). Several leadership studies have predominantly focused on affective empathy, and whether this emotional trait or the display of affective empathy affected outcomes of leadership in any way. One such example of a study cited by Jian (2022) is that by Watkins et al. (2019), in which empathy was found to moderate abusive supervision. Many leadership studies connected leadership styles and empathy.

There are three main criticisms of the entity approach to empathy in leadership, as outlined by Jian (2022). First, the mind-based or entity approach to empathy sees empathy as being fully formed within leaders' minds, and as a result, organisational members' responses are based on the leaders' thoughts and feelings. This approach does not consider the way empathy is constructed or constituted (relational view). Second, the entity approach to empathy in leadership studies often views leaders as empathisers and the members as empathised. Such an approach becomes unidirectional, and this view romanticises the leader, and emphasises the heroic view of leadership (see previous chapters for a critique of these views). Therefore, this view does not consider the likelihood that a leader might be the emphasised, or the mutual construction of empathy amongst multiple parties.

Third, many entity-based studies on leadership and empathy have examined this dyadically and have not considered how this may affect a rival community. For instance, in the context of the military, this could be about how the enemy is considered. It is important to consider empathy directed towards a '**collective other**' (Jian, 2022: 935) as decisions are often made by members of an organisation that have an impact on some social groups, even though they may not directly interact with them.

The emergence of the social constructionist approach to empathy can be attributed to Zahavi (2010, 2014). This approach is rooted in phenomenology (see Chapter 11 for further details). The two broad approaches within the social constructionist approach are the synchronic and diachronic. The **synchronic approach** involves the 'social construction of empathy in co-present dyadic interaction through conversation' (p. 936). This means that the synchronic approach within the social constructionist approach involves the immediate social and interactional context. For instance, imagine having interactions with a team member daily. On the other hand, the **diachronic** refers to the social construction of empathy towards a collective other. The collective other refers to social groups who are not in the immediate social or interactional context.

First, let us look at the synchronic approach. From a relational ontological perspective, empathy can be seen as an intersubjective process of an intentional act. The main premise of the relational ontology approach to empathy is the emphasis on observable behaviours. Emotions are seen as behaviours visible from the outside as opposed to aspects hidden in one's consciousness. Hence, emotions are seen as being intersubjectively reproduced in social contexts (Zahavi, 2010).

Empathy unfolds intersubjectively in many ways. First, it can be viewed as following a 'temporal flow' (Taipale, 2015; Jian, 2022: 936) which arises from the interaction between the self and the other. This can be understood through the metaphor of music, and how one might appreciate a melody, in which you listen to multiple notes, instead of trying to listen to a melody from a point of view of a single note. Similarly, empathy cannot be understood from the point of view of a particular mental state (Taipale, 2015).

Second, empathy must be viewed as a reciprocal process through which the context is mutually shaped. For instance, as Zahavi (2014) notes, when another individual appears on the scene, they influence the meaning or the context, because this individual becomes a centre of reference. In this way, this affects the self's relation to the world. Therefore, the existence of other people on the scene would inevitably affect how one views the world.

Third, empathy is not just about emotional sharing. It is essential to recognise that the empathised experience is located in the other and not the self, and this helps distinguish between the 'subject of empathic experience' and the 'subject of empathised experience' (Zahavi, 2010: 294). Therefore, this directs the attention to the other and points to the incompleteness of one's 'empathic grasp' of the other. This in turn requires further communication due to the incompleteness preserving the otherness (Levinas, 1969; Overgaard, 2005).

Finally, through expressive phenomena constituted by the mind and body, the direct experience of the other is made possible (Overgaard, 2005; Zahavi, 2010, 2014; Walsh, 2014). Here, expression does not mean the outer presentation of inner mental states, but expression is seen as constituting mental life.

Moreover, the research in counselling literature highlights that empathy involves communicative processes that take place sequentially. In addition, various conversational resources are used, such as facial expressions, mental verbs and follow-up questions in the construction of empathy (Jian, 2022).

Moving on to the diachronic approach, this is about the collective other. Organisational members often make decisions that affect social groups that do not directly interact with the decision makers in the organisation; these social groups can be referred to as the collective other. In this context, it is useful to understand narrative empathy. For instance, Keen (2007) argued that narrative empathy could be accomplished using fiction. This is done by authors using stories with the strategic purpose of increasing the understanding of particular social groups, which would result in stimulating empathy. This extends beyond fiction, where people's lives can be seen as being composed of stories, and such a narrative provides insight into the other's experience (Claire et al., 2016).

Therefore, we can conclude that empathic leadership practice needs to be viewed from a social constructionist lens, and it is important to move beyond an individual-centred view of empathy in which the individual can manipulate a relationship. Instead, it is important to recognise that empathic leadership unfolds intersubjectively through shaping meanings and interactions.

Gender and relational leadership

It is important to consider gender in relation to relational leadership. In order to do so, we return to authentic leadership. In Chapter 4, we discussed how women being seen as authentic had to do with women leaders performing in accordance with gender norms (Liu et al., 2015). It was Eagly (2005) who proposed the notion of relational authenticity and argued that it is harder for women to achieve relational authenticity.

Eagly (2005) defines relational authenticity as being made up of two components. The first component involves leaders promoting values that are in the interest of the larger community, and leaders being able to communicate these values to the audience. The second component involves followers identifying with these values and accepting these leaders as suitable for the community or organisation. This two-sided concept is understood as relational authenticity.

An example Eagly (2005) discusses is that of a female music conductor, in the field of conducting, which is a male-dominated field. She has to push her talent and charisma so far that the 'natural qualities' of being a woman are seen as being lost. As a result, despite performing to a high standard, conveying charisma and showing commitment to musicianship, the female conductor may be disliked by other musicians because of the challenge she poses to the gender norms by overturning the gender hierarchy that is expected. This is an example of prejudice that makes the achievement of relational authenticity more challenging. It can be argued that this definition of relational authenticity adopts an entity perspective as the emphasis is on individual leaders and followers.

Offering a relational perspective that focuses on interaction and processes as opposed to individual entities is Crevani's (2019) take on relational leadership and gender. Crevani (2019) points to the social construction of gender – the idea that the meanings of what is considered feminine may be constantly changing and evolving. Therefore, what it is to act as a woman may be constantly evolving and changing, and this is not fixed. However, traits attributed to successful leaders may relate to social constructions of masculinity. Importantly, Crevani (2019) points out that these constructions of masculinity may emphasise independence and moving away from interdependence. Such emphasis on celebrating independence becomes a challenge to practising leadership relationally, as relational leadership is about moving away from the focus on such individualism (Crevani, 2019).

Crevani (2019) highlights framing, positioning, and bridging and resonating as processes that form part of relational leadership. The notion of framing comes from Goffman (1959), and refers to being able to control the meaning that is presented to an audience. This can be done by using frames and moving between them as appropriate, depending on how we want a particular situation to be constructed.

Positioning involves how positions are constructed/shaped in conversations and interactions. For instance, some examples of this involve positioning oneself as an insider, a junior and so on. Positions are continually contested and negotiated. In this way, and in this context, positions differ from roles that are more well-defined, stable and fixed.

Bridging and resonating refer to the interdependencies between people, and how people are constantly dependent on one another. This can be interpreted by thinking of conversations as ripples in water resonating off one another, building movement, but without minimising difference.

Let us look at another example of an empirical study that explores gender and relational leadership. Smit (2014) provides a qualitative, narrative ethnographic account of a female school principal in a disadvantaged school in South Africa. Smit (2014) uses a feminist qualitative research frame which examines multiple categories of differences such as race, class and gender as well as one's material circumstances, which result in inequalities. A feminist qualitative research frame highlights the lived experiences of women and provides space for research participants to be able to share and be heard. Feminist research takes a subjective and relational approach to reality, by recognising that truth and knowledge may only be partial (Given, 2008, cited in Smit, 2014). Smit (2014) focused on the lived experiences of a female school principal to investigate relational leadership which encompassed observing interaction patterns, relationships and socio-cultural contexts. The findings of this ethnographic study validate the social process of leadership with a strong focus on relationships. The study highlights how a female school principal negotiates her role in a disadvantaged school by working collaboratively with people, with care and a moral code of conduct.

Mini case study 5.1

Future ways of working and relational leadership

In March 2020, we were impacted by COVID-19 in many ways. Our approach to work has completely changed given the increased proportion of people that were working from home. Dr Jane Parry, an Associate Professor in the Department of Organisational Behaviour and Human Resource Management at the University of Southampton, along with several colleagues, has been leading a large-scale research project about work after lockdown, which investigates how people might want to work in the future. Data were gathered through both quantitative questionnaires and in-depth semi-structured interviews from white collar workers in local authorities and law firms.

The findings of this research by Parry et al. (2021) reveal a mindset shift in the UK about how work is organised. The *Work after Lockdown* survey revealed that nine out of ten people thought they got more or as much done working from home than in their offices, and seven out of ten people expressed that they wanted to continue to work from home (Parry, 2020). The recommendation from the findings of this survey is that employees should be given the right to flexible work from the start of their employment, which might see productivity gains (Parry, 2020).

However, insights from this research also highlight deepening inequalities. For instance, extended periods of working from home, despite its massive productivity gains, have led to isolation amongst young people and increased concerns about skills development due to extended periods of working from home. Another group that was affected by these inequalities was young parents, particularly women, who had greater domestic responsibilities (Parry and Veliziotis, 2021).

This changing nature of how work has been thought about differently may have implications for relational leadership. Approached from a relational ontological perspective, relational leadership is understood as socially constructed by interactions and processes. Given new ways of working, everyday interactions may take place differently or not take place at all. The conversations that used to take place in the corridor of the workplace may not happen in the same way. With meetings largely taking place online, casual conversations such as chatting about the weather, may not take place in the same way. This change is likely to impact how relational leadership is constructed. For instance, Cunliffe and Ericksen (2011) examined the everyday interactions between Federal Security Directors and their teams in airports and found how relational leadership emerged in everyday interactions. It is therefore important to consider the consequences for relational leadership when such interactions do not take place in person and whether relational leadership can emerge through infrequent and limited interactions. It is also important to recognise how particular groups can especially be negatively impacted due to limited relationships.

Questions

1. Can relational leadership emerge through limited interactions?
2. What is the importance of relational leadership in work after lockdown?

Indigenous Māori perspective on relational leadership

It is important to move beyond Western conceptualisations of relational leadership, given that the ontological approach to relational leadership is rooted in indigenous cultures. We will now discuss the **Māori** perspective. The Māori are an indigenous group of Polynesian people in New Zealand (Walter et al., 2017). The Māori were compelled to assimilate to Western culture because of colonisation. However, since the 1960s, there has been a revival of the Māori culture (Te Ahukaramū, 2005). Adopting a relational ontological perspective, Henry and Wolfgramm (2018) have offered an indigenous, Māori approach to relational leadership. They used a longitudinal qualitative approach, utilising participant action research and life history narratives as methods, to investigate Māori leaders and practitioners in the screen industry. The findings of this longitudinal research revealed three relational leadership factors, which include embodying relational leadership, enacting relational leadership and enacting relational identity. Embodying relational leadership included the self-concept, the self in relation to others, as well as culture revitalisation. This emphasises the whole collective, and the ways of being in leadership. An example of a Māori term is *mana* which refers to empowering Māori voices and Māori storytelling (Henry and Wolfgramm, 2018: 214). It is useful to note that there has been an increase in the emphasis on life histories and storytelling within Western traditions of leadership (for example, Sparrowe, 2005). It is important to recognise that these traditions and practices of understanding have always existed in non-Western and indigenous cultures. However, due to the West centrism of theorising rooted in the history of colonisation, there is a dearth of diverse approaches to leadership theorising.

Enacting relational leadership included industry dimensions. Examples include training benefits, other political factors within the industry, Māori leaders and mentors as well as allies that were not Māori. The benefits of networking were also highlighted by participants.

Enacting relational identity includes the macro dimensions of relational leadership, which encompassed contextual and structural factors. The negatives include issues related to colonisation, racism as well as institutional racism. The positives include being part of leading-edge technology for indigenous storytelling, with Māori TV being the largest independent producer of New Zealand material.

Such an approach to relational leadership highlights the importance of considering cultural identity as well as macro contextual factors in the understanding of the practice of leadership.

Mini case study 5.2

Collective Māori Leadership (CML)

Collective leadership has been a way of life for a long time for Māori people (Spiller et al., 2020). The Māori worldview is underpinned by *whakapapa*, which refers to genealogy in Māori society. *Whakapapa* can be seen as a process of discovery that encompasses the relationships of the self with others including 'ancestors, mountains, rivers, and sacred guardians' (Spiller et al., 2020: 521). All entities have a genealogy, including humans, insects, birds, plants as well as rocks. Leadership in the Māori worldview is associated with *rangatira*, which refers to excelling at weaving people together by encouraging them to go on a journey together to bright light in a world in which all flourish. CML moves beyond traditional classifications of individuals as leaders and followers. Instead, each can be seen as simultaneously a leader and follower, recognising the whole. Spiller et al. (2020) extend Uhl-Bien's (2006) theoretical model of relational leadership by locating this in Māori praxis. To investigate CML, the researchers submitted themselves into the *wananga* process in which community members focus their intention on purpose. This allows insights to emerge from researchers' experiences and conversations with research participants. The process cannot be sequentially defined and categorised into the data collection, coding and analysis process. Instead, the analysis is based on the 'geneaological ordering of the world' (Spiller et al., 2020: 527). There are three watershed moments that the scholars describe, which form the findings of their research. The first is to do with the 'Iwi Chairs Forum', an organisation made up informally of a coalition of Māori representatives of their tribes. This organisation serves as a platform for sharing knowledge and information between Māori. They gather four times a year. During one such gathering in December 2017, on the new Minister of Māori Development's suggestion that the new government would interact with the Iwi chairs (individuals who represent their tribes), tensions rose, and there was a stimulation of lively discussion. While this could have resulted in bitterness, a well-respected elder launched into a well-known Māori song which led to all in attendance joining in. These songs are cultural messages. This saw a reduction in tension, and at that moment a state of peace was achieved between all parties. The second moment had to do with the claims process by tribes seeking redressal made against the British Crown for any breaches of the Treaty of Waitangi which was signed by many Māori tribal chiefs, and the representatives of the British Crown. The public humiliation encountered through the claims process by the elders of the Ngatiwai tribe, due to a cross-witness process, made them rethink whether to continue to participate in such claims processes. After the tensions between the Crown, Ngatiwai and other tribes in the region, the elders of the Ngatiwai tribe stepped back and decided to follow a process guided by Māori protocols in order to resolve issues with the Iwi. The group decided they would move fluidly across their obstacles, reflective of them being water people.

The third moment that the researchers offer is based on a *wai* (water) documentary showcasing Māori collective leadership addressing the government's

(Continued)

assumption that no one owned water. The Māori asserted their rights as custodians for water. The Māori collective leadership discussion resulted in the Te Awa Tupua Bill that meant that the Whanganui River would be considered a legal person with equal rights and responsibilities, and the Bill also reflects the agentic stewardship between the Whanganui Iwi and the river.

Questions

1. What lessons can be learned from the Māori perspective of collective leadership?
2. How is an ecosystems view of leadership helpful in advancing leadership theorising and praxis?

Collective leadership

Table 5.2 A map of collective approaches to leadership

		View of collectivity	
		Collective leadership as type	Collective leadership as lens
Locus of leadership	Leadership residing in the group	Cell 1 *Dual/co-leadership, Shared leadership, Social network leadership, Team leadership*	Cell 3 *Relational leadership, leadership-as-practice*
	Leadership residing in the system	Cell 2 *Multiteam systems leadership, Distributed leadership, Network leadership, Complexity leadership, Collective leadership practices*	Cell 4 *Collectivist constructionist perspectives, Discursive/communicative leadership, Some critical leadership studies*

Adapted from Ospina SM, Foldy EG, Fairhurst GT, et al. (2020) Collective dimensions of leadership: connecting theory and method. Human Relations 73(4): 441–463.

So far, we have seen how some forms of relational leadership emphasise the collective. It is useful to look at collective leadership which encompasses various types of scholarship that emphasise the collective aspects of leadership. We look at a useful categorisation which allows us to view various strands of leadership scholarship that fall within the broader umbrella of collective leadership.

Ospina, Foldy, Fairhurst and Jackson (2020) provide a map of collective approaches, which is a useful categorisation system for various studies that fit within collective leadership. This matrix involves two axes. The first axis is the 'locus of leadership', which is about how scholars theorise where to look for leadership. 'View of collectivity' is the second axis. There are four cells that they propose. The first cell is where leadership resides in interpersonal relationships. Here, collective leadership is viewed as a type. Examples include shared leadership, dual leadership, team leadership and social network leadership.

Cell 2, which also views collective leadership as a type, sees leadership as residing in the system, and within systemic dynamics. Examples include complexity leadership, distributed leadership and network leadership. A specific example of a study within both cell 1 and cell 2 is by Gibeau, Langley, Denis and van Schendel (2020). They look at dual leadership in four healthcare organisations with different institutional logics. This study looked at 'how 20 dyads tried to bridge competing logics across the different organisational levels' (Gibeau et al., 2020, cited in Ospina et al., 2020: 453). Gibeau et al.'s (2020) study fits within cell 1 due to the focus on dyads, which locates leadership in the group category. However, by examining the organisational level, this study also moves into cell 2 which locates leadership in the system.

Cell 3 views collective leadership as a lens, and leadership as residing in a group. Relational leadership, and leadership-as-practice are examples of this cell. An example that fits within cell 3 is that of Cunliffe and Eriksen's (2011) study of relational leadership in which they investigate the dialogic practice of leadership through ethnography and interviews. Cell 4 also views collective leadership as a theoretical lens, and views leadership as residing in the system. Discursive and communicative leadership, as well as collective constructionist leadership are examples that fit within this cell. Spiller, Wolfgramm, Henry and Pouwhare (2020) examine the Māori ecosystems view of leadership that 'encompasses the contributions of the entire ecological community – ancestors, animals, rivers, and trees' (Spiller et al., 2020, cited in Ospina et al., 2020: 454). In this way, Spiller et al. (2020) argue that true collective leadership is like a living system which is rooted in developing a kinship culture 'with each generation of leaders seeking to grow and enhance the collective toward intergenerational, interdependent flourishing' (Spiller et al., 2020: 533). The worldview of the Māori approach to the construction of knowledge is known as *wānanga* (Spiller et al., 2020: 516), which brings about an integrated collective intelligence by crossing space and time, involving a quality of consciousness. *Wānanga* is a process that is both a methodology and method that challenges quantitative and reductionist research by dissolving the separation between the researcher and the area of their focus, which gives rise to an eco-systemic view of leadership (Spiller et al., 2020). Hence, viewing collective leadership as a theoretical lens, as well as seeing leadership as residing in a system, the Māori ecosystems view of collective leadership can be placed in cell 4 (Ospina et al., 2020).

Conclusion

In this chapter, we began by examining the differences between entity and relational perspectives within relational leadership. We saw that relational leadership is not a style or type of leadership, but that it encompasses several leadership theories that emphasise a relational approach. We reviewed entity perspectives of leadership such as LMX, Hollander's relational theory, charismatic relationship, relational and collective self as well as network theories. We examined the relational perspective and explored the relational ontology that Cunliffe and Eriksen (2011) adopted in their ethnographic study. Within the relational, and social constructionist orientation of relational leadership, we explored empathy and empathic leadership practice. We explored gender in relation to relational leadership, drawing on Eagly (2005) and Crevani (2019), before exploring indigenous Māori perspectives of collective leadership, which took us to the larger umbrella of collective leadership consisting of a matrix proposed by Ospina et al. (2020) comprising four cells.

Decolonising leadership

Rosile, G. A., Boje, D. M. and Claw, C. M. (2018) 'Ensemble leadership theory: Collectivist, relational, and heterarchical roots from indigenous contexts'. *Leadership*, 14(3): 307–328.

The authors offer an ensemble theory of leadership, focusing on contemporary indigenous scholarship, which emphasises the collective over individual-centred views of leadership.

Key summary

- Relational leadership can be categorised into 'entity' and 'relational' perspectives.
- The 'entity' perspective focuses on individuals such as leaders or followers and views organisations and inviduals as stable or fixed entities.
- The 'relational' perspective within relational leadership views individuals and organisations as socially constructed, and focuses on the processes and practices of leadership. It focuses on leadership as being intersubjective.
- Collective leadership can be viewed through four cells set on two axes, based on where leadership is located and the type of collectivity.
- The indigenous Māori worldview challenges traditional paradigms, and proposes an ecosystems view of collective leadership.

Further reading

Fischer, D. (2019) 'Relational leadership and regional development: A case study on new agriculture ventures in Uganda'. *Journal of Developmental Entrepreneurship*, 24(02): 1950010.

Kinder, T., Stenvall, J., Six, F., et al. (2021) 'Relational leadership in collaborative governance ecosystems'. *Public Management Review*, 23(11): 1612–1639.

Sánchez, I. D., Ospina, S. M. and Salgado, E. (2020) 'Advancing constructionist leadership research through paradigm interplay: An application in the leadership–trust domain'. *Leadership*, 16(6): 683–711.

6

LEADERSHIP IN CRISIS: WHAT WE CAN LEARN FROM ENTREPRENEURS AND INTRAPRENEURIAL APPROACHES

Louisa Huxtable-Thomas and Russ Huxtable

Chapter objectives

The objectives of this chapter are:

- To introduce the concept of **entrepreneurial** leadership as a perspective of leadership in a period of persistent and unpredictable change.
- To illustrate that entrepreneurial leadership is a disputed concept that is growing in popularity in popular management practice.
- To consider the role of entrepreneurial leadership in society, particularly as it pertains to dealing with crisis and creating resilient organisations, and the creation of entrepreneurial leadership teams.

Introduction

In this chapter, we explore the concept of 'entrepreneurial' leadership. This phrase is increasingly used in the popular press and even in policy documents, but the academic theory behind it is still in the early stages of development. To understand the concept, the first part of this chapter considers the notion of the entrepreneurial person and the links between theories on the leader and the entrepreneur. The chapter will then develop theory around the definition and traits of the entrepreneurial 'leader' and consider the contemporary view which ascribes entrepreneurial leadership to a team, not just an individual starting a business. In decoupling the concept from traditional 'great man' theories, the chapter then focuses more on what the entrepreneurial leader(s) do, using leadership during a **crisis** as a lens to understand this alternative perspective on leadership.

The name alone suggests that entrepreneurs or entrepreneurial people are some-how excluded from the leadership concept. This chapter will explore why a new concept has been adopted, why it appears to cross cultural boundaries more readily than more established theories and how it can be used as an approach to leading through a crisis.

What does the entrepreneur have to do with leadership?

If you close your eyes and imagine an 'entrepreneur', what do you think of? If you imagine a middle-aged, affluent, somewhat pompous man or woman who has a great deal of money and is always in a rush to make more money for themselves, then you are not alone (Ogbor, 2000; Raible and Williams-Middleton, 2021). Incidentally, this stereotyping is something that is also true of leadership (Cann and Siegfried, 1987) but that will be covered elsewhere in this book.

Internationally popular programmes such as *The Apprentice* and *Dragon's Den* have made this stereotype even more prominent in the popular consciousness. The reality, in almost every territory around the world, is that we are surrounded by 'entrepreneurs' that do not conform to this image. At its simplest and perhaps most stereotypical – the definition of an entrepreneur is someone that starts a business; they bring together new ideas and concepts; they solve problems for their customers; and they work hard and achieve success through innovation and dedication. Entrepreneurs run our local global franchises and they create and sell bespoke artisan products. In spite of this, entrepreneurship is not all about corner shops and restaurants (Deakins and Scott, 2018). As market-led mixed economies develop worldwide, doctors, lawyers, cleaners, journalists, models, farmers and artists have to be entrepreneurs – setting up organisa-tions in order to trade their expertise or services. More complex definitions, as discussed by Howorth, Tempest and Coupland (2005), suggest that individuals can be included or excluded from the definition of entrepreneur purely because of the paradigm utilised to observe them. In addition, as society, and the global challenges we face, become more connected and more complex, corporate organisations and the public sector are adopting entrepreneurial ways of working in order to be more agile in response to change (Pinchot and Soltanifar, 2021; Smith, 2021).

Entrepreneurs are diverse, and the way that they lead is diverse. As described in Chapter 2, trait theories don't adequately explain leadership success or failure, and so it is unlikely that there can be a valid model for trait-based entrepreneurial leadership. This is made doubly difficult because, although many authors have suggested lists of traits, there is so far no validated model that can predict whether someone will become an 'entrepreneur'. Equally, when viewed through 'situational', 'transformational', 'authentic' and 'servant' leadership constructs, there is no clear preference for which one is most successful based on their context as an entrepreneurial (or **intrapreneurial**) individual or team (Leitch and Volery, 2017).

In an effort to create a definition for this chapter, two undeniable common factors of the entrepreneurial leader can be accepted: first, that they lead during times of fast-paced change and uncertainty; and second, that they lead whilst also participating in the business of their organisation (creating value).

…'ships' that pass in the night

The two '… ships', entrepreneurship and leadership, have equally ambiguous constructs (Leitch and Harrison, 2018), so it is no surprise that entrepreneurial leadership has not yet achieved **definitional consensus** and is still emerging as a theory. In 2014, a search of the major leadership literature identified that less than 1 per cent of articles on leadership were about entrepreneurial leadership (Dinh et al., 2014). This is in direct opposition to the amount of entrepreneurial leadership that must be enacted everyday: if less than 10 per cent of firms in most countries have multiple layers of management, being medium to large established firms, then surely 90 per cent of leadership must be by definition 'entrepreneurs'. A further complication exists in that prior to 2005, research suggested that the commonly observed characteristics of the entrepreneur: *driven, goal orientated, participative, autocratic*, were problematic to effective, contemporary leadership (Meyer and Dean, 1990). However, if we accept the statistics above, that every entrepreneur by definition must be the leader of their firm, especially in the early days of uncertainty where they, by default, are at the head, then either all entrepreneurial ventures are doomed to be poorly led, or there is a different set of 'rules' at play.

Given the ambiguity, four major schools or perspectives are identified in the literature.

The first is 'leadership that the entrepreneur does', as espoused by Kuratko (2007) and Leitch and Volery (2017). Kuratko takes the view that observing and duplicating the behaviour of successful entrepreneurs can make others more successful. However, this perspective is also a type of 'necessity' leadership (Kempster and Cope, 2010). If the entrepreneur needs to start leading just by virtue of owning or founding an organisation, in which employees are by default followers, then the task of leadership may not be a natural fit for them.

The second perspective is a development on the first and swaps the 'entrepreneur' for the entrepreneurial person in the larger organisation. This is called the behavioural perspective (Renko, 2005; Flamholtz, 2011) and applies to leaders in large organisations who are not necessarily 'entrepreneurs' but that exhibit entrepreneurial behaviours and attitudes. Understanding how a small business owner behaves and applying that to the creation of new ventures, products or services in a large organisation is seen as a way to overcome the entrenched management thinking that often stymies innovation. Surie and Ashley (2008) describe entrepreneurial leadership as a type of leadership capable of sustaining innovation and adaptation in high velocity and uncertain environments – these are the conditions that all entrepreneurial ventures face at the outset, whether a small business start-up or an intrapreneurial endeavour in a large corporation. Renko et al. (2015: 54) simplify it as 'influencing and directing the performance of group members toward the achievement of organizational goals that involve recognizing and exploiting entrepreneurial opportunities'. When considering the leadership that the entrepreneurial person does, this can also be thought about in terms of not only how the leaders display their own entrepreneurial characteristics, but how they encourage and consider followers in terms of their entrepreneurial passion and **self-efficacy**. They enhance followers' beliefs in their own entrepreneurial skills and abilities and ignite passion for innovation and creativity (Bandura, 1986; Cardon et al., 2009).

The third perspective is the skills perspective – this conceptualises entrepreneurial leadership as a set of skills belonging to the entrepreneurial leader that can be learned and displayed by anyone when it is relevant (Thornberry, 2006). This skills perspective borrows again from the first two perspectives – identifying the skills of the entrepreneur who leads, or the entrepreneurial person in the larger organisation – and it seeks to understand which skill set is appropriate to the achievement of certain tasks of value creation in an organisation. This is closely aligned to the discourses on entrepreneurial learning and leadership learning as described by Huxtable-Thomas et al. (2016).

The fourth perspective is the differential view – focusing on the similarities and differences between entrepreneurs and leaders. This last school asks two questions – the first is whether context (in this case the entrepreneurial endeavour) changes the style and behaviours of leadership. At its most extreme, this perspective suggests that entrepreneurial leadership is just 'leadership' and that there is no differentiation between the leadership that the entrepreneurial person does and what other people do that cannot be explained by other theories of leadership style. This was one of the earliest and most cited conceptual considerations of entrepreneurial leadership (Vecchio, 2003). Vecchio (2003) reviewed the literature and argued that entrepreneurship (as it applied to starting a small business) and leadership could not be disentangled, encouraging researchers to consider it purely as a context. For the purposes of this chapter, it is worth acknowledging Vecchio's critical viewpoint and using it to provide an alternative and critical view as we consider the role of entrepreneurial leadership in dealing with crisis. For instance, when considering Cunningham and Lischeron's very early (1991) definition that entrepreneurial leadership involves setting clear goals, creating opportunities, empowering people, preserving organisational intimacy, and developing a human resource system, it could equally apply to middle-tier leadership in the corporate context.

It is easy to see how Vecchio reached his conclusions. Again, from the differential perspective, the behaviours and characteristics of the successful entrepreneur and leader have much in common. At the intersection of entrepreneurship and leadership, Fernald et al. (2005) identify eight characteristics common to both successful entrepreneurs and leaders:

- the ability to motivate,
- achievement orientation,
- creativity,
- flexibility,
- patience,
- persistence,
- risk taking,
- vision.

This list identifies that there is a great deal of overlap between the two concepts.

Many of the subsequent definitions identify the tasks of the entrepreneurial leader and avoid defining the context as a small business or intrapreneurial endeavour.

Roomi and Harrison (2011: 2) focused on the role of the vision and gaining competitive advantage, concentrating on the role of leadership in developing the small business, 'having and communicating the vision to engage teams to identify, develop and take advantage of opportunity in order to gain competitive advantage'. While Renko et al. (2015) are more closely aligned with the intrapreneurial point of view, stating that it 'involves influencing and directing the performance of group members toward achieving those organizational goals that involve recognizing and exploiting entrepreneurial opportunities.' The concept of gaining competitive advantage comes from the heart of economics – the strategy of competition in order to win market share overriding all, whereas Renko et al.'s definition points to an important yet subtle notion – why the entrepreneurial person does what they do: to find and exploit opportunities. This subtlety comes about because it not only eschews the competitive stance taken by Roomi and Harrison, but points at the inherent nature of opportunities as being important. This is because opportunities differ from ideas in that they have a perceived value to a specific audience or 'market'. To paraphrase both definitions, the entrepreneurial leader is engaged in motivating others to create value.

Having identified that there are different ways of looking at the entrepreneurial leader, and accepting that the concept is still emerging, the remainder of this chapter will concentrate on entrepreneurial leadership as being the leadership associated with periods of persistent and unpredictable change, regardless of whether in the larger corporate or small start-up.

Why 'entrepreneurs?' and does entrepreneurial leadership exist at all?

The remainder of this chapter will focus on the *pragramatic* view of entrepreneurial leadership, i.e., while leadership is inherent in the concept of venture creation, the particular value of entrepreneurial leadership is that it describes the practice of achieving a useful change; in particular, in the context of dealing with the ambiguity of complex and fast-paced global change and crises. For this reason, the chapter also considers the context of 'crisis' – both as a critical contemporary perspective on entrepreneurship, and in considering the role of leadership in 'intrapreneurship'. Entrepreneurial leadership is likely to be the creation of new or novel ventures from within larger corporate firms or public sector organisations and often in response to unexpected events.

Entrepreneurs (and their corporate employee equivalents, the 'intrapreneurs') are key actors in the knowledge economy and are fundamental to any entrepreneurial and dynamic economic system. This is because they drive change and innovation by starting new ventures, growing businesses, and investing in new ideas. They spot viable opportunities, they mobilise resources, they take risks, and they are action focused (Vecchio, 2003).

It has been argued that environments with increasingly higher levels of uncertainty, unpredictability and complexity demand entrepreneurial responses (Gibb, 2012). The capacity and capability of entrepreneurs to lead and develop their ventures, whether alone as individuals or as an entrepreneurial team, affect future success and sustainability and this is especially the case when crisis or unforeseen incidents require people to be resilient and respond quickly to events.

It then appears logical that entrepreneurial *leaders* would be an even greater asset; retaining the action-oriented, opportunity-exploiting aspects of the entrepreneur while undertaking the common tasks of the leader: setting visions, thinking ambitiously and driving performance in their business but also influencing their sectors and regions. As described by Kempster and Cope (2010: 27), 'entrepreneurs are leaders by virtue of their position, being encouraged to take this role through organisational necessity'.

Student exercise

When are entrepreneurs not leaders? And when are leaders not entrepreneurs?

Entrepreneurial leadership – moving away from the blandness of corporate leadership

In developing nations, small businesses and entrepreneurs are used to representing and responding to the needs of people in their local populations. Large corporate firms are likely to be different. Large firms, defined by their multimillion - or billion-dollar turnovers and hundreds of staff, in multiple bases, are more likely to be international or global in their outlook. While they may undertake local community endeavours or seek to support local neighbourhoods with their facilities, the higher proportion of large firms originate in Western nations and so are likely to have a Western outlook – a phenomenon known as 'home country bias'. In fact, these global or multinational organisations have been accused of being 'bland' (Kingsnorth, 2011), creating environments and systems where 'one size fits all'. In every region, the local entrepreneurs and business owners are more attached to and more able to relate to their own region and in doing so are highly influential as community leaders. They embody local distinctiveness and local norms.

Measuring entrepreneurial leadership

Early in the quest for understanding entrepreneurial leadership came the mission to quantify it.

Gupta, MacMillan and Surie (2004) used secondary data from the GLOBE study to develop a scale to measure the roles of entrepreneurial leaders; however, the roles and scale do not feature the goals of opportunity recognition and exploitation. Renko et al. (2015) criticise this because it isn't clear from the responses how the measure is different to measures of other contemporary and enabling styles of leadership. In fact, many early attempts to measure entrepreneurial leadership inadvertently just measured 'leadership' or 'entrepreneurship' because the distinction between the two – entrepreneurs and leaders – wasn't adequately conceptualised. Therefore, any measures of leadership also measured entrepreneurship and vice versa, leading to issues with construct validity.

Thornberry (2006) conceptualised entrepreneurial leadership into four 'boxes' based on the individual's preferences. In this conceptualisation, the measure is more one of entrepreneurial leadership 'personality', and it considers which of the four boxes an individual fits with most closely, building on the concept that anyone can be an entrepreneurial leader if the circumstances fit. The boxes divide people according to whether they prefer to be 'internal facing' or 'externally oriented' and whether they are a facilitator of entrepreneurial activity in others, or if they prefer to act entrepreneurially themselves.

Since its inception, the most cited tool for measuring entrepreneurial leadership has been Renko et al.'s (2015) ENTRELEAD scale. Renko et al. deem entrepreneurial leadership to be a leadership style present in an organisation of any size, type or age. This scale was described as one of the first valid constructs of entrepreneurial leadership. To create this, the research team first had to conceptualise entrepreneurial leadership. The definition is oriented on the 'goals' of the entrepreneurial leadership activity, recognising and exploiting entrepreneurial opportunities – by doing this they took out the context of whether it was the *entrepreneur leading*, or the leader *acting entrepreneurially*. In doing so, the authors acknowledge the alignment of their model with transformational leadership (Bass and Avolio, 1994) and creativity enhancing leadership (Makri and Scandura, 2010) while from the entrepreneurship canon, concentrating on the concept of **'entrepreneurial orientation'** (Basso et al., 2009).

The measure is something of a chimera – leadership is often measured by asking followers about their 'leader' (Hammond et al., 2021). In contrast, entrepreneurial orientation is determined in organisations by measuring the objective output of entrepreneurial activity, and infers an organisational bias towards (or against) entrepreneurial behaviour as a result. Renko et al.'s concept takes a middle ground and measures the 'immediate supervisor' so doesn't rely on leadership being based at the top of an organisation. The work undertaken by Renko et al. was comprehensive in that it examined the constructs of entrepreneurial leadership and confirmed it was different to an entrepreneurial orientation of the organisation or supervisor creativity-supporting behaviours. Some key factors of transformational leadership were found to be common to entrepreneurial leadership – in particular, the elements of intellectual challenge and seeking new opportunities for the organisation. However, these were the only confirmed overlaps. The study suggested that the environmental and organisational context helped entrepreneurial leadership be 'distinctive', but what was also interesting was the idea that follower susceptibility to entrepreneurial leadership style affects the outcomes that it achieves. At its simplest, this is one of the new school of emergent leadership styles that are contingent not just on the 'control' of the leader, but the willingness of the follower to follow.

Finally, the measurement of entrepreneurial leadership does rely on the ability (or otherwise) to measure the entrepreneurial orientation of the leader. Kraus et al. (2019), in their study of public sector intrapreneurship, identified that the entrepreneurial orientation of the individuals in an organisation (both the leader *and* the followers), was vital to opportunity creation, identification and/or exploitation. They also found that the entrepreneurial *orientation* of followers could exist without the leader being entrepreneurial. If entrepreneurial orientation is defined as a bias towards being innovative, autonomous and risk accepting, and biases are 'malleable' as suggested by Krueger and Sussan (2017), then this suggests that entrepreneurial orientation can be 'adopted' if not learned. This chapter will not delve further into the literature on entrepreneurial learning, however Huxtable-Thomas et al. (2016) and Pittaway et al. (2019) provide further guidance on how entrepreneurs and leaders learn.

Entrepreneurial leadership theories – leadership during venture creation

The traits and tricks of the 'leaderpreneur' are starting to be expounded in the popular press, however the traits of these all-in-one business actors are of little practical use without understanding the processes or systems they create and how people can become entrepreneurial leaders. Or if, indeed, the concept of leadership can even be applied to entrepreneurs as separate from the state of entrepreneurship.

The suggestion that the concept may be a misnomer comes from two sources – first, Roomi and Harrison's 2011 review that aimed to 'offer a relatively stable definition' but was limited by the relatively sparse academic literature on the subject. The assumptions in that paper have not yet been critically analysed elsewhere but are starting to be cited in studies relating to gender, education and small firms (Clark, Harrison and Gibb, 2019). No studies directly address Roomi and Harrison's suggestions for future research into the field. In addition, there has been limited attention paid to the field compared to other forms of leadership (Dinh et al., 2014).

Reflective questions

1. Consider what you have read so far about leadership: Does every entrepreneur have to be a leader by default?
2. Consider the context in which businesses start up – these are often 'team' endeavours. Does a single 'leader' have to emerge for the business to be successful?

Two sides of the same leadership – is it what the entrepreneur does or how they lead?

To make sense of the definitions of entrepreneurial leadership, it is best to consider why the concept exists at all. As recently as the early 2000s, the academic literature about entrepreneurial leadership was sparse at best. Gupta, MacMillan and Surie (Gupta et al., 2004) set out to develop and measure the construct, and to identify whether it had traction across cultures. They identified only four seminal papers with only one directly mentioning the concept. That conceptual paper, authored by Kuratko and Hornsby (1999), identified 'corporate entrepreneurial leadership' as the future of leadership. Their framework combined the concepts of corporate venturing and leadership as a way of responding to issues of sophisticated and fast-moving competition and the loss of talent from corporate management to entrepreneurship. Kuratko and Hornsby (1998) acknowledged that the concept had been identified first in the popular business press, citing articles in *Forbes*, *Fortune* and *Business Week*, however hindsight over twenty years later has proven them right. Large corporate organisations have had to evolve at an accelerated rate to cope with global challenges such as the ubiquity of internet connectivity, an aging population and climate change, among others. Since the 1980s, there has been a suggestion that major business corporations have lost their competitiveness through an emphasis on management rather than leadership (Fernald et al., 2005).

Since Gupta et al.'s paper in 2004, the business press has been littered with stories of fast growth, high-tech start-ups and disruptive product and service innovations that have led to business model innovation and changes in market expectation. Added to this is the reported increasing global impact of natural and man-made crisis events because of the global economy; thus the need for new approaches is well founded. Quite simply, as this chapter is being published in 2023, what used to be impossible is no longer even improbable.

How the entrepreneur provides an opportunity to consider more diverse leaders and leadership

Traditional leadership theories for dealing with the fast paced and unpredictable changes (or crises) tend towards the traits approach and 'styles'. In both the Eastern and Western academic and philosophical cannon, leadership theory started with the aim of understanding and emulating the great military leaders – this is where the first 'great man' theories started. The ancient cultural and military roots of leadership (and by association, strategy) start with the writings of Sun Tzu in *The Art of War* in the East or Plato and Socrates in the West (Nice, 1998; Markham, 2012).

While the concept of the leader as a military construct is one that is almost ubiquitous across cultures, the eighteenth, nineteenth and twentieth centuries saw a proliferation of academic studies of leadership, heavily influenced by underlying Western culture and values. As academics generally build upon the work of others, the foundations of modern leadership studies assumed that societies were hierarchical, that leadership was passed down through generations alongside land ownership, that women were subservient to men, that other places and cultures should submit to colonisation, and that wealth and leadership were essentially the same thing (Nice, 1998; Van de Vliert, 2006). This book addresses some of these assumptions directly in Chapters 2 and 11.

As it pertains to entrepreneurial leadership, it is sufficient to say that in the Western cannon, entrepreneurs – those who endeavoured to earn wealth but weren't independently wealthy or hereditary landowners – were considered to be lower class citizens by the privileged people who could afford to study and become academics in the eighteenth and nineteenth centuries. The notion of the entrepreneur as leader did not have a strong role in the academic discourse until the study of strategy and innovation started to develop in the early to mid-twentieth century, between the First and Second World Wars. It is not a coincidence that this came at the same time that inherited hierarchies and dynasties started to lose their power and influence, superseded by large corporate organisations, and the entrepreneur became seen as a powerful actor in society.

The proliferation of business schools at this time in developed nations like the United Kingdom, the United States and Northern Europe saw large numbers of academics with military experience applying their knowledge to leadership and business (Adair, 2005). This was a period of significant upheaval, but also of opportunity. However, the basis of their work was still grounded in the assumptions of hierarchy, wealth and inherited privilege. Academic theory was, and still is, dominated by the study of successful individuals. Because of when and where these successful individuals were studied, they were often white men, many with either military training or a privileged upbringing, at the highest level of a hierarchy (Adair, 2005).

The study of entrepreneurs and how they lead, as well as the skills of leading they possess, provides a much more diverse and inclusive opportunity to study leadership practices. Entrepreneurs are found in every nation; they are not limited to people with a certain upbringing, personality type, landownership, creed, culture, religion or any other characteristic. Entrepreneurs are diverse; they often found businesses as partnerships or small teams, rather than as lone individuals, and so their leadership is equally diverse.

Equally, the role of entrepreneurial leadership has a global appeal. From the earliest days of the concept being developed, empirical work has identified that the construct of entrepreneurial leadership has a wider appeal across cultural boundaries (Gupta et al., 2004). While it may not be unexpected, the countries with high power distance such as Middle Eastern and Confucian societies are less likely to endorse entrepreneurial leadership. Interestingly, the study by Gupta et al. supports the theory that entrepreneurial approaches are more likely to be adopted in highly competitive and turbulent situations. Gupta et al.'s study concluded that entrepreneurial leadership was likely to be endorsed by individuals with a high need for achievement and value creation from any country.

Mini case study 6.1

Bureaucracy versus crisis

At over 90 years old, Al Futtaim is seen as one of the most progressive family business houses in the Gulf Region. Operating in over 20 countries, it prides itself on being the partner of choice for Western companies to operate in the UAE where they entrust their reputation and brand image to the Al Futtaim Company. The conglomerate now covers a diverse portfolio of business units that comprise well-known brands in the automotive, retail and media sectors as well as real estate and health. Within the automotive sector, FAMCO is the business unit that covers the heavier vehicle end of the market, including specialised plant and construction equipment, trucks and buses.

In 2011, FAMCO Al Futtaim won a lucrative contract to supply and support plant and specialist large vehicles to DynCorp, an American private military contractor. Al Futtaim created a new company to manage this multimillion-dollar contract.

Select Auto was created, and a leadership team sought who would not only ensure the financial success of the operation, but at the same time who had experience of operating in a volatile, potentially high-threat environment with all the additional planning and crisis/incident leadership that this contract would require.

The initial contract was delivered successfully, and the leadership team quickly set about looking to the future, in particular opportunities in the potentially lucrative and largely unexploited oil fields of southern Iraq – it was hoped that this would pave the way for other Al Futtaim companies to follow when the conditions were favourable.

The careful balancing act here was to meet the entrepreneurial requirement of a new business whilst at the same time having the appropriate leadership and contingency planning skills to operate in a post-conflict environment. This expansion was initially unsuccessful due to rapidly escalating terrorist activity in the region. However, the leadership team's focus on contingency planning, designed to protect or extract staff and resources in an emergency, allowed safe withdrawal. Being a small, highly capable and agile team, Select Auto had already identified alternative markets. They quickly transitioned into the Cabo Delgado region in Northern Mozambique, another emerging, high-risk but stabilising new opportunity where Select Auto would be able to differentiate itself. This operation normalised so much that Select Auto was absorbed back into the main Al Futtaim FAMCO business unit when the Board perceived the combined reduced risk and need for additional, entrepreneurial, leadership was no longer required.

Perhaps Al Futtaim transitioned to normal operations too quickly as Al Shaba undertook terrorist activity that disrupted Select Auto's Mozambique operation in March 2021. What was missing in 'normal' operations was the analysis of the changing threat environment that eventually undermined the business. Too much focus on day-to-day business and not on wider threat environments and contingency planning led to drastic failure.

Questions

1. This case study is an extreme but true-to-life example of how unexpected events can change a firm's strategy overnight. Do you think that Select Auto benefitted from having a leadership team that were focused on contingency planning?

2. Entrepreneurial leadership as a 'way of leading' as opposed to a theoretical framework suggests that it is the context that differentiates the theory from others. It is clear to see that it would be useful in a new start-up – but in which alternative contexts do you think the entrepreneurial leadership style or behaviour would be a suitable approach?

Panic stations…

You are the leader of an organisation. You have been informed that, during a period of political and social upheaval, there is an energy crisis. Your firm will not be able to rely on a stable or predictable source of electricity or oil to fuel its operations. In order to cope with this news and lead your organisation into the future – what do you need to do in the first 24 hours?

- Do you think that your approach to this event is 'entrepreneurial'? Why or why not?

How best to lead in a crisis?

Before trying to understand the role of leadership in a crisis, it is important to define what a crisis is. While there is no single accepted definition, most definitions of crisis in the organisational or business context agree that it can be characterised as an event or specific turning point (Boin, 2006) as opposed to the outcome of that event (Borodzicz, 2005; Boin et al., 2010). Scholars also agree that it is unpredictable or unexpected (i.e., rare) and extreme, in that it is likely to lead to catastrophic outcomes, potentially business or organisational failure (Doern, 2016). Others suggest that a crisis is significant, high impact, ambiguous, urgent, and involves high stakes (Simola, 2014).

Studies often focus on large complex organisations, with a view to responding to the crisis and preventing drops in productivity or business effectiveness. Kayes et al. (2012) describe crisis as a period when the core values of the organisation are under threat. This perspective, which focuses on the destabilising effect that the crisis has and the likelihood of issues for organisational norms as a result, provides something of a refreshing change from the other definitional literature which focuses on creating 'conditions' under which an event is either defined as a crisis or isn't. Kayes et al. instead focus on why a crisis causes so much trouble; it undermines the norm. This point is picked up in one of the most commonly used definitions, created by Pearson and Clair (1998: 60):

> An organizational crisis is a low probability, high impact event that threatens the viability of the organization and is characterized by ambiguity of cause, effect, and means of resolution, as well as by a belief that decisions must be made swiftly.

If we take this definition on board, received wisdom of how to lead in a crisis suggests that autocratic and dictatorial methods will be more effective than democratic or inclusive methods in a crisis situation. This is for two reasons – the first being that the time pressures of a crisis require decisiveness and autocracy; there is no time for discussion. The second comes from the underlying societal norms of which leadership is constructed and requires more unpicking.

Grint (2010) in his essay on the sacred in leadership, has suggested that the desire for a single 'heroic' leader (especially during a period of unpredictable change) comes about because people are keen to be led, not because they don't wish to be seen as a leader, but to avoid the risks associated with leadership – not least of which is being seen to 'fail'. In these times of crisis, the person that steps up and is willing to separate themselves from their followers and believes that the cause is worth the possible sacrifice and risk of failure, are likely to find themselves accepted as a leader because everybody else has relinquished the responsibility.

Renko et al.'s seminal paper on the measurement of the entrepreneurial leader in 2015 also suggested that a crisis may distract followers from the discovery and pursuit of entrepreneurial opportunities, reducing the effect of entrepreneurial leadership. Intuitively, this makes sense if the discovery and pursuit of entrepreneurial opportunities is considered to be an active task that requires creativity. This is because creativity is a cognitive process that requires the individual(s) doing it to have an available cognitive workload, i.e., the time and space to think. This viewpoint is confirmed by studies such as that by Elsbach and Hargadon (2006) that show that individuals will choose tasks that they are familiar with and can control over experimental or creative activity when workload pressure is high. However, both practical examples of entrepreneurial responses to crisis and deeper development of socio-cognitive theory suggest that this is a limiting view (Shao et al., 2019).

During the Japanese tsunami of 2011, critiques of the Japanese government suggested that the response was slow, and that the focus of the guidelines for reconstruction was exactly that – about returning things to the way that they were – dealing with essential requirements for life. In short, the challenge of returning things to the known and familiar was considered to be easier and more achievable than seeking and pursuing new and unproven opportunities. In that case, the opportunity recognition and innovation came from the business community. As described by the Kauffman Fellow Taro Sato (2012), it was young entrepreneurs and entrepreneurial leaders of large firms that took the opportunity to build back better. During Hurricane Katrina in 2005, again the government was responsible for protecting public order and concentrating on returning to 'normal' (Boin et al., 2010), however the Tulane University School of Medicine took the approach in the wake of the disaster to encourage entrepreneurship, asking staff to build a 'different health-care system, not rebuild' and 'turn adversity into opportunity'. Out of this came a completely different approach to primary care in New Orleans which led to a new slew of organisations providing community primary care clinics to 220,000 people (Kahn and Sachs, 2018).

In the final, and at the time of writing still ongoing, example, the COVID-19 pandemic led to the fastest change in work place practices seen in over 100 years, and the global necessity to do things differently led to the adoption of innovations as well as entrepreneurial responses becoming the norm (Akpan et al., 2021; Galanakis, 2020).

In all of these examples, the innovations and entrepreneurial responses were required in order to ensure welfare and health, not profitability or productivity, as demonstrated by Scheepers and Bogie (2021) in their case study on Alon Lits, Director and General Manager of Uber in Sub-Saharan Africa. Seeking to profit from a pandemic or any other natural disaster is not the value of the entrepreneurial leader. Being able to change what the organisation does quickly to add value to others, be they staff, suppliers or customers, appears to be the great difference.

Student exercise

Debate with four other students the following motion:

Not everyone can be an entrepreneurial leader – entrepreneurial leaders must have a natural talent for being 'entrepreneurial'.

- Do you think that leading in an entrepreneurial way is something that can be taught? Can it be learned or must you be born 'entrepreneurial'?

Why are entrepreneurial leaders useful in a crisis and not others?

Bennett and Lemoine (2014) further help us to understand why entrepreneurial leaders are useful in a crisis by helping us understand the different factors that make up the crisis context. Using the VUCA acronym: volatility, uncertainty, complexity, ambiguity, Bennett and Lemoine suggest that the low predictability and low information of 'ambiguity' call for experimental approaches – understanding cause and effect and applying lessons learned broadly. The other three are less entrepreneurial and this reminds us that the issue with crisis is that it is a specific and pivotal time of little information and high unpredictability. If it can be predicted (complexity, volatility), it is a job for data modelling, strategic scenario planning and preparedness exercises – having enough flexibility that the right people can do their jobs if required. If there is plenty of data but a situation is unpredictable (uncertainty), again the answer is to analyse the information and share it. This is demonstrated clearly in the case of a financial director. It is where information is missing that the entrepreneurial approach comes to the fore. When nobody knows what to (do), somebody needs to step up and do something and the entrepreneurial person in a leadership role is likely to be comfortable in the situation because of their experience in working in novel environments.

Eco-leadership, a type of meta-leadership, has arisen recently in response to a system of ongoing chronic climate emergency as well as the ongoing trends of Industry 4.0, globalisation (or hyper-globalisation as it is termed) and a greater societal requirement for a nurturing workforce that drives not only employee value but value in communities (Western, 2020). In eco-leadership, connectivity, networks and ethics are seen as being the central tenets of leadership. In this case, the crisis that eco-leadership considers is not as immediate – it is a much wider meta-context. That isn't to say that the two are contrary or in conflict. Entrepreneurial leadership may form part of the eco-leadership discourse. This is still an early area of study, but much merit may be had from considering the role of connectivity, networks and ethics in the life world of the entrepreneur as leader. This in turn could be used to inform leadership behaviours in mature and large organisations as they seek to adopt changes in response to the climate emergency.

Further, researchers have started to consider the concept of 'active' leadership as being of value during crisis. Active leadership (LaBrosse, 2007) suggests an active project management approach to leadership, where the same networks and connectivity as described in eco-leadership are utilised, but the focus is on the leader as the connecting force – actively moving between stakeholders to keep actions on track. This is certainly the case for entrepreneurs in small firms – presenting endless opportunities for followers to interact directly with their leader (Vecchio, 2003).

The entrepreneurial leader does this, but – as described earlier on, the differentiators are in their focus – the entrepreneurial leader does what all leaders do (Vecchio, 2003), however the concept of 'creating value', whether through innovation, opportunity recognition and capture or risk management, is 'why' they do it. If these things are not in place, they can neither set a vision nor inspire or enable followers to achieve it.

The right person at the right time

Wesmouth County Council in the UK is a public sector organisation employing over 1000 full- and part-time staff and with a portfolio of services including estates, finance, well-being, education, licensing and grants that at any one time provide services to over 20,000 people. The Council is led by an established leadership team that have been employed in public sector roles for the majority of their career. In an effort to prepare for anticipated issues of extreme weather, increasing physical and security threats, as well as other more likely incidents such as fire, chemical spills or major accidents, the management teams were brought together to conduct Incident Management training.

During an Incident Management training exercise, the Director of Finance had been nominated as the Silver Commander for the exercise. At the start of the exercise, the problem and many contingencies were analysed in detail, a process that meant that the Director took 90 minutes to make the first decision. At this point, the exercise was halted for a learning point.

The Finance Director was asked 'what do you anticipate has happened in the 90 minutes it took you to make the first decision and act? At this point, do you have any control or understanding of how events on the ground have developed?'

Our erstwhile Silver Commander, having needed 90 minutes to learn about the initial event, had to admit to having no control or understanding of the events on the ground over an hour later and no idea whether the decided upon action was still relevant or even actionable. She was a talented individual, used to operating day to day in an ordered domain with clear policies to work to and set processes to dictate what should happen when. When change was required, there was plenty of preparation time to plan and introduce those changes.

Like many business leaders who operate in well-ordered paradigms, the Finance Director was unprepared and ill-prepared for the paradigm shift of working in the chaotic realm of incident/crisis management. In 'chaotic' situations, where it is often difficult to establish a relationship between cause and effect, the primary goal should have been to establish order.

Questions

1. Based on this case study, to what extent do you think a more entrepreneurial style of leadership would have benefitted the Director?
2. What would be the downsides of this approach?
3. What other styles of leadership or leadership behaviours that you are aware of would work in this situation?

Entrepreneurial leadership at the top and bottom

Entrepreneurial individuals are at the operational level – they aren't always the CEO or Manager and this eschews upper echelon theory (Covin and Miller, 2014), according to which top executives view situations through their personalised lenses.

Vecchio (2003) suggested that the role of the follower in the entrepreneurial endeavour was equally, if not more, important than the charisma and communication ability to communicate that vision. Baum, Locke and Kirkpatrick (1998) identified the need for setting vision as central to the entrepreneur and this is perhaps the construct with the greatest intersection with leadership in general but the one that sets entrepreneurial leadership apart.

Followership is a subject still hotly debated (see Chapter 4). However, it is well established that followers either cede, or infer, power and control to leaders. In transformational leadership, it is the charisma and inspiration of the leader that followers cede to. In situational leadership, it is the perceived knowledge and experience of the leader that they follow. In ethical and authentic leadership, it is usually shared values and a consensus on the vision. This shared vision and values are the starting point to demonstrating the difference between entrepreneurial and other leaders in practice.

Entrepreneurs, by definition, must be servicing a consumer or market. The 'opportunity' doesn't exist without a customer need at the end of it and so the vision and the direction are set with a focus on creating value for those customers. This 'market' doesn't have to be the capitalist construct of the exchange of goods and services for financial gain. Consumers of value can do so from charitable, public sector or educational organisations as easily as the private sector. The concept of 'crisis' is exactly such a need.

As described in Renko et al. (2015), reflecting on the work of Cardon et al. (2009), entrepreneurial leaders enable their followers and expect them to act decisively, with passion and self-efficacy, and they expect innovation and creative responses. It is perhaps in this that the entrepreneurial leadership discourse is most divided. Entrepreneurial leaders create entrepreneurial leaders, transforming and enabling their followers, finding success when the follower becomes a leader in their own right. Encouraging others to be proactive, innovative or take risks are cultural factors of an organisation – the difference is that the entrepreneurial leader provides support and 'air cover' for others to do this *as long as* they achieve the ultimate goal of creating value and this culture is then passed down through the organisation.

These leaders are distributed through an organisation – the culture flows down from the top, but the activity is inherently led by operational staff; as described by

Kraus et al. (2019), the entrepreneurial orientation of the individual is key in driving these changes, and entrepreneurial leadership in the context of these large organisations eschews upper echelon theory (Covin and Miller, 2014), placing leadership firmly into the realm of lower-level employees and often in the hands of teams (Hensel and Visser, 2018, 2019).

The factor of identifying, measuring and managing risk that is so important to the definition of 'entrepreneurship' means that the individuals taking that risk must see the 'value' in doing so. This is perhaps why you see people rise through the ranks of an organisation into leadership during periods of change. Leading during periods of crisis and ambiguity is often a selfless task. It is a daunting and mentally challenging prospect with high levels of uncertainty and potentially personal risk. As described in mini case study 6.2, people rise during a crisis who are able to thrive in these conditions, but they are motivated by a need to provide a specific value or assistance to others. The traits of the entrepreneurial leader have been suggested by Gupta et al. (2004), Renko et al. (2015) and Leitch and Volery (2017) as being able to communicate a vision and rally a group behind it in order to achieve value. However, if, as has been suggested, they do this without being 'charismatic' or 'inspirational' then the vision – the 'why' must be the driver.

Reflective question

Entrepreneurial leadership is a disputed perspective. Some say that the leadership styles, behaviours or attitudes expressed by entrepreneurs are as diverse as the entrepreneurs themselves, and so it is not possible to define entrepreneurial leadership as a perspective in its own right. Conversely, others believe that it is not possible for an entrepreneur to be a 'leader' because entrepreneurs 'start' enterprises, and therefore they are not leading large groups of followers. However, entrepreneurs (and intrapreneurs) are inherently in a leading role in their endeavours.

1. What criteria would you use to determine if an entrepreneur is, in fact, a leader?
2. And how would you know if the leadership of an entrepreneur differs from any other leader?

Conclusion

In this chapter, we began by considering how the 'entrepreneur' as the individual leads and we justified the entrepreneurial context as valid as it is different from leadership since it is characterised as being at the head of a corporate organisation.

The value of entrepreneurial leadership as a construct was justified in that it can be, and has been, measured. The difference between the role of the leader in setting up a new venture and the leadership of the entrepreneurial individual in organisation contexts was established and provided a critical perspective from which we considered other leadership theories. Finally, we reviewed the role of this leadership style in the context of leading through a crisis.

Decolonising leadership

Gupta, V., MacMillan, I. C. and Surie, G. (2004) 'Entrepreneurial leadership: Developing and measuring a cross-cultural construct'. *Journal of Business Venturing*, 19(2): 241–260.

While the concept of entrepreneurial leadership originally came out of the corporate entrepreneurship constructs first identified in the US by Kuratko, it has now been adopted and is written about as widely in Asia and Africa as in the Anglo-American literature. This is perhaps because of this ground breaking paper. Gupta et al. (2004) have undertaken an empirical study which suggests that the construct of entrepreneurial leadership has a wider appeal across cultural boundaries.

Key summary

- The act of venture creation and business start-up provides a different point of view from which to examine the behaviours and requirements of the leader.
- The concept of leadership as it pertains to the individual leader (either as business owner or CEO) needs to be questioned in light of entrepreneurial and intrapreneurial individuals who perform as part of a team or wider organisation.
- Entrepreneurial leadership as a construct can be measured and developed in individuals.
- The culture of entrepreneurial endeavour is a requirement for entrepreneurial leadership styles to be accepted and to succeed in any organisation.
- Crisis as a context in which leadership needs to be swift and decisive presents an opportunity for entrepreneurial leadership behaviours and skills to come to the fore.
- Recognising those with the capacity for entrepreneurial leadership can be a way for a large firm to identify those individuals suitable to take over leadership when succession planning, or to lead specific projects likely to result in high levels of change or uncertainty such as mergers, acquisitions or introducing new innovations to market.

Further reading

Leitch, C. M. and Volery, T. (2017) 'Entrepreneurial leadership: Insights and directions'. *International Small Business Journal*, 35(2): 147–156.

An up-to-date review of the academic literature into entrepreneurial leadership, considering the developments since Renko's seminal paper in 2015.

Renko, M., El Tarabishy, A., Carsrud, A. L. and Brännback, M. (2015) 'Understanding and measuring entrepreneurial leadership style'. *Journal of Small Business Management*, 53(1): 54–74.

Maija Renko and colleagues were the first to try and measure the entrepreneurial leadership style. Consider the questions that were asked in order to create the ENTRELEAD scale. Do you agree that this is a suitable measure?

Roomi, M. A. and Harrison, P. (2011) 'Entrepreneurial leadership: What is it and how should it be taught?' *International Review of Entrepreneurship*, 9(3).

In 2011, Roomi and Harrison attempted to define entrepreneurial leadership with the aim of identifying how it could be taught. This paper assumes that the fundamentals of entrepreneurial leadership can be developed.

PART 3
CONTEMPORARY ISSUES AND LEADERSHIP

7

POWER AND THE DARK SIDE OF LEADERSHIP

James Wallace and Naveena Prakasam

Chapter objectives

The objectives of this chapter are:

- To explore the importance of power in the study of leadership.
- To critically review different perspectives of power.
- To review critical leadership studies.
- To explore the dark side of leadership.

Reflective question

1. Why do you think that it is important to study power when it comes to leadership?

Why study power and leadership?

The present chapter rests upon the premise that power is a crucial factor affecting the way in which leaders lead, and that an understanding of power will enhance our understanding of leadership. To some extent, the connection between leaders and power may seem obvious – after all, we generally understand a leader as a person who has the *power* to achieve certain objectives through the leadership of others, even if we may not normally use the word 'power' to express this idea. The aim of this chapter, however, is to suggest that the connection between power and leadership may be more complicated than it first appears.

One important consequence of the seemingly obvious connection between leadership and power is that often this relationship is overlooked or taken for granted. This is because studies of leadership often understand the power of the leader as something which occurs *naturally*, that the power a leader has over their followers is intrinsic to their position as leader. As such, the power of the leader over others is considered to be unproblematic and not something we, as students of leadership, should question. A key argument of this chapter is that, paradoxically, the very manner in which the relationship between leadership and power is assumed to be unproblematic is itself deeply problematic. As such, one of the key arguments advanced by this chapter is that, to understand leadership, we must de-naturalise the relationship between leadership and power. To understand **de-naturalisation**, we first must understand naturalisation. **Naturalisation** can be regarded as the process by which value-based choices come to be widely accepted and unchallenged (in other words, seen as natural). These choices can relate to any value held by society regarding what is right or wrong, good or bad. One example of the naturalisation of beliefs regarding leadership might be the idea that it is natural that leaders have power over followers. De-naturalisation is a process by which we seek to challenge ideas which have become taken for granted as the natural way of thinking or acting within a particular society (Fournier and Grey, 2000). Applying this process to leadership would involve asking questions such as 'why should leaders have power over followers?', or 'what gives leaders their power over followers?'. For this reason, we believe that questioning and challenging the power of leaders are a very important undertaking.

In the course of this chapter, we consider a number of key ways of understanding power and reflect on what these theories can tell us about the power of the leader. However, before moving on to this we will briefly consider two interesting consequences of the de-naturalised understanding of power and leadership that we are advocating.

Firstly, de-naturalising the relationship between leadership and power entails that we need to examine how it is that leaders come to have power in the first place, and who gets to become a leader. One way of examining this is to look at the issue of causality. If it is the case that power is a natural component of leadership then this would suggest that leaders have power *because* they are leaders. Crudely speaking, this is to say that leadership comes before power. Alternately, it could be the case that who gets to become a leader is determined by who has power, in other words people are leaders *because* they have power. Again, crudely speaking this would be to say that power comes before leadership.

We can see that this formulation seems to connect in some ways with the classic 'born or made' debate in leadership theory (explored in more depth in Chapter 2). In this manner, we might connect the idea that power comes before leadership with trait theories, which state that some people are born leaders (see Galton, 1869). Nowadays, looking at the way in which trait theory was formulated in the nineteenth century, we are much more likely to equate the characteristics associated with 'born' leaders with the societal privileges afforded to certain individuals – usually white, male and upper-class. In this sense, the social positioning of these individuals meant that they had power before they became leaders. By contrast, if we look at the idea that leadership comes before power – that power is a consequence of leadership – we are much more likely to equate this with the notion that leaders are 'made', and that having power is a consequence of the skills and qualities required to become a leader. In other words, power is earned through demonstrating ability. In either of these cases, it can be said that, broadly, what is at stake is the legitimacy of the leader's power; this, in turn, raises questions concerning to what extent it is right that leaders do have power.

A key consequence of the naturalised view of leadership and power is that leadership studies have tended to focus nearly exclusively on the figure of the leader. As Ford and Harding (2018) point out, traditionally, followers have generally been understood as passive recipients of leadership, and therefore largely ignored. This makes sense: if we believe that power and leadership are intrinsically connected then this suggests that followers are people lacking in power and therefore not very interesting. Put simply, followers merely follow the leader's orders. This brings us to the second implication of a de-naturalised understanding of the relationship between leadership and power: that we need to reconsider the relationship between leaders and followers. More recent developments in leadership studies have begun to consider the relationship between leader and follower in a more nuanced way (Collinson, Smolovic-Jones and Grint, 2018; Ford and Harding, 2018; Kempster, Schedlitzki and Edwards, 2021). This has been explored in more detail in Chapter 4. Generally speaking, a key idea here is that followers are an important factor in the relationship through which leadership takes place. In terms of the focus of the present chapter, this shift is important because it implies that followers are not merely passive recipients of leadership, simply subject to the leader's power. Rather, a relational understanding of leadership implies that there is a shifting power dynamic between leader and follower, and that followers may also exercise power within this relationship (most obviously, through resisting a leader's attempt to exercise power) (Collinson, 2020).

One way of understanding relational leadership is that it is premised on the **empowerment** of followers in a manner which may serve to fundamentally undermine the power of the leader. In considering this development, Gordon (2011) has highlighted an essential paradox in modern leadership, whereby to 'maintain their identity as a leader in contemporary organisations, leaders must establish a differential status, while simultaneously attempting to empower their followers' (Gordon, 2011: 198). Note that, whilst this idea may question the balance of power in the leader–follower relationship, the idea that leaders empower followers nevertheless still rests on the premise that leaders possess power and that they bestow this on followers.

What is power?

In the following sections, we consider the way in which several key theorists have conceptualised power, as well as the implications these understandings have for the way we understand leadership. As such, the following sections are guided by two questions: 'what is power?' and 'how is power exercised?'.

Dahl, Bachrach and Baratz, and Lukes: one-sided, two-faced and three-dimensional power

Power has been an object of study for philosophers and political thinkers for many centuries. The works of Aristotle and Plato considered how power should be used to rule well, and this tradition continued with diverse thinkers such as Thomas Hobbes and Niccolò Machiavelli. In 1974 Steven Lukes published a book which fundamentally changed how power was understood within society. In his book, *Power: A Radical View*, Lukes (2005) argued that power consisted of three dimensions, and that to understand how power operates we need to take account of all three of these dimensions. Lukes considered his three-dimensional understanding of power to be building upon the work of a number of thinkers, specifically Robert Dahl (1957) and Peter Bachrach and Morton Baratz (1962). In this section, we will briefly consider the understanding of power advanced by each of these thinkers, as well as considering how each understanding offers an answer to our two guiding questions.

In 1957 Dahl published an influential article titled 'The concept of power'. In the article, Dahl attempted to present a statement of the concept of power which would offer a means of determining who had power and what degree of power they possessed. In the article, Dahl provided the following formulation: '*A* has power over *B* to the extent that he (sic) can get *B* to do something that *B* would not otherwise do'

(Dahl, 1957: 202–203). Dahl went on to extend this definition by breaking power down into what he considered to be its constituent elements: its source (or base)[1], how it is exercised, and the amount (or extent) to which it could be exercised. Using these terms, Dahl proposed a means of measuring the relative power of different actors, thus meaning it would be possible to quantify one person's power in respect of another. Dahl's formulation offers us an understanding of power which corresponds to our intuitive or common-sense understanding of what we mean when we talk about power. Put simply, power is a means of getting others to do things they wouldn't otherwise do. We can also clearly understand how this concept of power relates to leadership: a leader is someone who can make others act in a way that they wouldn't if they were not being led.

Dahl's understanding of power also offers an answer to the second of our questions: how is power exercised? In looking at the answer Dahl provides, it is important to note that, at the time he was writing, a debate on the issue of power was raging between two positions known as 'pluralism' and 'elitism'. The pluralists, of which Dahl was a member, were mostly political scientists working to defend the traditions of American democracy against the elites, who were mostly sociologists, and who feared that power had become concentrated in the hands of those at the top levels of society. In contrast to the elites, the pluralists believed that democratic processes and the rule of law served to distribute power throughout society in a manner which stopped it becoming concentrated in the hands of a few. It is within this context that we can make sense of Dahl's formulation of power.

Crucially, the concern with legitimating legal-democratic practices meant that the pluralists' understanding of power centres around decision-making processes and conflict between parties. For this reason, the pluralists believed that power was exercised when parties participating in decision-making processes reached a decision affecting both parties. In concrete terms, in the case where A and B were involved in making a decision which resulted in B behaving in a manner which was contrary to their own wishes, then A has exercised power over B. Applying this idea to the realm of leadership, we might wish to consider a hypothetical situation where a leader feels that it would be beneficial for her employees to eat more healthily. In order to help them achieve this, she decides to consult her staff on the proposal to remove 'junk food' from the staff canteen and replace this with a healthier option. Unfortunately for her, the employees enjoy eating junk food, so they mostly express the opinion

---

The idea of 'bases' of power was extended by French and Raven (1959) in their influential article, 'The bases of social power'. In the article, the authors distinguish between five bases of power: coercive, reward, legitimate, referent and expert. In a later edition, they added the idea of informational power.

that they want things to remain the same. Nevertheless, the leader decides that she will remove the food anyway, perhaps using the few staff voices that were in favour as a justification. In this case, the leader has exercised power over her staff members through the decision-making process. This focus on decision-making processes, as well as conflict between parties involved in decision making, has important implications for the way that we understand power. As a result of this focus, for pluralists, power is something which is always, in principle, observable in the actions of an actor (be they individual or collective) upon another – if power is being exercised then we will be able to see it. Referring to our earlier discussion concerning the de-naturalisation of power, we can see that this point has important consequences for questions surrounding the legitimacy of power. For Dahl, an illegitimate exercise of power would be one which violated legal-democratic principles (that is to say something which was undemocratic and/or illegal). Fortunately, according to him, the very existence of these principles and the frameworks which codify them mean that it would be relatively unproblematic to establish if this had happened. In most instances, leadership is exercised within a legal-democratic legislative context; this means that, in principle, it should be easy to determine if a leader had abused their power. In our example above, our leader has exercised power but has not done so illegitimately because she has done nothing illegal. As we shall see, however, things become more complicated once we start to question the observability of power.

In sum, Dahl offers us a seductive understanding of power: one that corresponds with our intuitive understanding of the word, and which offers us a means of understanding, observing and even judging how it is exercised. Likewise, the application of this understanding to the realm of leadership provides us with a basis to understand the centrality of power to how leaders lead.

Whilst Dahl offered a substantial contribution to the understanding of power, the debate between pluralists and their critics continued. In 1962 Bachrach and Baratz published their article 'Two faces of power'. In this article, they described power as having two distinct elements, or 'faces'. According to Bachrach and Morton, whilst the pluralists – and Dahl in particular – had done much to advance our understanding of power, they were only accounting for one face of power, meaning that its other face remained hidden from us. Whilst an understanding of the first face of power can provide valuable insights, it nevertheless provides an incomplete picture of the way power operates within society. In this manner, Bachrach and Morton's key insight was to draw attention to the way power is exercised through controlling participation in decision-making processes; they refer to this as *nondecision-making*. As they put it:

> power is also exercised when *A* devotes his energies to creating or reinforcing
> social and political values and institutional practices that limit the scope of
> the political process to public consideration of only those issues which are

comparatively innocuous to *A*. To the extent that *A* succeeds in doing this, *B* is prevented, for all practical purposes, from bringing to the fore any issues that might in their resolution be seriously detrimental to *A's* set of preferences. (Bachrach and Baratz, 1962: 948)

We can see that this second 'face' of power significantly modifies Dahl and other pluralists' conception of power. No longer are we concerned solely with the power involved in making decisions, we are also concerned with the power involved in preventing actors from successfully having issues which concern them being the object of decision making.

To return to our earlier example, suppose that the people employed by our leader like to be able to make choices regarding what they buy from the staff canteen; however, what concerns them more are proposed changes to their contracts, extending the working hours of the company, meaning that they may need to work longer hours, possibly including weekends. Fortunately for our leader, she is aware that obesity amongst the working-age population is an issue attracting a lot of attention in the media at the moment. Using this knowledge, she is able to control decision-making processes to focus attention on the staff canteen, whilst ensuring that the impending change in contracts is not discussed, much to the dismay of trade unions who wish to properly debate the issue. Here we can see that our leader has, once again, exercised power over her staff members, this time through preventing an issue which was important to them being subject to decision-making processes.

It is important to note that despite their modification of the pluralist definition of power, there is significant affinity between the definition offered by Bachrach and Baratz and that of the pluralists. In this vein, it is important to stress that, according to Bachrach and Baratz, even nondecision-making processes are, in principle, observable to those wishing to study power. We can see this in our earlier example, where – although it was prevented from entering into the formal decision-making process – the issue of employment contracts was clearly observable, manifested in the conflict between the leader and trade union representatives. Again, this focus on observable exercises of power mean that, in our example, we would not consider the actions of our leader illegitimate because they do not violate the legal frameworks surrounding employment law. We can see, however, that the leader's power to circumvent decision-making processes does begin to give us cause for concern regarding the exercise of power.

Steven Lukes' book *Power: A Radical View* (2005) attempted to advance the way in which power was understood by, once again, adding an additional facet to the way in which power is conceptualised, thus giving us three 'dimensions' of power. According to Lukes, all of the theories of power we are concerned with in this section – the pluralist conception (represented by the work of Dahl), Bachrach and Baratz's subsequent revision, and his own third dimension – share the same basic formulation of power. He stated this as 'A exercises power over B when A affects B contrary to B's interests' (Lukes, 2005: 30). If all these theories share the same formulation of power, then the obvious question is: what separates these accounts? The answer, according to Lukes, rests in differing understandings of how interests are to be defined.

As we have seen, both Dahl and Bachrach and Baratz focus attention on the observable actions of actors, where the differing interests of these parties give rise to conflict. For Dahl, this took place through decision making; through Bachrach and Baratz, it also included nondecision-making. For Lukes, however, power could also be exercised through non-overt actions which were not easily observable, as he remarked: 'the most effective and insidious use of power is to prevent such conflict from arising in the first place' (2005: 27). How would it be possible to exercise power whilst preventing conflict? Lukes gives us some insight when he states, 'A may exercise power over B by getting him (sic) to do what he does not want to do, but he also exercises power over him by influencing, shaping or determining his very wants' (2005: 27). In other words, the most effective use of power lies in A shaping the desires of B in accordance with A's own desires, so that B believes that what A wants is also in his own best interests. Through shaping B's wants or interests, A can effectively stop any conflict from occurring.

Returning to our earlier example, remember that our leader had managed to divert attention away from her proposed changes to employees' working contracts, ensuring that the matter was not discussed fully with employees. Now imagine that rather than diverting employees' attention away from this change, instead our leader draws attention to it but also manages to persuade employees that it will actually benefit them. Perhaps this could be done by positioning this in terms of 'flexible working', a trend current within many organisations. Maybe the leader emphasises the way in which the shift in working times might be helpful to those with caring responsibilities or other commitments. There is also the fact that longer hours will mean increased wages. By whatever means this is done, employees are persuaded that this increase in working hours isn't too bad after all, and they agree to the change. Our leader has again exercised power over employees, in this case by shaping what they believe to be in their interests in order to stop any conflict occurring.

It is important to note that Lukes' formulation introduces some difficulty when considering individual interests because it raises a distinction between the interests an individual *believes* they have (but which they may have been manipulated into having by another actor) and the interests they *really* have (the ones they would have if they hadn't been manipulated). In other words, it assumes that interests can be objectively determined. We can illustrate this issue by looking at my preference for eating fried eggs rather than poached ones. I will insist that it is in my interest to eat fried eggs because they taste better than the poached ones, and therefore I will enjoy them more. You, on the other hand, might insist that it is in my *real* interest to eat the poached eggs because they are healthier for me. In this case, you would be maintaining a distinction between the interest I *believe* I have (for fried eggs) and the interest I *really* have (for poached eggs). It can be seen that we are potentially in difficult territory if we start insisting that individuals adopt certain behaviours contrary to what they want to do on the basis that they are not aware of their real interests and that we are better able to perceive these than they are. In fact, one of the authors of this chapter encountered just this situation when conducting research. In this case, a decision was made to remove fried eggs from the staff canteen and replace them with poached eggs on the basis that this was in employees' 'real' interests. Unfortunately, the employees were very unhappy about this change and eventually fried eggs were reinstated in the canteen.

Returning to the issue of legitimacy, we can see that Lukes' formulation introduces an interesting twist to the way in which this is conceived. In this sense, because Lukes appeals to objective notions of individual interest – rather than to legal-democratic frameworks – he is able to claim the legitimacy of power rests in whether its exercise violates individuals' interest. In our example, if we could objectively determine that it was in the interest of the employees to remain on their existing employment contract, then our leader would be exercising her power illegitimately through her attempts to distort employees' perception of their interests. However, as noted above, the ability to do this does rest on the claim that we can indeed determine these interests objectively, a somewhat problematic assumption.

Lukes' third dimension of power again significantly enhances our understanding of power by building on the previous two dimensions described by Dahl and Bachrach and Baratz. In considering his work to be building on these other thinkers, Lukes was clearly in dialogue with them. In the next section, we move on to another thinker who, in some ways, has a similar perspective on power to Lukes, but pushes this in a much more radical direction.

Foucault: power without the powerful

Michel Foucault was a twentieth-century French intellectual who engaged primarily in the history of thought and ideas. Over his career, he built up a body of work which looked to explain how we are to understand ourselves. He considered the analysis of power to be central to this project.

Foucault's work is of particular interest in our survey of power because his starting point was quite different from the thinkers we have previously considered. Lukes and his contemporaries understood power in terms of the actions of actors (either individuals or groups) upon other actors; in this sense, power takes the form of people doing things to other people. We can see from this that the study of power would be particularly concerned with understanding the actions of these actors – both those who have power and those who don't (with leaders (normally) being an example of the former, and followers (normally) being an example of the latter). By stark contrast, Foucault believed that power was not primarily to be understood in terms of the actions of actors upon others; rather, power 'is the name that one attributes to a complex strategical situation in a particular society' (1990: 93). Because society is composed of highly complex and enmeshed relationships, it is not possible for us to completely discern the effects that our actions have, rather 'people know what they do; they frequently know why they do what they do; but what they don't know is what they do does' (Foucault, quoted from personal correspondence, in Dreyfus and Rabinow, 1982: 187). For this reason, Foucault made the explicit claim that to comprehend power we need to move away from examining the actions of actors and instead look at the configuration of the mechanisms of power within society. Looking at the actions of 'powerful' figures like leaders and kings leads us nowhere, instead '[w]e need to cut off the king's head' (Foucault, 2010b: 63). Already we can see that Foucault's understanding takes us quite a long way from a traditional understanding of power! To be clear, Foucault was not denying that one actor could force another actor into changing their behaviour, he was merely saying that this was not a particularly interesting way of understanding power, or one that captures the most significant ways in which power works within society. Another way of understanding this is to say that whilst it is true that 'leaders' exist and they undertake a process referred to as 'leadership', to understand the way in which leadership works we need to understand the way in which it takes place in very complex social circumstances and through interdependence amongst many different actors – in other words, leaders don't know what leadership does!

To understand the claims Foucault made about the need to move beyond conceiving of power in terms of the specific actions of actors, we need to understand the way in which he understood society. Again, contrasting Foucault's perspective with that of Lukes, Dahl, and Bachrach and Baratz provides a useful starting point. Lukes and his colleagues were working within a liberal-humanist tradition of thought which focuses on innate human nature and individual rationality. This can be seen in their concern with legal-democratic processes. By contrast, Foucault can be understood to be working from a social constructionist perspective (although it is important to note that Foucault did not describe himself in this way). As such, Foucault considered social reality to be defined by the particular social circumstances we find ourselves in, rather than universal ideas such as 'human nature'. To illustrate this, we can see that the values that one society holds are quite different from ones held by other societies that exist elsewhere in the world, or even from the same society during an earlier period in history. These values are not necessarily better or worse, they are just different. This is not to say that there is no right or wrong, or that 'anything goes'; each society contains its own understanding of right or wrong and these understandings will be (for the most part) internally consistent. Another way of stating this is to say that truth and the knowledge on which it is based are not objective facts, instead they are bound up with the society we live in. For Foucault (and us), this point is crucial because knowledge, and therefore truth, are bound up in the workings of power; for this reason, 'power-knowledge' (Foucault, 2010a: 27) was a concept which came to be central to Foucault's work. Foucault expresses this idea as he says:

> Truth isn't outside power, or lacking in power … Truth is a thing of this world … [a]nd it induces regular effects of power. Each society has its regime of truth, its 'general politics' of truth: that is, the types of discourse which it accepts and makes function as true; the mechanisms and instances which enable one to distinguish true and false statements, the means by which each is sanctioned; the techniques and procedures accorded value in the acquisition of truth; the status of those who are charged with saying what counts as true. (2010b: 72–73)

This quote also contains another idea which is central to Foucault's understanding of power: that it is a productive – rather than merely repressive – force. We can see here that Foucault's social constructionism marks a key departure from Lukes and his contemporaries. Looking back to the earlier definitions of power, we can see that they mostly consist of A preventing B from doing something they want, or in restricting the options of B such that they have to take a particular course of action. However, for Foucault, power is a productive force, not in the sense that it is good, but rather in the sense that it produces knowledge and truth, and in doing so it defines what it is possible for us to know and understand, and, therefore, how we interact with the world. For Foucault, power doesn't only produce truth about the world around us, it also governs the way that we understand ourselves; in this sense, power also produces individuals who are subjects of power.

It is this de-naturalisation of the subject which caused Lukes, when he considered Foucault's work in the second edition of *Power: A Radical View*, to refer to Foucault's position as 'ultra-radical', ultimately rejecting his conclusions. As can be seen, Foucault's conceptualisation of power marks a departure from how we normally think of it. For this reason, it can be tricky to understand what this means in concrete terms. Fortunately, we can illustrate its consequences by, once again, returning to our hypothetical leader.

Remember that the original conflict between the leader and her staff members centred around the removal of junk food from the staff canteen, accompanied by the introduction of a healthy eating option. Staff members were dismayed at this possibility and expressed dissatisfaction; despite this, our leader decided to go ahead and make the choice anyway. Now instead imagine that the same substitution of unhealthy for healthy food is being proposed by the leader, however this time things are a bit different. Whilst our staff members do enjoy the taste of unhealthy eating options, they also live in a society (probably not much unlike your own) where there is constant emphasis on being healthy and looking a certain way. These employees are constantly bombarded with adverts featuring thin, fit, smiling people and they constantly hear about the dangers of life expectancy being shortened by unhealthy living. On top of this, the leader of the company has introduced a new employee benefit: a workplace well-being programme. Part of this features information, on how to eat healthily, as well as diet clubs for those wishing to lose weight. As a result of all of this information the employees decide that they want to eat more healthily at work, and as a result the change in the canteen menu is welcomed by everyone. In this situation, we can say that the action of our leader has significantly contributed towards a change in the behaviour of our employees. However, we cannot simply say that our leader has exercised power over her employees because to understand this change we need to understand the way they are embedded in a complex social arrangement which encompasses the employees, the leader, the government, advertising agencies, universities, and so on.

Taking this further, we can see that rather than turning our attention to the legitimacy of specific actions, instead we need to focus on the particular arrangements of knowledge and truth which enable certain actions to have legitimacy, whilst others do not. Applying this to the notion of leadership, rather than being concerned about whether the actions of a particular leader are legitimate, we might instead be interested in understanding how the power differential between leaders and followers is legitimated and how particular leaders position themselves so as to take advantage of this legitimacy.

Critical leadership studies

The earlier sections in the chapter have provided an in-depth overview of different approaches to power. This tells us that there is not necessarily one thing called power. Following Lukes and Foucault, we also know that power is not always overt and obvious. Critical perspectives of leadership studies or **critical leadership studies** (CLS) consider how power relations shape leadership understandings (Alvesson and Spicer, 2012). CLS draw on the more established field of critical management studies (CMS). In addition to being interested in power relations, CLS are interested in identity constructions through which leadership is constantly 'reproduced, rationalised, resisted and occasionally transformed' (Collinson, 2012: 89). While a brief overview of critical assumptions of leadership was provided in Chapter 1, we now delve deeper into approaches that sit within this perspective as you are now aware of how power works. These critical assumptions of leadership are fundamentally about questions of power.

There are three things that we would like to highlight about CLS. Firstly, it tries to de-naturalise leadership. At the start of this chapter, you were shown the meaning of 'de-naturalise' in this context. According to Alvesson and Spicer, critical studies de-naturalise leadership by showing that leadership is an outcome of an 'ongoing process of social construction and negotiation' (2012: 373). Secondly, reflexivity is of most importance to critical leadership studies scholars. They study leadership reflexively. **Reflexivity** refers to being aware of and reflecting on how the researchers and the methods these researchers use would play a role in the construction or production of leadership phenomena. Thirdly, leadership is treated non-performatively. To understand what this means, we need to look at what **performativity** is. Put simply, performativity is about using forms of knowledge to maximise efficiency and enhance performance (Lyotard, 1984). Hence, non-performativity in this context refers to resisting the tendency to reduce leadership to being merely a means of optimising performance and productivity.

There are various areas of focus within CLS. Drawing on Alvesson and Spicer's (2012) broad categorisations, we consolidate these themes into five categories. One might argue that the creation of such categories itself may be challenging and is exactly the kind of essentialist thinking that critical perspectives problematise. However, we think that understanding the plethora of approaches that sit within CLS would be made easier through categories within this field. The themes we identify include the excessive positivity associated with leadership; gendering of leadership; critique of a cult-ish approach (see Chapter 3 for a critique of transformational leadership); and anti-leadership. While these themes are considered by Alvesson and Spicer, we would also like to add to this categorisation another theme, which includes postcolonial perspectives that adopt a critical lens. Chapter 11 focuses more on this; hence we will only provide a brief overview in this chapter.

Excessive positivity

The first theme we discuss is the critique of the overwhelmingly positive approach to leadership studies. This has been drawn attention to by several scholars (for example, Ford and Harding, 2011; Alvesson and Spicer, 2012; Collinson, 2012; Alvesson and Kärreman, 2016). We draw on Collinson's (2012) notion of '**Prozac leadership**' to understand this. Leaders frame and manage meanings in excessively positive ways. In Chapter 1, we looked at Smircich and Morgan's (1982) definition of leadership which focused on the ability of an individual or individuals to frame and manage the reality of others. Such framing and managing of reality in excessively positive ways can be viewed as an influence tactic and is a key leadership skill. The way this is enacted is of interest to scholars in the understanding of the social construction of leadership (see Chapter 4). It is however important to recognise that while leaders' positivity may inspire followers and drive change, this is not necessarily always the case. To unpack this further, it is important to examine Collinson's (2012) definition of Prozac leadership. The term Prozac leadership is used as a metaphor to refer to the excessive positivity associated with leaders and followers in contemporary organisations. The term is borrowed literally from the drug 'Prozac' which is used as a treatment for depression. This drug has received criticism for its addictive nature given its ability to induce artificial happiness. Hence, figuratively, applied to leadership, Prozac in a way depicts the addiction to excessive positivity which is used by leaders to enact their power and influence. Such an addiction can get in the way of critical reflection, and it is therefore essential to question the underlying assumptions about positive thinking inspiring followers.

As Collinson (2012) notes, one reason for such proliferation of excessive positivity might be to do with positive thinking being embedded in American culture. In a US society that is highly competitive and individualistic, upbeat self-promotion is seen as a survival strategy. This led to the popularity of several self-help books which also had advice on leadership strategies. One example is Carnegie's *How to Win Friends and Influence People*. Carnegie (1994) argued that one way to get anyone (followers) to do anything was to use praise and appreciation as tools. In terms of its influence on academic disciplines, the emergence of positive psychology and positive organisational behaviour can be attributed to it (Seligman, 1998, 2002; Bernstein, 2003; Luthans, 2003; Luthans and Yousef, 2007; Wright, 2003 cited in Collinson, 2012). Such academic disciplines had an influence on how leadership was conceptualised. For instance, in Chapter 3, we reviewed and critiqued the Authentic Leadership Questionnaire (ALQ) which was a conceptualisation of authentic leadership that was based on perspectives from positive psychological capital.

Ehrenreich (2009) provides a critique of positive thinking in US society. One example of the dangers of positive thinking entrenched in US society is the refusal to consider negative outcomes such as mortgage defaults, which contributed to the 2008 financial crisis.

The 'underlying toxic message' (Collinson, 2012: 92) of the promotion of such positive thinking is that if a person doesn't think positively, they won't be successful, and it would be the individual's fault. In doing so, such positive thinking can place the blame solely on individuals should something go wrong, such as a business failure or a job loss (Ehrenreich, 2009). Placing such focus exclusively on individuals through positive psychology might divert attention from larger societal problems. In the context of positive organisational behaviour, Fineman (2006) compares such positivity to disciplinary pressure where the imposition of positivity as organisational practice might lead to penalties for those that do not fit in.

This brings us to an interesting argument by Cunha, Clegg and Rego (2013), who discuss the usefulness of Machiavelli as a response to the excessive positivity in leadership and organisation studies. Niccolò Machiavelli was a diplomat and political philosopher, best known for his treatise called *The Prince* which contained a controversial analysis of politics. The treatise is based on a premise that the ends justify the means, and that in order to retain power, the prince must follow any means necessary. Cunha et al. (2013) argue that Machiavelli advanced important knowledge related to leadership. They offer seven observations. Firstly, the study of Machiavelli will help scholars of leadership understand the complexity of power better, but Machiavelli is not exactly a source of best practice. Secondly, negativity is inescapable. Machiavelli's lessons point to the importance of being flexible in behaviour where, often, leaders and managers must make tough decisions. This relates to the third point. While Machiavelli was considered to be amoral and as not considering ethics, however, the most virtuous of values may be dangerous and not actually virtuous – see, for example, actions such as ethnic cleansing or organisational border control which are based on ideas of purity. Virtue can be understood as behaviour and/or a set of attitudes that display high moral standards. However, sometimes these moral standards may themselves be problematic to implement. Sacrifices must be made for the greater good and this warrants flexibility to move away from the existing social order, as well as to move away from a set of values when needed. Fourthly, the negative is essential to the positive. For instance, excessive positivity might lead to a tolerance of the normalisation of corruption. The fifth point is to do with the ideology of the positive which may be seductive and make it difficult for individuals to cope during organisational crises. To this end, Sinclair (1992) provides a critique of the team ideology where such an ideology in fact tyrannises the individual team member. Sixthly, managers and leaders must focus on how strategy is done in practice instead of solely focusing on prescriptive and normative approaches to leadership. Focusing on the here and now would be a more realistic way of approaching problem-solving. In this way, *The Prince* provides a realistic picture as Machiavelli focused on how government actually works instead of how it 'should' work. Finally, Cunha et al. (2013) offer as their seventh observation that Machiavelli and Machiavellianism must not be confused. The term 'Machiavellian' has become synonymous with corporate psychopaths, but the original descriptions of power in *The Prince* are less evil than commonly thought.

Such managerial and organisational emphasis on positivity has its roots in the **human relations movement** that was based on the notion that happier workers would be more productive workers (Collinson, 2012). Theories of motivation such as Maslow's hierarchy of needs and Herzberg's two-factor theory that form the fundamentals of organisation and management theories, arose out of that movement. While these theories still have value, critics have raised concerns. For instance, Michaelson (2005) emphasises the need for an ethical dimension without which individuals can be manipulated to suit the organisation's need for productivity. The impact of such positivity-focused theories can be seen in mainstream leadership studies such as charismatic leadership, transformational leadership, as well as authentic leadership (reviewed and critiqued in Chapter 3).

Student exercise

Can you think of a movie, or a scene from a movie, which has depicted excessive positivity only to later end up in a crisis or a tragedy? Discuss this in groups, then compare this movie to the themes within critical leadership studies.

Gendering of leadership

Another important theme that critical scholarship of leadership tackles is the masculinity associated with leadership. Feminist approaches to leadership have been offered that question the prevalent dominant masculine conceptualisations of leadership. Chapter 11 provides a detailed overview of gendered and racialised leadership. In the following paragraphs, we provide a brief overview of the connections between gender and critical perspectives.

There are different ways of looking at gender and femininity. Critical perspectives of leadership view gender as a social construction as opposed to a biological characteristic. The view that gender is a social construction is influenced by Butler (2015). On the other hand, the trait-focused view of leadership that we reviewed and critiqued in Chapter 2 views gender as a biological characteristic.

Critical feminist scholars have highlighted that leadership has been associated with male stereotypes and attitudes (Acker, 1990; Calás and Smircich, 1992). One of the reasons for the questioning of the treatment of gender in leadership studies is because notions of 'ideal managers' are more closely aligned to cultural images of masculinity. Organisational structures and everyday practices constitute such images of an ideal manager. Femininity, on the other hand, is associated with embodiment, emotions and sexuality, and is viewed as subordinate to 'male rationality' and is seen as out of place in rational organisations (Fournier and Keleman, 2001: 268). Such prevailing attitudes of rationality may affect recruitment processes where an ideal employee would be seen as a disembodied subject, and in doing so, the ideal employee becomes associated with masculinity. Disembodied subjects in this context can be seen as individuals who are not seen as people, but as rational beings that are purely associated with their jobs, devoid of their own identities. For instance, Sliwa and Johansson (2014) have questioned the meritocracy of such organisational processes where jobs are designed for disembodied and rational subjects.

A qualitative study by Stead (2014) examined gendered power relations in the context of leadership development using a feminist poststructuralist lens. Stead (2014) analysed six women's reflections through interviews about being involved in action learning which formed part of a leadership development programme for small businesses. The study sheds light on the importance of considering gendered power relations in action learning by showing that, firstly, power relations as perceived by women in that environment have an impact on their ideas of what it is to be a leader. This corresponds to dominant masculine understandings of leadership. Secondly, the study highlights the unspoken or what is left unsaid in action learning, which has a powerful effect on the women, causing feelings such as frustration that they are reluctant to disclose. Thirdly, not taking gender into account challenges the core action learning values focused on togetherness and assumptions of equality. Therefore, understanding gender and leadership by considering power relations enables a richer critical understanding of leadership. Such understandings have implications for practice as they allow for leadership development programmes that are truly inclusive. However, one thing to bear in mind is that the very notion of 'developing' leaders may get in the way of individual subjectivities (see Ford and Harding, 2011).

Cult-ish approach

We reviewed and critiqued the ideological approach to charismatic and transformational leadership in Chapter 3, so readers are already aware of some of the problems with mainstream approaches to leadership like charismatic-transformational leadership. In this section, we focus on the cult-ish approach to leadership studies, a characteristic of mainstream approaches to leadership that critical leadership studies attempt to address. Tourish and Pinnington (2002) offer a critique of transformational leadership and specifically focus on its cult-like status. They argue that the components of transformational leadership are similar to the traits of cults. A cult can be defined as a group or movement with the goal of advancing the interests of the group's leaders to the detriment of followers through unethical manipulation and excessive devotion to a person or a thing. Members demonstrate 'high commitment, replace their pre-existing beliefs and values with those of the group, work extremely hard, relinquish control over time, lose confidence in their own perceptions in favour of those of the group and experience social punishments, such as shunning by other group members' (Singer, 1987; Langone, 1988; Tourish and Pinnington, 2002: 157). Let us now look at how transformational leadership overlaps with cultism.

We have seen that there is an overlap between charismatic leadership and transformational leadership (Chapter 3), and in that way, charismatic leadership forms part of transformational leadership in Tourish and Pinnington's (2002) critique. They argue that charismatic leadership is one of the key ingredients of a cultic organisation. Examples include the Doomsday cults in the 1950s (Festinger, 1957) and the Jonestown cult of the 1970s (Layton, 1999). Followers over-attribute charisma and other larger-than-life qualities to leaders, contributing to a cult-like status. The over-attribution by followers has been detailed in Chapter 4 where we looked at Meindl's romance of leadership.

A compelling vision and intellectual stimulation lead to ideological totalism. What this means is that the group's leaders lead followers into believing that their vision can transform reality. Such ideas get embedded deeply amidst followers, constraining any doubts about the leader (Tourish and Pinnington, 2002).

Individualised consideration, another component of transformational leadership, also has several similarities to cults. Tourish and Pinnington (2002) point to two aspects. One is ingratiation, a term coined by Jones (1990) within the impression management literature. Ingratiation is a technique used to get people to like you through praise and saying nice things. This is akin to individualised consideration where followers would be taken in by this and give in to the objective of the cult to create a group identity. The second aspect relates to power imbalance. Leaders tend to be at a much higher position of power, and individuals (followers) of lesser status give importance to being liked by those of a higher status. In turn, this leads to followers agreeing with the leader's opinions, and giving in to their demands.

Finally, promoting a common culture is another similarity between transformational leadership and a cult. This is seen in the absence of dissent and promoting monoculturism where all group members are expected to follow the same norms. One of the dangers of such a culture is groupthink. Groupthink is a phenomenon that occurs when the desire to reach a consensus in a group leads to the absence of critical reasoning. An example of groupthink may be when a group of people with a similar view about their distrust for technology, results in their failure to use new technology intended to make tasks easier. Consequently, members might start to justify irrational behaviours when the dominant belief system is internalised. Such promotion of a common culture can be viewed as a form of social control which is covert, as opposed to being coercive and overt (Tourish and Pinnington, 2002) (see Lukes' dimensions, explained earlier in this chapter).

Mini case study 7.1

Karoshi and cultish work cultures

Karoshi is a Japanese term meaning 'death from overwork'. The term was coined in the 1970s in recognition of a growing number of deaths attributed to work-related issues. Around this time, authorities realised corporate culture in Japan was leading to employees feeling under pressure to work unhealthy amounts of overtime (commonly over 80 hours a week in total) and neglecting to take time off. In turn, this resulted in an increasing number of employees dying from lifestyle-related health conditions such as heart disease and stroke, as well as a striking number of workplace suicides. Whilst *karoshi* is associated with Japan, recent evidence from the World Health Organisation revealed a growing global trend in work-related death resulting from long working hours (WHO, 2021).

One way of understanding the phenomenon of *karoshi* is through the lens of cultish leadership, whereby leaders instil a corporate culture based upon individuals sacrificing their own interests to that of the collective. When discussing this kind of highly collectivist organisational culture, it is common to hear of workers feeling unable to take time away from work due to not wanting to let a leader down, or not wanting to differentiate themselves from others through being seen as not working hard enough. As we can see from the quote from Tourish and Pinnington (2002) above, critics of this leadership tendency point to the way it can undermine the individual's sense of self. It is important to note, however, that the leadership which

(Continued)

gives rise to *karoshi* is not normally attributable to characteristics found in the 'dark triad' of leadership (see Chapter 2); as such, this is not an overt exercise of power but relates to the way in which society naturalises certain power relations conducive to capitalist production.

In 2018, in recognition of the presence of a harmful organisational culture, the Japanese government introduced the Work Style Reform Bill. This legislation changed existing labour laws, putting caps on excessive working hours and requiring employers to designate annual leave for staff. Nevertheless, the cultish culture leading to *karoshi* remains a problem.

Questions

1. Why might leadership based on an attitude of 'excessive positivity' make it difficult to prevent *karoshi* from happening?
2. In what ways might the 4 I's of transformational leadership contribute to creating a workplace culture leading to *karoshi*?
3. How might the theories of power explored earlier be relevant to understanding *karoshi*?

Anti-leadership

Another category of studies that falls within CLS constitutes **anti-leadership** theories. While CLS emerged as a response to the problems with mainstream theories of leadership, anti-leadership, a stream within CLS, is built on the premise that leadership is 'beyond redemption' (Harding, 2021: 237). For instance, Alvesson and Sveningsson (2003) point to the importance of considering the non-existence of leadership. They arrived at this through six mini-case studies of leadership only to find that there was not one thing called leadership. Kelly (2014) views leadership as a negative ontology and states that organisational processes can be understood equally well without using the term leadership. Harding (2021) uses a reflexive auto-ethnographic methodology to contribute to anti-leadership studies set within the context of South Welsh communities. Providing a socio-historic context, Harding (2021) argues that there was a paradoxical sense of both superiority and inferiority amidst Welsh people who were colonised by England but who were also complicit in the British Empire's colonisation of other countries. There appeared to be a class divide during their Brexit vote, and Harding (2021) reflects on her own dual identity as a middle-class academic who grew up in a working-class Welsh mining town. Borrowing from postcolonial literature (Fanon, 1952/1970), Harding considers **Celtic**

postcolonialism as essential to analyse and understand Celtic nations with very different histories. Harding concludes that imposing leadership and followership into a culture that is neo-communitarian and leaderless would be an act of colonisation. The neo-communitarian philosophy is leaderless and contrasts presumptions about leadership theory, and is based on the idea of public service which is applied to the context of the South Wales Valleys. Therefore, through this reflexive account, Harding (2021) contributes to anti-leadership which opposes leadership in its entirety.

Postcolonial perspectives

We add this category to CLS. While there has been an increase in postcolonial and decolonial perspectives within CLS, most critical perspectives are Western centric, based on Western theorising. Nkomo (2011) offered a postcolonial and anti-colonial reading of African management and leadership in organisation studies. Both postcolonialism and **anti-colonialism** consider Western colonisation of non-Western subjects. They diverge on the issue of essentialism: where postcolonialism allows for multiplicity and hybridity, anti-colonialism can be seen as the epistemology of the colonised, that resists colonialism. Nkomo (2011) found tensions and contradictions in her review of the African leadership and management literature. She argues that Western texts essentialise African cultures in their depictions in African leadership and management texts, where African cultures are portrayed homogenously. Mainstream conceptualisations of culture such as Hofsetede's dimensions (explained in Chapter 3) are used to offer comparisons between African and American business cultures, but such theorising does not provide a deeper or a critical understanding of African culture. Wright (2002) explains that culture is not purifiable, and that the mutual effects of coloniser and colonised must be understood (Frenkel and Shehnav, 2006; Nkomo, 2011). Therefore, examining power relations through the lens of postcolonialism and anti-colonialism can offer a richer understanding of leadership in non-Western contexts.

Dark side: The toxic triangle

In the preceding sections, we have considered power and CLS. CLS points to the complexity of leadership theorising and considers power relations whilst doing so. We now move to a model of the dark side of leadership, where power is considered as a repressive force. We discuss Padilla, Hogan and Kaiser's (2007) **toxic triangle** which is a model that suggests that there are three realms of factors that lead to the emergence of destructive leadership: destructive leaders, susceptible followers, and conducive environments. Within destructive leadership, there is an overwhelming focus on positive outcomes of leadership as we have seen in the preceding sections of this chapter. Elements within destructive leaders include charisma, personalised power, narcissism, negative life themes and an ideology of hate. As we have discussed charisma as well as the dark side of charisma (see Chapters 2 and 3), we will not go over this again. Personalised power refers to power being misused by unethical leaders. In this context, power is a repressive force. Narcissism is a trait from the dark triad (see Chapter 2) which can contribute to the emergence of destructive leadership. Padilla et al. (2007) argue that negative life themes such as childhood adversity, socio-economic problems and parental discord may be contributing factors to the emergence of destructive leadership. These might then lead to an ideology of hate.

The second realm of factors within the toxic triangle is susceptible followers. Padilla et al. (2007) make a distinction between conformers and colluders. Conformers are defined as followers who have unmet needs, low core self-evaluations and low maturity. Colluders are seen as having high ambition, a similar worldview to the destructive leader, and unethical values, although as we have seen earlier, values can be subjective. The third realm of factors relates to a conducive environment, which includes instability, where leaders can enhance their power in unstable environments. Perceived threat is another factor which is constituted in a conducive environment. Research has shown (see Solomon, Greenberg and Pyszczynski, 1991) that perceived threat increases followers' support and identification with charismatic leaders. Cultural values that bring people together to solve conflicts can also create a conducive environment for destructive leadership as strong leaders that can take over are preferred in these circumstances. Finally, an absence of checks and balances with limited governance can lead to destructive leadership.

Hence, Padilla et al.'s (2007) toxic triangle moves away from a leader-centric view to include other factors which contribute to the emergence of destructive leadership. Pelletier, Kotke and Sirotnik (2019) apply the toxic triangle to a public university to analyse three case episodes through a qualitative approach. However, they point out some of the limitations of the toxic triangle and argue that several questions remain unanswered. For instance, as we have reviewed in Chapter 4 and in the CLS section above, the leader–follower distinction warrants careful consideration given that Padilla et al. (2007) assume a normative stance. Moreover, several essentialist assumptions are also made about characters, and cultural values as well as power. Despite these issues, the toxic triangle has descriptive power (Pelletier et al., 2019).

Uber

Travis Kalanick was the former CEO and founder of Uber, an American technology company and one of the largest firms in the gig economy that focused on lift-sharing. Kalanick resigned from the firm after pressure from the shareholders following a series of scandals. Several issues with the culture at Uber were highlighted, one of which included sexism. An example included a promotion in Lyon where Uber promised riders they would be paired with 'hot chick' drivers for 20 minutes. Another example comes from a *GQ* interview where Kalanick joked about a service for women in demand that he nicknamed 'Boob-er'. Uber was accused of breaking the rules by using a computer programme called Greyball which is claimed to have been used by officials to catch Uber drivers and deny them service in areas where Uber had not been authorised. Uber was also accused of stealing fingerprinting code technology from Apple iPhones and using serial numbers to track phones, which is against Apple's terms. Waymo, a firm owned by Alphabet, Google's parent company, accused Uber of stealing trade secrets. It was alleged by Waymo, a self-driving car firm, that a former employee who had later joined Uber had downloaded confidential documentation before leaving the firm. The employee was subsequently fired by Uber for failing to assist in the investigation (Kleinman, 2017). Kalanick's behaviour exemplified that he was driven but also ruthless. Kalanick was described as someone who would run through a wall to accomplish his goals, which became both his strength and a weakness (Kleinman, 2017).

In May 2021, Uber struck a deal with GMB, one of the UK's largest trade unions. This deal came about to end the exploitation of Uber drivers. Under this deal, Uber will formally recognise GMB to represent up to 70,000 drivers across the UK (*The Guardian*, 2021).

Questions

1. What factors from the toxic triangle can you apply to this case?
2. To what extent was Kalanick responsible for this culture at Uber?
3. What might be some ways to attain financial performance as well as maintain a healthy culture?

Conclusion

In this chapter, we began by discussing the importance of studying power to understand leadership. We looked at different perspectives of power including those of

Dahl, Bachrach and Baratz, Lukes, and Foucault. We then discussed in depth the field that has come to be known as critical leadership studies, which primarily focuses on how power relations influence leadership understandings. Within CLS, we discussed the various themes that oppose mainstream approaches to leadership, which include excessive positivity, gendering of leadership, a cultish approach, anti-leadership and postcolonial (and anti-colonial) perspectives. We then returned to a normative, more mainstream approach to leadership, the toxic triangle.

Decolonising leadership

Iwowo, V. (2015) 'Leadership in Africa: Rethinking development'. *Personnel Review*, 4(3): 408–429.

This paper takes a critical look at leadership development in Africa and highlights the importance of indigenous knowledge in relation to context and mainstream theory in order to propose a way forward.

Key summary

- Power affects the way leaders lead.
- It is important to de-naturalise the relationship between leadership and power.
- Naturalised or traditional views of leadership are centred around the leader.
- According to Dahl and Bachrach and Baratz, power is observable in conflict between actors. Lukes claims that power involves shaping others' interests to your own to prevent conflict from occurring. All of them primarily understand power as a repressive force.
- Foucault offers a very different understanding which focuses on power as a productive force. Power produces knowledge and truth and in doing so defines what it is possible for us to know and understand.
- Critical leadership studies is an emerging field within leadership studies that is interested in how power relations shape leadership understandings. This stream of studies is critical of mainstream approaches to leadership studies.
- Some of the themes within critical leadership studies focus on the excessive positivity of leadership, gendering, the cult-ish approach, anti-leadership and postcolonial perspectives.
- The toxic triangle, an uncritical model of destructive leadership, encompasses destructive leadership, susceptible followers and a conducive environment.

Further reading

Collinson, D. (2017) 'Critical leadership studies: A response to Learmonth and Morrell', *Leadership*, 13(3): 272–284.

Learmonth, M. and Morrell, K. (2017) 'Is critical leadership studies "critical"?', *Leadership*, 13(3): 257–271.

Thoroughgood, C. N., Sawyer, K. B., Padilla, A., et al. (2018) 'Destructive leadership: A critique of leader-centric perspectives and toward a more holistic definition'. *Journal of Business Ethics*, 151: 627–649.

8

LEADERSHIP, ETHICS AND STRATEGIC HRM

Geraint Harvey and Carl Rhodes

Chapter objectives

The objectives of this chapter are:

- To explore the ethics of leadership through the leadership of people and strategic HRM (SHRM).
- To unpack the ethical credentials of two influential approaches to SHRM: high involvement management and high commitment management.
- To present an alternative ethical approach to leadership in the management of people based on the political ideas of 'agonism' and 'dissensus'.

How do we determine the ethics of leadership? Before we grapple with the difficulties of defining ethics – efforts famously likened to 'nailing jello to a wall' (Lewis, 1985) – let's simply think about the outcomes of decisions made at the highest level of organisation. A problem here is in weighing the merit of leaders' decisions (Svensson and Wood, 2008). For instance, what is considered good (in either an ethical or a practical sense) from the perspective of an employee as an internal stakeholder (Rok, 2009), does not always align with the shareholder perspective (Friedman, 1965; Heath, 2006: 538) or the perspective of different external stakeholders (Rushton, 2002). The decision to invest in one area rarely entails outcomes that all would favour (Heath, 2006). One exception, some claim, is the decision to invest in human resource management (HRM). Advocates of **strategic HRM** (SHRM) aver that investment in workers is beneficial for workers, shareholders and other stakeholders alike. Workers benefit from extrinsic gains (as per the hard model of

SHRM that we discuss below) or intrinsic gains (as per the soft model of SHRM, again discussed below). Shareholders, on the other hand, benefit from improved organisational (and financial) performance if SHRM delivers on the promise of a return on investment in staff. As for external stakeholders, families of workers stand to enjoy a better quality of life as a consequence of the improved terms and conditions of those employed, while proximate businesses might benefit from more affluent workers as consumers.

Our purpose in this chapter is to consider the ethics of leadership with a specific focus on the leadership of people within the organisation and through the lens of SHRM introduced above. It is now well established that leadership manifest in SHRM and ethics are inextricably bound (Macklin, 2006; Sloan and Gavin, 2010; Greenwood, 2013; Greenwood and Freeman, 2018; Van Buren III, 2020). An organisational leader responsible for SHRM has the potential at least to become a 'guardian of ethics' (Lowry, 2006: 173), an ethical steward (Winstanley et al., 1996; Caldwell et al., 2010) or a 'champion of corporate ethics' (Gilley et al., 2008: 193). However, the ethics of leadership as it pertains to people management may become aligned with (or subservient to) the responsibility to achieve economic goals and meet the [competing] obligation to the shareholders, at the expense of others.

The chapter will first consider the ethical credentials of two popular approaches to the strategic leadership of people that underpin SHRM, these being high commitment management (HCM) and high involvement management (HIM). On the face of it, each of these might be understood as an ethical approach to the leadership of people – we explain why they might be understood in this way and why they might not. We then proceed to consider ethical leadership of the employment relationship that acknowledges SHRM as only one player in a contested political terrain. We return to the point that every organisation is characterised by multiple and potentially incommensurable interests, interpretations, and ethical standpoints. We thus suggest that ethics can arise not just through the actions of an organisation's leaders, but also, and potentially more meaningfully, through processes of political 'agonism' (Mouffe, 2000a, b, c) whereby conflicting positions on organisational matters are brought together in democratic interaction. We conclude with a discussion of the ethics and the leadership of people practised through dissent and resistance to SHRM.

Ethics and strategic HRM

There are two different conceptions of the strategic management of people that have enduring appeal, commonly referred to as hard and soft HRM (Cregan et al., 2021). The central thrust of these ideas, and the models from which they were derived,

remains pervasive in the HRM strategies of command and control, and high involvement and high commitment management (see Bamber et al., 2009; Thompson, 2011;
Bryson, 2017).

The Michigan model of SHRM as developed and advocated by Fombrun et al.
(1984) is the basis of what has come to be known as **hard HRM** (see Guest, 1987;
Storey, 1992). Hard HRM is a strategy designed to harness human capital to the benefit of the firm (Storey, 1989). It consequently downplays the interests of stakeholders
other than shareholders and avers that employees are solely a resource to be 'obtained
cheaply, used sparingly, and developed and exploited as fully as possible' (Sparrow
and Hiltrop, 1994: 7). The overt exploitation of the worker prescribed by this model
of SHRM has been questioned ethically on the grounds that it supports the pursuit of
organisational self-interest over any other interests. It does so either by disregarding
other interests or by assuming that organisational interests should be advanced at the
expense of any other interests (Hart, 1993). Consequently, it is claimed that such an
approach is 'morally and commercially inferior to "moral management" in the new
era of stakeholder accountable organizations' (Simmons, 2004: 601; see also Carroll,
1991). As much of the existing research into ethics and SHRM is rendered from an
explicit or implicit ethical critique of the hard SHRM model, what of '**soft HRM**'?

Soft HRM is a system of people management that enhances the work experience of
the employees and is beneficial to them in order to generate conditions for greater
levels of organisational commitment (Truss et al., 1997; Guest, 1999). Advocates claim
that SHRM practice can impact positively upon the attitudes of the employee so as to
align employee and organisational values and encourage behaviour that supports
organisational goals (Walton, 1985; Wood and Wall, 2007; Park et al., 2019; Aust
et al., 2020). Organisations consequently benefit from the heightened productivity,
efficiency and compliance of satisfied and committed employees. The Harvard model
(Beer et al., 1984) that inspired the concept of soft HRM adopts a putatively pluralist
approach, identifying the centrality of stakeholder interests to the success of its long-
term outcomes. The Harvard model has often been considered to be a more ethically
justifiable model of people management than that of the Michigan model in that it
was 'one of the earlier models to suggest that, as well as organizational well-being,
SHRM had to concern itself with the promotion of individual and societal well-being'
(Ho and Kuvaas, 2020; Winstanley and Woodall, 2000a:).

In relation to ethics, it is suggested that the affective commitment of employees
(Meyer and Allen, 1991; see also Cafferkey et al., 2019) can be enhanced if an organisation can establish its 'own conduct standards, systematize its ethical obligations
into clear, concise statements, and socialize its members toward understanding and
conformity' (Boling, 1978: 360; see also Sloan and Gavin, 2010). Employees may then
be rewarded for compliance with those values or disciplined for behaving in ways that

contravene them. Here the role of SHRM is inherently linked to employee control and performance. In more general debates, SHRM is best understood as a 'third order strategy', determined by the activities and goals of the organisation (first order strategy) and organisational structure and internal control mechanism (second order strategy) (see Purcell and Ahlstrand, 1989: 398). The HR function has also been described as a handmaiden to the corporate elite (see Bamber et al., 2017 for a summary).

In terms of ethics, this means that what is deemed ethical by the organisational leadership, necessarily becomes ethical for the employee. There is then the desire for employees to be organisationally compliant and complicit in their behaviour; not doing so would be deemed unethical outside of the discursive framework of the organisation. At the very least, HCM (by its own criteria of success) seeks to ensure that employees neither determine nor question the ethical position of the organisation but adhere to it.

Here the purpose of SHRM is to establish a harmonious, or at least congruent, set of interests between employees and the 'organisation' as it is understood in managerial terms. Moreover, with such a managerialist approach ethics ignores alternative frames of reference (Fox, 1966; Heery, 2016) and becomes a matter of unitarism. It is assumed that leadership ethics is consistent with managerial agency without the need for disharmony or contestation (Geare, et al., 2006; cf. Delbridge and Keenoy, 2010). As such, SHRM is designed to encourage employee docility (Townley, 1994) through the co-optation of employees within managerial moral discourse (cf. Fleming, 2009). In this sense, ethics in SHRM discourse can be seen as being 'deployed to legitimize […] inequalities of power and persuade social actors to accept and endorse managerial objectives' (Delbridge and Keenoy, 2010: 801).

Normative accounts of SHRM and ethics assert that HR leaders should adopt a role of ethical stewardship (Tasoulis et al., 2019) by becoming 'more aware of their ethical duties to their organizations and more effective in helping their organizations to create increased wealth, achieve desired organizational outcomes, and establish work environments that are more satisfying to employees' (Caldwell et al., 2010: 171). Again, with such thinking ethics becomes subsumed under SHRM which is in turn subservient to organisational strategy and focused on the achievement of bottom-line performance and competitive advantage (Becker and Gerhart, 1996; Guest, 2011; Chadwick and Flinchbaugh, 2021). SHRM is in many cases a third order strategy abeyant to superordinate organisational goals and structures (Purcell and Ahlstrand, 1989; see also Guest and Woodrow, 2012). So, if SHRM is to concern itself with ethical matters, such concern is also a part of this third order. Consequently, any ethics conceived by (or for) SHRM is somehow at the service of an organisation.

Here then ethical leadership of people 'is conditional on an appropriate fit between it and the organization's strategy' (Miller, 1996: 16). Derivative of and servile to business strategy, SHRM functions are invoked to assert their organisation's moral legitimacy. This occurs on two levels, first in terms of the ethicality of the policies and procedures through which HR is implemented and, second, through ensuring that employees behave in accordance with an organisationally sanctioned ethics. HR leaders are, then, beholden to 'have a responsibility for determining how ethical SHRM is in any organization' (Macklin, 2006: 211), such that 'prescriptive accounts of SHRM depict the HR manager as a type of guardian of organizational ethics' (Lowry, 2006: 182).

Again, we see from this position that leadership ethics in people management should reflect and succumb to other demands of the business, subordinate to organisational structure and organisational goals. In this vein, it has been asserted that 'HR can demonstrate a business-based rationale for the adoption of ethical corporate governance and HRM that is the key to sustainable organization development' (Simmons, 2008: 19). This position that HR practitioners are somehow to take on the responsibility for ensuring the ethicality of employee relations is notably one-sided in the sense that all ethical agency is placed within a managerial function that deems itself fit to control and direct ethics (cf. Guest and Woodrow, 2012). Moreover, this alignment has as its goal a certain 'ethical harmony' that is in the primary interest of leadership more generally. Even when stakeholder management is brought to bear within a more pluralist iteration of SHRM (see Boxall, 2021), its focus is on how organisations can achieve a 'stakeholder synthesis' on the basis of decisions made by organisational leaders (Simmons, 2008: 18) and why organisations should recognise that other groups have 'valid needs and interests with respect to the organization' (Greenwood, 2002: 267). Such an approach always assumes that the interests of others can be incorporated within those of the organisation itself and done so without conflict, contradiction or hypocrisy. This is an ethics that seeks 'to block off certain experiences that are, for various reasons, deemed to be unwelcome' (ten Bos, 2003: 267), which in this case are the experiences of dissent, resistance and difference more generally. As such, what are deemed as ethical SHRM arrangements would occur when everybody is happy on the same terms – terms defined within SHRM discourse in its function of validating managerial prerogative.

What about SHRM from a HIM perspective (Lawler, 1986; Wood and Wall, 2007; Garmendia et al., 2021)? HIM is associated with a shift in managerial strategy away from low discretion, control-based work practices of the traditional 'Taylorist-Fordist work models' towards 'a more empowering type of work design' (Boxall and Purcell, 2011: 134). HIM may be considered ethical if indeed it enhances employee discretion and freedom – these being positioned as positive ethical values. The ethics of empowerment have been subject to much debate (see Claydon, 2000). Those supportive of the ethics of HIM suggest that the value of empowerment strategies is that they offer '"win–win" outcomes for organizations and their employees' (Claydon and Doyle,

1996: 13). The goal here is to dismiss 'ethical frames of reference which [...] reflect the structured antagonism of employment relationship' (ibid.) in favour of the creation of what are seen to be mutual interests, i.e., increasing the discretion and autonomy for the worker, in turn making them responsible for the outcomes of their work and ultimately for the success of the organisation. Such an approach also increases the pressure on, and stress of, employees who are now entirely responsible for the task (Ramsay et al., 2000) – a stress that can be exacerbated if empowerment is construed as being morally righteous (Styhre, 2001). The moral responsibility that HIM entails is thus a double-edged sword in that any benefits gained in terms of 'empowerment' and discretion are offset by the intensified work (Boxall and Purcell, 2011: 139).

---Reflective questions---

1. What assumptions about i) organisational leaders and ii) the workforce underpin HCM and HIM?
2. Why are these assumptions problematic for the ethics of HCM and HIM?

Leadership ethics?

The central theme running through the discussion above is that responsibility for ethics rests in the hands of leaders who seek to bring employees into line with that for which they see themselves responsible. As its purpose is unambiguously one of achieving the strategic goals of management in relation to people, SHRM calls for the varied interests of other parties, most especially employees, to be subsumed into an ethical framework that ultimately serves the primary interests of organisational strategy. What goes unquestioned in such an arrangement of ethics is whether or not a congruence of values and interests between an organisation and its employees can or should be achieved.

It is helpful at this point to refer to Critchley's (2007) discussion of ethics that poses the fundamental question: '[h]ow does a self bind itself to whatever it determines as good?' With this question, Critchley points to the idea that the motivation to act morally arises out of one's 'ethical experience' – an experience that gives rise to a demand for action in the name of the 'good'. This notion of 'good' is not ultimately determined, universal or inevitable – as Critchley explains, '[t]he question of the metaphysical ground or basis of ethical obligation should simply be disregarded' because it is 'not cognizable' (p. 55).

The issue we are taking up with mainstream SHRM discourse is the way that it not only seeks to justify the morality of SHRM and management more generally, but also that it proposes that this morality be distributed to all stakeholders (especially employees). This amounts to the assumption that organisations can and should try to influence, even control, individual morality and ethical subjectivity – in other words, its ethics become a politics directed at hegemony. Moreover, what is issued as the desired ethical demand is itself based on the values embedded in SHRM discourse.

The 'good' as far as SHRM is concerned is something that can be organisationally defined and imposed on employees, with its ultimate justification being organisational performance. As such, the veracity of this demand is brought into question in that it appears more based on self-interest and prudence than it does on any concern for others on their own terms. Such an approach to leadership ethics 'represses rather than resolves the contradictory nature of the employment relationship interests and values' (Claydon and Doyle, 1996: 14). Such an approach likewise ignores the plurality of goods that might be in place amongst the variety of people and groups who hold a stake in SHRM practice. Dominant approaches to ethics and (soft) HRM concern a business-based rationale for ethically engaging with 'stakeholders', especially employees. In this way, co-option works first to determine the ethical demand that others 'should' respond to and then to insist on the manner through which they should respond. This, in turn, marks the ethics of SHRM as an attempt at subjective control at the level of ethics.

In the case of HCM, this operates in terms of the organisation setting a system of values that employees are expected to internalise irrespective of their own personal values. In the case of HIM, it operates in terms of the manner in which 'involvement' and co-determination become a smokescreen for employee co-option. With this in mind, it comes to bear that the central moral thrust of both soft and hard HRM is what is to be done in the name of the 'good' is that which is good for the organisation and that labour is a resource to be deployed for that 'good'. Where hard and soft HRM differ is ultimately not on moral grounds but just on different views of what might be the best way to use SHRM to ensure organisational success.

If we view ethics just as a socially constructed set of moral values then what we have been discussing can be considered as a matter of trying to influence how these values are constructed in organisations. In so doing, however, SHRM discourse runs the risk of seeking to 'totalise' ethics in the sense of setting the terms by which ethics is understood and practised, such that this ethics is subordinated to the politics of market capitalism. It is imperative that we look behind such a constructivist approach, to consider the 'ethical relation in general' (Derrida, 1978/2001: 138) that underlies and precedes particular systems of morality. This basis of ethics is not in rule, law or custom, but originates in a generosity towards the absolute difference of each and every other person – each person is to be respected and responded to as unique before systems of knowledge and categorisation are imposed upon them (Levinas, 1991). Moreover, considering ethics this way also suggests that the forms of ethical totalisation favoured in SHRM discourse are anathema to ethics in that they fail to acknowledge or account for difference in other people. While stakeholder theory approaches appear at face value to acknowledge difference, closer interrogation reveals that they too seek to subsume difference. This is an ethics where it is necessary that 'effective governance can be reconciled with social responsibility, and that incorporating stakeholder views in HR systems enhances organization performance and commitment' (Simmons, 2003: 129).

Picking up on Levinas's approach to ethics, Diprose (2003) locates injustice within 'normalizing social discourses' (p. 11) – for example, those that attempt to curtail ethical freedom by imposing their own morality on others. The concern here is not in establishing what might be considered 'good' in an overarching and universal sense, nor in establishing some kind of criteria for what is good, but rather ways in which such a good is constituted. What Diprose is calling to question are those powerful systems of knowledge that seek to determine and impose their own sense of what is thought of as 'good' and 'normal'. Such discourses, for Diprose, establish dominant conventions that deny difference by proffering rationalised prescriptions of what it means to be 'normal', with this normality being unquestioningly associated with the 'good'. Diprose refers to these conventions as 'familiar ideas' – ideas that produce a 'closed circle of totality' which enacts an 'imperialism and violence of self knowledge' (p. 137), thereby limiting the possibilities open to others. Moreover, these limits extend not only to what other people should do, but also to whom they should be. And so, what passes as ethical in SHRM is located in a powerful normalising discourse that actually seeks to limit and control the 'moral impulse' (Bauman, 1993) that is borne out of a respect for difference.

For both Diprose (2003) and Critchley (2007), it is resistance to power (rather than subsumption within it) that marks ethical action (see Pullen and Rhodes, 2014; Alakavuklar and Alamgir, 2018). For instance, ethics is that which opens 'modes of living and paths of thinking beyond the imperialism of familiar ideas' (Diprose, 2003: 145). Moreover, in practice, this is a political matter – 'a passionate politics and an impatience for justice' (p. 187) provoked by a respect for difference and a desire to reanimate different ways of being (p. 195). This resonates with Critchley's (2007) 'politics of resistance' where 'ethics is the disturbance of the status quo […] the continual questioning from below of any attempt to impose order from above' (p. 13). For the purposes of our discussion, the implication of this is that the ethical demand is to challenge and resist the unitarist and normative ethics portrayed in SHRM discourse.

What matters here is not so much what SHRM can or should do in order to be ethical (the predominant focus of current debates), but rather the de-centring of SHRM as the focal point of ethical authority so as to bring SHRM practice into ethical question from the outside. This ethics eschews the normality of the 'familiar ideas' (Diprose, 2003) embedded in SHRM discourse in favour of a politics of dissensus (Rhodes et al., 2020) that calls authority into question (Critchley, 2007). And, by working through Critchley's more general discussion of politics, we can surmise that this is a process of democratisation emergent through political activism that seems to disturb and disrupt the 'consensual idyll' (p. 130). SHRM discourse is then cast as an attempt at 'depoliticising moralisation' and as such requires, of scholars, 'the development of alternative frameworks' (p. 130).

Agonism and ethical leadership in people management

An alternative relationship between ethics and leadership in people management is of the democratic type – one that understands this aspect of leadership 'in the context of the wider socio-economic, political and cultural factors which shape – if not determine – those practices' (Delbridge and Keenoy, 2010: 801). We use the term democracy not as it relates to the specificities of state politics but as it relates to the 'manifestation of dissensus' (Critchley, 2007: 131) in society more generally. From this perspective, consensus is not necessarily a 'bad' thing, and all forms of managerial practice should not necessarily be challenged and contested. In this sense, disagreement is not to be understood as a goal in itself but rather it is necessary for disagreement to be articulated and acted upon when it arises. The need for ethical action presents itself precisely when people do not agree and when organisational structures institutionalise the repression and/or oppression of difference. To explore the possibilities of such a political dissensus, we turn to Mouffe's (2000a, b) connection between democracy and what she calls 'agonism' – a term that refers to non-violent political difference and conflict as a central feature of democracy. Mouffe's discussion of agonism speaks directly to the core aspects of the ethical discourse of SHRM. As she writes, what has become fashionable in recent years is a form of ethics, whose 'leitmotif is the need for consensus, shared values and involvement in "good causes"', all of which amount to a 'retreat from the political' (Mouffe, 2000c: 85).

Mouffe registers that conflict is an important part of social organisation and that such conflict is a necessary condition for democracy if differences are to be articulated and confronted. With agonism, it is dissensus rather than (false or imposed) consensus that is valued as the basis for political interaction. Agonism promotes respect for the particularity of every person and for structural and personal differences. It is in this way that agonism is related to, but different from, antagonism. The purpose of agonism is not the conquest over and destruction of the opponent, but rather the perpetuation of democracy through the respect for difference amongst legitimate opponents. Thus, antagonism is a 'relation between enemies', while agonism is a 'relation between adversaries' (Mouffe, 2005: 50). The political process is then to combat both false consensus and destructive antagonism so as to enable difference to be addressed through democratic means.

Traditionally, of course, it is organised labour that has taken on the role of contesting organisations. It is precisely in acts of resistance, whether formally organised or not, that agonism (understood in relation to ethics) can be identified. Considering industrial relations and trade unionism in terms of its resistance to management is of course also not unproblematic. Some time ago, Wright Mills (1948: 119) commented that 'the leaders of labour will deliver a responsible, which is to say, a well-disciplined, union of contented workers in return for a junior partnership in the productive process, security for the union, and high wages for the workers of the industry' (quoted in Hyman, 1971: 20).

Such promises have inspired many trade unions to sign partnership agreements with management (see Boxall and Purcell, 2016: 138), raising considerable concerns about the conflation of labour and management agendas (Johnstone and Wilkinson, 2018). Notwithstanding these accounts, it remains that an independent trade union is more resilient to incorporation due to its fundamentally democratic nature (see, for example, Lewis and Vandekerckhove, 2018; see also Harvey et al., 2017). So it is that the greatest potential for ethical leadership in HRM may not be in new innovations, but rather more mundanely in resorting to its personnel management heritage, embracing radical pluralism (Edwards, 2014) and traditional industrial relations. To realise ethical credibility, the organisation must have conflict: continual challenge to the party line. At a fundamental level, the trade union represents an agonism with capital, or as Anderson (1967: 274) puts it, 'the very existence of a trade union de facto asserts the unabridgeable difference between Capital and Labour' (quoted in Hyman, 1971: 25). Debates over CEO remuneration, unfair discrimination, downsizing and redundancies, the abuse of benefits programmes and so forth all feature regularly in public debate. With a powerful, independent trade union, management has not only a formidable adversary but also an ethical check on its prerogative (see also Harvey et al., 2017).

---Student exercise---

Thinking about the differences between agonism and antagonism, consider the following questions:

- How might trade unions act in the role of a) enemy or b) adversary of management?
- What are the shortcomings of trade unions as an adversarial otherthan in the context of diminishing trade union membership?
- How does trade union partnership and acquiescence with management complicate the role of the trade union as the adversarial other?

---Mini case study 8.1---

Ryanair

The European low-fares airline, Ryanair, has impressive economic credentials. The airline is an outstanding performer in European civil aviation in the 20 years prior to the pandemic, with profit increasing from £500 million in 2008 to almost £1.5 billion a decade later. Moreover, it has achieved this feat through its people and through a distinctive SHRM with a hard orientation (see Harvey and Turnbull, 2020). It might be difficult to make a case for the ethics of leadership that is unconnected to economic performance at an airline whose CEO, Michael O'Leary has said of his staff:

> MBA students come out with: 'My staff is my most important asset.' Bullshit. Staff is usually your biggest cost. We all employ some lazy bastards who need a kick up the backside, but no one can bring themselves to admit it.

> I'm Europe's most underpaid and underappreciated boss. I'm paid about 20 times more than the average Ryanair employee and I think the gap should be wider. (Hogan, 2013)

Indeed, O'Leary once promised that if Ryanair were to set up a transatlantic service then first-class passengers would be offered 'beds and blowjobs' (Noonan, 2008; Platt, 2008; Reilly, 2010). Employment practices at the airline have been documented extensively elsewhere (see, for example, Harvey and Turnbull, 2020) as an exemplar of what has been labelled neo-villeiny in other contexts (see Harvey et al., 2017):

(Continued)

- The airline relies heavily on self-employed workers, especially among its flight crew, leading authorities to investigate the status of the self-employed pilots based in Germany;
- Cabin crew have been required to pay for their own training over the first six months of a temporary, zero-hours contract;
- Employees are bound to the airline by financial penalties.

Until 2017, the airline operated independently of trade unions, drawing on union suppression policies to keep trade unions from organising workers. Indeed, Michael O'Leary has previously announced that he would prefer to cut off his own hands than sign an agreement with trade unions (Ritholtz, 2017). Since trade unions have been recognised, leadership has adopted a highly adversarial approach to organised labour.

Questions

1. Drawing on the logic of SHRM, make a case for the ethics of leadership at Ryanair.
2. In what ways might leadership change at the airline in order to be ethical according to the logic of dissensus?

Conclusion

The purpose of this chapter has been to offer an evaluation of the ethics of leadership through the lens of SHRM as presented in mainstream approaches. In contrast, we presented an alternative perspective that considers ethics as emerging from contestation, difference, dissensus and resistance. Here, ethical leadership is not one that is pre-determined but one that might arise from such dissensus, most especially dissensus over what constitutes the 'good'. Practically, this is an ethics that might manifest in the democratic experience of political 'agonism' that cannot be controlled by a function that is dominated by one of the adversaries.

The alternative ethics of leadership arises not when an ethical system is enforced through SHRM, but when leadership decisions as they relate to people management are brought into question through dissent and resistance from the outside. This alternative ethical leadership of people does not place SHRM at its centre, as the sole arbiter of organisational ethics, but rather sees SHRM as being merely an actor in a set of socio-ethical relations.

Decolonising leadership

Pullen, A., Rhodes, C., McEwen, C. and Liu, H. (2019) 'Radical politics, intersectionality and leadership for diversity in organizations'. *Management Decision*, 59(11): 2553–2566.

The paper draws on Black feminist indigenous perspectives such as the Combahee River Collective and their focus on intersectionality to examine the role of politically engaged leadership in encouraging equality and diversity.

Key summary

- Leadership of people is a critical component of organisational leadership.
- Leadership of people is most obviously manifest in SHRM and so the ethics of this aspect of leadership can be discussed in relation to SHRM.
- Hard HRM and soft HRM (both high commitment and high involvement management) are ethically problematic in that they impose on staff the beliefs of leaders and diminish contestation and conflict.
- An alternative approach to leadership connects with the concept of agonism and notions of democracy and dissensus.
- Accordingly, ethical leadership is the acknowledgement of the legitimacy of interests other than shareholders.
- Ethical leadership can be understood as the creation of conditions for contest rather than capitulation.

Further reading

Alakavuklar, O.N. and Alamgir, F. (2018) 'Ethics of resistance in organisations: A conceptual proposal'. *Journal of Business Ethics*, 149(1): 31–43.

Branicki, L., Brammer, S., Pullen, A. and Rhodes, C. (2021) 'The morality of "new" CEO activism.' *Journal of Business Ethics*, 170(2): 269–285.

Rhodes, C. and Badham, R. (2018) 'Ethical irony and the relational leader: Grappling with the infinity of ethics and the finitude of practice'. *Business Ethics Quarterly*, 28(1): 71–98.

Parts of this chapter are adapted from Rhodes, C. and Harvey, G. (2012) 'Agonism and the possibilities of ethics for HRM'. *Journal of Business Ethics*, 111(1): 49–59.

9

LEADERSHIP AND THE DIGITAL AGE

Desireé Joy Cranfield, Isabella Venter and Andrea Tick

Chapter objectives

The objectives of this chapter are:

- To introduce the concept of the '**digital age**' and the influence it has on business today.
- To present the influence of the digital age on leadership and management.
- To provide views of the leadership styles, behaviours and approaches to be considered, given the digital age and fast-paced environment we live in.
- To introduce and review the leadership competencies required for the digital age.

Mini case study 9.1

Cape Town, South Africa

Uwe Koetter Jewellers (https://uwekoetter.com), a family business, was started in 1968 by Magda and Uwe Koetter, in Cape Town, with a small loan as seed capital. Uwe, an experienced goldsmith, completed his studies in Germany. The business focused, from the start, on designing and creating bespoke and unique pieces of jewellery. A strong point of this fledgeling business was Uwe's ability to design and quote with the client being present. The client base were professionals, businesspeople, farmers and

(Continued)

politicians (the Baby Boomer generation). The importance of the tourism industry was realised very early on, and the workshop became a tourist attraction.

The business environment during that period was less complicated, less costly and with little government interference. The South African post office and railways functioned as well as in similar institutions in First World countries and its supporting infrastructure was reliable. What was lacking was the accurate collection and collation of data for optimising business efficiency – such as client frequency, amounts spent and preferences – as such information relied on personal note keeping.

Business management in South Africa today is much more challenging than it was prior to the 1990s. A much bigger skill set is required – in this business, one has to understand both the creative and the manufacturing process and the fast-changing market. Over and above business management, skills like financial management and accounting as well as understanding and responding to conditions laid down by law are important to legally conduct business. For Uwe Koetter Jewellers, it became apparent that to run the business effectively, a team approach would be necessary. Each team member contributes a different skill and thus this combined skill set would ensure that the business leader can make the best-informed decisions. The style of leadership is currently consultative and informal. The hierarchical system has become flatter, resulting in easy interaction between management and staff. The digital age brought faster communication with the limiting effect of time and distance largely being negated. Information on best practices is instantly available. The challenge for leaders is to constantly upskill as new technologies become available and which are imperative to adopt.

Adapting as a leader during the disruptive COVID-19 period meant learning to use and embrace new technologies and approaches. Being aware of the many shortcomings of these technologies was challenging, but the paradigm shift was also exciting and has created new opportunities.

Questions

1. What do you consider to be the leadership skill set required of an innovative small business and entrepreneur?
2. How do you think the re-skilling of employees should be managed?

Introduction

Digitally connected technologies have caused profound changes in all domains of life during the 21st century, signalling a new age: the 'digital age' (Saykili, 2019).

These dramatic changes could and can still be seen in education, industry, health services, and government due to new ways of working and they created both opportunities and challenges for leaders in these sectors. The coronavirus pandemic that emerged in 2019 demanded unusual and unexpected expertise of leaders in all walks of life, which D'Auria and De Smet (2020: 2) suggest was and is a 'landscape scale crisis: an unexpected event or sequence of events of enormous scale and overwhelming speed, resulting in a high degree of uncertainty that gives rise to disorientation, a feeling of lost control, and strong emotional disturbance'. The pressures of the digital age as well as the 'landscape-scale crisis' of the pandemic have necessitated rethinking leadership, with certain behaviours and associated mindsets now required to help leaders navigate the challenges and opportunities presented (D'Auria and De Smet, 2020).

This chapter, 'Leadership and the digital age', introduces the idea of the digital age, and how leadership as a concept and practice has become a pressing concern for all, especially given the COVID-19 pandemic and the drastic changes that society, the world of work, and in particular, businesses, have been forced to embrace. 'Leadership in the digital age' and 'Digital leadership' are two different concepts. The latter, 'Digital leadership', refers to leadership in the fundamental sectors of the knowledge society – computing, communications, and content (broadcasting and print or multimedia) – while the former refers to leadership in any organisation or sector rooted in the broader changes toward a more knowledge-intensive society (Wilson, 2004). This chapter focuses on the former.

The different approaches, styles, behaviours and competencies required of leadership in an increasingly digital age are explored. This chapter furthermore provides a diverse and inclusive view of leadership throughout, and it also explores the skills, qualities and practices that are required of managers and leaders in this age.

The chapter is structured as follows. It starts with an introduction to the digital age, with an explanation of technology and digitisation, disruptive technologies, as well as the challenges and opportunities that the digital age presents. The chapter then considers the digital age and its implications for management and leadership; more specifically, it considers the importance of leadership in the digital age, providing a summary of the competencies, responses, attitudes and behaviours leaders should exhibit, and ends with a discussion of leadership and decolonisation. Case studies of three organisations are presented (one already discussed), discussing the background of the organisation; their challenges prior to the digital age; how they perceive leadership; how the digital age has necessitated changes in their leadership; the new challenges they now face; and how the pandemic has impacted their organisation – and these form part of this chapter.

The digital age
Technology, digitalisation and digitisation

Over the past decades, the proliferation of technology has enabled new ways of working and socialising, which has had a profound effect on the way businesses conduct their business, with most of previously manual processes and relations being converted to digital form (Owie, 2017). Technology like the internet, the World Wide Web and mobile platforms have transformed businesses (Chaffey, Hemphill and Edmundson-Bird, 2019) and have introduced new, innovative business models which are transforming the global business environment and practices for managing and organising businesses (Laundon and Laudon, 2020). Globalisation – and the emergence of the internet as an international communications system, which substantially reduced transacting and operating costs on a global scale (Laundon and Laudon, 2020) – expanded markets and their reach, and thus presents both challenges and opportunities for businesses. The conditions for a fully digital firm, 'one in which nearly all of the organisation's significant business relationships with customers, suppliers and employees are digitally enabled and mediated', are thus now possible (Laundon and Laudon, 2020: 44).

Digitisation and **digitalisation** are related but quite different terms. *Digitisation* refers to the conversion of data and documents etc. into digital formats, whilst *digitalisation* is the adaptation of business processes to using digital technologies. Digitalisation can be understood from a technical perspective, and on the other hand, it can also be seen as a development of society as a whole, triggered by technological developments in electronic data processing (Hensellek, 2020). Digitalisation has been happening over the past decades and Davenport (2014) defines it as the transformation of manual business processes to digital, interconnected business processes supported by personal and work computers. A further definition is offered by Bamsode (2008: 13) who defines digitisation as 'the conversion of an item – be it printed text, manuscript, image, or sound, film and video recording – from one format (usually print or analogue) into a digital format'. Hensellek (2020) purports that digitalisation has led to both new challenges and opportunities and has imposed major transformations at all levels of the economy and society, primarily transforming the way people engage with each other and the way companies function in the market.

In the next section, the influences of '**disruptive technologies**' and new business models on leadership and business are explored. Furthermore, the change in leadership style required for the new digital firm and the digital age, is considered. The question thus is: 'Have the changes to the way in which businesses conduct their business and core operations, changed leadership and management styles, and furthermore, what are the fundamental characteristics and responses of leaders required for the digital age?'.

The influence of disruptive technologies and business models on leadership and management

Disruptive technologies

When our lives are disrupted, we are forced to deal with the associated changes that this can bring, which each of us experience in different ways and to different degrees. These disruptions can be triggered by political, economic, environmental, medical and/or social events, and don't always present as single, standalone incidents. Distinct global and local disruptions may co-exist, adding to the complexity of a situation; however, while these disruptions are inconvenient, and on occasion, can potentially be life-threatening, they can offer opportunities for transformative change (Davison, 2020).

Disruption can also be triggered by a new technology. Daneels (2004: 247) asks the question 'What makes a technology disruptive?'. Chaffey et al. (2019) suggest that disruptive digital technologies offer opportunitie's for new business processes, products and services along the organisations value chain. A widely cited definition by Daneels (2004: 249) suggests that 'a disruptive technology is a technology that changes the bases of competition by changing the performance metrics along which firms compete. Customer needs drive customers to seek certain benefits in the products they use and form the basis for customer choices between competing products'. Disruption occurs when those overlooked segments are successfully targeted and more suitable functionality – often at a lower cost – is offered, and customers start to adopt offerings in volume (Christensen, Raynor and Mcdonald, 2015).

The exponential rate of the development of various technologies converges and can trigger an even faster growth (Diamandis and Kotler, 2020), requiring high flexibility, an agile response, and fast changes in business as well as organisational and management practices. Disruptive technologies question traditional organisational structures and traditional management and leadership styles. Traditional management approaches for example towards business strategy development, the processes are quite sequential in nature and leaders address the process in a chronological manner (see Figure 9.1).

However, when developing a digital business strategy, Kalakota and Robinson (2000), cited in Chaffey, Hempill and Edmunson-Bird (2019) suggest that the process is more of a dynamic and cyclical one where managers and leaders have to be aware of the environment, continually analysing it, and being flexible in being able to adapt to triggers or events within the environment where appropriate, see Figure 9.2. As the environment is so dynamic compared to previous eras, leaders have to adapt to this and develop the responses and attitudes to survive in this new environment.

Generic strategy process model

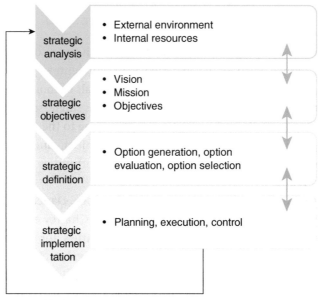

Monitor, evaluate, respond

Figure 9.1 A generic strategy process model

Adapted from Chaffey, D., Hemphill, T., and Edmundson-Bird, D. (2019: 194). Digital Business and e-Commerce Management (seventh ed.). United Kingdom: Pearson.

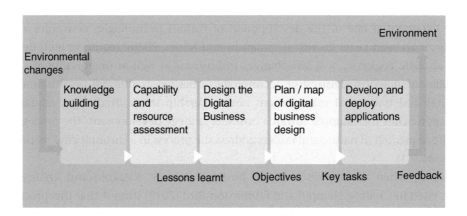

Figure 9.2 A dynamic digital business strategy process model

Source: Adapted from Chaffey, D., Hemphill, T., and Edmundson-Bird, D. (2019). Digital Business and e-Commerce Management (seventh ed.). United Kingdom: Pearson.

Diamandis and Kotler introduced a six dimensioned model for the exponential development of technology (Kotler and Diamandis, 2015), which can be applied to business models and leadership and management changes. They describe it as a chain of reactive technological advances with rapid development, that causes upheaval but also provides opportunities (Kotler and Diamandis, 2015). The six dimensions defined are (see Figure 9.3):

Digitised: If a business becomes digitised, it enters a new phase of exponential growth. Digital technology triggers new business processes, higher efficiency and cost cuttings. Consequently, the business model should adapt to the digitised business processes.

Deceptive: If a business is digitised, the revolutionary threshold is high. The first growth phase takes a relatively long time until convergent processes meet and speed up business processes. At the managerial level, this is a deceptive phase.

Disruptive: When the digitisation of business processes reaches the state of having a tangible impact on business performance, it starts to become disruptive and changes products, processes and services, and thus digital technologies boost effectiveness and cost-cutting in business. New business models are introduced.

Demonetised: Due to disruptive technology products, technologies disappear from the market, or may turn into services. Certain services have become free or are provided at almost a cost approaching zero. For example, consider the cost of taking photos or making videos using a phone and listening to music via applications (apps such as Apple Music, Deezer, SoundCloud). Apps have changed the way these services are purchased. Therefore, CDs and cameras are not being bought as before.

Dematerialised: Industry 4.0 introduces the digital twin concept: a product life cycle is prolonged with digital services that do not require physical devices. Separate functions are built into a single device such as a smartphone which has the functionality of a radio, a camera, a global positioning system (GPS), a video, maps, etc., or a smart television (TV) equipped with internet access which can act as a big computer screen. Products like cheque books, tapes, a video home system (VHS), calculators and encyclopaedias have disappeared from the market, and even paper might become a commodity that disappears in the near future.

Democratised: When something is digitised, it becomes accessible to everyone by means of computers and smartphones. Self-driving cars and 3D (three-dimensional) printing are expected to be democratised in the future. Even business processes are democratised, as with self-service cashiers and paperless online public administrations where customers take over specific tasks that used to be the responsibility of the business firm. New business models eliminate these steps from their business processes, making the operation more effective and reducing costs.

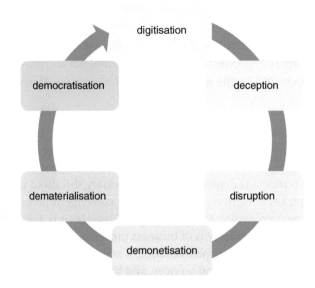

Figure 9.3   The six dimensions of exponential growth

Adapted from Kotler, S., and Diamandis, P. (2015). BOLD - How to Go Big, Create Wealth and Impact the World. New York: Simon and Schuster.

Each of the six dimensions will require: the utilisation of a specific skill set; appropriate leadership behaviours and characteristics; and the ability to be flexible and adaptable to the dynamic and rapidly changing environment. This demands of the leader constant surveying of the external environment and the impact of the six dimensions on the business to remain successful. These characteristics and competencies of leaders are discussed and defined later in the chapter.

Westerman, Bonnet and McAfee (2014) suggest that there are three main areas where digital technologies can serve leaders and managers to a great extent. The first is customer experience, through which customers become active participants in the business process; they are given new responsibilities, new tasks and become content creators. The second is operational processes, through which the product life cycle is extended, adding new features and services like creating digital twins of physical products, for instance. The third is business models, through which novel forms of value creation and value capturing are introduced. The business might need to undergo a transformation such as entering the sharing economy market or turning into a software company from a physical product producer. For each of these two models discussed above, leaders need to be innovative and agile in their decision making, creating a collaborative and participative environment, enabling customers to become co-creators in the process of decision making, which is different to previous models of leadership.

Business models

The digital age has necessitated leaders to adopt digital business and e-commerce models. A traditional business model is defined as 'a set of planned activities designed to result in a profit in a marketplace' (Laudon and Traver, 2021: 326); it is 'a summary of how a company will generate revenue identifying its product offering, value added services, revenue sources, and target customers' (Chaffey, Hemphill and Edmundson-Bird, 2019: 651). On the other hand, an e-commerce business model is a model that aims to 'leverage the unique qualities of the internet, the Web, and the mobile platform' (Laudon and Traver, 2021: 326), therefore utilising digital technologies to conduct business.

Business models are situated between the company's strategic and operative layer (Osterwalder, 2004) and focus on the company's core activity. When the core activity is disrupted, either by technologies or innovation, business models alter and need to adapt to the new market situation to keep the business operational and fulfil customer and market demand.

From this perspective, leaders and managers are responsible for following the industrial trend and striving to fit the 'core activity' to the digital market demands and trends. For example, advanced manufacturing capabilities and trends – 3D printing, advanced robotics, real-time collaboration, and digital prototyping – will have an impact on how leaders and managers deal with productivity increases and labour costs (Bhattacharya, Reeves, Lang and Augustinraj, 2017).

New (digital) business models are built on digital and internet technologies, and influenced by mainly advanced technology developments, as seen in Table 9.1.

Table 9.1 Six developments that contributed to new (digital) business models

Connectivity
- increasing number of connected people and devices
- real-time connection

Data Analytics and AI
- data mining
- customer-centricity, customised business
- sharing-knowledge

Digital Platform
- consolidation of buyers and sellers

Industry 4.0
- connected digital devices, IoT, digital twins, 3D printing, customised products

(Continued)

Table 9.1 (Continued)

Digital Ecosystem

- connected and mobile users
- value chains become value networks
- P2P model including ICT systems, social and knowledge networks

Economies of Scale and Cost Restructuring

- protectionism and state capitalism
- lower deployment costs, administrative costs, customer access costs, cross-border cooperation costs

Adapted from Bhattacharya, A., Reeves, M., Lang, N., and Augustinraj, R. (2017). New Business Models for a new global landscape. BCG Henderson Institute. Retrieved August 21, 2021, from https://www.bcg.com/publications/2017/globalization-new-business-models-global-landscape

These advanced technologies help businesses move towards more collaborative models, become modular, expand across borders, and become more connectable and shareable, which has an impact on leadership and management styles.

Bhattacharya et al. (2017) identified several digital business models, not mutually exclusive, nor exhaustive, but it does provide a view of the expanding set of possibilities for accessing new markets and finding new avenues for growth as perceived important by leadership:

1. *Cross-border servitisation:* The proliferation of the IoT (Internet of Things) and data analytics allows for delivering digital services and end-to-end solutions instead of selling physical products. The owning of a physical product loses its importance and the pay-per-use concept becomes the business (e.g., car-sharing; city bike; remote maintenance support via the internet.).

2. *Asset light market entry:* The network economy – utilising partnerships – allows for less upfront investment, low distribution costs, and faster reach of potential customers (e.g., Xiaomi teamed with Flipcart in India).

3. *Adding value through software:* A shift from firmware to software licensing and software support is available thanks to digital technology and the increasing interconnectivity (e.g., Tesla; GE airplane engine support).

4. *Global ecosystem:* Digitalised enterprises combine and aggregate the various services of partner companies. These companies transform 'value chains' to 'value networks', covering the end-to-end business process (e.g., Google's Android; Booking.com).

5. *Global personalisation:* Customer time and interest are precious. Personalised offers through digital platforms anywhere and anytime have massively over-taken offers for everyone. Data analytics and Artificial Intelligence (AI) heavily support personalised services (e.g., Netflix; HBO Go; personalised ads and newsfeeds).

6. *Multilocal manufacturing:* Digital technological advances allow the breakdown of manufacturing facilities and the relocation of production plants closer to end-users. Therefore, more customised products can be offered at lower costs, using additive manufacturing and robotics.
7. *Developing multiple national identities:* The local premises of global companies strive to adapt to local norms and requirements. Companies are involved in job-creation, address local and national priorities, and serve local workforce needs through which a more robust local identity is established.

As the global marketplace is reshaped by technological, political and societal influences, new business models are being deployed to exploit opportunities and develop competitive advantage over the long term. However, these potential opportunities must be supported by the appropriate capabilities, approaches and organisational structures (Bhattacharya et al., 2017). Leaders and managers will need to be able to identify these potential opportunities and exploit them for competitive advantage to ensure success and in certain cases their survival. If leaders and managers do not stay abreast of technological innovations, businesses lose their position in the market, thus their competitive advantage, and this could have an impact on their business surviving long term (Chaffey, Hemphill and Edmundson-Bird, 2019).

The influence of globalisation on leadership and management

Digital technologies have contributed to the concept and practice of globalisation, which presents opportunities as well as threats to businesses (Bennett and Lemoine, 2014a). The simplest definition of **globalisation** is that it describes the increased interconnectedness between different countries. From a business perspective, Ali (2001) suggests that globalisation 'means the ability of a corporation to conduct business across borders in an open market, the maximizing of organisational benefits, without inflicting social damage or violating the rights of people from other cultures' (Ali, 2001: 5). Furthermore, globalisation, as it relates to the increase in cross-border transactions, e-commerce, and information and communications technology (ICT), has resulted in a robust global framework for carrying out international business (Owie, 2017). ICT have not only driven globalisation but dramatically changed the way business is conducted. The framework for the conduct of international business has changed and continues to do so. As businesses go 'global', 'leadership and managerial roles, as well as styles and structures would have to change to accommodate societal differences' (Owie, 2017: 212).

Although globalisation has many benefits, in some cases it has facilitated the transfer of jobs to cheaper and lower skilled economies, allowing businesses to take advantage of the imperatives of globalisation to maximise profits by cutting down on the local labour work-force and outsourcing (Owie, 2017). In addition, Ali (2001) suggests that certain highly connected, informed and elite individuals and corporations are able to maximise their networks to serve their own interests and to seize opportunities for themselves and clients, which Owie (2017) indicates undermines the progress towards unification and social good.

Given the challenges and opportunities globalisation presents leaders and managers with, it is imperative for leadership to be able to develop the competencies of an effective global leader, described by Javidan et al. (2021) as the ability to engage in the multicultural and establish global collaborations. Javidan et al. (2021) further suggest that global leadership effectiveness is influenced by an individual's multicultural life exposure, which shapes their own global mindset, underpinned by their embedded-ness in their own culture. All of these factors contribute to developing an effective global leader. Every business leader and manager who engages in global trade will need to be an effective global leader. This view is supported by Owie (2017), who suggests that leadership competencies should include communication skills, motivation to learn, flexibility, open-mindedness, respect for others, and sensitivity.

Opportunities and challenges of the digital age
Opportunities
The influence of the digital age on work

Digitalisation has transformed work practices within the digital age, however the crisis of the coronavirus pandemic has presented employers and employees with challenges as well as opportunities to continue work practices remotely, away from the office (Owie, 2017). Prior to COVID-19, very few employees worked from home and most organisations were not prepared for supporting this practice. Millions of employees globally were suddenly expected to become remote workers in 2020, with the outbreak of the pandemic inadvertently leading to a de facto global experiment of remote working (Wang, Liu, Qian and Parker, 2021: 17). Remote working was expected almost overnight and now has become the 'new normal' (Kniffin et al., 2021). Leaders need to be aware of the impact of these changed circumstances on their employees' home–work environment, workload and well-being.

Where this remote working was possible during the COVID-19 pandemic, businesses and industries were able to continue providing services to their customers, and hence, continue their 'business', a huge advantage over those who were not innovative and able to adapt to the changed circumstances.

Another influence of the digital age on work is that using technology to conduct work practices has created the opportunity to improve work processes, streamlining them to improve efficiency (Sedziuviene and Vveinhardt, 2009; Owie, 2017).

Knowledge management and intellectual capital

With the proliferation of the internet, access to information has become ubiquitous, the amount of information and data has amplified, and the concept of 'big data' has established importance, providing untold benefits to organisations. Owie (2017) suggests that employees' knowledge is shaped by the culture and practices evident in the workplace and can be managed to create value for an organisation.

The management of 'knowledge' and 'intellectual capital' within the workplace is said to be critical to an organisation's competitive advantage. But what is '**knowledge management**' or '**intellectual capital**'? The concept of knowledge management was first introduced by an American scientist, Karl Wiig, in 1986. Wiig (1995: 1) presents the notion that 'knowledge, perceptions, understandings, and practical know-how that everyone possesses, is the fundamental resource that allows us to function intelligently – as individuals and organisations'. He continues to add that over time this knowledge can be converted into other forms, for example into books, technology, practices and traditions, which can result in cumulated expertise and increased effectiveness. Over time, organisations have shown more interest in evaluating, managing and developing their intellectual assets (Kianto, Vanhala, Ritala and Hussinki, 2018). Two knowledge-related factors considered important for the success of an organisation are suggested by Wiig (1995: 1):

- *Knowledge assets* – valuable knowledge available to individuals and organisations that needs to be used, nurtured and preserved.
- *Knowledge-related processes* – these processes include: to create, build, compile, organise, transform, transfer, pool, apply and safeguard knowledge, which must be managed very carefully.

The concept of 'intellectual capital' refers to 'intellectual material – knowledge, information, intellectual property, experience – that can be put to use to create wealth' (Steward, 1997: x). Intellectual capital is an intangible value driver, an important resource and a crucial contributor to the financial success and value creation in any business (Abdulaali, 2018). Digital technologies have made the process of managing and accessing intellectual capital, knowledge, knowledge assets and knowledge processes much easier, and ubiquitous. Given the ubiquitous nature of the internet and the dynamics of the digital age, it is imperative that organisational leaders continue to invest in secure knowledge management systems, and encourage knowledge sharing to ensure relevant information is continuously available at the right time to the right staff to create competitive advantages.

Challenges for leadership in the digital age

The volatility, uncertainty, complexity and ambiguity (VUCA) environment

Digitisation and digitalisation have created a profound impact on leadership and management. Hensellek (2020) suggests that digitalisation 1) has enabled new entrants to markets to have lower barriers to entry, consequently changing the way competition occurs and driving down innovation cycles; 2) has changed the way customers communicate, changed the values they hold, and has therefore changed consumer behaviour; and 3) has changed the way the world of work happens, especially around the needs and design of the workplace.

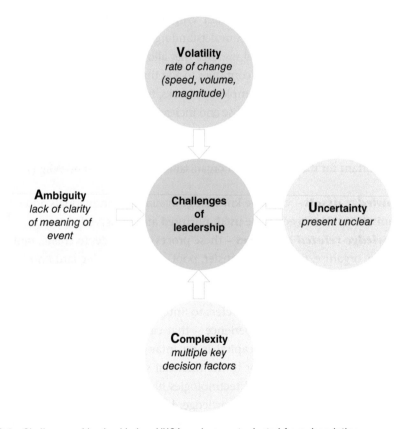

Figure 9.4 Challenges of leadership in a VUCA environment adapted from description

Adapted from Hensellek, S. (2020). Digital Leadership:A Framework for Successful Leadership in the Digital Age. Journal of Media Management and Entrepreneurship, 2(1). Retrieved August 31, 2021, from https://www.igi-global.com/article/digital-leadership/246066;Bennett, N., and Lemoine, G. J. (2014). What a difference a word makes: Understanding. Business Horizon, 1126, 1-7. Retrieved from https://www.researchgate.net/publication/263926940_What_VUCA_really_means_for_you

The digital age has in essence contributed to the volatility, uncertainty, complexity and ambiguity (VUCA) of the business environment (Bennett and Lemoine, 2014b), with the characteristics of the VUCA environment imposing different challenges on leaders (see Figure 9.4).

Hensellek (2020: 58) suggests that in the VUCA environment, leaders can face several challenges:

- *in a volatile* environment, developing a vision for the future can be difficult for leaders
- *in an uncertain* environment, understanding future directions relevant for the success of an organisation can be challenging
- *in a complex* environment, there is a need to increase flexible adaptation to changes as well as openness to adjust and reformulate existing goals
- *in an ambiguous* environment, higher levels of ambiguity demand that leaders develop strategies for the clear communication and actions of leaders to ensure unambiguous messages.

Each of the challenges requires a different and appropriate response from leaders, especially in relation to where to invest their time, money and effort (Bennett and Lemoine, 2014b). The digital age and globalisation have erased the safety of the predictability of markets, with leadership needing to be able to respond swiftly to the increased speed of shifting markets in response to worldwide environmental changes and events, like the pandemic, for example (Jurkiewicz, 2018). The relative comfort of feeling secure in the legal and ethical systems that protect us is not there any longer, and leaders need to be acutely aware of the current economic, political and social markets to be able to take immediate action to maintain success (Jurkiewicz, 2018). Sustainable leadership is therefore critical to the long-term success of businesses in an increasingly globalised and digitalised market (Hensellek, 2020).

Skills development and shortages

As we live in the digital age, all sectors rely on digital technology to be able to conduct their business. The move to digital technologies requires the reskilling and retraining of employees and the recruiting of employees with the necessary digital skills for the industry. A report titled 'Disconnected: exploring the digital skills gap' (WorldskillsUK, 2021) investigates the digital skills needed and the future of the labour market in the United Kingdom (UK) from the perspectives of employers in terms of demand for skills and the digital skills gap. The education of the young has been interrupted by the COVID-19 pandemic and the labour market disadvantaged due to the pandemic contributing to exacerbating educational inequalities. Digital skills will be crucial for the future of the UK economy as countries emerge from the coronavirus pandemic, hence improving digital skills will both help build on the UK's status as a world leader in digital technology, and help drive growth, productivity and innovation across the rest of the economy (WorldskillsUK, 2021). The challenge is for the young to be encouraged to participate in digital skills training, which the report by *WorldSkillsUK* (2021) suggests is declining – the number of young people taking Information Technology (IT) subjects in the UK at school-leaving level has fallen by 40 per cent since 2015. Additionally, the competencies required for the new disruptive technologies present a potential worldwide IT shortage. As of 2020, 35 per cent of chief information officers (CIOs) worldwide who took part in the research study indicated that they were facing a skills shortage in cyber security functions (*Statista*, 2020). This function received the highest responses in comparison to all the other functions (for example, big data, AI).

Big data, privacy and security

The central elements of the concept of '**big data**' refer to the 'massive volumes of information collected through technological means, accumulating at such a velocity that continually innovating information processing is required to keep pace' (Jurkiewicz, 2018: S47). The value of big data has increased in currency and changed the way businesses conduct their business. Every opportunity to leverage a competitive advantage and maximise productivity and efficiencies in service by collecting data on citizens via digital gateways and platforms, is sought by businesses (Jurkiewicz, 2018). However, there can be privacy and cybersecurity issues related to accessing and collecting 'big data' for businesses and therefore leaders need to be fully aware of the security and privacy issues and policies that need to be in place, and the impact of any legal charges if misused in any way.

Additional issues can be related to access to big data, which can include the ability of governments to be able to spy on citizens; to be able to profile individuals using criminal justice analytics; the ability to generate fake identities and the use of cyber theft; student cheating and a decreasing trust in Higher Education (Jurkiewicz, 2018). Despite these challenges, the value of access to big data is immense, which leaders need to be fully aware of, but they also need to be aware of the consequences of violating any cyber security or privacy issues, which can cause legal implications and financial loss. What about the ethical issues that could be related to accessing or collecting 'big data'?

Ethical issues related to big data

There is the potential to collect personal data from anyone that utilises a digital platform either for work or for socialising. The scope of the ethical issues introduced by big data, while collecting personal data on virtually everyone about anything, is astounding.

Despite this, Jurkiewicz (2018) suggests that there are many benefits to be realised from big data, however there is a need for governments to establish more robust policies, protections and solutions for citizens harmed by big data related personal infractions. Some of the types of ethical issues that big data presents are listed below (Jurkiewicz, 2018):

1. *Data collected under the guise of social betterment* – collecting personal data like customer behaviours and preferences for profit, without the knowledge of the customer, is an ethical concern. An example of this is the new iPhone X, whose facial recognition system is advertised as a security benefit while in the meantime this data is collected to create saleable content.
2. *Facilitating unequitable wealth distribution* – AI enables the dehumanisation of individual choice; in addition, unskilled jobs are the ones that are eliminated first, which will negatively affect the lower social economic groups dissimilarly, protecting those of greater intricacy and further exacerbating the divide between economic classes.
3. *Increasing social hostilities for political furtherance* – social media websites allow for the targeting of specific demographics that enable access by hate groups, which aids discrimination.
4. *Concealed data collection for profit* – ubiquitous camera systems, allegedly for safety or convenience, generate data that are accumulated and resold at a substantial profit.
5. *Facilitating human dependency on technology* – deeper, complex and logical thinking is being reduced in humans as technology undertakes some of these tasks, reducing these skills in humans and increasing dependency on technology.

Each of these ethical concerns requires leaders and managers to understand the nature of the concerns, and understand each of the policies in place to mitigate it. The scope and range of ethical concerns have changed since the heralding of the digital age. Leaders are responsible for their data and information – both private and organisational – and for understanding any concerns and their impact on the business, as well as understanding the key actions to take.

Workload

The digital age has enabled employees and employers to be connected with all stakeholders along the value chain of the business. Different businesses have taken advantage of becoming fully digital, while others use technology in specific areas of the business. Remote working is one of those areas that has taken on a new meaning during the COVID-19 pandemic and lockdown, when most businesses were forced to close their physical doors to their customers as well as employees. Leaders grappled with the introduction of new forms of working to ensure business continuity. Wang et al. (2021) define four challenges for remote working: home interference; ineffective communication; procrastination; and loneliness. They also found that virtual work characteristics such as social support, job autonomy, monitoring and workload affected the experience of the employees – the employees' self-discipline played a moderating role within these relationships (Wang, Liu, Qian and Parker, 2021).

Those businesses who were unable to conduct their work remotely and online, were not able to continue with their core functions, and in certain cases were soon put into administration. Although the 24/7 access to work, work files and management communication is very beneficial for businesses and staff as indicated before, it has created an unforeseen pressure on staff who could feel obliged to be contactable 24/7 and feel the need to respond, as well as work more than the allocated weekly hours. This immense pressure put on staff members – sometimes not only by managers but by different stakeholders – required a deliberate leadership strategy that took the well-being of staff members into account.

Leaders therefore need to be agile enough to recognise the developing challenges around different situations and be able to respond appropriately. Owie (2017) continues to add that unfortunately these improvements in work practices can lead to redundant roles, and subsequent job losses, which can eventually become a social issue.

Mini case study 9.2

Admiral Insurance (Cardiff, Wales)

Admiral Group Plc – a large financial services company headquartered in Cardiff, Wales and founded in 1993 by Henry Engelhardt – provides products that include home insurance, van and travel insurance, personal loans, and car finance. Admiral's aim is to provide customers with the best possible customer service.

Admiral's initial advertising campaigns took the form of physical channels, placing advertisements on buses. The leadership style was authoritative with the co-founders driving the company. The business operated in silos where functions were dealt with independently. It started as a relatively small business (approximately 57 employees) and hence, despite the silos, people knew each other, so communication was not a challenge and work could get done. As the business grew, communication and styles of leadership had to improve since the focus of the business changed from being a market disruptor to focusing on staying abreast of the industry.

Leadership needed to rethink their competitive advantage, how to remain relevant and to adapt to environmental changes. Admiral adopted a more democratic leadership style, which was more participative in nature, involving people across the organisation in decision making as well as accountability. Admiral moved from working in silos to creating small cross-functional teams from each of the functions, to ensure that the business used efficient and effective means to manage their services. An agile methodology was applied in different parts of the business to ensure the responsiveness of leadership to environmental changes.

Advancement in technology enabled more efficient customer service and different communication channels to be used. Admiral questioned what this meant for leadership if the workforce and ways of working changed, and decided to create a cultural board-level role, which enabled staff issues to be raised. A coaching style of leadership was used to unlock the potential of staff, enabling a wide array of opportunities.

To maximise opportunities that the digital age presents, leaders need to be agile, aware of both opportunities and challenges, and need to become innovative in their approach to their business to ensure competitiveness. While focusing on improved services, and trying to stay abreast of the industry, decision making needs to become quicker and more efficient. Admiral is a regulated business and therefore it was important to work towards getting the balance right between decision-making expedience and compliance. The challenge was to ensure that decisions could be made in response to the environmental changes timeously.

Questions

1. How do you think leaders should support their remote working staff?
2. What is considered an agile leadership style?

The digital age and the implications for management and leadership

Importance of leadership in the digital age

Leadership is an important aspect of management, justified by the scope of responsibility leaders have which includes initiating activities, guiding and motivating others, developing confidence in staff, building morale and the work environment, the coordination of staff and aligning personal interests with organisational goals (Juneja, 2021). Bennis and Thomas (2020: 62) suggest that 'everyone is tested by life, but only a few extract strength and wisdom from their most trying experiences. They are the ones we call leaders'.

Leaders play a critical role in the management of transformation and change, critical during the pandemic, as well as pre-COVID-19, to keep abreast of the changing environment. Leaders prepare their organisation for change and help the organisation and its workers to cope with inevitable change. As leaders of change, it is important that leaders can inspire others to be confident, loyal and to work hard during challenging times. Leadership is in fact the ability to cope with rapid changes. The COVID-19 pandemic has globally catapulted everyone into a vastly different world, where leadership has become paramount as changes had to be made rapidly, which is still an ongoing 'reset' that will be taking place, with considerable changes required from all.

The influence of the digital age and the changing demands of leadership

Digitisation has unquestionably altered how organisations are led and are managed (Owie, 2017). New social constructs are engendering new leadership styles, with the different eras producing new kinds of leadership, with diverse forms of hierarchical authority, different skill sets and attitudes, and different institutional incentives (Wilson, 2004). Hensellek (2020) suggests that classic leadership styles do not adequately address the opportunities and challenges stemming from digitalisation.

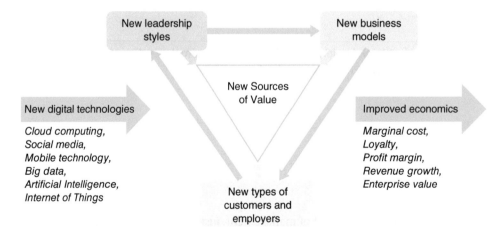

Figure 9.5 Disruption caused by new technology

Adapted from Libert, B., Wind, J., and Fenley, M. B. (2015, February 6). Is Your Leadership Style Right for the Digital Age? Retrieved August 29, 2021, from Knolwedge @ Wharton: https://knowledge.wharton.upenn.edu/article/the-right-leadership-style-for-the-digital-age/

As depicted in Figure 9.5, markets are being transformed by technological advancements and digital technologies (social media, cloud computing, big data analytics, mobile technology and the Internet of Things), creating new, intangible sources of value, delivered by new business models, and creating a new profile of customers and employees who are technology savvy and connected, introducing new ways of engaging with new businesses. These changing demands have put pressure on leaders to develop new skills to be able to attract, satisfy and retain both their customers and employees, thus requiring new leadership styles. The traditional directive and authoritarian leadership styles had to transform into more consultative and collaborative ones (Neubauer, Tarling and Wade, 2017), taking a relational view, as suggested by Uhl-Bien (2006) (see Chapter 5 for more on relational leadership). This can be quite challenging for leaders without the necessary training, skills and competencies. Improved economics is said to be experienced by businesses and leaders who can adapt to this new environment (Libert, Wind and Fenley, 2015). Research conducted by Libert et al. (2015) suggests that 1) businesses that value intangible assets, for example valuing relationships with customers and suppliers (Facebook, LinkedIn, Airbnb, TripAdvisor), and investors, have the highest price to revenue ratios; and 2) different leadership styles complement different business models, since each business model leverages different types of assets (for example, physical assets like shoes, or intellectual assets like software).

Leadership competencies, personality and behaviours for the digital age

Research conducted by the Global Center for Digital Business Transformation, a Cisco Initiative (DBT Center) and the human resources (HR) consultancy metaBeratung, conducted between October 2016 and January 2017, found that 'agile leaders', leaders who measured highly on competencies and behaviours, tended to significantly outperform other leaders on measures such as work engagement and leadership effectiveness (Neubauer, Tarling and Wade, 2017).

Libert et al. (2015) provide a framework that suggests new digital technologies impact the creation of new leadership styles, new business models and new relationships, with employers and customers providing opportunities to engage differently with the business. This creates new sources of value, in turn having a positive impact on economic growth. On the other hand, Neubauer et al. (2017) address the behaviours (hyper-awareness, informed decision making, fast execution) and characteristics (being engaged, humble, visionary, adaptable) leaders need to have in the digital age (see Figure 9.6).

Owie (2017) suggests that the digital age has transformed leadership and management from a top-down approach to a more collaborative one. To lead successfully in any era requires a specific set of competencies and behaviours that align with the current demands of the time (Neubauer, Tarling and Wade, 2017). Digital innovations and the related pace of change are making it more challenging for leaders to achieve competitive advantage and sustain the position, hence Neubauer et al. (2017) suggest that executives who are successful in disruptive environments, in particular those who are characterised by digital disruption, are called agile leaders. To be agile as a leader and as an organisation, requires a different mindset; it requires a paradigm shift as it is a co-operative, open, interconnected, self-sustaining, cross-functional, flexible form of working (Juneja, 2021). Four characteristics of agile leaders (H.A.V.E.) are suggested by Neubauer et al. (2017: 3):

1. **Humble**: the leader is open to feedback from others and recognises that others can know more than they do.
2. **Adaptable**: the leader is open to change, recognises that change is constant and that being flexible is a strength rather than a weakness.
3. **Visionary**: the leader can develop long-term strategies in the face of uncertainty.
4. **Engaged**: the leader is open to listening to others, can interact and communicate with internal and external stakeholders with a strong awareness of emerging trends.

The agile leader characteristics point to leaders being able to advise but also to being able to take advice and feedback from others. Being flexible and agile to situational circumstances, having a long-term view, and being ready to engage with all stakeholders, are key to being successful in this digital age. In addition, research conducted by Neubauer et al. (2017: 3) suggests that agile leaders exhibit three key behaviours which help to successfully navigate disruptive environments:

1. *Hyper-awareness*: the leader is constantly surveying and scanning the micro and macro environments for opportunities and threats.
2. *Informed decision making*: the leader can use data and information to enhance decision making based on evidence.
3. *Fast execution*: the leader values speed over perfection, therefore they can move quickly to implement decisions.

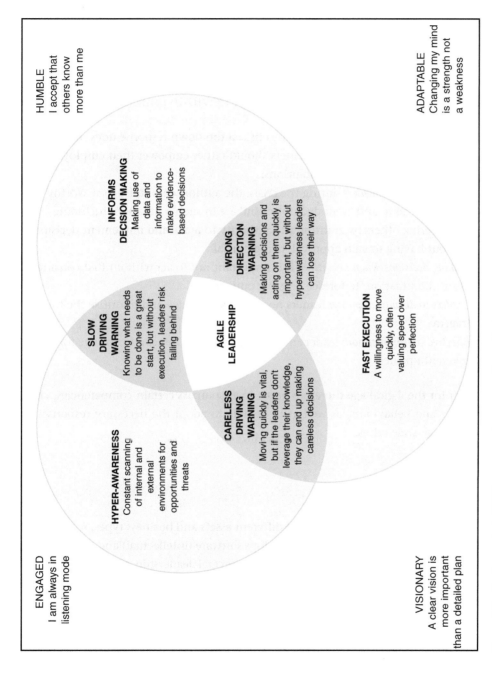

Figure 9.6 Neubauer et al. (2017) competencies, personality and behaviours for agile leadership, presentation adapted

Figure 9.6 brings together the leadership characteristics and behaviours for agile leadership that Neubauer et al. (2017) have suggested are needed in the digital age. Certain warnings are highlighted, as indicators for success or failure, provided in the intersections of the Venn diagram.

In addition to the leadership characteristics and behaviours for agile leadership, D'Auria and De Smet (2020) suggest five leadership responses and competencies to counter crises. For example, a crisis such as the COVID-19 pandemic requires:

1. *A team approach* as a response to the crisis: a top-down response does not necessarily provoke stability; leaders should rather empower their employees to search, find and implement solutions.
2. *Leaders to elevate leaders* during the crisis: the authors emphasise how worthy 'deliberate calm' and 'bounded optimism' are in such a situation, including empowering others by granting the authority to make and implement decisions without having to gain approval, being crucial.
3. *Making decisions when uncertain:* it is important not to act without first pausing to assess the situation, to foresee possible outcomes.
4. *Leaders to display empathy:* leaders need to acknowledge and prioritise the human tragedy.
5. *Effective communication:* leaders need to be open and direct and arrange for frequent updates.

A leader for the digital age therefore needs to encompass certain competencies, characteristics and behaviours, as well as to be able to adopt the necessary responses to counter large-scale crises.

Leadership styles for the digital age

Most businesses are a complex mix of different assets and business types, for example Nike produces shoes (physical), also develops software (intellectual) and is developing Nike+ (network); most leaders therefore use several leadership styles to lead their organisations based on the situation, business model, and purpose (Libert, Wind and Fenley, 2015).

Libert, Wind and Fenley (2015) suggest four leadership styles (see Figure 9.7):

1. Commander: sets the goal and tells others how to accomplish it. Works well with machinery, and with direct subordinates who prefer to simply execute; less effective with employees and customers who want choice and participation. This style is limited by the commander's vision and capabilities.

2. Communicator: sets a vision and a plan but communicates it to inspire and develop buy-in. Works better with employees and customers who want to at least understand where 'the firm is headed.' It enables them to act in line with the leader's vision, but it does not encourage innovation. This style is suited to services firms where all employees must work to fulfil the mission.

Collaborator: works together with customers and employees to achieve the organisation's goals, which is empowering and enabling. This style inspires innovation of people and drives the creation of new intellectual capital.

Co-Creator: allows other stakeholders to pursue their individual goals in parallel with the goals of the organisation. As a result, he or she drives both rapid scaling (due to the high level of participation) and innovation. This style is at the heart of network companies where value is shared by the company and the network participants, such as Airbnb, Uber and Innocentive.com.

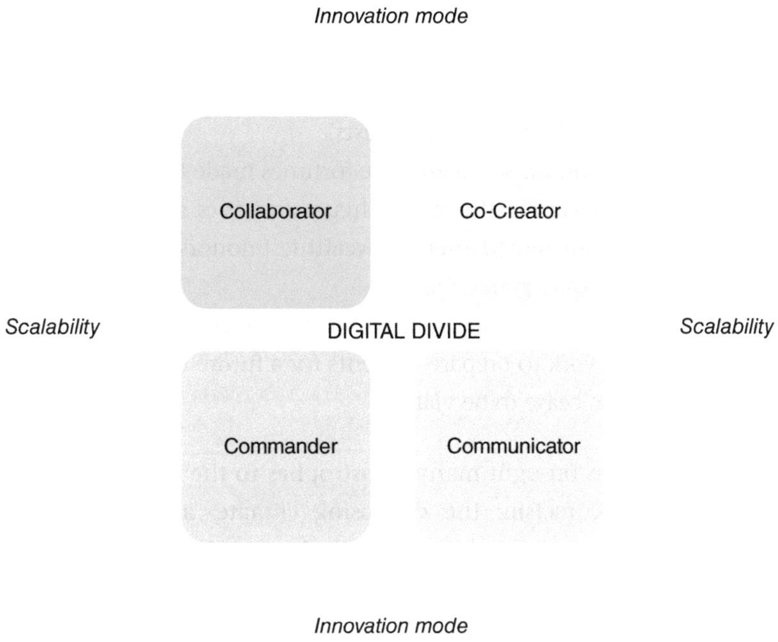

Innovation mode

Collaborator	Co-Creator

Scalability　　DIGITAL DIVIDE　　*Scalability*

Commander	Communicator

Innovation mode

Figure 9.7　Four leadership styles

Adapted from Libert, B., Wind, J., and Fenley, M. B. (2015, February). Leadership: Is Your Leadership Style Right for the Digital Age? Retrieved from Knowlege @ Wharton: https://knowledge.wharton.upenn.edu/article/the-right-leadership-style-for-the-digital-age/

Most leaders are able to engage several styles effectively, perhaps with the exception of co-creation which is relatively new, however using different leadership styles effectively and when appropriate is not simple or easy (Libert, Wind and Fenley, 2015).

Leadership training considerations

Business management academics rarely both know and can identify the roots of the theories and disciplines. Frederic Taylor's 'Scientific Management' underpins the understanding of management as a scientific discipline. Much of business scholarship grew out of Taylor's experience of his grandfather's slave ownership (Kemper, 2020). This awareness, of the close links between the concept of management and the control of enslaved peoples by overseers and accountants, cannot be ignored (Kemper, 2020). The situation we find ourselves in, in 2023, raises the importance of responsible business leadership, and the need for business management schools to recognise their responsibility in the development and training of future leaders. Kemper (2020) suggests that business schools have maintained so-called 'colonial processes' in the following ways:

1. The financial training of students can at times be traced back to colonial structures.
2. Researchers theorise and test systems of refining and replicating systems of wealth transfer from labourers to capitalists.
3. Administrators and fundraisers legitimise fortunes made in the past and those to be made with little regard to the moral circumstances of such fortunes. Schools and research chairs are named after the wealthiest donors with little regard to the way these funds were generated.
4. Few business scholars research or teach alternative forms of commerce, and almost no scholars work to prepare students for a future in which the prevailing models of capitalism cease to be viable.

The COVID-19 crisis has brought many catastrophes to the fore: income inequality and precarity; systemic racism; the collapsing climate; and each one of these demands responsible business leaders. These leaders need to be developed by business schools, requiring business schools to consider their role in the broader system, which, according to Kemper (2020), seems to be failing spectacularly. Professor Kemper (2020) purports that creating responsible leadership requires decolonisation. 'Decolonisation is about the consciousness and rejection of values, norms, customs and worldviews imposed by the [former] colonisers' (Césaire, 2000: 89). Decolonisation of leadership training is the first step in the right direction to ensuring ethical, responsible leadership.

Conclusion

In this chapter, the concept of the digital age was introduced, presenting both challenges and opportunities for businesses and society at large. The influence of the digital age has transformed how leadership should be considering the concept and practice of leadership and management, given the changing demands on leadership due to the macro and micro environmental shifts. Several characteristics, behaviours and leadership styles, as well as advice on leadership responses to crises, have been presented (see Figure 9.8), given the digital age and fast-paced environment we live in, focusing on the recent crisis of the COVID-19 pandemic.

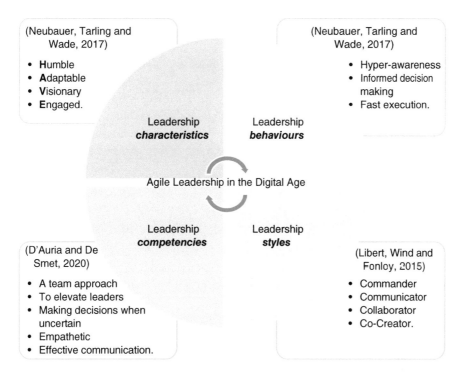

Figure 9.8   Agile leadership framework for the digital age

Given the digital age and the pandemic, now, more than ever, it is important for leadership to rethink their leadership style, be agile in their approach, taking on different leadership styles and combining approaches where appropriate for the situation. There is broad consensus that these are challenging times for leaders (Bennett and Lemoine, 2014a).

Decolonising leadership

An article by Cecilia, F. (2020), titled "E-leadership: The Implication of Digital transformation for Leadership in Organizations in Africa", examines the competencies of e-leadership to lead a digital transformation agenda of an organization in a highly and digitally competitive marketplace in Africa. This paper proposes that having effective e-leaders in an organisation would lead to adequate appropriation of digital technologies to digitally transform an organisation

Cecilia, F. (2020), "E-leadership: The Implication of Digital transformation for Leadership in Organizations in Africa.

The following journal article by De Boer, A.-L., Bothma, J. and Olwagen, J., titled "Library leadership: Innovative options for designing training programmes to build leadership competencies in the digital age" examines the role of leadership in the development of Library leaders in Africa, and suggest that they may not be fully equipped to deal with the demands and rigours of the digital age and its consumers (this article is still of relevance even though it is published in 2012).The authors argue that the thinking preferences of these library leaders could enable or detract from their readiness to develop the appropriate competencies in the digital age. Recommendations are made by the authors on how best to overcome this to prepare library leaders in Africa to deal with the requirements of the digital age consumer.

De Boer, A.-L., Bothma, J., & Olwagen, J. (2012). Library leadership : innovative options for designing training programmes to build leadership competencies in the digital age. *South African Journal of Libraries and Information Science, 78*(2). Retrieved December 13, 2021, from https://hdl.handle.net/10520/EJC133017

Reflective question

1. Now that you have read through the chapter on leadership in the digital age, what are the behaviours, competencies, attitudes, characteristics and skills you think you need to work on and develop to be a good leader in the digital era?

Student exercise

Imagine that you are a senior manager in a technology firm. What would your main priorities be as a leader? What kind of a working environment would you want to create?

Mind System Consulting Ltd (Hungary)

Mind System Consulting Ltd, a Hungarian IT consulting small and medium-sized enterprise (SME), established in 2004, used to operate in a large office, conducting regular project meetings offline. Internal and external communication occurred via email or telephone. The owners, responsible for centrally managing projects, kept an extensive table for tracking and scheduling projects and allocating assignments. They followed an intuitive type of leadership where fast decisions could overwrite priority.

Three areas posed challenges: ongoing HR problems, training and recruitment, and communication. The owners had to deal with an overwhelming number of emails and phone calls, resulting in ineffective communication. Employees were overloaded with work; tasks could not be completed due to a lack of assignment or assignment to the wrong employees. Projects, without proper workflows, were prolonged, or not completed on time, causing a loss to the company. The demand for an internal digital administration system arose to solve the tracking of workloads and projects, with employees demanding a home office option too.

By 2019, a digital tracking and task assignment system, 'TOTIS' (Today Ticket System), was developed for workflow management and employee administration. It solved HR and communication problems, resulting in more efficient management, improved performance and higher competitiveness.

During the COVID-19 lockdown, the cloud-based TOTIS enabled full home office working and ensured the continuity of business operations. The owners used 'task and progress' conference calls twice a day – but this communication option turned out to be ineffective. Ad hoc solutions forced the owners to think over their intuitive leadership style.

In 2020, a prioritising add-in for employees and a direct communication and password management add-in were developed. Consequently, the owners' active involvement was reduced while they could still monitor processes. A higher rate of digitalisation, the sudden shift to home and online office working and decentralised business operations brought in democratised leadership.

Leaders became more understanding, flexible and caring but were still able to motivate and inspire employees. They learnt administrative and operational skills, such as assisting colleagues with tasks and as system administrators could overwrite task assignments. Their human management skills improved, as they needed to pay more attention to the well-being of their employees and partners. In TOTIS,

(Continued)

both managers and colleagues work similarly. Clearing with partners is no longer debated – transparent accounting is fully accepted by the company and its partners – internal project workflows are developed and 'TOTIS' is fully accepted. The owners believe that this digitalisation has proved to be a success.

Questions

1. How did the TOTIS system support leadership?
2. What other leadership style could positively influence employee performance?

Key summary

- The *digital age* has emerged through a combination of new technologies, particularly computers and the internet.
- *Digitisation* refers to the conversion of data and documents into digital formats, and *digitalisation* is the adaptation of business processes to using digital technologies.
- Disruptive technologies are those technologies that have been able to 'disrupt' a market or an industry, offering opportunities for new products and services, new business models, and the transformation of business processes.
- Leaders need to be agile and aware of their environment, continually scanning and monitoring it to capitalise and exploit the potential opportunities available for competitive advantage and achieve ultimate success in the digital age.
- Digital technologies have contributed to the concept of globalisation which presents opportunities and threats for leadership and management, however globalisation should mean enabling cross-border business in an open market, allowing for the maximising of organisational benefits, without inflicting social damage or violating the rights of people from other cultures.
- There are several opportunities and challenges related to the digital age which include transformed work practices, ubiquitous access to information, knowledge management and intellectual capital, knowledge assets and knowledge-related processes.
- Leaders play a critical role in the management of transformation and change, and help prepare their organisation for change, inspiring their employees and helping them cope with rapid change.
- Digital innovations and the rapid pace of change have exacerbated the challenges leaders need to navigate to achieve and sustain competitive advantage.

- The four main characteristics of an agile leader are humility, adaptability, visionary, and vision and engagement. Key behaviours will help leaders navigate disruptive environments: hyper-awareness, informed decision making and fast execution.
- Leaders need: to have a team approach: empowering employees to search, find and implement solutions; to be able to elevate leaders: granting authority to make and implement decisions without having to gain approval; to make decisions when uncertain: it is important to pause to assess the situation and possible outcomes; to display empathy: to have empathy and acknowledge human tragedy; to have effective communication: to be open and give frequent updates.

Further reading

Dirani, K.M., Abadi, M., Alizadeh, A., Barhate, B., Garza, R.C., Gunasekara, N., Ibrahim, G. and Majzun, Z. (2020) 'Leadership competencies and the essential role of human resource development in times of crisis: a response to Covid-19 pandemic', *Human Resource Development International*, 23(4): 380–394.

Goran, J., LaBerge, L. and Srinivasan, R. (2017) 'Culture for a digital age', *McKinsey Quarterly*, 3: 56–67.

Hensellek, S. (2020) 'Digital leadership: a framework for successful leadership in the digital age', *Journal of Media Management and Entrepreneurship (JMME)*, 2(1): 55–69.

Jäckli, U. and Meier, C. (2020) 'Leadership in the digital age: its dimensions and actual state in Swiss companies', *International Journal of Management and Enterprise Development*, 19(4): 293–312.

Klus, M. and Müller, J. (2020) 'Identifying leadership skills required in the digital age', *CESifo Working Paper No. 8180*, https://papers.ssrn.com/sol3/papers.cfm?abstract_id=3564861 (accessed 14 December 2021).

Sarrazin, H. and Willmott, P. (2016) 'Adapting your board to the digital age', *McKinsey Quarterly*, 2016(3): 89–95.

10
DATAFICATION, SURVEILLANCE AND LEADERSHIP

Naveena Prakasam

Chapter objectives

The objectives of this chapter are:

- To explore **datafication** and **surveillance** in contemporary society.
- To examine the issues arising from datafication and surveillance against the wider context of leadership and power relations.
- To consider the implications of datafication and surveillance on issues of inclusion.

Introduction

We live in a datafied society. This means that our everyday interactions and activities can be translated into data that can be processed. Simply put, datafication is the conversion of phenomena into data points. For example, if you were to visit a website, then you leave behind data points that can be collected, analysed and interpreted in many ways. It is probably also likely that third parties get access to your data. We live in an age in which our everyday activities and interactions are monitored, and such monitoring extends to our personal as well as professional lives.

Consider Ron Swanson from the TV series *Parks and Recreation*. A self-proclaimed **libertarian**, after learning that he may be monitored by the government, he throws away his computer and other electronic devices. If you think about it, his fears about being monitored are not entirely misplaced because entities such as corporations or governments may be able to access individuals' data, which could lead to serious ramifications. For example, America's high-tech surveillance could track abortion seekers by analysing their digital footprints. One example of this includes a woman in Granger, Indiana who was convicted of feticide and neglect. In this instance, data from her iPad and cell phone were used as evidence by the prosecutor (Chowdhury, 2022). It is thus vital to consider the implications of living in a datafied society as this could enable extensive surveillance and monitoring.

This chapter begins by exploring what surveillance means, and its relevance and implications for leadership. We then explore various theories of surveillance and examine datafication and surveillance in the context of power relations. Finally, we review inclusion and surveillance, and the disproportionate impact of surveillance on racialised individuals.

Student exercise

Think about your most recent use of social media. Reflect on what this involved. What data did you share? With whom did you intend to share it? Who are the parties that you think had access?

The relevance of leadership

Before we explore the implications of surveillance and datafication on leadership, let us understand the connection between datafication and surveillance.

The conversion of phenomena into data is referred to as datafication or 'a modern technological trend turning many aspects of our life into computerized data' (Mayer-Schönberger and Cukier, 2013: 8). There is a 'self-evident relationship between data and people' (Van Dijck, 2014: 199) because individual behaviour can be predicted by the interpretation of aggregated data. Aggregate data refers to information that has been collected from multiple sources that are compiled into data summaries or reports for statistical data analysis, revealing insights and information (*Ed Glossary*, 2015).

In the context of the internet, users' online activities are converted into data points and kept in databases by service providers as well as public and private organisations, as online activities leave behind digital traces, which enable surveillance and commercial exploitation (Lomborg, Dencik and Moe, 2020). Hence, datafication and surveillance are connected because datafication enables surveillance. We will look at some surveillance theories in a subsequent section.

In this context, it is important to understand what big data means. 'Big data refers to the binding of advanced predictive tools with large data sets on human activity, with the aim of tracking, monitoring, analysing, and disseminating this information' (Boyd and Crawford, 2012; Lohr, 2012; Warner and Sloan, 2014, cited in Andrew and Baker, 2021: 566). There are three main sources of big data: organisational records, websites, and the physical movement of people. Data from organisational records might include 'economic transactions, contracts, or registrations with companies of governmental institutions' (Andrew and Baker, 2021: 566). The use of websites includes social media exchanges, browser searches, and e-commerce activities. Data pertaining to physical movement of people is collected through smartphones, surveillance cameras and satellites (Andrew and Baker, 2021).

Questions of leadership are significant to such issues pertaining to datafication. It is leaders that are in positions of power (see Chapter 7 for a discussion of power) and surveillance is largely carried out on those individuals who have less power. This presents a power asymmetry between subjects that are exposed to surveillance, and leaders in charge of organisations that carry out such surveillance. Let us examine one example that illustrates such power asymmetry.

Facebook came under immense scrutiny because of the Cambridge Analytica scandal that broke in 2018. Cambridge Analytica was a political consultancy that was hired by Donald Trump's 2016 election campaign team. The company was able to gain access to 50 million Facebook users' private data and claimed to be able to use the information to categorise different types of voters and influence their behaviour. It was Carole Cadwalladr's reporting in *The Guardian* and *The Observer* that led to the downfall of Cambridge Analytica. Cadwalladr worked with whistle-blower and former employee Christopher Wylie to unearth that Cambridge Analytica played a role in the 2016 US elections as well as the Brexit vote (Cadwalladr and Glendinning, 2018).

Whistle-blower Christopher Wylie revealed that the entire foundation of Cambridge Analytica was to target the 'inner demons' of millions of Facebook users by harvesting their data to build models that would facilitate this interference (Cadwalladr and Graham-Harrison, 2018). An app called 'thisisyourdigitallife' was developed by a Cambridge University academic, Aleksandr Kogan, through his company Global Science Research in collaboration with Cambridge Analytica. This app facilitated the data collection of hundreds of thousands of users that were paid to take a personality test and had agreed for their data to be collected for academic purposes. Importantly, the test also led to the collection of the test-takers' Facebook friends' data that led to a data pool of tens of millions, which was against Facebook's platform policy. The policy only permitted the collection of friends' data for improving the app experience and barred it from being sold for advertising purposes. More than two years after the data breach being initially reported, and upon *The Observer's* request for comments from Facebook, Facebook announced the suspension of Cambridge Analytica as well as Aleksandr Kogan from the platform (Cadwalladr and Graham-Harrison, 2018).

In 2019 Facebook was fined 5 billion dollars and in 2022, Washington DC's attorney general Karl Racine sued Mark Zuckerberg, co-founder of Facebook, for his role in allowing Cambridge Analytica to harvest the data of millions of people during the 2016 United States presidential elections (Rushe and Milmo, 2022).

The scandal and the aftermath have highlighted the power of corporations such as Facebook, given its continued growth in revenue and net income (*Statista*, 2022) despite the scandal. Moreover, empirical research suggests that not much has changed in terms of people's use of such social media platforms or the decisions to leave them. Despite the scandal revealing such a significant data breach, a qualitative study by Hinds, Williams and Joinson (2020) involving semi-structured interviews with individuals based at a UK university, showed the scandal did not result in people deleting their Facebook accounts and that people did not express much concern. They did not anxiously change their privacy settings due to the scandal's revelations about data breaches. In fact, these individuals considered themselves immune to the tailored advertisements, and the study also revealed that there was an absence of understanding of how **algorithms** work by harvesting personal data (Hinds et al., 2020).

Similarly, Brown (2020) found that while participants expressed privacy concerns over Facebook, none of them left Facebook, and they believed that participation in social media required a degree of exchange of personal data. Additionally, Afriat, Dvir-Gvirsman, Tsuriel and Ivan (2021) found in their qualitative study that young adults in Israel saw economic surveillance as innate to the digital world, and one needed to accept this if they wanted to take part in it.

Snowden and surveillance

Even before the Cambridge Analytica scandal, there was another event that had a large-scale impact on how we think about surveillance. It is important to discuss the revelations of whistle-blower Edward Snowden about mass surveillance conducted by the US National Security Agency (NSA) and the UK Government Communications Headquarters (GCHQ). Edward Snowden revealed the large-scale secret surveillance conducted by these agencies that he believed did more harm than good (Greenwald, 2013). Of most significance in these leaks was not the political or business espionage, but the large-scale monitoring of the everyday communications of ordinary citizens (Dencik and Cable, 2017). While mass surveillance is used in liberal democracies for national security reasons, these very actions run up against individuals' right to privacy. Given the extent to which people rely on digital communications, there is substantial potential for state intrusion into privacy through mass surveillance. The Snowden leaks in 2013 exemplify the complicated struggle between individuals' right to privacy on one hand, and security on the other (Bakir, 2021).

People's views on Snowden appeared to be dependent on where one was located. In the immediate aftermath of the leak, 51 per cent of Americans saw Snowden as a hero; 49 per cent saw him as a traitor threatening Western intelligence. In the UK, 60 per cent viewed it positively, and 67 per cent of Canadians also viewed him positively (Reid, 2013; Bauman, Bigo, Esteves et al., 2014). Dencik and Cable (2017) argue that despite the exposé of widespread data collection and monitoring of everyday communication platforms utilised by citizens, the public reaction in the United Kingdom as well as other parts of the world has been subdued. After collecting and analysing data from NGOs and smaller grassroots organisations across the UK, they introduced the notion of 'surveillance realism' (Dencik and Cable, 2017: 763). Surveillance realism is the result of control and lack of knowledge about how one's personal data might be used online, and refers to the simultaneous discomfort as well as normalisation of such surveillance characterised by 'widespread resignation, not consent to the status quo' (Dencik and Cable, 2017: 763). This highlights the complexity in which citizens are intertwined within systems of contemporary forms of surveillance.

Reflective question

1. Did you or would you change your social media use? Why or why not?

Surveillance theories

In simple terms, surveillance refers to watching a person, usually a suspected person or a prisoner for the purposes of control (*Oxford English Dictionary*, n.d., 2022). An increase of surveillance of persons and places in the second half of the century has led to a scholarly discipline known as 'surveillance studies', which is a multidisciplinary field encompassing accounts of surveillance in society (Galič, Timan and Koops,

2017: 10). In the following sections, we examine some popular theories of surveillance, which include Foucault and Bentham's approaches, Deleuze and the more recently popular surveillance capitalism put forth by Zuboff (2015).

Foucault and Bentham

One of the most widely known concepts associated with surveillance is Foucault's notion of **panopticism**. Panopticism is 'a type of power that is applied to individuals in the form of continuous individual supervision, in the form of control, punishment, and compensation, and in the form of correction, that is, the modelling and transforming of individuals in terms of certain norms' (Foucault, 2002: 70) where 'panoptic' refers to 'seeing everything, everyone, all the time' (Foucault, 2006: 52). Foucault used the context of the prison to theorise panopticism. However, Foucault's **panopticon** can be applied to other parts of society to understand and analyse power relations. The panopticon is active in many aspects of society, and the key thing to note is the hiddenness of these systems and the fact that they are ever present in daily life, which makes them more powerful. For instance, this can be seen in various institutions from schools to hospitals, and factories. When everyone can potentially be under surveillance at any time, this leads to individuals disciplining their own behaviours. Individuals will internalise control, morals and values, and in this way such a type of society becomes a disciplinary society. This is the key premise of Foucault's disciplinary power, which he explained using the panopticon.

While the panopticon has been popularised due to Foucault's panopticism, it was actually first put forth by Jeremy Bentham. Bentham in fact came up with four panopticons. The most well-known one, which was subsequently used by Foucault, and briefly explained earlier, is the 'prisoner-panopticon' which portrays a prison which is designed as a circular building, with an inspector at the central tower overseeing the activities of convicts in their cells (Galič et al., 2017: 11). The power lies with the inspector, as the architectural design of the panopticon creates an illusion of constant surveillance. The central tower is designed in a way that the prisoners can be seen at any time, but they are not able to see the one who watches them. This increases the disciplinary panoptic power of the inspector because the possibility of the inspector seeing the prisoners at any point creates discipline in the prison-panopticon. Therefore, in the prisoners' perception, 'the inspector is all-seeing, omniscient and omnipotent' (Galič et al., 2017: 12). However, Bentham's vision was to remove the need for watching at all within the panopticon as 'discipline would be internalised' (Galič et al., 2017: 12).

Galič et al. (2017) argue that Bentham's idea of the panopticon is different to Foucauldian conceptualisations. In order to understand the differences, it is important to explore the three lesser known types of panopticon: pauper-panopticon; chrestomatic-panopticon; and constitutional-panopticon. Pauper-panopticon, or industry house, is like Foucault's panopticism as it encompasses methods of control, albeit more complex than the prison-panopticon. The difference is that paupers are part of this voluntarily and can leave when they want to. This involves surveillance conducted by Guardian Elders through methods like book-keeping and other rules on heating and feeding. For instance, no pauper would be fed or could leave the panopticon until their share of work had been completed, so there are some forms of control.

Chrestomatic-panopticon is a school-based panopticon in which advanced pupils teach the less advanced. There are limits to the level of panoptic control here compared to the previous two panopticons, given that the students are only subjected to this whilst in school. Moreover, the class structures are not fixed, allowing for the change of categories and classes based on their age, achievement levels and subjects, leading to possible changes in specific forms of panoptic control (Brunon-Ernst, 2013, cited in Galic et al., 2017).

The fourth panopticon is the constitutional-panopticon, which has two main features. The first feature is that this has also been referred to as a reversed or inverted panopticon, because in this instance, instead of the few watching the many, the many watch the few. The citizens watch the governors who are observed through panoptic methods to prevent misrule. The second feature is like the chrestomatic-panopticon, in that the governors are not necessarily constantly visible, but only during their public duties. The governors can leave the citizens' gaze when they want some privacy. The architectural design for a constitutional-panopticon looks a bit different. The prime minister is at the centre of the building, and communication between the prime minister and his ministers is conducted through communication tubes, with each ministerial office being a thirteen-sided polygon with a public/private waiting room on each side for people to come and visit the ministers. The central inspection tower (as in the prison-panopticon) is a metaphor, rather than a real tower. This is because inspection is not central but dispersed, as many people ensure their rulers' good behaviour through publicity via newspapers. The newspaper as a tool plays an important role in criticising any misrule that might occur (Galič et al., 2017).

It can be observed that the panoptic characteristics reduce as we move towards the chrestomatic and constitutional panopticons. This is because despite the wider gaze made possible by the school-based and the constitutional panopticans, there are 'intentional limitations' (Galič et al., 2017: 15) placed on their panoptic power.

This is exemplified by the fact that the children are only being observed whilst they are in school, and the governors are only being watched whilst they are performing their public duties, with the gaze being reversed to oversee the rulers in the case of the constitutional-panopticon. The act of watching is hence not just negative, but also positive given that the panoptic gaze is reversed in the case of the constitutional panopticon. According to Brunon-Ernst (2013), it is these features that refer to Bentham's panoptic paradigm, which encompass 'architectural projects operating as a model for governing the behaviour of individuals and groups and the operations of social practices or institutions and having the potential to function in non-disciplinary environments' (Galič et al., 2017: 15).

Therefore, this means that the panopticon is not uniquely disciplinary (Foucault's disciplinary power) but in fact similar to another one of Foucault's concepts, which is 'governmentality' (Brunon-Ernst, 2013: 36). Governmentality refers to managing entire populations to regulate behaviour, as opposed to managing individual bodies. Foucault referred to governmentality as 'conduct of conduct' (Madsen, 2014: 814), which means that citizens are controlled in a subtle way through techniques that are empowering to them, such as 'self-esteem' (p. 814). As you may remember from Chapter 7, power is not only a repressive force, but can be a productive one. This happens by power manifesting itself in a positive way through the production of certain discourses that can be internalised by individuals, which can result in guiding the behaviour of these populations. Such form of control becomes more effectual as knowledge allows individuals to govern themselves. For example, consider 'self-esteem' which can be seen as a technology of the self which is effective through individuals governing themselves in order to be healthy so that doctors, police or judges don't have to (Madsen, 2014: 815), hence there is an economic imperative for the state in this. This is an example of **neoliberal governmentality**. The main premise of neoliberal governmentality is to aspire to a political arrangement which would ensure that the population is as wealthy as possible (Oksala, 2013). The example of the rise of psychology-related disciplines exemplifies such neoliberal governmentality. This is because of psychology's focus on 'measuring, controlling, manipulating the subject's desires and needs which fits in line with state's goals' and, by being a technology of expertise, can be seen as resulting in the professional status of such disciplines (Rose, 1996, 1999; Madsen, 2014: 815).

Deleuze and surveillance

Deleuze is seen as the founding father of post-panoptical literature. He moves away from panoptical thinking, and views discipline not as a goal or a 'driving force of governing' (Galic et al., 2017: 19) but as something found in the forms of control.

Instead of focusing on the disciplinary society like Foucault, Deleuze argues that the current system is a control society, which is governed by the corporation (Braatvedt, 2020). He argues that institutions like schools, hospitals and factories are becoming like corporations. As a result, instead of a long-term, stable and docile society, corporations focus on short-term goals for profit. This has happened due to the increase in globalisation and capitalism and these short-term goals are achieved by the means of constant monitoring of markets. Deleuze (1992) uses a metaphor of a carpenter as a coded figure in order to illustrate this view of the corporation. A carpenter cannot rely on having a steady trade, as his skills may no longer be needed due to changes in the markets. This notion of skills being useful on one day and useless the next is referred to as modulation (Deleuze, 1992: 2). This reflects the constant changes of systems of institutions. It is useful to note the differences to Foucault's panopticon. With Foucault's panopticon, while the power itself is less visible, the discipline is effective because it is visible. For instance, one would have to follow certain rules in particular institutions, and there might be visible penalties for not doing so. However, with Deleuze's notion, modulations happen in ways that are invisible to subjects/citizens because they take place in networks that are concealed from individuals.

For Deleuze, the surveillance is no longer about individuals, but about their representations; he refers to people as data-bodies. For instance, it is the consumers and their purchasing behaviour that are of significance. **Dividual** refers to the division of the individual into different parts, depicting a fragmentation of the individual. The idea is that individuals should not be viewed as 'uniform beings' (p. 20) but as entities with many different roles represented in many different data banks. Interestingly, Deleuze came up with this idea before the internet and computers were ubiquitous, and the issue of datafication is now more relevant than ever (Galic et al., 2017).

Surveillance capitalism

Zuboff (2015) put forth the idea of **surveillance capitalism**, a recent popular theory of surveillance. This refers to the economic imperative of extracting online users' data in order to better target customers. For example, if one were to use the Google search engine, the search query leads to collateral data such as a pattern of search terms. Such data can be harvested by machine intelligence to predict what products are likely to attract customers (Garrett, 2021). A connection can be drawn to Deleuze's theory, as the focus here is also on corporations having power and control.

The relevance of surveillance capitalism to leadership is that CEOs are the key players who benefit from the tenets of surveillance capitalism, as the initial few months of the COVID-19 pandemic show, with a surge in the wealth of leading surveillance capitalist CEOs (Garrett, 2021). The wealth of Amazon CEO Jeff Bezos, and Facebook

CEO Mark Zuckerberg increased by 25 billion dollars and 22 billion dollars respectively (*BBC News*, 2020, cited in Garrett, 2021).

Google is an example of a corporation that epitomises surveillance capitalism. Google's uniqueness is in its capability for 'hunting, capturing, and transforming surplus into predictions for accurate targeting' (Zuboff, 2019: 80; Garrett, 2021). Just like Facebook, Google can be perceived as a giant advertising platform.

Unfortunately, the **General Data Protection Regulations** (GDPR) that came into effect in 2018 do not safeguard people from the extraction of their behavioural data that characterises surveillance capitalism. This is pointed out by Andrew and Baker (2021) who highlight the tensions within the GDPR. While the GDPR has made progress in terms of protecting individual privacy, it does not sufficiently protect citizens from the surveillance risks, with the collection, analysis and trade of behavioural data. Drawing on Zuboff (2019), Andrew and Baker (2021) point out that behavioural data is treated as a free commodity, which is not governed by legal frameworks. Such behavioural data is completely decoupled from its subjects. While the GDPR was designed to protect individuals, its focus on individual privacy may be 'unintentionally providing data controllers with a legal mandate to pursue market surveillance practices as they attempt to avoid the costly constraints and procedures required by the regulation' (Andrew and Baker, 2021: 574). Such de-identification safeguards, intended to protect individuals' privacy, paradoxically may be facilitating the exchange of their behavioural data. This is because the GDPR, whilst focusing on whether data can be tied to a person, does not identify the issues relating to behavioural data (Andrew and Baker, 2021) and its subsequent use by large corporations. Therefore, such safeguarding measures can be seen as unintentionally furthering surveillance capitalism. It can be discerned from this discussion that there are complex power relations at play. The following section explores this in further detail.

Mini case study 10.1

Space surveillance

Elon Musk is a billionaire SpaceX CEO who is promising to deliver high-speed broadband to as many people as possible by launching satellites into orbit. Starlink, a less-known venture from Musk, and a division within SpaceX, intends on selling internet connections to anyone via private satellites. There are over 2000 operational satellites, however there will need to be at least 10,000 satellites for coverage over most of the globe. Currently, this is only available in some parts of the world including the United States, the United Kingdom, France, Canada and Germany, but in future the intention is to provide internet coverage in less accessible places (Crist, 2022).

Despite the intention of providing internet access to more people globally, concerns have been raised about the increase in satellites, potentially leading to increased surveillance, which would have implications for people's privacy. For instance, remote sensing is extremely valuable, and many businesses are going after it. Remote sensing refers to scanning the earth by satellite or high-flying aircraft for obtaining information. There is a danger that despite being helpful in times of disasters such as helping with the California wildfires, there may be an increase in human-based activity monitoring (Clifford, 2019).

In response to Starlink, and its potential national security concerns, Chinese military experts are developing ways to destroy Starlink satellites should they threaten national security, by advising surveillance systems to monitor Starlink satellites. However, Musk believes that more satellites can be launched than adversaries can destroy in a given time frame (Winfrey, 2022).

Musk's donation to Starlink in the aftermath of Russia's invasion of Ukraine had increased China's alertness of the usefulness of low-earth orbit satellites to strengthen communication during times of war. There are also concerns about a possible scenario in which Musk's satellites could be deployed to conduct surveillance on China (White and Olcott, 2022).

While Musk's satellites aided collapsed Ukrainian cities to keep a link with Kyiv and the rest of the world, China have increased suspicions due to data and security implications (While and Olcott, 2022).

Questions

1. What are the implications of the space satellites providing internet connections in our already datafied society?
2. What inclusion issues can you think of?

Social relations, power and datafication

It is important to move beyond focusing on data and to consider the power relations and other social dimensions that relate to such data collection and its consequences. We have already explored surveillance theories that help shed light on control and power, for instance through panopticism, disciplinary power, neoliberal governmentality and Deleuze's emphasis on the corporation being the driving source. Dencik (2019) points out that there is a trend which seeks to reduce everything to mere data, including social identities, without recognising the power relations produced by these activities. Dencik (2019) argues that it is important to move beyond focusing solely on data and algorithms, or the institutions that produce such data, and instead we should combine the concerns arising from both of them in order to gain an insight into the underlying social mechanisms such as organisational limitations, the ideology underpinning the organisation and resource allocation in relation to the agents within this context. A key thing to note here is that adopting such an approach emphasises the power relations underpinning the use of data.

To explain further, it is important to analyse the social dimensions of data in response to the prevalent functionalist approaches that dominate such understandings and to suggest situating data in a manner which might reveal the relationship of such data to dominant agendas (Dencik, 2019). For instance, in the example of Cambridge Analytica and Facebook discussed earlier in the chapter, we saw how the data were collected to be used as part of an election campaign, clearly revealing dominant agendas behind such actions. It was therefore the combination of the data itself, as well as the social and power-laden context in which it was collected, that sheds light on the complete picture, and the implications of datafication and surveillance. In this way, datafication can be seen as being continuously constructed. This necessitates a paradigm shift in examining issues pertaining to datafication, which involves a move from functionalist approaches to constructionist methods.

Dencik (2019) argues that a practice approach to datafication is important because data systems have the power to implicitly define agents or entities in a relevant realm. This can be explained by examining the case of predictive policing, which aims to create automated forms of decision making by subtracting the human element using data. However, such data practices should be viewed within the context of organisational and institutional practices. There is a hierarchy that data practices are part of, and they have consequences for how other practices may be defined. For example, there are two forms of anchoring practices within institutional contexts that shed light on how data systems are situated: integration and outsourcing. Integration involves the use of big data analysis along with other types of intelligence-gathering practices by the police. Outsourcing, the other form of anchoring practice, involves systems that are not developed within the organisation, but predominantly from private companies, leading to a focus on marketing-driven discourses. Marketing-driven categories then get shifted into policing in this way. There is hence a dependence on pre-existing external knowledge that sits outside of data analytics. It is important to look at data practices linked to other social practices instead of only focusing on the data, as this reveals how data processes are situated in power relations, and other agendas. Focusing on these practices would then help us examine questions of how data relates to social justice (Dencik, 2019).

Reproductive rights and surveillance

On 24 June 2022, the *Roe v. Wade* verdict was overturned by the Supreme Court in America. The *Roe v. Wade* ruling was a landmark verdict in 1973, which made it a US constitutional right for women to have abortions. This came about when a woman with a pseudonym 'Jane Roe' challenged the criminal abortion laws in Texas in 1969. Henry Wade, the district attorney, defended the anti-abortion laws. Hence, this came to be known as *Roe v. Wade*. At the time, this case was rejected, and Jane Roe was forced to give birth, despite having been made pregnant due to rape. However, her appeal in 1973 reached the US Supreme Court, and after the hearing of her case alongside another woman from Georgia, 'the court justices ruled that governments lacked the power to prohibit abortions' (*BBC News*, 2022). This led to women's right to terminate a pregnancy being protected under the US constitution. However, as Alavi (2021) argues, applying Foucault's concept of governmentality to this context indicates that this type of choice generates conditions for governance, and reproductive choice can be said to be determined by the capacity to be able to govern oneself. This is because a woman's decision regarding the pregnancy might be subject to moral assessment, and evaluated to the degree to which she was choosing responsibly (Alavi, 2021). Moreover, neoliberal practices of governing enable our own subjectivity (Oksala, 2013). Individuals are responsible for their own choices, as well as a number of problems under neoliberal governmentality. There are disproportionate implications for Black women due to this as the regulation of individuals is largely based on white supremacist and patriarchal norms (Alavi, 2021).

Since the 1973 ruling, several changes, notably the one with most impact, *Planned Parenthood v. Casey* in 1992, saw further restrictions across states regarding abortions, such as states being able to restrict them without medical reasons even in the first trimester (*BBC News*, 2022).

The overturning of the *Roe v. Wade* judgement in June 2022 might mean that several states in the United States might see the introduction of more abortion restrictions, with huge consequences for women's reproductive rights and privacy.

It is important to consider the implications of this verdict for the surveillance of women, as women's phones could be tracked (Bushwick, 2022). Databrokers or private companies that collect large amounts of data through apps on people's phones could be asked by law enforcement to provide personal health information that could potentially be used to prosecute someone (Bushwick, 2022).

Questions

1. Apply any one theory of surveillance to this situation in order to analyse it.
2. What underlying issues of inclusion can you stop? How are surveillance and inclusion connected?

Surveillance, datafication and inclusion

Surveillance has had a disproportionate effect on marginalised groups (Clarke, Parsell and Lata, 2021). In this section, we begin by discussing the socio-historical context pertaining to Māori people's surveillance, and then examine the concerns of inclusion more broadly.

Cormack and Kukutai (2022) investigate how Māori people were regulated and managed by surveillance in the context of **coloniality**. Coloniality refers to 'Eurocentred colonial structures of power' (Mignolo, 2011, cited in Jimenez-Luque, 2021: 155). According to Mignolo (2011), this Eurocentric perspective has shaped a worldview that the Eurocentered social order is superior to the rest of the world, which has created an asymmetrical distribution of power by forming a hierarchy between races, cultures and identities (Jimenez-Luque, 2021).

In particular, Cormack and Kukutai (2022) shed light on data colonialism and the way, as part of the larger Indigenous Data Sovereignty movements, Māori are resisting this form of data colonialism by asserting rights to **Māori Data Sovereignty** to unsettle the existing data relations. Māori Data Sovereignty holds that Māori data should be subject to Māori governance (Taiuru, 2022), which would facilitate the advancement of self-determination. The main assumption of Indigenous self-determination is about Indigenous people having a fundamental right 'to be in control of their destinies and to create their own political and legal organisations' (Toki, 2017, cited in Cormack and Kukutai, 2022: 123). Therefore, Indigenous jurisdiction over Indigenous data becomes part of their fundamental right to self-determination.

Historically, many Māori tribes in Aotearoa, New Zealand saw census-taking with suspicion. This is because in settler colonial societies, race-based classification practices went beyond creating divisions between coloniser and colonised by creating hierarchies of difference within native people based on cultural closeness to Europeans. The growth of a 'Māori-European half-caste population' was monitored closely and seen as an indicator of 'racial amalgamation', relative to 'Māori full bloods' (Cormack and Kukutai, 2022: 124). Such categorisation of Indigenous people into racial categories represents asymmetric power relations, which also constructed the coloniser as a 'knowing subject' and Indigenous peoples as 'knowable objects' (Quijano, 2007, cited in Cormack and Kukutai, 2022: 125). The surveillance resulted in framing Indigenous people's deviance as a biological threat. Sophisticated forms of control were developed through documentation and surveillance (Berda, 2013: 628). This enabled state intervention where it was needed. This can be seen as being linked to biopolitics, which is a Foucauldian term that refers to state interventions in managing entire populations. There was a breaching of human rights by positioning some groups as worthy of protection, and others as potentially dangerous.

There is an extensive use of 'big data and linked government datasets' (Cormack and Kukutai, 2022: 122). These are used for various purposes, which also include predictions for future behaviours and outcomes. Aotearoa, New Zealand, is seen as leading in terms of data innovation. An example of this is the Integrated Data Infrastructure or IDI which connects census data for the whole population to several survey datasets. Despite safety mechanisms such as the de-identification of data in IDI, concerns have been raised, because such data linkage could allow forms of surveillance that are not based on individuals' informed consent.

Innovative data-linking technologies have resulted in being able to track individuals and families. Surveillance also involves the use of predictive analytics, which allows for the prevention of future risks. In fact, governments have increasingly started using algorithms for decision making with the motivation to reduce costs. Unfortunately, such decisions made by algorithms are not without bias, as human beings input their beliefs, values as well as biases into these algorithms. Māori are disproportionately negatively affected by predictive analytics due to their historic over-surveillance by various institutions which has meant that more data about Māori are likely to be included in government databases. For instance, 52 per cent of the prison population in 2020 were Māori so there is a danger in that the use of actuarial risk models taking a predictive risk approach would disproportionately affect Māori (Te Uepu HIpai i te Ora, 2019; Cormack and Kukutai, 2022).

It is important to recognise that Māori have 'collective data rights' (Cormack and Kukutai, 2022: 133), which include not being known by the state or constructed as racialised and colonial subjects. Unfortunately, the Māori people are part of data aggregations, and regulatory frameworks do little to address privacy concerns. Indigenous Data Sovereignty compels us to embed collective rights and interests and relational understandings of data into contemporary data practices. Resistance efforts are aimed at disrupting colonial data practices. These resistance efforts include holding to account the government agencies responsible for these issues. In response, government initiatives have been developed while structural inequities remain (Cormack and Kukutai, 2022).

In the age of big data, and Artificial Intelligence, it is important that those designing algorithms must be actively anti-racist. For instance, Owens and Walker (2020) point out that health algorithms have been shown to reinforce racial inequities by prioritising white patients over patients of colour, which calls for active anti-racist interventions while designing such algorithms. It is important that these anti-racist interventions extend to all spheres that utilise Artificial Intelligence algorithms.

Conclusion

This chapter focused on datafication and surveillance, and their widespread implications for contemporary society. Given that our everyday personal as well as professional lives are so intertwined with online communication channels, it is necessary to consider the consequences that large-scale surveillance can have. The chapter began by exploring the relationship between datafication and surveillance and reviewed its relevance to leadership, by discussing contemporary issues such as the Cambridge Analytica scandal and the Snowden leaks. Theories of surveillance, starting with Foucault and Bentham, then Deleuze and Zuboff's (2015) surveillance capitalism were explored. We discussed the importance of taking into consideration power and social relations alongside issues of datafication, as purely functionalist interpretations of datafication do not give us the complete picture. Finally, we considered the disproportionate impact of data practices on historically marginalised groups such as the Māori, by exploring the perils of data colonialism.

Decolonising leadership

Stavig, L. I. (2022) 'Unwittingly agreed: Fujimori, neoliberal governmentality, and the inclusive exclusion of Indigenous women'. *Latin American and Caribbean Ethnic Studies*, 17(1): 34–57.

This paper examines the unwitting role of the Reproductive and Sexual Rights assemblage, a group of feminists in Peru, in the violation of Indigenous women's rights by downplaying the scale of their forced sterilisations in the 1990s.

Key summary

- Datafication refers to the conversion of phenomena into data.
- Surveillance refers to watching a person, usually a suspected person or a prisoner, for the purposes of control.
- The relationship between datafication and surveillance is that surveillance in contemporary societies happens via datafication.
- Surveillance is related to leadership because the CEOs of large companies have been responsible for making decisions about harvesting the data of millions of people.

- Surveillance theories include Bentham's and Foucault's notion of the panopticon, as well as neoliberal governmentality.
- Surveillance capitalism is the economic imperative of extracting online users' data in order to better target customers.
- Surveillance has a disproportionately negative impact on marginalised individuals such as Indigenous communities due to coloniality.

Further reading

Darmody, A. and Zwick, D. (2020) 'Manipulate to empower: Hyper-relevance and the contradictions of marketing in the age of surveillance capitalism'. *Big Data & Society*, 7(1): 2053951720904112.

Mishra, P. and Suresh, Y. (2021) 'Datafied body projects in India: Femtech and the rise of reproductive surveillance in the digital era'. *Asian Journal of Women's Studies*, 27(4): 597–606.

Sparkes, M. (2022) 'How can we prevent AI from being racist, sexist and offensive?'. *New Scientist*, 254(3392): 14.

11
GENDER, RACE AND LEADERSHIP

Naveena Prakasam

Chapter objectives

The objectives of this chapter are:

- To critically examine gender and race in relation to leadership.
- To critically analyse the importance of considering intersectional perspectives and being more inclusive about leadership.
- To review postcolonial and decolonial approaches to leadership.

Introduction

As of 2021, only 8.2 per cent percent of CEOs were women in the Fortune 500 list (Fortune, 2021). If we consider race and ethnicity, 92.6 per cent of the CEOs in the Fortune 500 list are white (Zweigenhaft, 2021). These statistics are just some of the reasons for investigating gender and race in relation to leadership, but as we will learn in further detail in this chapter, discrimination on the grounds of one's gender and race, as well as other dimensions of difference which result in inequalities, is quite complex.

While the traditionally masculine nature of leadership has been critiqued by several scholars (for example, see Acker, 1990, 1998, 2006; Calás and Smircich, 1992; Fournier and Kelemen, 2001; Liu, Cutcher and Grant, 2015), matters of **intersectionality** (explained in further detail in a subsequent section) and race remain relatively underexplored, as much work on gender and leadership has only captured white women's experiences (Ospina and Foldy, 2009). This is now changing with an increase in studies that attempt to remedy the current state of affairs. For instance, Rosette, Koval and Livingston (2016) point out that the gendered and racial group of the target (the leader) influences perceptions of leadership potential, and the degree to which they would encounter backlash because of their non-stereotypical behaviours. This suggests that race matters for women leaders, and that both gender and race need to be considered whilst we conceptualise notions of leadership.

Even though there has been an increase in leadership research that focuses on women's lived experiences (for example, Brescoll, 2016; Zheng, Kark and Meister, 2018), and scholarship that has taken into account both the gender and race of women leaders focusing on intersectional experiences (Jean-Marie, Williams and Sherman, 2009; Ospina and Foldy, 2009; Liu, Cutcher and Grant, 2015; Gause, 2021), there have been recent calls to re-radicalise intersectionality in organisation studies (Liu, 2018). Moreover, the domination of whiteness in the leading discourses of leadership continues to be questioned (Liu and Baker, 2016).

This chapter explores the importance of examining gender and race in relation to leadership to shed light on racial and gender inequality in conceptualisations of leadership. This chapter will also be examining postcolonial and decolonial approaches to leadership, which are strongly connected to conceptualisations of race, and emphasise moving away from Western-centred theorising of leadership. This chapter will review further contemporary studies that examine multiple categories of difference (such as race, gender and migration status to name a few), shedding light on intersectionality in depth. However, before considering gender and race in relation to leadership, it would be useful to situate multiple categories of difference (intersectionality) in practice through a mini case study. The following mini case study demonstrates that even when leadership is explored outside of the corporate sector, for instance in the context of social activism, ethnic minorities' role in fighting for climate justice are often ignored in the media, this particularly being the case for female ethnic minorities.

Mini case study 11.1

Power, racism and climate activism

People of colour are often erased from the discussion around activism surrounding climate change. While most people have heard of Greta Thunberg due to extensive media attention, there are several people of colour whose achievements in climate activism are often ignored. Vanessa Nakate was cropped out of group photos that also featured the well-known climate activist, Greta Thunberg. As a result of the outcry from supporters over the incident, the media agency that cropped out her photo apologised and claimed no ill intent. Despite this apology, Nakate remained sceptical of the intentions of the media agency. Due to this experience of marginalisation, Nakate said she felt a responsibility to amplify the voices of climate activists of colour (Evelyn, 2020). Climate researchers have argued that such erasure of marginalised voices in climate science narratives are not new (Evelyn, 2020). Rafaely and Barnes' (2020) study of Nakate's accusation of racism in the media shows that her accusation was undermined by journalists where they challenged her claims of representing Africa and attempted to sow doubt about whether the incident was really racist. The journalists tried to attribute this to her emotionality which rendered her irrational. In addition to a racialised element, there is a gendered one, which can be observed due to the reference to Nakate's emotionality (Barnes, 2021).

Barnes (2021) sheds light on the triple bind that is Nakate being African, female and young, and highlights how youth activists such as Nakate can negotiate their agency in relation to these binds. Despite the oppressive structures that try to undermine her (such as the media agency), her activism has continued to become stronger. The incident of cropping out her photo led to Nakate's use of her personal, temporal and political agency in order to create a space for African, female youth climate activism. Temporal agency in this situation refers to her being able to move between the different temporal (time) dimensions. For instance, she can move between the past, present and future. This can be explained by an example of a journalist suggesting a historical position that indicates that female youth activists are emotional, which would be a link with the past dimension. In response to this, a female climate activist could dismantle this criticism in the present by suggesting the importance of genuineness, emotional connection, and authenticity as essential qualities of climate activism. In future, climate activists could then argue for the need for more authenticity and genuineness in climate activism.

Questions

1. What are the multiple forms of discrimination that you can identify? How are they interrelated?
2. Can you identify where the power lies in this situation with Vanessa Nakate?

Gender and leadership

There are several reasons why there are fewer women in powerful leadership positions. Existing normative attitudes about gender that result in prescribed gender roles is one reason. The other aspect that has already been touched on in Chapter 2, is that male rationality is considered the norm, that is, white heterosexual men are seen as ideal leaders which automatically excludes women and ethnic minorities from being considered ideal leaders. From a trait perspective (see Chapter 2), I highlighted the importance of questioning gendered and racialised assumptions of leadership. In this section, we examine how male rationality has been the norm (Acker, 2006), and how organisational structures and processes tend to be implicitly masculine. As Fournier and Kelemen (2001) argue, the organisational cultures, structures and everyday practices in organisations that constitute the 'ideal employee' (Fournier and Kelemen, 2001: 268) align more closely to the cultural images of masculinity as opposed to femininity. This is also the case for the 'ideal manager' where ideal managers are presented as rational and **disembodied** figures (Fournier and Kelemen, 2001: 268). By disembodied, they mean that these notions of ideal managers are separate from their bodies, which separates the rationality associated with being ideal managers from the people they are. Such processes and practices in organisations that implicitly exclude women have made it harder for women to thrive in organisations because 'femininity is associated with embodiment, emotions and sexuality' (Fournier and Kelemen, 2001: 268) and is seen as being out of place in rational organisations. This has resulted in femininity being inferior to rationality, which is quintessentially seen as masculine. Unfortunately, it is the masculine voice that oversees the worlds of communication and economy (Burrell, 1992; Harding, 2003; Ford, 2005), which has resulted in inequalities.

Some of the issues within the organisational and leadership discourses can be traced back to earlier writings from philosophy which have come to shape organisational theorising. The male body was often the reference point for many of these writings, which automatically led to the exclusion of the female body and women. Irigaray (1985) uses the term **phallogocentrism**, which is defined as a strong Western tradition that consigns the feminine to a position of material, matter or object against which the masculine defines itself. Through Irigaray's (1985) work, Fotaki, Metcalfe and Harding (2014) conclude that the feminine has been met with disapproval in organisational discourse. Irigaray deconstructs male philosophers' theories (such as Freud and Plato) by engaging in dialogue with them, and often uses their own paradoxical words in deconstructing these theories. Through her work, Irigaray shows that the female or feminine in dominant discourse is shown as 'less than masculinity' and 'distorted' due to the binary classification of sex and gender (Fotaki et al., 2014: 1245). Such a classification has come about through the 'male logic of sameness', which refers to masculine and feminine subjects being caught up in the masculine production of truth, which implicitly depicts the feminine as inferior (Fotaki et al., 2014). The next section focuses on **feminist phenomenology** in order to gain a deeper understanding of the gendered nature of leadership.

Feminist phenomenology and leadership

This section focuses on feminist phenomenology. Here, I draw on Gardiner's paper 'Hannah and her sisters: Theorizing gender and leadership through the lens of feminist phenomenology' in which she discusses the contributions of four feminist thinkers who have contributed to phenomenology by challenging dominant masculine discourses. Gardiner (2018) argues that these perspectives contribute towards thinking about leadership relationally.

Gardiner (2018) proposes that feminist phenomenology can strengthen the field of gender and leadership by adding conceptual richness to it. Hence, Gardiner (2018) draws on the work of four influential feminist thinkers, Hannah Arendt, Simone De Beauvoir, Sarah Ahmed and Iris Marion Young. However, to get a comprehensive understanding of each of these thinkers' work and how they can advance leadership, it is first important to examine what phenomenology entails.

Phenomenology is attributed to Edmund Husserl and continued to be developed by Western philosophers such as Heidegger, Derrida and Sartre. Phenomenology is concerned with how we experience the world. To understand this, Husserl focused on consciousness, and the point of view of the first person. This would mean that the phenomenologist would study their own experience by living through that experience (Gallagher, 2012). The way in which we come to share a similar understanding of the world is of primary interest to phenomenologists. Furthermore, phenomenology is concerned with our distorted sense of the world. For instance, Husserl argued that genuine insight could be achieved if we were to strip back our preconceptions (Gallagher, 2021). The methodological approach that Husserl adopted included researchers describing things themselves as this would encourage researchers to suspend any bias in relation to the phenomena to allow for the phenomena to appear as they are. However, Heidegger (1962) argued that it was not possible for researchers to suspend their biases and prejudices completely, as some of these prejudices remain unknown to us. Heidegger (1962) viewed phenomenological enquiry as a way for researchers to be able to grasp the meaning of a phenomenon intuitively (Gardiner, 2018).

Student exercise

Ask your peer what their experience of leading a project was like. Make notes about this. Now, based on these notes, try to make sense of your peer's experience of leading that project.

As Gardiner (2018) argues, such study of phenomena, and of conscious experience from the first-person point of view, is relevant to leadership studies, as it focuses on the relational component of leadership (see Chapter 5 for more on relational leadership). For example, Ladkin (2013) argues that phenomenology can help researchers further their understanding of the relational space that exists between leaders and employees. It is therefore necessary to connect leadership actions with everyday concerns.

Feminist phenomenology can be seen as a field that is concerned with questions relating to gendered experiences and sexual difference. As Gardiner (2018) explains, many feminist phenomenologists are interested in investigating the effects of ideology, power and language on lived experience. Importantly, it is not just what is said, but also what is left unspoken that is of interest to phenomenologists.

Drawing on Hannah Arendt, Gardiner (2018) argues that Arendt's ideas are pertinent to leadership because they emphasise the importance of adopting a relational approach to leadership and highlight collective freedom (see Chapter 5 for more about relational leadership). Arendt argues that the Western tradition since Plato has prescribed egotistical understandings of leadership, with an emphasis on the individual leader more than collective action. She argues that it is such individual-centric, egotistical interpretations of leaders, which emphasise self-mastery, that might lead to authoritarian and totalitarian leadership. She offers a way out by suggesting that every individual's uniqueness unfolds in a 'web of relationships' (Arendt, 1958: 183), which underscores the importance of taking on a relational approach to leadership.

Simone De Beauvoir, a French feminist theorist, in her book *The Second Sex*, focused on women's lived experiences. Beauvoir's primary argument was that the male was always the reference point, and that the woman was considered the other. Gardiner (2018) points out that Beauvoir also offers insights into racism as well as discussing oppressive social systems, which include both racism and sexism. Beauvoir's premise was that we must consider concrete conditions that create oppression, and not just consider freedom in an abstract way. It is only by doing so that we would be able to move beyond the oppressive social systems of racism and sexism. As a result, when we consider contemporary leadership, women leaders have to work hard to obtain people's confidence, due to notions of leadership traditionally being associated with masculinity (Gardiner, 2018).

Iris Marion Young was a feminist and social activist who was influenced by Beauvoir. She argued that male phenomenologists paid little attention to women's lived experience. Young particularly critiques Mearleau-Ponty (1962, 2007) for using the male body as the norm. Young argues that as women encounter the world differently, they experience 'inhibited intentionality' as opposed to 'open intentionality' (Gardiner, 2018: 299). **Intentionality** refers to how each conscious act is oriented towards an object. This is because women's bodies are often objectified by others as well as themselves. Merleau-Ponty (1962) talks about the connection between body and space, and argues that it is through this connection that we obtain knowledge of this world. Such knowledge is embodied as it is unique to us due to our own specific experiences. However, Young argues that there is a contradiction that women experience, as there are limitations imposed upon them which affect their ability to transcend their situation. This results in the tension and failure of some women not being able to put forth their whole bodies whilst engaging in physical tasks. This is relevant to leadership because gendered embodiment influences leadership potential due to women's suspicion of their bodies, which may lead to their doubting of abilities. While Young acknowledges that there may be generational differences with regard to women's doubting of their abilities – for instance, she notes that her daughter's generation had opportunities and confidence in their abilities that Young's generation lacked – she argues that the connection between the materiality of gendered embodiment and inequality continues to be relevant. Young's work on feminist phenomenology helps us understand how socio-structural processes 'enable certain bodies to flourish whilst constraining others' (Gardiner, 2018: 299). For example, we could consider organisational structures and processes that might constrain certain groups of individuals such as women and other minorities from flourishing. Scholars have argued that organisational structures both directly and indirectly contribute to the reproduction of inequality (Ray, 2019; Amis, Mair and Munir, 2020).

Sarah Ahmed focuses on queer phenomenology. Ahmed draws on the ideas of Husserl to argue that when we focus on a particular object, 'it is not just how we orientate ourselves to the object that matters' (Gardiner, 2018: 300), but also how other objects fade into the background. Ahmed uses the metaphor of Husserl's writing desk to highlight the unequal nature of gender roles. While he is focused on the writing desk, he imagines what he cannot see, his children playing in the summerhouse. However, what Husserl does not imagine, like other male philosophers, is the kitchen and the domestic labour that goes into it, and the others that enable his needs and wants. This allows him to focus on his writing and be comfortable whilst doing so. Ahmed compares this experience with that of a female Black feminist writer, Audre Lorde, who describes being disrupted by her children every time she attempts to 'orientate' herself to her writing. As she is constantly interrupted by her children, her focus is diverted away from her writing and onto the children's lives. What this suggests is that for many women, what matters is often at odds with one another. When we apply this to women taking on leadership roles, Gardiner (2018) suggests that the challenges of balancing both personal and career priorities might inhibit women's eagerness to take on leadership roles. What we can learn from this is that given that many women still must take on increased domestic responsibility due to prescribed gender roles, this affects what they are able to achieve in the public sphere. While we may note exceptions to this, for instance Marissa Mayer only took two weeks maternity leave whilst taking on the role of CEO for Yahoo, this was met with intense debate and criticism. Perhaps the privilege afforded to her at the time was not afforded to others.

Some people may feel marginalised in certain surroundings due to structural inequalities such as sexism and racism, where they feel silenced by their surroundings as well as silencing themselves, which creates a double dilemma. In this section, we have reviewed the contributions of feminist phenomenologists, which helps us think more deeply about gendered experiences in leadership.

Race and leadership

This section provides an analysis of race and leadership by drawing on Ospina and Foldy's (2009) review of three different categories of research: first, the effects of race-ethnicity on perceptions of leadership; second, how perceptions of race-ethnicity impact leader enactment; and third, how leaders/followers engage with race-ethnicity.

Ospina and Foldy (2009) provide an in-depth critical review of race and ethnicity in the leadership literature. The first category in their review of research on race-ethnicity and leadership focused on the effects of race-ethnicity on perceptions of leadership. This category of research takes an individual orientation, in that both race and leadership are viewed as individual characteristics that are impacted by power inequities. Here, the target, that is, the leader, is the passive recipient of the perceptions of subordinates or followers. In this category of research, race-ethnicity was viewed as an independent variable. An independent variable in the statistical sense means that the perceptions of leadership depend on the race-ethnicity of leaders or followers. The dependent variables here are the perceptions of leadership. Some researchers have investigated how the race-ethnicity of followers or the leader impact the perceptions of leadership, whether positively or negatively. For example, an early study by Bartol, Evans and Stith (1978) found that Black managers were rated more negatively compared to white managers. Several studies seemed to indicate that race was a constraint that needed to be managed. This is because the research was carried out in contexts in which white people were the dominant group. Ospina and Foldy argue that this type of research implies that racial identities as well as contexts have an impact on 'racially-based power inequities' (p. 879). For instance, Rosette, Leonardelli and Phillips (2008) argue that 'being white'

(Ospina and Foldy, 2009: 880) is a part of the prototype of an ideal business leader, meaning that white people are more likely to be seen as leaders, indicating the presence of negative racial bias.

However, a recent study by Ubaka, Lu and Gutirrez (2022) replicated the study by Rosette et al. (2008) and found that leadership perceptions have now become more racially inclusive. Ubaka et al. (2022) highlight the broader trends in American society such as the Obama presidency, as well as Harris' vice presidency, which indicate a change in leadership perceptions. They found that despite the ongoing phenomenon of implicit racial bias, this appears to be moving in a positive direction given the weakening of the standard of white leadership. However, in practice, large disparities in leadership continue to remain, with only 6.8 per cent of Fortune 500 US corporations' CEOs being non-white (Ubaka et al., 2022).

The second category of studies that Ospina and Foldy (2009) discuss focuses on how the race-ethnicity of leaders influence leader enactment, that is, the manner in which leaders enact their leadership. An example of this would be how race-ethnicity might impact leadership styles. While race-ethnicity is an independent variable in this case as well, this stream of research focuses more on the leaders as opposed to followers' assessments of the leaders. This category of leadership includes how individuals construct leadership due to race-ethnicity. For example, a study by Pitts (2005) found that school superintendents of colour were less empowering to their staff than white superintendents, even though it was hypothesised that the opposite would be true. This is likely because superintendents of colour felt more vulnerable considering there were such few superintendents of colour.

Another example of a study that is relevant to this category is to do with leadership understandings in the Chinese context. Ma and Tsui (2015) conducted a qualitative study by interviewing 15 Chinese leaders to discuss three Chinese philosophies, **Daoism**, **Confucianism** and **Legalism**. Daoism is complicated to define and is associated with a mystery that cannot be explained. An in-depth review of Daoism is beyond the scope of this textbook, but based on Ma and Tsui's (2015) interpretation of Daoism in relation to leadership, it involves dialectics, which means the balancing of opposites. It is about recognising that sometimes no action is better than wasting time on unnecessary actions. Daoism also relates to selflessness and promotes the view that having no personal agenda is essential to leadership effectiveness. Confucianism is about virtuous leadership. 'Examples of Confucian virtues include unselfishness, a desire to pursue noble causes, loyalty to relationships, full engagement in core business tasks, empathy with others' feelings, and willingness to work tirelessly for the common good, to treat family members well, and to serve the king loyally' (Ma and Tsui, 2015: 16). Serving the king loyally can also be construed as serving the government loyally. Legalism comes from Han Fei and is about establishing and maintaining detailed policies and systems in the preservation of power. In terms of contemporary leadership, transactional elements of leadership and initiating structure can be linked to Legalism. Ma and Tsui (2015) argue that all of these traditional philosophies are interwoven with contemporary leadership, and they found that all of the 15 leaders they interviewed had elements of all of these philosophies. It is essential to move away from Western philosophies and obtain an understanding of diverse philosophies that might shed a different light on leadership.

The third category of leadership studies that focuses on race-ethnicity that Ospina and Foldy (2009) came up with relates to how leaders/followers engage with race-ethnicity. In this case, race-ethnicity is not viewed as an individual characteristic but is seen as having both personal and collective meaning, which is dependent on the context within which leadership is produced. Within this category, Ospina and Foldy (2009) further categorise these studies into two sub-categories. The first sub-category takes a social identity approach from a social psychological point of view. Examples of studies that fit within this sub-category are those that focus on shared and collective identities to induce followers to move beyond their own personal interests and perform beyond expectations (see Lord and Brown, 2003). The second sub-category is about looking into leaders' responses to the external environment in which systemic inequities occur due to the influence of race-ethnicity. The difference between the two sub-categories is the emphasis on power dynamics. The latter places emphasis on power dynamics in their analysis. An example of this is a study by Gause (2020). Gause (2020) adopted a narrative inquiry method to obtain an insight into the lived experiences of women of colour who were leading community colleges. The study sheds light on the resilience of these women, as well as their motivations and intentions in transforming the community college presidency. This study provides an insight into the way these women navigate through the hurdles posed by the institution and emphasise the power dynamics at play within these institutions.

Another example of a study that highlights how leadership has traditionally heroicised whiteness is one by Liu and Baker (2016). In their study, they examine media representations of white Australian leaders and highlight how depictions of images in which white Australian leaders are shown as mastering aboriginal culture demonstrate white people as protectors and stewards of Aboriginal traditions. Such media portrayals highlight the implicit manner in which the invisible dominance of whiteness is perpetuated. This study again highlights power dynamics, and shows how the dominance of whiteness in portrayals of leadership is almost hidden.

An example of a style of leadership that links to the idea of straight whiteness as the norm is authentic leadership (see Chapter 4). This is because authentic leadership is linked to the notion of presenting one's true self. Authentic leadership being portrayed in a way that is consistent with the norms of straight white men, creates difficulties for minorities to be able to present their true self (Ladkin, 2021). The same issues that we encounter in notions of ideal leadership or the ideal manager can be applied to authentic leadership because the conceptualisation of authentic leadership is not inclusive of all people. It is also worth remembering that leadership can be viewed as a social construction (see Chapter 4). What this implies for authentic leadership is that leaders who are perceived by followers as being more similar to them are more likely to be seen as authentic. Hence this could pose problems for minorities if they are different to the group that they are leading. Ladkin (2021) explains this problem further by drawing on the concept of 'double-consciousness'. Double-consciousness is a term that African American scholar W.E.B. DuBois came up with, and describes how African Americans were only able to experience their own self-consciousness through the eyes of the other. This therefore creates a problem for anyone wanting to act authentically because there may not be one true self. What this means is that African Americans may not experience 'one identity' or 'one true self' (Ladkin, 2021: 397).

Ray (2019) argues that racial inequalities are hidden in structures at the micro, meso and institutional levels, evidenced by empirical studies in these categories. Examples of this at the micro level include stereotypes and in-group favouritism. At a meso or organisational level, examples include wage differentials and racialised tracking, and at the macro or institutional level, examples include racialised laws, and state racial categorisation. Ray particularly points to how organisational structures themselves are racialised. He argues that the notion that organisational structures, hierarchies and processes are race-neutral must be abandoned. Instead of questioning whether discrimination exists, scholars must start with the assumption that organisational norms include 'discrimination, racial sorting and an unequal distribution of resources' (Ray, 2019: 46). Therefore, intersectional approaches to the understanding of systemic inequalities are essential to consider if we want leadership to be more inclusive. Intersectionality is discussed in detail in the following section.

Reflective question

1. If you were a human resource manager at an organisation, what steps would you take to tackle organisational-level racial inequalities?

Intersectionality and leadership

While intersectionality stems from Black feminism (Combahee River Collective, 1977/1995; Davis, 1981; hooks, 1989; Collins, 1990; Crenshaw, 1991), it has currently become a tool for examining multiple intersecting identities (Czarniawska and Sevon, 2008; Johansson and Śliwa, 2014).

As Rodriguez, Holvino, Fletcher and Nkomo (2016) point out, there are two approaches to intersectionality within organisation studies. The first approach examines the subjective experiences of marginalised individuals with multiple categories of difference where individuals have membership of more than one group. The second approach looks at how these inequalities are embedded in systemic dimensions of power. Addressing the latter, Netto, Noon and Hudson (2020) conducted 31 interviews with female and male migrants employed in five large organisations in England and Scotland. They adopted a feminist approach in analysing the data and found that patriarchy in the home interacts with racism within the workplace. They found that multiple constraints intersect with the gendered and racialised identity work that go on to create barriers for progression. Furthermore, migrants as a group do not have the same access to diverse resources. Therefore, it is important to recognise structural factors through policy actions. The findings of Netto et al. (2020) have implications for leadership, as barriers to career progression would inevitably prevent individuals from rising to senior leadership positions. Another study that examines intersectional experiences shows a complex picture and blurred lines between privilege and disadvantage – Hwang and Beauregard (2022) examine East Asian women's life in the United Kingdom and shed light on their context-specific and fluid experiences, showing that the line between privilege and disadvantage may not be so rigid. They used semi-structured interviews to investigate these experiences. An interesting finding of their research was the existence of ambiguous privilege among these women, exemplified by positive perceptions due to their East Asian communication styles which could benefit them. However, there is also a danger in that positive perceptions such as seeing East Asian women as hardworking, in the long term could result in forcing them to comply with white understandings of how they should behave.

Intersectionality has not been limited to studying the experiences of women. For instance, Fernando, Reveley and Learmonth (2020) reconceptualise Goffman's (1963) concepts of covering and accenting in intersectionality by adopting an auto-ethnographic approach, focused on the experiences of a male, non-white 'immigrant' business scholar, adding to the growing and important field of research about race, and foreign workers' experiences. Covering involves hiding an outsider identity by consciously changing an impression one is making. Accenting is the opposite of covering, in that it is about the accentuation of a particular identity element (Fernando et al., 2020). Particularly, Fernando et al. (2020) discuss intersectionality in relation to a multiple-identified individual – however, not with respect to gender, but the author's intersecting identities of being a non-white immigrant, as well as being a Christian. The individual in question changed their name to a Christian-Italian name exemplifying 'covering'. Mario's identity work encompasses covering his Sinhalese identity and accenting his Christianity – done in order not to be labelled as an oppressor or to be seen as a refugee who fled war. The complexity of intersectional identity work is highlighted by Fernando et al. (2020) wherein, on one hand accenting and covering may successfully be used as strategies to overcome 'oppressive structures' (p. 779), by making a distinction between the 'discreditable' and 'potentially discreditable' (p. 779). On the other hand, when this fails to challenge identity misunderstandings, the oppressive structures may be intensified – leading to the challenges of being a minoritised, racialised and immigrant subject.

Adopting an intersectional approach, Jean-Marie, Williams and Sherman (2009) investigate Black women leaders' constructions of leadership by applying **critical race theory** and an Afrocentric epistemological framework. Critical race theory originated in the field of critical legal studies and is associated with the writings of Derrick Bell in the 1960s (Morris, 2001; Bernal, 2002, cited in Jean-Marie et al., 2009). Critical race theory is about racism, discrimination and the subordination of racialised individuals. This approach uses storytelling to name one's own reality and considers the intersection of gender, race and class. The authors used narrative inquiry in order to gain an insight into the participants' life stories. The participants, who are now in senior leadership positions in academia (such as dean, vice chancellor etc.), were all children of the civil rights movement, so they recounted their experiences of being marginalised as they were growing up. Studies such as this provide us with a deeper understanding of intersectionality, by focusing on the lived experiences of Black women leaders. The study showed that race, class and gender are all markers of power which reinforce forms of oppression. The narratives of these women reveal that their leadership practices involve collaborative leadership in order to work towards the best interest of students. By analysing the narratives of Black women's leadership, it will be possible to develop educational opportunities for the 'disenfranchised' (Jean-Marie et al., 2009: 577).

Diversity policies

A *Financial Times* article by Liebig (2021) discusses the importance of bearing in mind how diversity policies sometimes benefit those who are already privileged. For instance, an OECD (2020) study of HR professionals shows that in the US, the positive effect of affirmative action has been strongest for white women, and there was much less impact on Black women, Black men, or Hispanics. In this case, the affirmative action involved setting targets for women, disabled people, ethnic minorities, and migrants amid one in 10 companies. While Jarvis Thomson (2013) points out that affirmative action programmes are justified due to Black employees in the US receiving privileges commensurate with privileges reserved for white males in the past, despite such initiatives, white people, through their higher status throughout these decades, have been able to benefit from a higher level of confidence.

Socio-economic disadvantage stands out the most, especially considering that income inequalities were exacerbated during the pandemic. Nonetheless, socio-economic background was an issue before the pandemic. Despite this, Liebig (2021) points out that socio-economic background is rarely considered in corporate diversity efforts and it is limited to the categories discussed above.

According to the same OECD (2020) study, policies that support ethnic minorities without paying attention to their socio-economic status tend to favour those who are socio-economically better off as fewer than half of the OECD countries contain anti-discrimination legislation that includes socio-economic status. Similarly, with gender, Bertrand, Black, Jensen and Lleras-Muney (2019) found that in Norway, gender quotas had no impact on the advancement of women at lower levels in Norway, which suggests that having female members on boards does not change opportunities for women working in the firm.

While socio-economic disadvantage is most definitely a factor that must be considered, scholars have pointed to the historic inequalities that necessitate diversity measures. An interesting perspective is offered by an anonymous letter in the *Journal of Management Inquiry* in which an academic and woman of colour notes her experience in the academy. Her success is often implicitly attributed merely to affirmative action in the US, and not her 'merit', praise of which only seems to be reserved for white male academics. Such negative experiences of marginalised individuals due to negative attitudes to affirmative action, pose problems.

Do certain characteristics make it easier to gain socio-economic advantage? Perhaps moving away entirely from diversity measures on race and gender is not the best course of action.

Questions

1. How can the understanding of intersectionality help organisations navigate the issues around socioeconomic disadvantage?
2. In what ways can diverse leadership in boards spill over to other levels in the organisation?

Decolonial and postcolonial approaches

Both **postcolonialism** and **decolonial theory** 'contest the world order established by European empires' (Bhambra, 2014: 119). Challenging dominant conceptual frameworks is central to postcolonial studies. According to Bhambra, postcolonial studies should disrupt Western discourses and transform these narratives. Decolonial approaches, too, are about disrupting Western-dominated discourses of theory. As Bhambra (2014) highlights, while postcolonialism came about because of the work of diasporic scholars from the Middle East and South Asia, and refer to those specific geographical contexts and their connections to Western imperialism, decoloniality came out of the work of South American scholars and refers to those specific contexts. There is also a difference in focus between the two regarding the time periods. Postcolonialism refers to the nineteenth and twentieth centuries, whereas decoloniality focuses on periods when Europeans conquered the lands which then came to be known as the Americas. Scholars of postcolonialism and decoloniality focus on challenging Western-dominant discourses, and these have largely been applied to the field of management and organisation studies.

In terms of the application of these approaches to leadership studies, it would be useful to focus on an empirical qualitative study on decolonial leadership. Jimenez-Luque (2021) proposes the construct of decolonial leadership by conducting a multi-method qualitative study in the context of a Native American organisation. This Native American organisation specialised in providing health services to the Native American community by focusing on Indigenous and holistic approaches to hospitality. Decolonial leadership can be defined as a type of leadership that highlights the emancipatory processes undertaken by an organisation which aims to decolonise society. Emancipatory processes refer to setting free from the control of the dominant Western narratives of leadership. For instance, transformational leadership is a very individual-centric style of leadership (see Chapters 3 and 4 for a detailed overview of charismatic-transformational leadership), whereas decolonial leadership is about collective action. Such collective action in this context involves challenging the accounts that are imposed by the dominant Eurocentric social order. By doing so, the organisation was able to gain back control of their reality from their own cultural perspectives. Jimenez-Luque (2021) found that safe spaces and platforms are important for decolonial processes of leadership to develop, which moves away from mainstream leadership approaches that offer a limited view of leaders that are centred on individual leaders.

Another contemporary study that focuses on non-mainstream leadership by non-dominant groups is one that draws on both intersectionality and postcolonialism. Raman (2020) conducted an ethnographic study in which he applied intersectionality to postcolonial organisation studies in studying the protests carried out by Dalit women at tea plantations in India. The study highlights gender, **caste** and class, and reveals the process through which women self-organised against the powerful. Raman (2020) points to a critique of postcolonial organisation studies that most management research, including critical management research, has been Eurocentric (Prasad, 2012). This idea is shared by postcolonial theory and represents an 'epistemic position' from the Global South. Raman's work addresses the issue of the unspeakability and unrepresentability of **subalterns**. The term subaltern was coined by Antonio Gramsci within postcolonial studies to refer to social groups that were excluded from the hierarchy of power of an imperial colony (Ludden, 2002). Through this study, Raman (2020) found that, first, Dalit women could speak for themselves; second, these women were self-organising, moving away from dominant organisational forms. This is an example of 'self-organising by the mis-organised refusing to comply with the traditional Marxist idea that workers are to be represented instead of representing themselves' (Raman, 2020: 282). Finally, these women challenged the hegemony of the state and trade unions by becoming conscious of their own acts of resistance.

Hence, both Jimenez-Luque (2021) and Raman's (2020) research sheds light on how collective action can challenge the dominance of the social order. These studies highlight how leadership can occur in non-traditional contexts where the power does not lie with the individual leaders but where symbolic power is generated through solidarity and collaboration by the marginalised. This challenges the prevailing power dynamics where the marginalised have less power. Both these examples emphasise the importance of moving away from an individual-centric theorising of leadership.

Conclusion

This chapter began with a case study that focused on intersectionality in the context of climate change activism, where the implicit censuring of faces that were not considered mainstream by the media points to how it is more challenging for individuals that are battling against multiple dimensions of difference. However, we saw how Nakate used her agency to challenge these implicit forces. The chapter focused on gender and leadership by examining how masculinity has always been the norm, which rendered organisational processes, structures and spaces as male. To explore this further, Gardiner's (2018) writings on four women feminist phenomenologists were explored. These ideas emphasised how the lived experiences of women are affected by masculine norms. I discussed the implications for leadership studies that emphasised more relational forms of leadership. We then explored race and leadership by examining three categories of leadership research as characterised by Ospina and Foldy (2009). We explored more contemporary studies of leadership that relates to race, which highlight the challenges experienced by racialised individuals and challenges the power structures that favour whiteness. My discussion of intersectionality by exploring Black women's lived experiences, demonstrates how their multiple categories of difference (being women and being Black) interact with power structures that are both implicit and explicit. The second case study examined the complexity of intersectionality by forcing learners to consider socio-economic disadvantage. Finally, we explored decolonial and postcolonial approaches to leadership by examining two contemporary studies of leadership in non-Western contexts.

Decolonising leadership

Johnson, D. E., Parsons, M. and Fisher, K. (2021) 'Indigenous climate change adaptation: New directions for emerging scholarship', *Environment and Planning E: Nature and Space*, 5(0): 25148486?11022450.

This paper is about decolonising and reframing climate change adaptation in line with Indigenous lived experiences.

Key summary

- Leadership has been considered a masculine and white construct, where attributes related to good leadership often corresponded to masculine rationality, automatically excluding women and minorities.
- Multiple dimensions of difference such as gender and race lead to heightened inequalities, which is why intersectional approaches to examining leadership are extremely important.

- Feminist phenomenology helps shed light on the importance of adopting a relational view of leadership.
- There are different categories of research within race-ethnicity and leadership. These include: how race-ethnicity influences perceptions of leadership; how race-ethnicity influences how leaders enact their leadership (for example, leadership styles); and how leaders/followers engage with race-ethnicity. The last category also takes into account power dynamics.
- Critical race theory is about the discrimination and subordination of racialised individuals and uses storytelling as an approach to gain insight into the experiences of marginalised individuals.
- Experiences of Black women leaders demonstrate how they have had to navigate through oppressive structures in order to overcome barriers to then go on to hold powerful leadership positions.
- Postcolonial and decolonial approaches to leadership challenge the Western dominant social order. In the context of leadership theorising, they offer alternative ways of conceptualising leadership by moving away from individual-centric theorising and embracing collective action.

Further reading

Roberson, Q. and Perry, J. L. (2021) 'Inclusive leadership in thought and action: A thematic analysis'. *Group & Organization Management*: 10596011211013161.

Smith, A. N., Watkins, M. B., Ladge, J. J., et al. (2019) 'Making the invisible visible: Paradoxical effects of intersectional invisibility on the career experiences of executive Black women'. *Academy of Management Journal*, 62(6): 1705–1734.

Spiller, C., Evans, M., Schuyler, K. G. and Watson, L. W. (2021) 'What silence can teach us about race and leadership'. *Leadership*, 17(1): 81–98.

12
CONCLUSION

Naveena Prakasam

Intentions

The intention of this textbook was to offer a diverse, inclusive and critical approach to leadership. This involved engaging with various theories and perspectives of leadership, starting with traditional individual-centric trait-focused approaches to leadership styles, social constructions of leadership, and a relational approach to leadership. Topics such as power, ethics, gender, race and intersectionality were examined in the context of contemporary practice, and the digital age and the implications of the surveillance-laden context we inhabit were explicitly explored. Throughout the book, readers were exposed to critical questions about the mainstream theorising of leadership and to diverse approaches moving beyond hegemonic discourses, which are accorded to 'white, cis-gender, heterosexual, elite class and able-bodied men' (Liu, 2021: 127).

The theories of leadership were critically reviewed against the contemporary contexts that we inhabit, through examples and mini case studies. Several case studies in this book focus on non-Western and/or diverse individuals and contexts. For example, issues relating to contemporary surveillance practices and the management of the COVID-19 pandemic were explored in relation to their implications for the marginalisation of certain groups of individuals as well as macro contextual power relations between the Global North and Global South, which will hopefully allow readers to critically review extant leadership knowledges in relation to pressing contemporary issues.

Addressing the need to decolonise the curriculum, through the decolonising leadership feature in every chapter, the book has pointed learners to additional readings that challenge dominant Western perspectives of leadership. This was done through providing examples of publications that focus on non-Western perspectives/contexts, those that adopt postcolonial or decolonial approaches to leadership and/or those that focus on inclusion, by explicitly highlighting the experiences of marginalised individuals. This has been embedded throughout the book.

Personal reflections and lessons

As editor, through the process of writing several chapters, and reading insightful chapters from the contributors, I have been able to gain valuable insights about leadership and explore further questions about the field. Writing this book required reviewing several leadership scholars' work, and also involved reviewing scholarship from beyond mainstream leadership disciplines such as surveillance studies. This was one of the main premises of this book – to offer a diverse perspective. Below, I outline some key lessons learnt, and end with some future concerns.

Lesson one: There is not one thing called leadership

I started with the notion that leadership is difficult to pin down, and I end with the same thought. This was pointed out in Chapter 1 in which I argued that there are several definitions of leadership. While I personally find Smircich and Morgan's (1982) definition particularly helpful, there are various other definitions that are insightful. We have also explored various perspectives of the phenomenon from leader-centred approaches to relational perspectives and focused on power and race. We have seen that Indigenous approaches to leadership are markedly different to traditionally Western notions as they emphasise the relational and collective elements of leadership and adopt a relational ontology (see Chapter 5). Hence, if I were to be asked to define leadership, then my answer would be that it is not possible to define it in narrow terms, but that it is useful to recognise the different approaches to leadership.

Lesson two: Power is central to leadership

As mentioned in lesson one, Smircich and Morgan's definition takes into account the underlying power dynamics of leadership by emphasising the framing of reality. I provide the definition here again: 'Leadership is realised in the process whereby one or more individuals succeed in attempting to frame and define the reality of others' (Smircich and Morgan, 1982: 258). Many critical scholars highlight the importance of power. Here I do not just refer to power within individuals but to the complex interplay of various entities from corporations, states and markets to individual subjects. It is difficult to be optimistic about leadership with the cost-of-living crisis engulfing the world, wars being fought in Europe, and the disastrous impact on the environment that has been the result of profit-driven decision making. At an organisational level, individuals in leadership positions can be said to have more power, however power is everywhere, and is embedded in structures, processes and interactions.

Lesson three: Diverse and inclusive perspectives are more important than ever

We have seen that traditional trait-focused approaches to leadership, by not taking into account tacit assumptions about traits, had contributed to leadership being exclusionary to those who did not fit the white, masculine and Western characteristics of what it takes to be a leader. Even though critical perspectives of leadership challenge such individual-centric notions, critical theorising of leadership also needs to be more inclusive. While critical diversity scholars have made an invaluable contribution to the field, we need more scholarship in leadership that engages with issues of gender, race, and colonial effects on the knowledge of leadership in order to redeem leadership (Liu, 2021). Not all critical theorising of leadership considers the fundamental matters of inclusion and diversity, and there is a need for all scholars, including critical scholars, to explicitly engage with these issues in order to create inclusive knowledges. The mini case study in Chapter 10 examined the *Roe v. Wade* verdict in relation to surveillance, which has huge ramifications for the reproductive rights of women but will likely continue to have a disproportionate effect on women of colour due to the double marginalisation that they face.

Current and future trends

It is important to consider climate change and environmental sustainability in relation to leadership. This is a really important issue that is afflicting humankind. Interestingly, it was recently revealed that Big Oil companies were aware of the environmental damage they have been doing since the 1950s (Franta, 2021). Exxon and Shell's internal reports suggested that they knew about the catastrophic effects of burning fossil fuels, but they did not do anything to stop it. In fact, in the late 1980s, Exxon and other oil companies came together through global effort to dispute climate science, block fossil fuel controls, and keep their products flowing. These powerful companies created the Global Climate Coalition in 1989, which, despite sounding like a pro-environmental group, in fact worked towards creating doubt in people's minds about the effects of climate change. They actively blocked clean energy legislation throughout the 1990s. While things have changed now, in that energy companies do not completely deny the effects of burning fossil fuels on the environment, they still do little in terms of investing in clean energy (Franta, 2021).

Pressing issues such as this need to be considered through the lens of leadership and power. Thinking about leadership differently and collectively is more important than ever, where individualist understandings of leadership only focus on furthering one's own interests, and there is an urgent need to move beyond such tendencies.

However, it is important to resist the actions of such powerful companies in an inclusive way. For instance, we saw through our case study on climate activism in Chapter 11 that people of colour are frequently left out of media recognition, despite their contributions. It is hence imperative to be inclusive in such resistance initiatives. It is important that we remember that Wangari Maathai was the first African woman to win a Nobel prize for sustainable development.

GLOSSARY

Agency   refers to masculinity in the context of trait-based leadership studies.

Algorithm   an algorithm is a set of instructions to be followed and used for problem-solving.

Anti-colonialism   can be seen as the epistemology of the colonised, that resists colonialism.

Anti-leadership   a stream within critical leadership studies, is built on the premise that leadership is 'beyond redemption'.

Authenticity   refers to being what one professes to be in simple terms. Philosophically, it is a complex term which has roots in existentialism.

Axiom   an axiom is a statement accepted as true.

Big data   refers to the application of predictive tools on large data sets based on human activity in order to track, monitor and analyse this information.

Brexit   refers to the withdrawal of the United Kingdom from the European Union.

Caste   refers to a social category, which is a result of social stratification through occupation and ritual status in a hierarchy.

Celtic postcolonialism   is a field of study that borrows from postcolonialism to analyse and understand Celtic nations with very different histories.

Charismatic-transformational leadership   refers to both charismatic and transformational leadership, and due to the overlap between the two styles, it is referred to in conjunction.

Collective other   the collective other refers to social groups that organisational decision-making members may not have direct interactions with but that have an impact on through their decisions.

Collective self   the collective self emerges from being part of a group such as an organisation, or a community.

Coloniality   refers to structures of power that have promoted a worldview that the Eurocentred social order is superior to the rest of the world, creating a power asymmetry through forming a hierarchy between races, cultures and identities.

Communion   refers to feminine traits in the context of trait-based leadership studies.

Confucianism   is a Chinese philosophy based on the teachings of Confucius.

Corporate-led cultural globalisation   looks at how multinational corporations influence culture.

Crisis   refers to a difficult time during which a significant decision must be made.

Critical leadership studies (CLS)   considers how power relations shape leadership understandings.

Critical race theory   is an epistemological framework developed by Derrick Bell about racism, discrimination, and the subordination of racialised individuals.

Daoism   is a Chinese philosophy that emphasises harmony and selflessness, and the idea that sometimes no action is required.

Dark triad   refers to three personality traits – narcissism, Machiavellianism and psychopathy.

Datafication   refers to the conversion of phenomenon into data.

Decolonial theory   is a framework originating in Latin America, which rejects a Eurocentred supremacy of the social order.

Deconstruction   is a form of analysis that French philosopher Derrida came up with. This type of analysis is used to examine texts.

Definitional consensus   refers to having a single agreed definition.

De-naturalisation   is a process by which we seek to challenge ideas which have become taken for granted as the natural way of thinking or acting within a particular society.

Diachronic approach   the diachronic approach refers to the social construction of empathy towards social groups that are not within the immediate social and interactional context.

Dialectical analysis   refers to a dialogue and analysis between two opposing points of view.

Digital age   the digital age refers to the start of the time period that saw the introduction of computers and widespread use of the internet.

Digitalisation   is the adaptation of business processes to using digital technologies.

Digitisation   refers to the conversion of data and documents etc. into digital formats.

Discursive leadership   is an approach to leadership that focuses on talk and interaction.

Disembodied   refers to being separated from the body.

Disruptive technologies   refer to innovations that change the way in which businesses operate by offering new opportunities.

Dividual   is a term introduced by Delueze, which refers to the division of the individual into different parts, depicting a fragmentation of the individual.

Dramaturgical analysis   is a type of analysis, adopting a symbolic interactionist approach, which uses theatre as a metaphor.

Empathic leadership   empathic leadership approaches stem from a relational ontological perspective to offer a social constructionist view of empathy in leadership.

Empowerment refers to the extent to which people have authority to make decisions.

Entity perspective the entity perspective focuses on individual cognitions and perceptions as they engage in relationships.

Entrepreneurial refers to a business attempt characterised by risk and individual initiative.

Entrepreneurial orientation is determined in organisations by measuring the objective output of entrepreneurial activity and infers an organisational bias towards (or against) entrepreneurial behaviour as a result.

Expressive harmonious collectives mean that there is a tendency within leadership studies which favours collective work over rupturing power where leadership is portrayed as seeking dialogue and harmony.

Expressive leadering refers to the commitment to collective work in the self-expression of leadership which emphasises an overly positive view of leadership.

Feminist phenomenology can be seen as a field that is concerned with questions relating to gendered experiences and sexual difference by investigating the effects of ideology, power and language on lived experience.

Followership approach refers to an approach to followers which focuses on how followers view their own behaviour.

Framing comes from Erving Goffman's frame analysis. It refers to controlling the meaning of the message that is presented.

Functionalism is a paradigm that relates to scientific method and uses quantifiable measures.

General Data Protection Regulations (GDPR) the GDPR is a European Union law on privacy and data protection with the primary aim of enhancing individual control and rights over their personal data.

Globalisation broadly refers to the growing interconnectedness of people, businesses, economies and cultures.

Governmentality is a Foucauldian term which refers to managing entire populations to regulate behaviour, as opposed to managing individual bodies.

Great Man Theory refers to a manner of understanding leadership based on traits and characteristics that a few 'great men' possessed.

Hard HRM is a strategy designed to harness human capital to the benefit of the firm.

Heteronormative describes the ideology that there are two opposing genders that are the same as assigned sex.

Hofstede's cultural dimensions is a framework developed by Geert Hofstede to understand how different cultures around the world impact organisations.

Human relations movement the human relations movement was based on the notion that happier workers would be more productive workers.

Implicit followership theories can be defined as the individual assumptions people have about the traits and behaviours of followers.

Implicit leadership theories (ILTs) are unconscious mental representations of leaders that followers have which help them distinguish leaders from non-leaders.

Intellectual capital is the value associated with an organisation's intangible resources.

Intentionality refers to how each conscious act is oriented towards an object in the context of phenomenology.

Interpretivism is a paradigm that emphasises interpreting means through social interactions.

Intersectionality is a term that stems from Black feminism that focuses on considering multiple intersecting categories of difference and how they impact oppression.

Intrapreneurial refers to an individual within an organisation responsible for coming up with innovative ideas.

Knowledge management broadly refers to the processes through which an organisation gathers, shares and analyses knowledge.

Leader effectiveness is the extent to which one performs well in the role of a leader.

Leader emergence refers to the extent to which an individual is recognised as a leader in a group.

Leader-member exchange (LMX) theory is about the dyadic relationship between two people (the leader and follower) as they interact with one another.

Leadership style refers to manifestations or constructions of leader behaviour patterns and characteristics.

Legalism is a Chinese philosophy that comes from Han Fei and is about establishing and maintaining detailed policies and systems in the preservation of power.

Libertarian an individual ascribing to a political ideology that maximises autonomy and political freedom and minimises government's so-called violation of individual freedoms.

Machiavellianism is the philosophy of Niccolò Machiavelli. It is also a personality trait that refers to being manipulative and callous and is part of the dark triad.

Māori are an Indigenous group of Polynesian people in New Zealand.

Māori Data Sovereignty is the idea that Māori data should be subject to Māori governance, which would facilitate the advancement of self-determination.

Marxist characterises the philosophy named after Karl Marx and focuses on the effects of capitalism.

Meta-analysis is a statistical analysis which combines the results of multiple scientific studies. In this case, the scientific studies include studies about leadership.

Narcissism refers to the extent to which individuals have exaggerated views of their own self-worth. It is one of the personality traits which is part of the dark triad.

Naturalisation can be regarded as the process by which value-based choices come to be widely accepted and unchallenged (in other words, seen as natural).

Neo-bureaucratic organisation is a hybrid organisation that presents a combination of market and bureaucracy, centralised and decentralised control.

Neo-colonialism is the idea that the State, in theory, may be independent from colonial rule, but such a State's economic system and political policies are still affected by outside interests.

Neoliberal governmentality refers to the aspiration of a political arrangement which would ensure that the population is as wealthy as possible by controlling populations in a subtle way through certain discourses that can be internalised by individuals, which can result in guiding the behaviour of these populations.

Neo Marxist is the philosophy adapted from Marx to apply to contemporary problems relating to the global economy.

Normalisation is a process by which identities are constructed through organisational practices that absorb individuals into their logic and strategic aims.

Panopticism is a theory introduced by Michel Foucault that refers to a power applied to individuals through individual supervision by controlling, punishing, compensating and transforming individuals in line with certain types of norms.

Panopticon is a circular architectural design that was initially proposed by Jeremy Bentham which consists of a central inspection tower from which the inspector could observe the prison cells around them. This is designed in a way that the inspector could observe the prisoners at any point, but they may not be aware of exactly when they are being observed.

Paradigm refers to approaches or a set of assumptions that researchers have.

Performativity is about using forms of knowledge to maximise efficiency and enhance performance.

Phallogocentrism is defined as a strong Western tradition that consigns the feminine to a position of material, matter or object against which the masculine defines itself.

Phenomenology refers to a philosophical approach that focuses on direct experience and consciousness.

Postcolonialism   refers to the field of study by diasporic scholars from the Middle East and South Asia in the aftermath of Western colonialism which disrupts Western discourses by examining the impact of the exploitation of colonised people.

Postmodernism   is a philosophy that rejects the idea of a universal objective truth.

Post-structuralism   refers to an intellectual movement or a school of thought which provided a critical response to structuralism, and highlighted the instability of meanings.

Proactive work behaviours   can be defined as individuals' proactive efforts in order to improve their work and organisation.

Prozac leadership   is used as a metaphor to refer to the excessive positivity associated with leaders and followers in contemporary organisations.

Reflexivity   refers to being aware of and reflecting on how the researchers and the methods these researchers use play a role in the construction or production of leadership phenomena.

Relational leadership theory   is an overarching leadership framework that focuses on social influence processes.

Relational ontology   refers to understanding social experience as intersubjective at the philosophical level.

Relational perspective   sees organisations and individuals as ongoing multiple constructions made in the processes themselves.

Relational self   the relational self develops from the role of the self in relationship with significant others. The self is entangled in relationships, as self-worth comes from the satisfaction of the other person in the relationship.

Roe v. Wade   was a landmark ruling in 1973, which made it a US constitutional right for women to have abortions.

Romance of leadership   is a theory put forth by James Meindl, which refers to a tendency of exaggerating leaders' contributions and treating leadership as causal and explanatory.

Romanticism   refers to a term that was used in the early nineteenth century in order to describe a movement in art and literature which emphasised the expression of personal feelings.

Second wave feminism   refers to feminist activity which took place between the 1960s and 1980s in the United States and then spread to the rest of the Western world. The movement was aimed at increasing equality for women and went beyond voting rights and property rights, including issues such as sexuality, reproductive rights, workplace and the family.

Self-efficacy   refers to our views about our own ability to complete a particular task.

Self-regulation   is a process through which authentic leaders can align their values with their intentions and actions.

Social constructionism   is the idea that meanings and knowledges are socially constructed.

Soft HRM   is a system of people management that enhances the work experience of the employees and is beneficial to them in order to generate conditions for greater levels of organisational commitment.

Strategic HRM   is an approach to HRM that focuses on the long-term goals of an organisation.

Subaltern   refers to a social group that was excluded from the hierarchy of power of an imperial colony.

Surveillance   refers to watching a person, usually a suspected person or a prisoner, for the purposes of control.

Surveillance capitalism   refers to the economic imperative of extracting online users' data in order to better target customers.

Synchronic approach   the synchronic approach, within the social constructionist approach to empathy, involves the immediate social and interactional context and takes a dyadic approach to empathy.

Tabula rasa   refers to the idea that we are all born with a 'blank slate' of mind, and that individuals are then shaped by knowledge and experiences.

Toxic triangle   is a model that suggests that there are three realms of factors that lead to the emergence of destructive leadership. These factors include destructive leaders, susceptible followers, and conducive environments.

Trumpism   broadly refers to the political ideology of Donald Trump.

Validity   refers to the extent to which a tool measures what it is set out to measure.

Vroom's expectancy theory   is a process theory of motivation developed by Victor Vroom. The idea is that people tend to believe that their effort would lead to desirable outcomes, which in turn would contribute to performance.

Chapter 1

Adapa, S. and Sheridan, A. (eds) (2018) *Inclusive Leadership: Negotiating Gendered Spaces. Palgrave Studies in Leadership and Followership*. Cham: Palgrave Macmillan.

Ahonen, P., Tienari, J., Meriläinen, S. and Pullen, A. (2014) 'Hidden contexts and invisible power relations: A Foucauldian reading of diversity research', *Human Relations*, 67 (3): 263–286.

Alvesson, M. and Kärreman, D. (2016) 'Intellectual failure and ideological success in organization studies: The case of transformational leadership', *Journal of Management Inquiry*, 25 (2): 139–152.

Alvesson, M. and Spicer, A. (2012) 'Critical leadership studies: The case for critical performativity', *Human Relations*, 65 (3): 367–390.

Bass, B. M. (1985) *Leadership and Performance Beyond Expectations*. New York: Free Press.

Bennis, W. G. and Nanus, B. (1985) *Leaders: Strategies for Taking Charge*. New York: Harper and Row.

Bligh, M. (2011) 'Followership and follower-centric approaches', in D. Collinson, A. Bryman, K. Grint, B. Jackson and M. Uhl Bien (eds), *Handbook of Leadership Studies*. London: SAGE.

Bolden, R. and Kirk, P. (2009) 'African leadership: Surfacing new understandings through leadership development', *International Journal of Cross-Cultural Management*, 9 (1): 69–86.

Burrell, G. and Morgan, G. (1979) *Sociological paradigms and organisational analysis: Elements of the sociology of corporate life*. London: Heinemann.

Chapman, S., McNeill, P. and Mcneill, P. (2005) *Research Methods* (3rd ed.). London: Routledge.

Denzin, N. K. (2004) 'Symbolic interactionism', in U. Flick, E. von Kardoff and I. Steinke (eds), *A Companion to Qualitative Research*. London: SAGE.

Eden, D. and Leviatan, U. (1975) 'Implicit leadership theory as a determinant of the factor structure underlying supervisory behaviour scales', *Journal of Applied Psychology*, 60 (6): 736.

Edwards, G. (2015) 'Anthropological accounts of leadership: Historical and geographical interpretations from indigenous cultures', *Leadership*, 11 (3): 335–350.

Fairhurst, G. T. and Grant, D. (2010) 'The social construction of leadership: A sailing guide', *Management Communications Quarterly*, 24 (2): 171–210.

Fiedler, F. E. (1967) *A Theory of Leadership Effectiveness*. New York: McGraw Hill.

Ford, J. (2010) 'Studying leadership critically: A psychosocial lens on leadership identities', *Leadership*, 6: 47–66.

Ford, J. and Harding, N. (2011) 'The impossibility of the "true self" of authentic leadership', *Leadership*, 7 (4): 463–479.

Ford, J. and Harding, N. (2018) 'Followers in leadership theory: Fiction, fantasy and illusion', *Leadership*, 14 (1): 3–24.

Foucault M (1998) *The Will to Knowledge: The History of Sexuality Vol. I*. Penguin Books.

Greedharry, M., Ahonen, P. and Tienari, J. (2020) 'Race and identity in organizations', in A. D. Brown (ed.) (2020), *The Oxford Handbook of Identities in Organizations*. Oxford: Oxford University Press. pp. 654–668.

Grint, K. (2020) 'Leadership, management and command in the time of the Coronavirus', *Leadership*, 16 (3): 314–319.

Hartnell, C. and Walumbwa, F. (2011) 'Transformational leadership and organizational culture', in N. Ashkanasy, C. Wilderon and M. Peterson (eds) *The Handbook of Organizational Culture and Climate*, 2nd edn. Thousand Oaks, CA: SAGE.

Hassard, J. (1991) 'Multiple paradigms and organizational analysis: A case study', *Organization Studies*, 12 (2): 275–299.

Hassard, J. and Wolfram Cox, J. (2013) 'Can sociological paradigms still inform organizational analysis? A paradigm model for post-paradigm times', *Organization Studies*, 34 (11): 1701–1728.

Hollander, E. P. (1992) 'Leadership, followership, self and other', *Leadership Quarterly*, 3 (1): 43–54.

House, R. J. and Aditya, R. N. (1997) 'The social scientific study of leadership: Quo vadis?', *Journal of Management*, 23 (3): 409–473.

Kelly, S. (2008) 'Leadership: A categorical mistake?', *Human Relations*, 61 (6): 763–782.

Kuhn, T. S. (1970) *The Structure of Scientific Revolutions*, 2nd edn. Chicago: University of Chicago Press.

Linnehan F and Konrad AM (1999) Diluting diversity: Implications for intergroup inequality in organizations. *Journal of management inquiry* 8(4): 399–414.

Liu, H. (2010) 'When leaders fail: A typology of failures and framing strategies', *Management Communication Quarterly*, 24 (2): 232–259.

Liu, H. (2018) 'Leadership from the margins: Practising inclusivity with "Outsiders Within"', in S. Adapa and A. Sheridan (eds), *Inclusive Leadership: Negotiating Gendered Spaces. Palgrave Studies in Leadership and Followership*. Cham: Palgrave Macmillan.

Liu, H. and Baker, C. (2016) 'White Knights: Leadership as the heroicisation of whiteness', *Leadership*, 12 (4): 420–448.

Meindl, J. R. (1995) 'The romance of leadership as a follower-centric theory: A social constructionist approach'. *The Leadership Quarterly*, 6 (3): 329–341.

Nkomo, S. M., Bell, M. P., Roberts, L. M., Joshi, A. and Thatcher, S. M. (2019) 'Diversity at a critical juncture: New theories for a complex phenomenon', *Academy of Management Review*, 44 (3): 498–517.

Noon M (2007) The fatal flaws of diversity and the business case for ethnic minorities. *Work, employment and society* 21(4): 773–784.

Ospina, S. and Foldy, E. (2009) 'A critical review of race and ethnicity in the leadership literature: Surfacing context, power and the collective dimensions of leadership', *The Leadership Quarterly*, 20 (6): 876–896.

Pondy, L. (1978) 'Leadership is a language game', in M. McCall and M. Lomardo (eds), *Leadership: Where Else Can We Go?* Durham, NC: Duke University Press.

Prakasam, N. (2014) 'Authentic performances: The role of impression management in audience understanding of leaders' authenticity'. Doctoral thesis, Durham University.

Rush, M. C., Thomas, J. C. and Lord, R. G. (1977) 'Implicit leadership theory: A potential threat to the internal validity of leader behaviour questionnaires', *Organizational Behaviour and Human Performance*, 20 (1): 93–110.

Sashkin, M. (2004) 'Transformational leadership approaches: A review and synthesis', in J. Antonakis, A. T. Cianciolo and R. J. Sternberg (eds), *The Nature of Leadership*. Thousand Oaks, CA: SAGE.

Smircich, L. and Morgan, G. (1982) 'Leadership: The management of meaning', *Journal of Applied Behavioural Science*, 18 (3): 257–273.

Uhl-Bien, M. (2006) 'Relational leadership theory: Exploring the social processes of leadership and organizing', *Leadership Quarterly*, 17 (6): 654–676.

Walumbwa, F. O., Avolio, B. J., Gardner, W. L., Wernsing, T. S., Peterson, S. J. (2008) 'Authentic leadership: Development and validation of a theory-based measure', *Journal of Management*, 34 (1): 89–126.

Zanoni P, Janssens M, Benschop Y, et al. (2010) Guest editorial: Unpacking diversity, grasping inequality: Rethinking difference through critical perspectives. *Organization* 17(1): 9–29.

Chapter 2

Ahmadian, S., Azarshahi, S. and Paulhus, D. L. (2017) 'Explaining Donald Trump via communication style: grandiosity, informality, and dynamism', *Personality and Individual Differences*, 107: 49–53.

Allport GW (1961) *Pattern and growth in personality*. Oxford, England: Holt, Reinhart & Winston.

Angell JR (1907) The province of functional psychology. *Psychological Review* 14: 61–91.

Antonakis, J., Day, D. V. and Schyns, B. (2012) 'Leadership and individual differences: At the cusp of a renaissance', *The Leadership Quarterly*, 23 (4): 643–650.

Babiak P and Hare RD (2006) *Snakes in suits: When psychopaths go to work* New York Harper Collins Publishers.

Badura, K. L., Grijalva, E., Newman, D. A., Yan, T. T. and Jeon, G. (2018) 'Gender and leadership emergence: A meta-analysis and explanatory model', *Personnel Psychology*, 71 (3): 335–367.

Baron RA and Byrne D (1987) *Social psychology: Understanding human interaction* Boston: Allyn & Bacon.

Barsade, S. G. and Gibson, D. E. (2007) 'Why does affect matter in organizations?', *The Academy of Management Perspectives*, 21: 36–59.

Bass, B. M. (1985) 'Leadership: Good, better, best', *Organizational Dynamics*, 13 (3): 26–40.

Bass BM (1990) From transactional to transformational leadership: Learning to share the vision. *Organizational dynamics* 18(3): 19-31.

Bauer NM (2020) A feminine advantage? Delineating the effects of feminine trait and feminine issue messages on evaluations of female candidates. *Politics & Gender* 16(3): 660–680.

Berlew, D. E. (1974) 'Leadership and organizational excitement', *California Management Review*, 17 (2): 21–30.

Bird, C. (1940). *Social psychology*. New York: Appleton-Century.

Blum ML, Naylor JC and Naylor JC (1956) *Industrial psychology; Its theoretical and social foundations*. Harper & Row.

Boddy CR (2011) The corporate psychopaths theory of the global financial crisis. *Journal of Business Ethics* 102(2): 255–259.

Bratton, J. (Ed.). (2020). *Organizational leadership*. Sage.

Braun, S. (2017) 'Leader narcissism and outcomes in organizations: a review at multiple levels of analysis and implications for future research', *Frontiers in Psychology*, 8: 773.

Buchanan DA and Huczynski AA (2017) *Organizational behaviour*. Pearson UK.

Burns, J. M. (1978) *Leadership*. New York: Harper and Row.

Byrne CL, Shipman AS and Mumford MD (2010) The effects of forecasting on creative problem-solving: An experimental study. *Creativity Research Journal* 22(2): 119–138.

Calàs, M. B. (1993) 'Deconstructing charismatic leadership: Re-reading Weber from the darker side', *The Leadership Quarterly*, 4 (3–4): 305–328.

Carroll B, Taylor S and Ford J (2019) Leadership: Contemporary critical perspectives. *Leadership*. 1–384.

Chabrol H, Van Leeuwen N, Rodgers R, et al. (2009) Contributions of psychopathic, narcissistic, Machiavellian, and sadistic personality traits to juvenile delinquency. *Personality and Individual Differences* 47(7): 734–739.

Clarke, J. (2005), *Working with Monsters: How to Identify and Protect Yourself from the Workplace Psychopath*, Random House.

Cleckley, H. (1941). *The mask of sanity: An attempt to reinterpret the so-called psychopathic personality*. The C. V. Mosby Company.

Colbert, A. E., Judge, T. A., Choi, D. and Wang, G. (2012) 'Assessing the trait theory of leadership using self and observer ratings of personality: The mediating role of contributions to group success', *The Leadership Quarterly*, 23 (4): 670–685.

Colbert AE, Judge TA, Choi D, et al. (2012) Assessing the trait theory of leadership using self and observer ratings of personality: The mediating role of contributions to group success. *The Leadership Quarterly* 23(4): 670–685.

Conger JA and Kanungo RN (1987) Toward a behavioral theory of charismatic leadership in organizational settings. *Academy of management review* 12(4): 637–647.

Conger JA (1989) *The charismatic leader: Behind the mystique of exceptional leadership.* Jossey-Bass.

Conger JA and Kanungo RN (1998) *Charismatic leadership in organizations.* Sage Publications.

Cunha, M. P. e, Clegg, S. and Rego, A. (2013) 'Lessons for leaders: Positive organization studies meets Niccolò Machiavelli', *Leadership*, 9 (4): 450–465.

Day DV and Zaccaro SJ (2007) Leadership: A critical historical analysis of the influence of leader traits. *Historical perspectives in industrial and organizational psychology.* Erlbaum, pp.383–405.

Deluga RJ (2001) American presidential Machiavellianism: Implications for charismatic leadership and rated performance. *The Leadership Quarterly* 12(3): 339–363.

Derue N Wellman, & Humphrey.(2011). *Trait and behavioral theories of leadership: An integration and meta-analytic test of their relative validity* 64(1): 7–52.

Desvaux G, Devillard-Hoellinger S and Meaney MC (2008) A business case for women. *The McKinsey Quarterly* 4(4): 26–33.

Dingler-Duhon M and Brown BB (1987) Self-disclosure as an influence strategy: Effects of Machiavellianism, androgyny, and sex. *Sex Roles* 16(3): 109–123.

Dinh, J. E. and Lord, R. G. (2012) 'Implications of dispositional and process views of traits for individual difference research in leadership', *The Leadership Quarterly*, 23 (4): 651–669.

Dow TE (1978) An analysis of Weber's work on charisma. *British Journal of Sociology.* 83–93.

Drory A and Gluskinos UM (1980) Machiavellianism and leadership. *Journal of Applied Psychology* 65(1): 81.

Eagly AH and Karau SJ (2002) Role congruity theory of prejudice toward female leaders. *Psychological Review* 109(3): 573.

Eagly AH (2016) What does social science say about how a female president might lead? *The Conversation.*

Eden, D. and Leviatan, U. (1975) 'Implicit leadership theory as a determinant of the factor structure underlying supervisory behaviour scales', *Journal of Applied Psychology*, 60 (6): 736.

Felfe, J. and Schyns, B. (2010) 'Followers' personality and the perception of transformational leadership: Further evidence for the similarity hypothesis', *British Journal of Management*, 21 (2): 393–410.

Fiedler FE (1964) A contingency model of leadership effectiveness. Advances in experimental social psychology. *Elsevier*, pp.149–190.

Fletcher JK (2004) The paradox of postheroic leadership: An essay on gender, power, and transformational change. *The Leadership Quarterly* 15(5): 647–661.

Foldy EG, Goldman L and Ospina S (2008) Sensegiving and the role of cognitive shifts in the work of leadership. *The Leadership Quarterly* 19(5): 514–529.

Foti RJ, Bray BC, Thompson NJ, et al. (2012) Know thy self, know thy leader: Contributions of a pattern-oriented approach to examining leader perceptions. *The Leadership Quarterly* 23(4): 702–717.

Furnham, A., Richards, S. C. and Paulhus, D. L. (2013) 'The Dark Triad of personality: A 10 year review', *Social and Personality Psychology Compass*, 7 (3): 199–216.

Galton F (1869) *Hereditary genius: An inquiry into the consequences*. New York, Appleton.

Galvin BM, Waldman DA and Balthazard P (2010) Visionary communication qualities as mediators of the relationship between narcissism and attributions of leader charisma. *Personnel Psychology* 63(3): 509–537.

Gardner WL and Avolio BJ (1998) The charismatic relationship: A dramaturgical perspective. *Academy of management review* 23(1): 32–58.

Gartzia L and Baniandrés J (2019) How feminine is the female advantage? Incremental validity of gender traits over leader sex on employees' responses. *Journal of Business Research* 99: 125–139.

Ghiselli EE and Brown CW (1955) *Personnel and industrial psychology*. New York, NY, US: McGraw-Hill.

Gibb CA (1947) The principles and traits of leadership. *The Journal of Abnormal and Social Psychology* 42(3): 267.

Gino, F. (2015) 'Introverts, extroverts, and the complexities of team dynamics', *Harvard Business Review*, 16 March. Available at: https://hbr.org/2015/03/introverts-extroverts-and-the-complexities-of-team-dynamics (accessed 23 September 2022).

Greenfeld L (1985) Reflections on two charismas. *British Journal of Sociology*. 117–132.

Grint, K. (2011) 'A history of leadership'. In A. Bryman, D. Collinson, K. Grint, B. Jackson and M. Uhl-Bien (eds), *The SAGE Handbook of Leadership*. London: SAGE. pp. 1–14.

Harrison, C. (2018) 'Entrepreneurial leadership in a developing economy: a skill-based analysis', *Journal of Small Business and Enterprise Development*, 25 (3): 521–548. Available at: https://doi.org/10.1108/JSBED-05-2017-0160 (accessed 23 September 2022).

Helgesen S (1990) *The feminine advantage: Women's ways of leadership*. New York: Doubleday.

Heydon, T. (2015) 'The 10 greatest controversies of Winston Churchill's career'. Available at: https://www.bbc.co.uk/news/magazine-29701767 (accessed 20 February 2022).

Hoffman BJ, Woehr DJ, Maldagen-Youngjohn R, et al. (2011) Great man or great myth? A quantitative review of the relationship between individual differences and leader effectiveness. *Journal of occupational and organizational psychology* 84(2): 347–381.

Hooijberg R, Hunt JG and Dodge GE (1997) Leadership complexity and development of the leaderplex model. *Journal of management* 23(3): 375–408.

House RJ (1977) *A 1976 theory of charismatic leadership*. In: Hunt JG and Larson LL (eds) Leadership: the cutting edge: A symposium held at Southern Illinois university, Carbondale, October 27–28, 1976

Carbondale, IL: Southern Illinois University Press.

House, R. J. and Aditya, R. N. (1997) 'The social scientific study of leadership: Quo vadis?', *Journal of Management*, 23 (3): 409–473.

House, R. J., Spangler, W. D. and Woycke, J. (1991) 'Personality and charisma in the U.S. presidency: A psychological theory of leadership effectiveness', *Academy of Management Proceedings*, 1990 (1): 216–220.

Huffman RC and Hegarty WH (1993) Top management influence on innovations: Effects of executive characteristics and social culture. *Journal of management* 19(3): 549–574.

Jenkins WO (1947) A review of leadership studies with particular reference to military problems. *Psychological Bulletin* 44(1): 54.

Joseph DL, Dhanani LY, Shen W, et al. (2015) Is a happy leader a good leader? A meta-analytic investigation of leader trait affect and leadership. *The Leadership Quarterly* 26(4): 557–576.

Judge TA, Bono JE, Ilies R, et al. (2002) Personality and leadership: a qualitative and quantitative review. *Journal of applied psychology* 87(4): 765.

Judge TA, Colbert AE and Ilies R (2004) Intelligence and leadership: a quantitative review and test of theoretical propositions. *Journal of applied psychology* 89(3): 542.

Judge TA, LePine JA and Rich BL (2006) Loving yourself abundantly: relationship of the narcissistic personality to self-and other perceptions of workplace deviance, leadership, and task and contextual performance. *Journal of Applied Psychology* 91(4): 762.

Judge, T. A., Piccolo, R. F., & Kosalka, T. (2009). The bright and dark sides of leader traits: A review and theoretical extension of the leader trait paradigm. *The leadership quarterly*, 20(6): 855–875.

Kaiser RB, Hogan R and Craig SB (2008) Leadership and the fate of organizations. *American Psychologist* 63(2): 96.

Katz R (1974) *Skills of an effective administrator*: Harvard Business School Press.

Katz D and Kahn RL (1978) Organizations and the system concept. *Classics of organization theory* 80: 480.

Landay K, Harms P and Credé M (2019) Shall we serve the dark lords? A meta-analytic review of psychopathy and leadership. *Journal of applied psychology* 104(1): 183.

Lieberman, C. (n.d.) 'The essential Audre Lorde', in *Writing on Glass* [blog]. Available at: https://www.writingonglass.com/audre-lorde (accessed 23 September 2022).

Lindebaum D and Zundel M (2013) Not quite a revolution: Scrutinizing organizational neuroscience in leadership studies. *Human relations* 66(6): 857–877.

Locke J (2000) An essay concerning human understanding. London: Routledge

Lord, R. G., Foti, R. J., De Vader, C. L. (1984) 'A test of leadership categorization theory: Internal structure, information processing, and leadership perceptions', *Organizational Behavior and Human Performance*, 34 (3): 343–378.

Lord RG, De Vader CL and Alliger GM (1986) A meta-analysis of the relation between personality traits and leadership perceptions: An application of validity generalization procedures. *Journal of applied psychology* 71(3): 402.

Machiavelli N (1961) *The Prince*. Harmondsworth: Penguin.

Marcy RT (2015) Breaking mental models as a form of creative destruction: The role of leader cognition in radical social innovations. *The Leadership Quarterly* 26(3): 370–385.

Meindl JR (1990) On leadership-an alternative to the conventional wisdom. *Research in organizational behavior* 12: 159–203.

Morgeson, F. P., Campion, M. A., Dipboye, R. L., Hollenbeck, J. R., Murphy, K. and Schmitt, N. (2007) 'Reconsidering the use of personality tests in personnel selection contexts', *Personnel Psychology*, 60 (3): 683–729.

Muchinsky PM (1983) Vocational behavior and career development, 1982: A review. *Journal of Vocational Behavior* 23(2): 123–178.

Mumford MD, Zaccaro SJ, Harding FD, et al. (2000) Leadership skills for a changing world: Solving complex social problems. *The Leadership Quarterly* 11(1): 11–35.

Mumford MD, Marks MA, Connelly MS, et al. (2000) Development of leadership skills: Experience and timing. *The Leadership Quarterly* 11(1): 87–114.

Mumford TV, Campion MA and Morgeson FP (2007) The leadership skills strataplex: Leadership skill requirements across organizational levels. *The Leadership Quarterly* 18(2): 154–166.

Mumford, M. D., Todd, E. M., Higgs, C. and McIntosh, T. (2017) 'Cognitive skills and leadership performance: The nine critical skills', *The Leadership Quarterly*, 28 (1): 24–39.

Nadler, D. A. and Tushman, M. L. (1990) 'Beyond the charismatic leader: Leadership and organizational change', *California Management Review*, 32: 77–97.

Ones, D. S., Dilchert, S., Viswesvaran, C., Judge, T. A. (2007) 'In support of personality assessment in organizational settings', *Personnel Psychology*, 60: 995–1027.

Oxford University P (2000) *Oxford English dictionary*.

Parry, K. and Kempster, S. (2014) 'Love and leadership: Constructing follower narrative identities of charismatic leadership', *Management Learning*, 45 (1): 21–38.

Paulhus, D. L. and Williams, K. M. (2002) 'The Dark Triad of personality: Narcissism, Machiavellianism, and psychopathy', *Journal of Research in Personality*, 36: 556–563.

Pullen, A., Rhodes, C., McEwen C and Liu, H (2019) 'Radical politics, intersectionality and leadership for diversity in organizations', *Management Decision*, 59 (11): 2553–2566.

Rekret, P. (2018) 'The posthumanist tabula rasa', *Research in Education*, 101 (1): 25–29.

Robbins, S. P. and Judge, T. A. (2016) *Organizational Behavior, Global Edition*. London: Pearson.

Sashkin M (1988a) *The visionary leader*. Jossey-Bass.

Schedlitzki D and Edwards G (2014) *Studying leadership: Traditional and critical approaches*. Sage.

Schyns B and Sanders K (2007) In the eyes of the beholder: Personality and the perception of leadership. *Journal of Applied Social Psychology* 37(10): 2345–2363.

Schyns, B., Kiefer, T., Kerschreiter, R. and Tymon, A. (2011) 'Teaching implicit leadership theories to develop leaders and leadership: How and why it can make a difference', *Academy of Management Learning Education*, 10 (3) :397–408.

Secord P and Backman, CW (1974) *Social Psychology* (2nd edition). New York, McGraw-Hill.

Shahzad, K., Raja, U. and Hashmi, S. D. (2020) 'Impact of Big Five personality traits on authentic leadership'. *Leadership & Organization Development Journal*, 42 (2): 208–218.

Shamir, B., Dayan-Horesh, H. and Adler, D. (2005) 'Leading by biography: Towards a life-story approach to the study of leadership', *Leadership*, 1 (1): 13–29.

Schoemaker PJ, Krupp S and Howland S (2013) Strategic leadership: The essential skills. *Harvard Business Review* 91(1): 131–134.

Shondrick, S. J., Dinh, J. E. and Lord, R. G. (2010) 'Developments in implicit leadership theory and cognitive science: Applications to improving measurement and understanding alternatives to hierarchical leadership', *The Leadership Quarterly*, 21 (6): 959–978.

Shondrick, S. J. and Lord, R. G. (2010) 'Implicit leadership and followership theories: Dynamic structures for leadership perceptions, memory, and leader–follower processes', in G. P. Hodgkinson and J. K. Ford (eds), *International Review of Industrial and Organizational Psychology*. pp. 1–33.

Silver, C. H., Benitez, A., Armstrong, K. and Tussey, C. M. (2018) 'Voices of leadership: wisdom from women leaders in neuropsychology', *The Clinical Neuropsychologist*, 32 (2), 252–262.

Spoelstra, S. (2019), 'The paradigm of the charismatic leader', *Leadership*, 15 (6): 744–749.

Stogdill, R. J. (1948) 'Personal factors associated with leadership: A survey of the literature', *Journal of Psychology*, 25: 35–71.

Taylor S (2019) Trait theories of leaders and leadership. *Leadership* 2: 49–67.

Tichy, N. M. and Devanna, M. A. (1986) 'The transformational leader', *Training Development Journal*, 40 (7): 27–32.

Visser BA, Book AS and Volk AA (2017) Is Hillary dishonest and Donald narcissistic? A HEXACO analysis of the presidential candidates' public personas. *Personality and Individual Differences* 106: 281–286.

Walter, F. and Scheibe, S. (2013) 'A literature review and emotion-based model of age and leadership: New directions for the trait approach', *The Leadership Quarterly*, 24 (6): 882–901.

Watson D and Clark LA (1984) Negative affectivity: the disposition to experience aversive emotional states. *Psychological Bulletin* 96(3): 465.

Zaccaro S, Kemp C and Bader P (2004) The nature of leadership. Antonakis, J., Cianciolo, AT y Sternberg, RJ *The nature of leadership.* London: Sage.

Zaccaro, S. J. (2007) 'Trait-based perspectives of leadership', *American Psychologist*, 62 (1):6–16.

Zaccaro SJ (2012) Individual differences and leadership: Contributions to a third tipping point. *The Leadership Quarterly* 23(4): 718–728.

Zaccaro, S. J., Green, J. P., Dubrow, S. and Kolze, M. (2018) 'Leader individual differences, situational parameters, and leadership outcomes: A comprehensive review and integration', *The Leadership Quarterly*, 29(1): 2–43.

Chapter 3

Algera PM and Lips-Wiersma M (2012) Radical authentic leadership: Co-creating the conditions under which all members of the organization can be authentic. *The Leadership Quarterly* 23(1): 118–131.

Alvesson M and Sveningsson S. (2003) The great disappearing act: difficulties in doing 'leadership'. *The Leadership Quarterly* 14: 359–381

Alvesson, M. and Kärreman, D. (2016) 'Intellectual failure and ideological success in organization studies: The case of transformational leadership', *Journal of Management Inquiry*, 25 (2):139–152.

Alvesson, M. and Spicer, A. (2012) 'Critical leadership studies: The case for critical performativity', *Human Relations*, 65 (3): 367–390.

Alvesson M and Einola K (2019) Warning for excessive positivity: Authentic leadership and other traps in leadership studies. *The Leadership Quarterly* 30(4): 383–395.

Anderson, M. H. and Sun, P. Y. (2017) 'Reviewing leadership styles: Overlaps and the need for a new "full-range" theory', *International Journal of Management Reviews*, 19 (1): 76–96.

Antonakis J and House R (2002) An nnalysis ofhe full–range leadership theory: The way forward Transformational and Charismatic Leadership, n. 2. In: Avolio BJ and Yammarino FJ (eds) *Transformational and Charismatic Leadership: The Road Ahead.* Amsterdam: JAI Press, pp.3–33.

Antonakis J, Simonton D and House R (2016) Can super smart leaders suffer from too much of a good thing. *The Curvilinear Effect of Intelligence on Perceived Leadership Behavior Unpublished manuscript.*

Arnold JA, Arad S, Rhoades JA, et al. (2000) The empowering leadership questionnaire: The construction and validation of a new scale for measuring leader behaviors. *Journal of organizational behavior* 21(3): 249–269.

Avolio BJ and Gardner WL (2005) Authentic leadership development: Getting to the root of positive forms of leadership. *The Leadership Quarterly* 16(3): 315–338.

Banks, G. C., Engemann, K. N., Williams, C. E., Gooty, J., McCauley, K. D. and Medaugh, M. R. (2017) 'A meta-analytic review and future research agenda of charismatic leadership', *The Leadership Quarterly*, 28 (4): 508–529.

Bass, B. M. (1985) 'Leadership: Good, better, best', *Organizational Dynamics*, 13 (3): 26–40.

Bass B (1998) *Transformational management: Industry, military, and educational impact.* Mahwah. NJ: Lawrence Erlbaum Associates, Inc.

Bass, B.M. (1990) From transactional to transformational leadership: Learning to share the vision. *Organizational dynamics*, 18(3): 19–31.

Bass BM and Steidlmeier P (1999) Ethics, character, and authentic transformational leadership behavior. *The Leadership Quarterly* 10(2): 181–217.

Bedeian, A.G. and Hunt, J.G. (2006) Academic amnesia and vestigial assumptions of our forefathers. *The Leadership Quarterly*, 17(2): 190–205.

Bennis, W. G. and Nanus, B. (1985) *Leaders: Strategies for Taking Charge.* New York: Harpers and Row.

Berlew, D. E. (1974) 'Leadership and organizational excitement', *California Management Review*, 17 (2): 21–30.

Berson, Y. and Avolio, B. J. (2004) 'Transformational leadership and the dissemination of organizational goals: A case study of a telecommunication firm', *The Leadership Quarterly*, 15 (5): 625–646.

Bryman, A. (1992) *Charisma and Leadership in Organizations.* London: SAGE.

Buchanan, D.A. and Huczynski, A.A. (2017) *Organizational behaviour.* Pearson UK.

Collinson, D (2012) Prozac leadership and the limits of positive thinking. *Leadership* 8(2): 87–107.

Cooper CD, Scandura TA and Schriesheim CA (2005) Looking forward but learning from our past: Potential challenges to developing authentic leadership theory and authentic leaders. *The Leadership Quarterly* 16(3): 475–493.

Conger, J. A. (1999) 'Charismatic and transformational leadership in organizations: An insider's perspective on these developing streams of research', *The Leadership Quarterly*, 10 (2): 145–179.

Deci EL and Ryan RM (2003) Intrinsic motivation inventory. *Self-determination theory* 267.

Desmet, P. T., Hoogervorst, N. and Van Dijke, M. (2015) 'Prophets vs. profits: How market competition influences leaders' disciplining behavior towards ethical transgressions', *The Leadership Quarterly*, 26 (6): 1034–1050.

Diddams M and Chang GC (2012) Only human: Exploring the nature of weakness in authentic leadership. *The Leadership Quarterly* 23(3): 593–603.

Drucker, P.F. (1988) The coming of the new organization. *Harvard Business Review*, 45–53.

Du, S., Swaen, V., Lindgreen, A. and Sankar, S. (2013) 'The roles of leadership styles in corporate social responsibility', *Journal of Business Ethics*, 114 (1): 155–169.

Edwards, G., Schedlitzki, D., Turnbull, S., et al. (2015) Exploring power assumptions in the leadership and management debate. *Leadership & Organization Development Journal*.

Edwards G, Schyns B, Gill R, et al. (2012) The MLQ factor structure in a UK context. *Leadership & Organization Development Journal*.

Fairhurst, G. T. (2001) 'Dualisms in leadership research', *The New Handbook of Organizational Communication: Advances in Theory, Research, and Methods*, 379–439.

Fiedler, F. E. (1978) 'The contingency model and the dynamics of the leadership process', *Advances in Experimental Social Psychology*, 11: 59–112.

Gardner WL, Fischer D and Hunt JGJ (2009) Emotional labor and leadership: A threat to authenticity? *The Leadership Quarterly* 20(3): 466–482.

Garman, A. N., Davis-Lenane, D. and Corrigan, P. W. (2003) 'Factor structure of the transformational leadership model in human service teams', *Journal of Organizational Behavior: The International Journal of Industrial, Occupational and Organizational Psychology and Behavior*, 24 (6): 803–812.

Gavan O'Shea, P., Foti, R. J., Hauenstein, N. M. and Bycio, P. (2009) 'Are the best leaders both transformational and transactional? A pattern-oriented analysis', *Leadership*, 5 (2): 237–259.

Gill R (2006) *Theory and practice of leadership*. Sage.

Gray JH and Densten IL (2007) How leaders woo followers in the romance of leadership. *Applied Psychology* 56(4): 558–581.

Grint K (2005) Problems, problems, problems: The social construction of 'leadership'. *Human Relations* 58(11): 1467–1494.

Grint, K. (2020) 'Leadership, management and command in the time of the Coronavirus', *Leadership*, 16: 314–319.

Hales, C. (2002) 'Bureaucracy-lite' and continuities in managerial work. *British Journal of Management*, 13(1): 51–66.

Hickman, C. (1990) The Winning Mix: Mind of a Manager, Soul of a Leader. *Canadian Business*, 63: 69–72.

Hoch B and Bommer J Dulebohn and Wu.(2016) Do Ethical, Authentic, and Servant Leadership Explain Variance Above and Beyond Transformational Leadership? A Meta-Analysis. *Journal of management* 44.

Hofstede G (1991) Empirical models of cultural differences.

House RJ (1971) A path goal theory of leader effectiveness. *Administrative science quarterly*. 321–339.

House RJ (1977) *A 1976 theory of charismatic leadershi*. In: Hunt JG and Larson LL (eds) Leadership: the cutting edge: A symposium held at Southern Illinois university, Carbondale, October 27–28, 1976

Carbondale, IL: Southern Illinois University Press.

Howell JM and Shamir B (2005) The role of followers in the charismatic leadership process: Relationships and their consequences. *Academy of management review* 30(1): 96–112.

Judge TA and Piccolo RF (2004) Transformational and transactional leadership: a meta-analytic test of their relative validity. *Journal of applied psychology* 89(5): 755.

Judge TA, Piccolo RF and Ilies R (2004) The forgotten ones? The validity of consideration and initiating structure in leadership research. *Journal of applied psychology* 89(1): 36.

Kang, J. H., Solomon, G. T. and Choi, D. Y. (2015) 'CEOs' leadership styles and managers' innovative behaviour: Investigation of intervening effects in an entrepreneurial context', *Journal of Management Studies*, 52 (4): 531–554.

Karakitapoğlu-Aygün, Z. and Gumusluoglu, L. (2013) 'The bright and dark sides of leadership: Transformational vs. non-transformational leadership in a non-Western context', *Leadership*, 9 (1): 107–133.

Kark, R., Van Dijk, D. and Vashdi, D. R. (2018) 'Motivated or demotivated to be creative: The role of self-regulatory focus in transformational and transactional leadership processes', *Applied Psychology*, 67(1): 186–224.

Kearney, E. and Gebert, D. (2009) 'Managing diversity and enhancing team outcomes: the promise of transformational leadership', *Journal of Applied Psychology*, 94 (1): 77.

Kernis MH (2003) Toward a conceptualization of optimal self-esteem. *Psychological inquiry* 14(1): 1–26.

Koo B and Lee E-S (2022) The Taming of Machiavellians: Differentiated Transformational Leadership Effects on Machiavellians' Organizational Commitment and Citizenship Behavior. *Journal of Business Ethics* 178(1): 153–170.

Kotter, J.P. (1988) *The leadership factor.* New York: Free Press; London: Collier Macmillan.

Kotter, J. (1990) *A force for change: How leadership differs from management* (pp. xi, 180). London: Collier Macmillan.

Kruglanski AW, Pierro A, Mannetti L, et al. (2006) Groups as epistemic providers: need for closure and the unfolding of group-centrism. *Psychological Review* 113(1): 84.

Le H, Schmidt FL, Harter JK, et al. (2010) The problem of empirical redundancy of constructs in organizational research: An empirical investigation. *Organizational Behavior and Human Decision Processes* 112(2): 112–125.

Nkrumah K (1965) *Neo-colonialism: The last stage of imperialism.* Nelson London.

Nyberg D and Sveningsson S (2014) Paradoxes of authentic leadership: Leader identity struggles. *Leadership* 10(4): 437–455.

Mangham IL (1986) In search of competence. *Journal of General Management*, 12(2): 5–12.

Meindl, J. R. (1995) 'The romance of leadership as a follower-centric theory: A social constructionist approach', *The Leadership Quarterly*, 6(3): 329–341.

Mintzberg H (2009) *Managing.* Pearson Education.

Mintzberg, H. (1980) *The Nature of Managerial Work*, Prentice – Hall, Englewood Cliffs, NJ.

Mowlam M (2002) *Momentum. The struggle for Peace. Politics and the People* (London 2002).

Nelson, M. (1994) *Long Walk to Freedom* (The Autobiography of Mandela. little Brown and Company.

Nimako, K. (2010) 'Nkrumah, African awakening and neo-colonialism: How black America awakened Nkrumah and Nkrumah awakened black America', *The Black Scholar*, 40 (2): 54–70.

Obama B (2007) *Dreams from my father: A story of race and inheritance*. Canongate Books.

Oc, B. (2018) 'Contextual leadership: A systematic review of how contextual factors shape leadership and its outcomes', *The Leadership Quarterly*, 29 (1): 218–235.

Oc, B., Bashshur, M. R., Daniels, M. A., Greguras, G. J. and Diefendorff, J. M. (2015) 'Leader humility in Singapore', *The Leadership Quarterly*, 26 (1): 68–80.

Perinbanayagam, R. S. (1971) 'The dialectics of charisma', *The Sociological Quarterly*, 12 (3): 387–402.

Peterson SJ, Abramson R and Stutman R (2020) How to develop your leadership style. *Harvard business review* 98(6): 68–77.

Prakasam N (2014) *Authentic performances: The role of impression management in audience understanding of leaders' authenticity*. Durham University.

Price TL (2003) The ethics of authentic transformational leadership. *The Leadership Quarterly* 14(1): 67–81.

Randolph-Seng B and Gardner WL (2013) Validating measures of leader authenticity: Relationships between implicit/explicit self-esteem, situational cues, and leader authenticity. *Journal of Leadership & Organizational Studies* 20(2): 214–231.

Rees, L. (2012) *The Dark Charisma of Adolf Hitler*. New York: Random House.

Rooney, D. (2007) *Kwame Nkrumah: Vision and Tragedy*. Ghana: Sub-Saharan Publishers and Traders. ProQuest Ebook Central.

Rost, J. C. (1991) *Leadership for the Twenty-first Century*. Westport, CT: Greenwood Publishing Group.

Sadler P (1997) Leadership. Kogan Page Publishers.

Sandberg, J. and Alvesson, M. (2021) 'Meanings of theory: Clarifying theory through typification', *Journal of Management Studies*, 58: 487–516.

Salaman G (2004) 'Competences of Managers, Competences of Leaders', in J. Storey (ed.) *Leadership in Organizations: Current Issues and Key Trends*, pp. 58–78. Milton Park: Routledge.

Schedlitzki D and Edwards G (2018) *Studying leadership: Traditional and critical approaches*. Sage.

Schepker DJ, Kim Y, Patel PC, et al. (2017) CEO succession, strategic change, and post-succession performance: A meta-analysis. The Leadership Quarterly 28(6): 701–720.

Schodl MM and Van Dijk D (2014) I Have a Dream but Ought to Do Something Else: Time Allocation to Prevention and Promotion Goals. *Academy of Management Proceedings*. Academy of Management Briarcliff Manor, NY 10510, 12946.

Shannon MR, Buford M, Winston BE, et al. (2020) Trigger events and crucibles in authentic leaders' development. *Journal of Management Development*.

Shin, S. J. and Zhou, J. (2007) 'When is educational specialization heterogeneity related to creativity in research and development teams? Transformational leadership as a moderator', *Journal of Applied Psychology*, 92 (6): 1709.

Somech, A. (2006) 'The effects of leadership style and team process on performance and innovation in functionally heterogeneous teams', *Journal of Management*, 32 (1): 132–157.

Sparrowe RT (2005) Authentic leadership and the narrative self. *The Leadership Quarterly* 16(3): 419–439.

Spoelstra, S. (2019) 'The paradigm of the charismatic leader', *Leadership*, 15 (6): 744–749.

Sturdy, A., Wright, C. and Wylie, N. (2016) Managers as consultants: The hybridity and tensions of neo-bureaucratic management. *Organization*, 23(2): 184–205.

Syed, F., Naseer, S., Nawaz, J. and Shah, S. Z. A. (2021) 'When the victim becomes vicious: Combined effects of pseudo transformational leadership and epistemic motivation on contempt and deviant behaviors', *European Management Journal*, 39 (2): 236–246.

Tengblad, S. (2006) Is there a 'new managerial work'? A comparison with Henry Mintzberg's classic study 30 years later. *Journal of management studies*, 43(7): 1437–1461.

Tiger L (1963) Ghana: A Charismatic Nation. *Current History* 45(268): 335–340.

Tourish, D. and Pinnington, A. (2002) 'Transformational leadership, corporate cultism and the spirituality paradigm: An unholy trinity in the workplace?', *Human Relations* 55: 147–172.

Tourish D and Vatcha N (2005) Charismatic leadership and corporate cultism at Enron: The elimination of dissent, the promotion of conformity and organizational collapse. *Leadership* 1(4): 455–480.

Uhl-Bien, M. (2006) 'Relational leadership theory: Exploring the social processes of leadership and organizing', *The Leadership Quarterly*, 17 (6): 654–676.

Van Dijk D, Seger-Guttmann T and Heller D (2013) Life-threatening event reduces subjective well-being through activating avoidance motivation: A longitudinal study. *Emotion* 13(2): 216.

van Knippenberg, D. and Sitkin, S. B. (2013) 'A critical assessment of charismatic – transformational leadership research: Back to the drawing board?', *Academy of Management Annals*, 7 (1): 1–60.

Walter F and Bruch H (2009) An affective events model of charismatic leadership behavior: A review, theoretical integration, and research agenda. *Journal of management* 35(6): 1428–1452.

Walumbwa, F.O., Avolio, B. J., Gardner, W. L., Wernsing, T. S. and Peterson, S. J. (2008) 'Authentic leadership: Development and validation of a theory-based measure', *Journal of Management*, 34 (1): 89–126.

Wang X-HF and Howell JM (2010) Exploring the dual-level effects of transformational leadership on followers. *Journal of applied psychology* 95(6): 1134.

Watson, T.J. (1994) Managing, crafting and researching: words, skill and imagination in shaping management research. *British Journal of Management*, 5: 77–87.

Yukl G (1999) An evaluation of conceptual weaknesses in transformational and charismatic leadership theories. *The Leadership Quarterly* 10(2): 285–305.

Chapter 4

Alvesson, M. and Kärreman, D. (2016) 'Intellectual failure and ideological success in organization studies: The case of transformational leadership', *Journal of Management Inquiry*, 25 (2): 139–152.

Alvesson, M. and Karreman, D. (2000) Varieties of discourse: On the study of organizations through discourse analysis. *Human Relations*, 53(9): 1125–1149.

Alvesson, M. and Spicer, A. (2012) 'Critical leadership studies: The case for critical performativity', *Human Relations*, 65 (3): 367–390.

Bell, E. and Taylor, S. (2016) 'Vernacular mourning and corporate memorialization in framing the death of Steve Jobs', *Organization*, 23 (1): 114–132.

Benjamin, W. (1996) *Selected Writings: 1938–1940*. Harvard University Press.

Berger, P. and Luckmann, T. L. (1966) *The Social Construction of Reality: A Treatise on the Sociology of Knowledge*. Garden City, NY: Doubleday.

Boussebaa, M. (2020) 'From cultural differences to cultural globalization: towards a new research agenda in cross-cultural management studies', *Critical Perspectives on International Business*, 17 (3): 381–399.

Burr, V. (2015) *Social Constructionism*. Abingdon, Oxfordshire: Routledge.

Butler, J. (1988) Performative acts and gender constitution: An essay in phenomenology and feminist theory. *Theatre Journal*, 40(4): 519–531.

Butler, J. (1999) *Gender Trouble: Feminism and the Subversion of Identity*. New York: Routledge.

Carsten, M. K., Uhl-Bien, M., West, B. J., Patera, J. L., McGregor, R. (2010) 'Exploring social constructions of followership: A qualitative study', *The Leadership Quarterly*, 21 (3): 543–562.

Clegg SR and Hardy C (1996) Organizations, organization and organizing. *Handbook of Organization Studies*. 1–28.

Collinson, D. (2006) 'Rethinking followership: A post-structuralist analysis of follower identities', *The Leadership Quarterly*, 17 (2):179–189.

Collinson, D., Smolović Jones, O. and Grint, K. (2018) '"No more heroes": Critical perspectives on leadership romanticism', *Organization Studies*, 39 (11): 1625–1647.

Cooren, F. (2020) Beyond entanglement: (Socio-) materiality and organization studies. *Organization Theory*, 1(3): 2631787720954444.

Clifton, J. and Mueni, J. (2020) 'The romance of human leaders? A socio-material analysis of a follower's account of being inspired', *Culture and Organization*, 1–17.

Cunliffe, A. L. (2008) 'Orientations to social constructionism: Relationally responsive social constructionism and its implications for knowledge and learning', *Management Learning*, 39 (2): 123–139.

Cunliffe, A. L. (2009) *A Very Short, Fairly Interesting and Reasonably Cheap Book about Management*. Los Angeles, CA: SAGE.

Daft, R.L. and Weick, K.E. (1984) Toward a model of organizations as interpretation systems. *Academy of Management Review*, 9(2): 284–295.

Fairhurst, G. T. and Grant, D. (2010) 'The social construction of leadership: A sailing guide', *Management Communication Quarterly*, 24 (2): 171–210.

Fairhurst, G. T. (2008) 'Discursive leadership: A communication alternative to leadership psychology', *Management Communication Quarterly*, 21 (4): 510–521.

Felfe J and Schyns B (2014) Romance of leadership and motivation to lead. *Journal of Managerial Psychology*, 29(7): 850–865.

Fiske ST and Taylor SE (1991) *Social Cognition*. Mcgraw-Hill Book Company.

Ford, J. and Harding, N. (2018) 'Followers in leadership theory: Fiction, fantasy and illusion', *Leadership*, 14 (1): 3–24.

Foucault, M. (1972) *The Archaeology of Knowledge*. New York: Random House.

Foucault, M. (1980) *Power/knowledge: Selected interviews and other writings*, 1972–1977. Vintage.

Giddens, A. (1979) *Central Problems in Social Theory: Action, Structure, and Contradiction in Social Analysis*. Oakland, CA: University of California Press.

Giddens, A. (1984) *The Constitution of Society: Outline of the Theory of Structuration*. Oakland, CA: University of California Press.

Giddens, A. (1991) *Modernity and Self-Identity: Self and Society in the Late Modern Age*. Cambridge: Polity Press.

Gioia, D. A. (2003) 'Give it up! Reflections on the interpreted world (a commentary on Meckler and Baillie)', *Journal of Management Inquiry*, 12 (3): 285–292.

Goffman E (1959) *The Presentation of Self in Everyday Life*. Harmondsworth (Penguin) 1959.

Graen GB and Uhl-Bien M (1995) Relationship-based approach to leadership: Development of leader-member exchange (LMX) theory of leadership over 25 years: Applying a multi-level multi-domain perspective. *The Leadership Quarterly*, 6(2): 219–247.

Grint K (2000) *The arts of leadership*. OUP Oxford.

Gronn P (2000) Distributed properties: A new architecture for leadership. *Educational Management & Administration*, 28(3): 317–338.

Gronn P (2002) Distributed leadership. *Second International Handbook of Educational Leadership and Administration*. Springer, pp.653–696.

Guthey E and Jackson B (2005) CEO portraits and the authenticity paradox. *Journal of management studies* 42(5): 1057–1082.

Iszatt-White M, Stead V and Elliott C (2021) Impossible or just irrelevant? Unravelling the 'authentic leadership'paradox through the lens of emotional labour. *Leadership*, 17(4): 464–482.

Kempster S and Carroll B (2016) *Responsible leadership: Realism and romanticism*. Routledge.

Kempster, S., Schedlitzki, D. and Edwards, G. (2021) 'Where have all the followers gone?', *Leadership*, 17 (1), 118–128.

Konst D and Van Breukelen W (2005) Effects of hierarchical positions of target persons on social inference: Schema use and schema content in perceiving leaders and subordinates. *Implicit leadership theories: Essays and explorations, Information Age*, Publishing, Greenwich, CT. 305–332.

Krzyżanowski, M. (2020) 'Normalization and the discursive construction of "new" norms and "new" normality: discourse in the paradoxes of populism and neoliberalism', *Social Semiotics*, 30 (4): 431–448.

Lawler J and Ashman I (2012) Theorizing leadership authenticity: A Sartrean perspective. *Leadership*, 8(4): 327–344.

Light, D. W. (1967) 'Berger and Luckmann: *The Social Construction of Reality*: A Treatise in the Sociology of Knowledge (Book Review)', *Sociology of Religion*, 28 (1): 55.

Liu, H. (2010) 'When leaders fail: A typology of failures and framing strategies', *Management Communication Quarterly*, 24 (2): 232–259.

Liu, H., Cutcher, L. and Grant, D. (2015) 'Doing authenticity: The gendered construction of authentic leadership', *Gender, Work and Organization*, 22 (3): 237–255.

Londono E and Milhorance F (2021)The New York Times 'Brazil passes 500,000 Covid deaths, a tragedy with no sign of let up.' Available at: https://www.nytimes.com/2021/06/24/world/americas/brazil-500000-covid-deaths.html

Meindl, J. R. (1995) 'The romance of leadership as a follower-centric theory: A social constructionist approach', *The Leadership Quarterly*, 6 (3): 329–341.

Meindl JR, Ehrlich SB and Dukerich JM (1985) The romance of leadership. *Administrative science quarterly*. 78–102.

Milgram S (1963) Behavioral study of obedience. *The Journal of Abnormal and Social Psychology* 67(4): 371.

Miller, L. B. (1972) 'From legitimacy to legitimations', *Kansas Journal of Sociology*, 123–131.

Morrison EW and Milliken FJ (2000) Organizational silence: A barrier to change and development in a pluralistic world. *Academy of management review* 25(4): 706–725.

Padilla, A., Hogan, R. and Kaiser, R. B. (2007) 'The toxic triangle: Destructive leaders, susceptible followers, and conducive environments', *The Leadership Quarterly*, 18: 176–194.

Pfeffer J (1977) Toward an examination of stratification in organizations. *Administrative science quarterly*. 553–567.

Pondy, L. (1978) 'Leadership is a language game', in M. McCall and M. Lomardo (eds), *Leadership: Where Else Can We Go?* Durham, NC: Duke University Press.

Prakasam, N. and Huxtable-Thomas, L. (2021) 'Reddit: Affordances as an enabler for shifting loyalties', *Information Systems Frontiers*, 23 (3): 723–751.

Romani, L., Boussebaa, M. and Jackson, T. (2020) 'Critical perspectives on cross-cultural management', in B. Szkudlarek, L. Romani, D. V. Caprar and J. S. Osland, *The SAGE Handbook of Contemporary Cross-Cultural Management*, 51.

Rose N (1989) *Governing the soul: The shaping of the private self.* London: Routledge.

Rosenberg S and Jones R (1972) A method for investigating and representing a person's implicit theory of personality: Theodore Dreiser's view of people. *Journal of Personality and Social Psychology* 22(3): 372.

Salancik GR and Pfeffer J (1978) A social information processing approach to job attitudes and task design. *Administrative science quarterly*. 224–253.

Salancik GR and Meindl JR (1984) Corporate attributions as strategic illusions of management control. *Administrative science quarterly*. 238–254.

Sayed Z and Agndal H (2020) Neo-colonial dynamics in global professional service firms: a periphery perspective. *Culture and Organization* 26(5–6): 425–443.

Schedlitzki, D., Ahonen, P., Wankhade, P., Edwards, G. and Gaggiotti, H. (2017) 'Working with language: A refocused research agenda for cultural leadership studies', *International Journal of Management Reviews*, 19 (2): 237–257.

Schyns B and Meindl JR (2005) *Implicit leadership theories: Essays and explorations.* IAP.

Sergi V, Lusiani M and Langley A (2021) Highlighting the plural: Leading amidst romance (s). *Journal of Change Management* 21(2): 163–179.

Shamir B (2007) From passive recipients to active co-producers: Followers' roles in the leadership process. *Follower-centered perspectives on leadership: A tribute to the memory of James R. Meindl* 9: 39.

Shamir B (1992) Attribution of influence and charisma to the leader: The romance of leadership revisited 1. *Journal of Applied Social Psychology* 22(5): 386–407.

Sharma A and Grant D (2011) Narrative, drama and charismatic leadership: The case of Apple's Steve Jobs. *Leadership* 7(1): 3–26.

Simpson G (1967) Review of The Social Construction of Reality. *American Sociological Review*, 32(1): 137–138

Sinclair A (2013) Essay: Can I really be me? The challenges for women leaders constructing authenticity. *Authentic Leadership*. Edward Elgar Publishing, pp.239–251.

Smircich, L. and Morgan, G. (1982) 'Leadership: The management of meaning', *Journal of Applied Behavioural Science*, 18 (3): 257–273.

Smolović Jones, S., Smolovi⊠ Jones, O., Winchester, N. and Grint, K. (2016) 'Putting the discourse to work: On outlining a praxis of democratic leadership development', *Management Learning*, 47(4): 424–442.

Steets, S. (2016) 'Taking Berger and Luckmann to the realm of materiality: architecture as a social construction', *Cultural Sociology*, 10 (1): 93–108.

Strati A (2000) Theory and method in organization studies. Theory and Method in *Organization Studies*. 1–256.

Sy, T. (2010) 'What do you think of followers? Examining the content, structure, and consequences of implicit followership theories', *Organizational Behavior and Human Decision Processes*, 113 (2): 73–84.

Urbach, T., Den Hartog, D. N., Fay, D., Parker, S. K. and Strauss, K. (2021) 'Cultural variations in whether, why, how, and at what cost people are proactive: A followership perspective', *Organizational Psychology Review*, 11 (1): 3–34.

Uhl-Bien, M. (2021) 'Complexity and COVID-19: Leadership and followership in a complex world', *Journal of Management Studies*, 58 (5): 1400–1404.

Uhl-Bien M and Pillai R (2007) The romance of leadership and the social construction of followership. *Follower-centered perspectives on leadership: A tribute to the memory of James R. Meindl*. 187–209.

Uhl-Bien, M., Riggio, R. E., Lowe, K. B. and Carsten, M. K. (2014) 'Followership theory: A review and research agenda', *The Leadership Quarterly*, 25 (1): 83–104.

Vine B, Holmes J, Marra M, et al. (2008) Exploring co-leadership talk through interactional sociolinguistics. *Leadership* 4(3): 339–360.

Chapter 5

Andersen, S. M. and Chen, S. (2002) 'The relational self: an interpersonal social-cognitive theory', *Psychological Review*, 109: 619.

Avolio, B. J. (2011) *Full Range Leadership Development*. Thousand Oaks, CA: SAGE.

Bass, B. M. and Bass, R. (2008) *The Bass Handbook of Leadership: Theory, Research, and Managerial Applications*. New York, NY: Simon and Schuster.

Blau, P. (1964) Exchange and Power in Social Life. Wiley, New York, NY, USA.

Crevani, L. (2019) 'Relational leadership', in B. Carroll, J. Ford and S. Taylor, *Leadership: Contemporary critical Perspectives*, London: SAGE. pp. 223–247.

Crevani, L., Lindgren, M. and Packendorff, J. (2010) 'Leadership, not leaders: On the study of leadership as practices and interactions', *Scandinavian Journal of Management*, 26 (1): 77–86.

Cunliffe, A. L. and Eriksen, M. (2011) 'Relational leadership', *Human Relations*, 64: 1425–1449.

Dachler, H. P. (1992) Management and leadership as relational phenomena. *Social representations and the social bases of knowledge* 1: 169–178.

Dansereau, Jr F., Cashman, J. and Graen, G. (1973) 'Instrumentality theory and equity theory as complementary approaches in predicting the relationship of leadership and turnover among managers', *Organizational Behavior and Human Performance*, 10 (2): 184–200.

Dienesch, R. M. and Liden, R. C. (1986) 'Leader-member exchange model of leadership: A critique and further development', *Academy of Management Review*, 11: 618–634.

Diprose, R. (2002) *Corporeal Generosity: On Giving with Nietzsche, Merleau-Ponty, and Levinas.* New York, NY: State University of New York Press.

Drath WH (2001) *The deep blue sea: Rethinking the source of leadership.* Jossey-Bass San Francisco, CA.

Drath, W. H., McCauley, C. D., Palus, C. J. and Van Velsor, E. (2008) 'Direction, alignment, commitment: Toward a more integrative ontology of leadership', *The Leadership Quarterly*, 19 (6): 635–653.

Eagly, A. H. (2005) 'Achieving relational authenticity in leadership: Does gender matter?', *The Leadership Quarterly*, 16 (3): 459–474.

Foucault, M. (1977) *Discipline and Punish: The Birth of the Prison.* London: Allen & Lane.

Gibeau É, Langley A, Denis J-L, et al. (2020) Bridging competing demands through co-leadership? Potential and limitations. *Human Relations* 73(4): 464–489.

Given, L. M. (2008) *The SAGE Encyclopedia of Qualitative Research Methods.* Thousand Oaks, CA: SAGE.

Gottfredson, R. K., Wright, S. L. and Heaphy, E. D. (2020) 'A critique of the leader-member exchange construct: Back to square one', *The Leadership Quarterly*, 31: 101385.

Henry E and Wolfgramm R (2018) Relational leadership–An indigenous Māori perspective. *Leadership* 14(2): 203–219.

Hinkin, T. R. and Schriesheim, C. A. (2008) 'An examination of "nonleadership": from laissez-faire leadership to leader reward omission and punishment omission', *Journal of Applied Psychology*, 93 (6): 1234.

Hogg, M. A. (2001) 'A social identity theory of leadership', *Personality and Social Psychology Review*, 5(3): 184–200.

Hollander, E. P. and Julian, J. W. (1969) 'Contemporary trends in the analysis of leadership processes', *Psychological Bulletin*, 71: 387.

Homans, G. C. (1961) 'The humanities and the social sciences', *American Behavioral Scientist*, 4 (8): 3–6.

Hosking, D. M. (1988) 'Organizing, leadership and skilful process', *Journal of Management Studies*, 25 (2):147–166.

Jacobs, T. O. (1971) *Leadership and Exchange in Formal Organizations.* Alexandria, VA: Human Resources Research Organization.

Jian, G. (2022) 'From empathic leader to empathic leadership practice: An extension to relational leadership theory', *Human Relations*, 75 (5): 931–955.

Kandade, K., Samara, G. and Parada, M. J. and Dawson, A. (2021) 'From family successors to successful business leaders: A qualitative study of how high-quality relationships develop in family businesses', *Journal of Family Business Strategy*, 12: 100334.

Keen, S. (2007) *Empathy and the Novel*. Oxford: Oxford University Press on Demand.

Levinas, E. (1969) *Totality and Infinity: An Essay on Exteriority* (A. Lingis, trans.). Pittsburgh, PA: Duquesne University Press.

Levinas, E. (1998) *Otherwise than Being or Beyond Essence* (A. Lingis, trans.). Pittsburgh, PA: Duquesne University Press.

Liden, R. C. and Maslyn, J. M. (1998) 'Multidimensionality of leader-member exchange: An empirical assessment through scale development', *Journal of Management*, 24 (1): 43–72.

Liu, H., Cutcher, L. and Grant, D. (2015) 'Doing authenticity: The gendered construction of authentic leadership', *Gender, Work and Organization*, 22 (3): 237–255.

Lord, R. G. and Maher, K. J. (1991) 'Cognitive theory in industrial and organizational psychology', *Handbook of Industrial and Organizational Psychology*, 2: 1–62.

Murrell, K. L. (1997) 'Emergent theories of leadership for the next century: Towards relational concepts', *Organization Development Journal*, 15: 35–42.

Nodding, N. (2013) *Caring: A Relational Approach to Ethics and Moral Education*, 2nd edn. Berkeley, CA: University of California Press.

Ospina, S. M., Foldy, E. G., Fairhurst, G. T. and Jackson, B. (2020) 'Collective dimensions of leadership: connecting theory and method', *Human Relations*, 73 (4): 441–463.

Oxford University P (2000) *Oxford English dictionary*.

'empathy, n.' *OED Online*, Oxford University Press (n.d.). Available at: www.oed.com/view/Entry/61284 (accessed 2 July 2022).

Overgaard S (2005) Rethinking other minds: Wittgenstein and Levinas on expression. *Inquiry* 48(3): 249–274.

Parry, J. (2020) 'Flexible working: lessons from the great work-from-home mass experiment', *The Conversation*, 18 December. Available at: https://theconversation.com/flexible-working-lessons-from-the-great-work-from-home-mass-experiment-152268 (accessed 26 September 2022).

Parry, J. and Veliziotis, M. (2021) 'COVID a year on: inequalities and anxieties about returning to workplaces are becoming clearer', *The Conversation*, 24 March. Available at: https://theconversation.com/covid-a-year-on-inequalities-and-anxieties-about-returning-to-workplaces-are-becoming-clearer-157548 (accessed 26 September 2022).

Parry, J., Young, Z., Bevan, S., Veliziotis, M., Baruch, Y., Beigi, M., Bajorek, Z., Salter, E. and Tochia, C. (2021) 'Working from home under COVID-19 lockdown: Transitions and tensions', *Economic & Social Research Council (ESRC)*, February.

Phillips, A. S. and Bedeian, A. G. (1994) 'Leader-follower exchange quality: The role of personal and interpersonal attributes', *Academy of Management Journal*, 37: 990–1001.

Robert, V. and Vandenberghe, C. (2021) 'Laissez-faire leadership and affective commitment: the roles of leader-member exchange and subordinate relational self-concept', *Journal of Business and Psychology*, 36: 533–551.

Rost, J. C. (1991) *Leadership for the Twenty-first Century*. Santa Barbara, CA: Greenwood Publishing Group.

Rost, J. C. (1993) 'Leadership development in the new millennium', *Journal of Leadership Studies*, 1 (1): 91–110.

Sayles, L. R. (1964) *Managerial Behavior: Administration in Complex Organizations*. New York City, NY: McGraw-Hill.

Scandura, T. A. and Graen, G. B. (1984) 'Moderating effects of initial leader–member exchange status on the effects of a leadership intervention', *Journal of Applied Psychology*, 69 (3): 428.

Skogstad, A., Hetland, J., Glasø, L. and Einarsen, S. (2014) 'Is avoidant leadership a root cause of subordinate stress? Longitudinal relationships between laissez-faire leadership and role ambiguity', *Work & Stress*, 28 (4): 323–341.

Smit, B. (2014) 'An ethnographic narrative of relational leadership', *Journal of Sociology and Social Anthropology*, 5 (2): 117–123.

Sparrowe RT (2005) Authentic leadership and the narrative self. *The Leadership Quarterly* 16(3): 419–439.

Spiller C, Maunganui Wolfgramm R, Henry E, et al. (2020) Paradigm warriors: Advancing a radical ecosystems view of collective leadership from an Indigenous Māori perspective. *Human Relations* 73(4): 516–543.

Taipale, J. (2015) 'Empathy and the melodic unity of the other', *Human Studies*, 38 (4): 463–479.

Te Ahukaramū, C. R. (2005) 'Māori – Urbanisation and renaissance', Te Ara – the Encyclopedia of New Zealand, Available at: http://www.TeAra.govt.nz/en/maori/page-5 (accessed 3 July 2022).

Uhl-Bien, M. (2006) 'Relational leadership theory: Exploring the social processes of leadership and organizing', *The Leadership Quarterly*, 17: 654–676.

Uhl-Bien M (2011) Relational leadership and gender: From hierarchy to relationality. *Leadership, gender, and organization*. Springer, pp.65–74.

Uhl-Bien M, Graen GB and Scandura TA (2000) Implications of leader-member exchange (LMX) for strategic human resource management systems: Relationships as social capital for competitive advantage. *Research in personnel and human resources management* 18: 137–186.

Walsh, P. J. (2014) 'Empathy, embodiment, and the unity of expression', *Topoi*, 33 (1): 215–226.

Walter, R., Buckley, H., Jacomb, C. and Matisoo-Smith, E. (2017) 'Mass migration and the Polynesian settlement of New Zealand', *Journal of World Prehistory*, 30 (4): 351–376.

Watkins, T., Fehr, R. and He, W. (2019) 'Whatever it takes: Leaders' perceptions of abusive supervision instrumentality', *The Leadership Quarterly*, 30 (2): 260–272.

Zahavi, D. (2010) 'Empathy, embodiment and interpersonal understanding: From Lipps to Schutz', *Inquiry*, 53 (3): 285–306.

Zahavi D (2011) Empathy and direct social perception: A phenomenological proposal. *Review of Philosophy and Psychology* 2(3): 541–558.

Zahavi, D. (2014) *Self and other: Exploring Subjectivity, Empathy, and Shame*. London: Oxford University Press.

Chapter 6

Adair, J. E. (2005) *How to Grow Leaders: The Seven Key Principles of Effective Leadership Development*. London: Kogan Page.

Akpan, I.J., Soopramanien, D. and Kwak, D-H. (2021) Cutting-edge technologies for small business and innovation in the era of COVID-19 global health pandemic. *Journal of Small Business & Entrepreneurship* 33(6): 607–617.

Bandura, A. (1986) 'The explanatory and predictive scope of self-efficacy theory', *Journal of Social and Clinical Psychology*, 4 (3), 359–373.

Bass, B. M. and Avolio, B. J. (1994) 'Transformational leadership and organizational culture', *The International Journal of Public Administration*, 17 (3–4), 541–554.

Basso, O., Fayolle, A. and Bouchard, V. (2009) 'Entrepreneurial orientation: The making of a concept', *The International Journal of Entrepreneurship and Innovation*, 10 (4), 313–321.

Baum, J. R., Locke, E. A. and Kirkpatrick, S. A. (1998) 'A longitudinal study of the relation of vision and vision communication to venture growth in entrepreneurial firms', *Journal of Applied Psychology*, 83 (1): 43.

Bennett, N. and Lemoine, J. (2014) 'What VUCA really means for you', *Harvard Business Review*, 92 (1/2).

Boin, A. (2006) 'Organisations and crisis: The emergence of a new research paradigm', in D. Smith and D. Elliott (eds) *Key Readings in Crisis Management*. London: Routledge.

Boin, A., Hart, P. T., McConnell, A. and Preston, T. (2010) 'Leadership style, crisis response and blame management: The case of Hurricane Katrina', *Public Administration*, 88 (3): 706–723.

Borodzicz, E. (2005) *Risk, Crisis and Security Management*. Oxford: Wiley.

Cann, A. and Siegfried, W. D. (1987) 'Sex stereotypes and the leadership role', *Sex Roles*, 17 (7): 401–408.

Cardon, M. S., Wincent, J., Singh, J. and Drnovsek, M. (2009) 'The nature and experience of entrepreneurial passion', *Academy of Management Review*, 34 (3): 511–532.

Clark, C. M., Harrison, C. and Gibb, S. (2019) 'Developing a conceptual framework of entrepreneurial leadership: A systematic literature review and thematic analysis', *International Review of Entrepreneurship*, 17 (3): 347–384.

Covin, J. G. and Miller, D. (2014) 'International entrepreneurial orientation: Conceptual considerations, research themes, measurement issues, and future research directions', *Entrepreneurship Theory and Practice*, 38 (1): 11–44.

Cunningham, J. B. and Lischeron, J. (1991) 'Defining entrepreneurship', *Journal of Small Business Management*, 29 (1): 45–61.

Deakins, D. and Scott, J. M. (2018) *Entrepreneurship: A Contemporary and Global Approach*. London: SAGE.

Dinh, J. E., Lord, R. G., Gardner, W. L., Meuser, J. D., Liden, R. C. and Hu, J. (2014) 'Leadership theory and research in the new millennium: Current theoretical trends and changing perspectives', *The Leadership Quarterly*, 25 (1): 36–62.

Doern, R. (2016) 'Entrepreneurship and crisis management: The experiences of small businesses during the London 2011 riots', *International Small Business Journal*, 34 (4): 276–302.

Elsbach, K. D. and Hargadon, A. B. (2006) 'Enhancing creativity through "mindless" work: A framework of workday design', *Organization Science*, 17 (4) 470–483.

Fernald, L. W., Solomon, G. T., and Tarabishy, A. (2005) 'A new paradigm: Entrepreneurial leadership', *Southern Business Review*, 30 (2): 1–10.

Flamholtz, E. G. (2011) 'The leadership molecule hypothesis: implications for entrepreneurial organizations', *International Review of Entrepreneurship*, 9 (3): 1–23.

Galanakis CM (2020) The food systems in the era of the coronavirus (COVID-19) pandemic crisis. *Foods* 9(4): 523.

Gibb, A. A. (2012) 'Exploring the synergistic potential in entrepreneurial university development: towards the building of a strategic framework', *Annals of Innovation and Entrepreneurship*, 3: 1–24.

Grint, K. (2010) 'The sacred in leadership: Separation, sacrifice and silence', *Organization Studies*, 31 (1): 89–107.

Gupta, V., MacMillan, I. C. and Surie, G. (2004) 'Entrepreneurial leadership: developing and measuring a cross-cultural construct', *Journal of Business Venturing*, 19 (2): 241–260.

Hammond, M. M., Schyns, B., Lester, G. V., Clapp-Smith, R. and Thomas, J. S. (2021) 'The romance of leadership: Rekindling the fire through replication of Meindl and Ehrlich', *The Leadership Quarterly*, 101538.

Hensel, R. and Visser, R. (2018) 'Shared leadership in entrepreneurial teams: the impact of personality', *International Journal of Entrepreneurial Behavior and Research*, 24 (6): 1104–1119.

Hensel, R. and Visser, R. (2019) 'Explaining effective team vision development in small, entrepreneurial teams: A shared mental models approach', *Journal of Small Business Strategy*, 29 (1): 1–15.

Howorth, C., Tempest, S. and Coupland, C. (2005) 'Rethinking entrepreneurship methodology and definitions of the entrepreneur', *Journal of Small Business and Enterprise Development*, 12 (1): 24–40.

Huxtable-Thomas, L. A., Hannon, P. D. and Thomas, S. W. (2016) 'An investigation into the role of emotion in leadership development for entrepreneurs: A four interface model', *International Journal of Entrepreneurial Behavior and Research*, 22 (4): 510–530.

Kahn MJ and Sachs BP (2018) Crises and turnaround management: lessons learned from recovery of New Orleans and Tulane University following Hurricane Katrina. *Rambam Maimonides medical journal* 9(4).

Kayes, D.C., Allen, N.C. and Self, N. (2012) 'Integrating learning, leadership, and crisis in management education: Lessons from army officers in Iraq and Afghanistan', *Journal of Management Education*, 37 (2): 180–202.

Kempster, S. and Cope, J. (2010) 'Learning to lead in the entrepreneurial context', *International Journal of Entrepreneurial Behavior and Research*, 16 (1): 5–34.

Kingsnorth, P. (2011) *Real England: The Battle Against the Bland*. London: Portobello Books.

Kraus, S., Breier, M., Jones, P. and Hughes, M. (2019) 'Individual entrepreneurial orientation and intrapreneurship in the public sector', *International Entrepreneurship and Management Journal*, 15 (4): 1247–1268.

Krueger, N. and Sussan, F. (2017) 'Person-level entrepreneurial orientation: clues to the "entrepreneurial mindset"?', *International Journal of Business and Globalisation*, 18 (3): 382–395.

Kuratko, D. F. and Hornsby, J. S. (1999) 'Corporate entrepreneurial leadership for the 21st century', *Journal of Leadership Studies*, 5 (2): 27–39.

Kuratko, D. F. (2007) 'Entrepreneurial leadership in the 21st century: Guest editor's perspective', *Journal of Leadership and Organizational Studies*, 13 (4): 1–11.

LaBrosse, M. (2007) 'Project management's role in disaster recovery', *Leadership and Management in Engineering*, 89 (1).

Leitch, C. M. and Harrison, R. T. (2018) 'The evolving field of entrepreneurial leadership: An overview', in R. T. Harrison and C. Leitch (eds) *Research Handbook on Entrepreneurship and Leadership*. Cheltenham: Edward Elgar Publishing. pp. 3–34.

Leitch, C. M. and Volery, T. (2017) 'Entrepreneurial leadership: Insights and directions', *International Small Business Journal*, 35 (2): 147–156.

Makri, M. and Scandura, T. A. (2010) 'Exploring the effects of creative CEO leadership on innovation in high-technology firms', *The Leadership Quarterly*, 21 (1): 75–88.

Markham, S. E. (2012) 'The evolution of organizations and leadership from the ancient world to modernity: A multilevel approach to organizational science and leadership (OSL)', *The Leadership Quarterly*, 23 (6): 1134–1151.

Meyer, G. D. and Dean, T. J. (1990) 'An upper echelons perspective on transformational leadership problems in high technology firms', *The Journal of High Technology Management Research*, 1 (2): 223–242.

Nice, D. C. (1998) 'The warrior model of leadership: classic perspectives and contemporary relevance', *The Leadership Quarterly*, 9 (3): 321–332.

Ogbor, J. O. (2000) 'Organizational leadership and authority relations across cultures: Beyond divergence and convergence', *International Journal of Commerce and Management*, 10 (1): 48–73.

Pearson, C. and Clair, J. (1998) 'Reframing crisis management', *The Academy of Management Review*, 23 (1): 59–76.

Pinchot, G. and Soltanifar, M. (2021) 'Digital intrapreneurship: The corporate solution to a rapid digitalisation', in M. Soltanifar, M. Hughes and L. Göcke (eds), *Digital Entrepreneurship*. Cham: Springer. pp. 233–262.

Pittaway, L., Huxtable-Thomas, L. and Hannon, P. D. (2018) 'Entrepreneurial learning and educational practice', in R. Blackburn, D. De Clercq and J. Heinonen (eds), *SAGE Handbook for Entrepreneurship and Small Business*. London: SAGE. pp. 471–490.

Raible, S. E. and Williams-Middleton, K. (2021) 'The relatable entrepreneur: Combating stereotypes in entrepreneurship education', *Industry and Higher Education*, 09504222211017436.

Renko, M., El Tarabishy, A., Carsrud, A. L. and Brännback, M. (2015) 'Understanding and measuring entrepreneurial leadership style', *Journal of Small Business Management*, 53 (1): 54–74.

Roomi, M. A. and Harrison, P. (2011) 'Entrepreneurial leadership: What is it and how should it be taught?', *International Review of Entrepreneurship*, 9 (3).

Sato, T. (2012) 'Kauffman fellow journal: Japan's challenge an entrepreneurial approach to disaster recovery'. Available at: https://www.kauffmanfellows.org/journal_posts/japans-challenge-an-entrepreneurial-approach-to-disaster-recovery

Scheepers CB and Bogie J (2020) Uber Sub-Saharan Africa: contextual leadership for sustainable business model innovation during COVID-19. Emerald Emerging Markets Case Studies.

Shao, Y., Nijstad, B. A. and Täuber, S. (2019) 'Creativity under workload pressure and integrative complexity: The double-edged sword of paradoxical leadership', *Organizational Behavior and Human Decision Processes*, 155: 7–19.

Simola, S. (2014) 'Teaching corporate crisis management through business ethics education', *European Journal of Training and Development*, 38 (5): 485–503.

Smith, R. (2021) *Entrepreneurship in Policing and Criminal Contexts*. Yorkshire: Emerald Group Publishing.

Surie, G. and Ashley, A. (2008) 'Integrating pragmatism and ethics in entrepreneurial leadership for sustainable value creation', *Journal of Business Ethics*, 81 (1): 235–246.

Thornberry, N. (2006) *Lead Like an Entrepreneur*. New York, NY: McGraw Hill Professional.

Van de Vliert, E. (2006) 'Autocratic leadership around the globe: Do climate and wealth drive leadership culture?', *Journal of Cross-Cultural Psychology*, 37 (1): 42–59.

Vecchio, R. P. (2003) 'Entrepreneurship and leadership: common trends and common threads', *Human Resource Management Review*, 13 (2): 303–327.

Western, S. (2020) 'Covid-19: an intrusion of the real the unconscious unleashes its truth', *Journal of Social Work Practice*, 34 (4): 445–451.

Chapter 7

Acker, J. (1990) 'Hierarchies, jobs, bodies: A theory of gendered organizations', *Gender and Society*, 4 (2): 139–158.

Alvesson, M. and Kärreman, D. (2016) 'Intellectual failure and ideological success in organization studies: The case of transformational leadership', *Journal of Management Inquiry*, 25 (2): 139–152.

Alvesson, M. and Spicer, A. (2012) 'Critical leadership studies: The case for critical performativity', *Human Relations*, 65 (3): 367–390.

Alvesson, M. and Sveningsson, S. (2003) 'The great disappearing act: difficulties in doing "leadership"', *The Leadership Quarterly*, 14: 359–381.

Bachrach, P. and Baratz, M. S. (1962) 'Two faces of power', *The American Political Science Review*, 56 (4): 947–952. doi: https://doi.org/10.2307/1952796

Bernstein, S. (2003) Positive organizational scholarship: Meet the movement. *Journal of Management Inquiry* 12(3): 266–271.

Butler, J. (2015) *Notes Toward a Performative Theory of Assembly*. Cambridge, MA and London, UK: Harvard University Press.

Calás, M. B. and Smircich, L. (1992) 'Using the F word: Feminist theories and the social consequences of organisational research', in A. J. Mills and P. Tancred (eds), *Gendering Organisational Analysis*. Thousand Oaks, CA: SAGE.

Carnegie, D. (1994) *How to win friends and influence people*. London: Cedar.

Collinson, D. L. (2020) '"Only connect!": Exploring the critical dialectical turn in leadership studies', *Organization Theory*, 1 (2): 2631787720913878.

Collinson, D., Smolović Jones, O. and Grint, K. (2018) '"No more heroes": Critical perspectives on leadership romanticism', *Organization Studies*, 39 (11): 1625–1647.

Cunha, M. P. e, Clegg, S. and Rego, A. (2013) 'Lessons for leaders: Positive organization studies meets Niccolò Machiavelli', *Leadership*, 9 (4): 450–465.

Dahl, R. A. (1957) 'The concept of power', *Behavioral Science*, 2 (3): 201–215. doi: https://doi.org/10.1002/bs.3830020303

Dreyfus, H. and Rabinow, P. (1982) *Michel Foucault: Beyond Structuralism and Hermeneutics* (1st edn). Hertfordshire: Harvester Press.

Ehrenreich B (2009) *Bright-sided: How positive thinking is undermined America*. Metropolitan Books.

Fanon F (1970) *Black skin, white masks*. Paladin London.

Fanon F (1952) The fact of blackness. *Postcolonial studies: An anthology* 15(32): 2–40.

Fineman S (2006) On being positive: Concerns and counterpoints. *Academy of management review* 31(2): 270–291.

Festinger, L. (1957) *A Theory of Cognitive Dissonance*. Evanston, IL: Row and Peterson.

Foucault, M. (1990) *The History of Sexuality – Volume 1: An Introduction*. New York: Vintage Books.

Foucault, M. (2010a) *Discipline and Punish* (2nd edn). New York: Vintage Books.

Foucault, M. (2010b) 'Truth and power', in P. Rabinow (ed.), *The Foucault Reader*. New York: Vintage Books. pp. 51–75.

Ford, J. and Harding, N. (2011) 'The impossibility of the "true self" of authentic leadership', *Leadership*, 7 (4): 463–479.

Ford, J. and Harding, N. (2018) 'Followers in leadership theory: Fiction, fantasy and illusion', *Leadership*, 14 (1): 3–24.

Fournier, V. and Grey, C. (2000) 'At the critical moment: Conditions and prospects for critical management studies', *Human Relations*, 53 (1): 7–32. https://doi.org/10.1177/0018726700531002.

Fournier, V. and Kelemen, M. (2001) 'The crafting of community: Recoupling discourses of management and womanhood', *Gender, Work and Organization*, 8 (3): 267–290.

French, J. R. P. and Raven, B. (1959) 'The bases of social power', in D. Cartwright (ed.) *Studies in Social Power*. Ann Arbor: University of Michigan. pp. 150–167.

Frenkel M and Shenhav Y (2006) From binarism back to hybridity: A postcolonial reading of management and organization studies. *Organization studies* 27(6): 855–876.

Gordon, R. (2011) 'Leadership and power', in A. Bryman, D. Collinson, K. Grint, B. Jackson and M. Uhl-Bien (eds), *The SAGE Handbook of Leadership*. London: SAGE. pp. 195–202.

Harding, N. (2021) 'Leadership without "the led": A case study of the South Wales Valleys', *International Journal of Public Leadership*, 17: 236–246.

Jones EE (1990) *Interpersonal perception*. WH Freeman/Times Books/Henry Holt & Co.

Kelly S (2014) Towards a negative ontology of leadership. *Human Relations* 67(8): 905–922.

Kempster, S., Schedlitzki, D. and Edwards, G. (2021) 'Where have all the followers gone?', *Leadership*, 17 (1): 118–128.

Kleinman, K. (2017) 'Uber: The scandals that drove Travis Kalanick out', *BBC News*, 21 June. Available at: https://www.bbc.co.uk/news/technology-40352868 (accessed 26 September 2022).

Langone, M. (1988) *Cults: Questions and Answers*. Weston, MA: American Family Foundation.

Layton, D. (1999) *Seductive Poison: A Jonestown Survivor's Story of Life and Death in the People's Temple*. London: Aurum Press.

Lukes, S. (2005) *Power: A Radical View* (2nd edn). Basingstone: Palgrave Macmillan.

Luthans, F. (2003) The need for and meaning of positive organizational behaviour. *Journal of Organizational Behavior* 23: 695–706.

Luthans, F. and Yousef, C. (2007) Emerging positive organizational behavior. *Journal of Management* 33(3): 321–349.

Lyotard J-F (1984) *The postmodern condition: A report on knowledge*. U of Minnesota Press.

Machiavelli N (1961) *The Prince*. Harmondsworth: Penguin.

Michaelson C (2005) Meaningful motivation for work motivation theory. *Academy of management review* 30(2): 235–238.

Nkomo, S. M. (2011) 'A postcolonial and anti-colonial reading of "African" leadership and management in organization studies: Tensions, contradictions and possibilities', *Organization*, 18 (3): 365–386.

Padilla, A., Hogan, R. and Kaiser, R. B. (2007) 'The toxic triangle: Destructive leaders, susceptible followers, and conducive environments', *The Leadership Quarterly*, 18: 176–194.

Pelletier, K. L., Kottke, J. L. and Sirotnik, B. W. (2019) 'The toxic triangle in academia: A case analysis of the emergence and manifestation of toxicity in a public university', *Leadership*, 15 (4): 405–432.

Seligman, M., Abramson, L., Semmel, A., et al. (1998) *Learned Optimism*. New York: Pocket Books.

Seligman, M. (2002) *Authentic Happiness*. New York: Free Press.

Sinclair A (1992) The tyranny of a team ideology. *Organization studies* 13(4): 611–626.

Singer, M. (1987) 'Group psychodynamics', in R. Berkow and M. Sharp (eds), *The Merck Manual of Diagnosis and Therapy*. Rahway, NJ: Dohme Research Laboratories.

sliwa M and Johansson M (2014) The discourse of meritocracy contested/reproduced: Foreign women academics in UK business schools. *Organization* 21(6): 821–843.

Solomon S, Greenberg J and Pyszczynski T (1991) A terror management theory of social behavior: The psychological functions of self-esteem and cultural worldviews. *Advances in experimental social psychology*. Elsevier, pp.93–159.

Stead V (2014) The gendered power relations of action learning: A critical analysis of women's reflections on a leadership development programme. *Human Resource Development International* 17(4): 416–437.

The Guardian (2021) 'GMB leader and Uber boss to discuss next step on workers' rights', 26 August. Available at: https://www.theguardian.com/business/2021/aug/26/gmb-leader-uber-boss-workers-rights-drivers (accessed 26 September 2022).

Tourish, D. and Pinnington, A. (2002) 'Transformational leadership, corporate cultism and the spirituality paradigm: an unholy trinity in the workplace?', *Human Relations*, 55: 147–172.

World Health Organization (WHO) (2021) 'Long working hours increasing deaths from heart disease and stroke: WHO, ILO'. Available at: https://www.who.int/news/item/17-05-2021-long-working-hours-increasing-deaths-from-heart-disease-and-stroke-who-ilo? (accessed 27 September 2022).

Wright, H. K. (2002) 'Notes on the (Im) possibility of Articulating Continental African identity', *Critical Arts*, 16(2): 1–18.

Wright, T.A. (2003) Positive organizational behaviour: An idea whose time has truly come. *Journal of Organizational Behaviour* 24: 437–442.

Chapter 8

Alakavuklar, O. N. and Alamgir, F. (2018) 'Ethics of resistance in organisations: A conceptual proposal', *Journal of Business Ethics*, 149 (1), 31–43.

Anderson, P. (1967) 'The limits and possibilities of trade union action', in R. Blackburn and A. Cockburn (eds), *The Incompatibles: Trade Union Militancy and Consensus*. Penguin: Harmondsworth. pp. 263–280.

Aust, I., Matthews, B. and Muller-Camen, M. (2020) 'Common good HRM: A paradigm shift in Sustainable HRM?', *Human Resource Management Review*, 30 (3): 100705.

Bamber, G. J., Bartram, T. and Stanton, P. (2017) 'Strategic HRM and workplace innovations: formulating research questions', *Personnel Review*, 46 (7): 1216–1227.

Bamber, G. J., Gittell, J. H., Kochan, T. A. and von Nordenflycht, A. (2009) *Up in the Air: How Airlines Can Improve Performance by Engaging Their Employees*. Ithaca: ILR Press.

Bauman, Z. (1993) *Postmodern Ethics*. London: Blackwell.

Becker, B. and Gerhart, B. (1996) 'The impact of human resource management on organizational performance: Progress and prospects', *Academy of Management Journal*, 39 (4): 779–801.

Beer, M., Spector, B., Lawrence, P. R., Quinn Mills, D. and Walton, R. E. (1984) *Managing Human Assets*. New York: Free Press.

Boling, T. E. (1978) 'The management ethics "crisis": An organizational perspective', *Academy of Management Review*, 3 (2): 360–365.

Boxall, P. (2021) 'Studying mutuality and perversity in the impacts of human resource management on societal well-being: Advancing a pluralist agenda', *Human Resource Management Journal*, 31 (4): 834–846.

Bryson, A. (2017) 'Mutual gains? is there a role for employee engagement in the modern workplace?', *IZA Discussion Papers*, 11112. Bonn: Institute of Labor Economics (IZA).

Boxall, P. and Purcell, J. (2011) *Strategy and Human Resource Management* (3rd edn). London: Palgrave.

Boxall, P. and Purcell, J. (2016) *Strategy and Human Resource Management* (4th edn). London: Palgrave.

Cafferkey, K., Heffernan, M., Harney, B., Dundon, T. and Townsend, K. (2019) 'Perceptions of HRM system strength and affective commitment: the role of human relations and internal process climate', *The International Journal of Human Resource Management*, 30 (21): 3026–3048.

Caldwell, C., Truong, D. X., Linh, P. T. and Tuan, A. (2010) 'Strategic human resource management as ethical stewardship', *Journal of Business Ethics*, 98 (1): 171–182.

Carroll, A. B. (1991) 'The pyramid of corporate social responsibility: Toward the moral management of organizational stakeholders', *Business Horizons*, 34 (4): 39–48.

Chadwick, C. and Flinchbaugh, C. (2021) 'Searching for competitive advantage in the HRM-firm performance relationship', *Academy of Management Perspectives*, 35 (2): 181–207.

Claydon, T. (2000) 'Employee participation and involvement', in D. Winstanley and J. Goodall (eds), *Ethical Issues in Contemporary Human Resource Management*. London: MacMillan. pp. 208–244.

Claydon, T. and Doyle, M. (1996) 'Trusting me, trusting you? The ethics of employee empowerment', *Personnel Review*, 25 (6): 13–25.

Cregan, C., Kulik, C. T., Johnston, S. and Bartram, T. (2021) 'The influence of calculative ("hard") and collaborative ("soft") strategic HRM on the layoff-performance relationship in high performance workplaces', *Human Resource Management Journal*, 31 (1): 202–224.

Critchley, S. (2007) *Infinitely Demanding: Ethics of Commitment, Politics of Resistance*. London: Verso.

Crossley, N. (2003) 'Even newer social movements? Anti-corporate protests, capitalist crises and the remoralization of society', *Organization*, 10 (2): 287–305.

Delbridge, R. and Keenoy, T. (2010) 'Beyond managerialism?', *International Journal of Human Resource Management*, 21 (6): 799–817.

Derrida, J. (1978/2001) *Writing and Difference*. London: Routledge.

Diprose, R. (2003) *Corporeal Generosity: On Giving with Nietzsche, Merleau-Ponty, and Levinas*. New York, NY: SUNY.

Edwards, P. (2014) 'Were the 40 years of "radical pluralism" a waste of time? A response to Peter Ackers and Patrick McGovern', *Warwick Papers in Industrial Relations*, No. 99. University of Warwick, Industrial Relations Research Unit, Coventry.

Fleming, P. (2009) *Cultural Politics of Work: New Forms of Informal Control*. Oxford: Oxford University Press.

Fombrun, C., Tichy, N. M. and DeVanna, M. A. (eds) (1984) *Strategic Human Resource Management*. New York: Wiley.

Fox A (1966) Industrial sociology and industrial relations: An assessment of the contribution which industrial sociology can make towards understanding and resolving some of the problems now being considered by the Royal Commission. HM Stationery Office.

Friedman, M. (1965) 'The Social Responsibility of Business Is to Increase its Profits', 34

Garmendia, A., Elorza, U., Aritzeta, A. and Madinabeitia-Olabarria, D. (2021) 'High-involvement HRM, job satisfaction and productivity: A two wave longitudinal study of a Spanish retail company', *Human Resource Management Journal*, 31 (1): 341–357.

Geare, A., Edgar, F. and McAndrew, I. (2006) 'Employment relationships: Ideology and HRM practice', *The International Journal of HRM*, 17 (7): 1190–1208.

Gilley, J. W., Anderson, S. K. and Gilley, A. (2008) 'Human resource management as a champion for corporate ethics: Moving towards ethical integration and acculturation in the HR function and profession', in S. A. Quattro and R. R. Sims (eds), *Executive Ethics: Ethical Dilemmas and Challenges for the C-suite*. Charlotte, NC: Information Age Publishing. pp.215–228.

Greenwood, M. R. (2002) 'Ethics and HRM: A review and conceptual analysis', *Journal of Business Ethics*, 36 (3): 261–278.

Greenwood, M. (2013) 'Ethical analyses of Strategic HRM: A review and research agenda', *Journal of Business Ethics*, 114 (2): 355–366.

Greenwood, M. and Freeman, R. E. (2018) 'Deepening ethical analysis in business ethics', *Journal of Business Ethics*, 147 (1): 1–4.

Guest, D. E. (1987) 'Human resource management and industrial relations', *Journal of Management Studies*, 24 (5): 503–521.

Guest DE (1999) Human resource management-the workers' verdict. *Human resource management journal* 9(3): 5–25.

Guest, D. E. (2011) 'Human resource management and performance: Still searching for some answers', *Human Resource Management Journal*, 21 (1): 3–13.

Guest, D. E. and Woodrow, C. (2012) 'Exploring the boundaries of human resource managers' responsibilities', *Journal of Business Ethics*, 111 (1): 109–119.

Hart, T. J. (1993) 'Human resource management: Time to exercise the militant tendency', *Employee Relations*, 15 (3): 29–36.

Harvey G and Turnbull P (2020) Ricardo flies Ryanair: Strategic human resource management and competitive advantage in a Single European Aviation Market. *Human resource management journal* 30(4): 553–565.

Harvey, G., Hodder, A. and Brammer, S. (2017) 'Trade union participation in CSR deliberation: an evaluation', *Industrial Relations Journal*, 48 (1): 42–55.

Heath, J. (2006) 'Business ethics without stakeholders', *Business Ethics Quarterly*, 533–557.

Heery E (2016) Framing work: unitary, pluralist, and critical perspectives in the twenty-first century. Oxford University Press.

Hendry, J. (2004) *Between Ethics and Enterprise: Business and Management in a Bimoral Society.* Oxford: Oxford University Press.

Ho, H. and Kuvaas, B. (2020) 'Human resource management systems, employee well-being, and firm performance from the mutual gains and critical perspectives: The well-being paradox', *Human Resource Management*, 59 (3): 235–253.

Hogan, M. (2013) 'Michael O'Leary's 33 daftest quotes', *The Guardian*, 8 November.

Johnstone S and Wilkinson A (2018) The potential of labour– management partnership: a longitudinal case analysis. *British Journal of Management* 29(3): 554–570.

Lawler, E. E. (1986) *High-Involvement Management.* San Francisco: Jossey-Bass.

Levinas, E. (1991) *Totality and Infinity.* Dordrecht: Kluwer.

Lewis, D. and Vandekerckhove, W. (2018) 'Trade unions and the whistleblowing process in the UK: An opportunity for strategic expansion?', *Journal of Business Ethics*, 148 (4): 835–845.

Lewis, P. V. (1985) 'Defining "business ethics": Like nailing jello to a wall', *Journal of Business Ethics*, 4 (5): 377–383.

Macklin, R. (2006) 'The moral autonomy of human resource managers', *Asia Pacific Journal of Human Resources*, 44 (2): 211–221.

Meyer, J. P. and Allen, N. J. (1991) 'A three component conceptualization of organizational commitment', *Human Resource Management*, 1: 61–89.

Miller, P. (1996) 'Strategy and the ethical management of human resources', *Human Resource Management Journal*, 6 (1): 5–26.

Mouffe, C. (2000a) *Deliberative Democracy or Agonistic Pluralism.* Vienna: Institute for Advanced Studies.

Mouffe, C. (2000b) *Deliberative Democracy or Agonistic Pluralism.* Vienna: Institute for Advanced Studies.

Mouffe, C. (2000c) *The Democratic Paradox.* London: Verso.

Mouffe, C. (2005) *On the Political.* London: Routledge.

Noonan, L. (2008) 'Membership of mile-high club goes on offer', *Independent.ie*, 19 June.

Park, O., Bae, J. and Hong, W. (2019) 'High-commitment HRM system, HR capability, and ambidextrous technological innovation', *The International Journal of Human Resource Management*, 30 (9): 1526–1548.

Platt, C. (2008) 'Ryanair CEO talks free sex on flights', *Sydney Morning Herald*, 27 June.

Pullen, A. and Rhodes, C. (2014) 'Corporeal ethics and the politics of resistance in organizations', *Organization*, 21 (6), 782–796.

Purcell, J. and Ahlstrand, B. (1989) 'Corporate strategy and the management of employee relations in the multi-divisional company', *British Journal of Industrial Relations*, 27: 396–417.

Ramsay, H., Scholarios, D. and Harley, B. (2000) 'Employees and high performance work systems: Testing inside the black box.', *British Journal of Industrial Relations*, 38 (4): 501–531.

Rhodes, C., Munro, I., Thanem, T. and Pullen, A. (2020) 'Dissensus! Radical democracy and business ethics', *Journal of Business Ethics*, 164 (4): 627–632.

Reilly, G. (2010) 'The best (and worst) of Michael O'Leary's surprise announcements', *The Journal*, 12 September. Available at https://www.thejournal.ie/the-best-and-worst-of-michael-olearys-surprise-announcements-23015-Sep2010/ (accessed 19 September 2022).

Ritholtz, B. (2017) 'Ryanair's caught between rebellious pilots and the wrath of investors', *Irish Examiner*, 14 November.

Rok, B. (2009) 'Ethical context of the participative leadership model: taking people into account', *Corporate Governance*, 9 (4): 461–472.

Rushton, K. (2002) 'Business ethics: A sustainable approach', *Business Ethics: A European Review*, 11 (2): 137–139.

Svensson, G. and Wood, G. (2008) 'A model of business ethics', *Journal of Business Ethics*, 77 (3): 303–322.

Truss, C., Gratton, L., Hope-Hailey, V., McGovern, P. and Stiles, P. (1997) 'Soft and hard models of human resource management: a reappraisal', *Journal of Management Studies*, 34 (1): 53–73.

Lowry, D. (2006) 'HR managers as ethical decision-makers: Mapping the terrain', *Asia Pacific Journal of Human Resource Management*, 44 (2): 171–183.

Simmons, J. (2003) 'Balancing performance, accountability and equity in stakeholder relationships: Towards more socially responsible HR practice', *Corporate Social Responsibility and Environmental Management*, 10 (3): 129–140.

Simmons, J. (2004) 'Managing in the post-managerialist era: Towards socially responsible corporate governance', *Management Decision*, 42 (3/4): 601–611.

Simmons, J. (2008) 'Ethics and morality in human resource management', *Social Responsibility Journal*, 4 (1/2): 8–23.

Sloan, K. and Gavin, J. H. (2010) 'Human resource management: Meeting the ethical obligations of the function', *Business and Society Review*, 115 (1): 57–74.

Sparrow, P. and Hiltrop, J.-M. (1994) *European Human Resource Management in Transition*. Hemel Hempstead: Prentice Hall.

Storey, J. (1989) *New Perspectives on Human Resource Management*. London: Routledge.

Storey, J. (1992) *Developments in the Management of Human Resources*. Oxford: Blackwell.

Styhre, A. (2001) 'Kaizen, ethics, and care of the operations: Management after empowerment', *Journal of Management Studies*, 38 (6): 795–810.

Tasoulis, K., Krepapa, A. and Stewart, M. M. (2019) 'Leadership integrity and the role of human resource management in Greece: Gatekeeper or bystander?', *Thunderbird International Business Review*, 61 (3): 491–503.

ten Bos, R. (2003) 'Business ethics, accounting and the fear of melancholy', *Organization*, 10 (2): 267–285.

Thompson, P. (2011) 'The trouble with HRM', *Human Resource Management Journal*, 21 (4): 355–367.

Thompson, P. and Ackroyd, S. (1995) 'All quiet on the workplace front? A critique of recent trends in British Industrial Sociology', *Sociology*, 29 (4): 615–633.

Townley, B. (1994) *Reframing Human Resource Management: Power, Ethics and the Subject at Work*. London: SAGE.

Van Buren III, H. J. (2020) 'The value of including employees: a pluralist perspective on sustainable strategic HRM', *Employee Relations*, 44 (3): 686–701.

Walton, R. (1985) 'From control to commitment in the workplace', *Harvard Business Review*, 63 (2): 77–84.

Winstanley, D. and Woodall, J. (2000a) 'The ethical dimension of human resource management', *Human Resource Management Journal*, 10 (2): 5–20.

Winstanley, D., Woodall, J., and Heery, E. (1996). Business ethics and human resource management: Themes And issues. Personnel Review, 25(6), 5–12.

Wood, S. J. and Wall, T. D. (2007) 'Work enrichment and employee voice in human resource management-performance studies', *International Journal of Human Resource Management*, 18 (7): 1335–1372.

Wright Mills, C. (1948) *The New Men of Power: America's Labor Leaders*. New York: Harcourt, Brace.

Chapter 9

Abdulaali, A. (2018) 'The impact of intellectual capital on business organization', *Academy of Accounting and Financial Studies Journal*, 22 (6). Available at: https://www.abacademies.org/articles/the-impact-of-intellectual-capital-on-business-organization-7630.html (accessed 6 September 2021).

Ali, A. (2001) 'Globalization: The great transformation', *Advances in Competitiveness Research*, 9 (1): 1–9. Available at: https://www.proquest.com/docview/211369540?pq-origsite=gscholarandfromopenview=true (accessed 27 September 2022).

Bamsode, S. (2008) 'Creation of digital library of manuscripts at Shivaji University, India', *Library Hi Tech News*, 1: 13–15.

Bennett, N. and Lemoine, G. J. (2014a) 'What a difference a word makes: Understanding', *Business Horizon*, 1126: 1–7. Available at: https://www.researchgate.net/publication/263926940_What_VUCA_really_means_for_you (accessed 27 September 2022).

Bennett, N. and Lemoine, G. J. (2014b) 'What VUCA Really Means for You', *Harvard Business Review*, January–February. Available at: https://hbr.org/2014/01/what-vuca-really-means-for-you (accessed 6 September 2021).

Bennis, W. and Thomas, R. (2020) 'Crucibles of leadership', in R. P. Vecchio (ed.), *Leadership: Understanding the Dynamics of Power and Influence in Organisations* (2nd edn). Notre Dame, IN: University of Notre Dame Press.

Bhattacharya, A., Reeves, M., Lang, N. and Augustinraj, R. (2017) 'New business models for a new global landscape', *BCG Henderson Institute*. Available at: https://www.bcg.com/ publications/2017/globalization-new-business-models-global-landscape (accessed 6 August 2021).

Césaire, A. (2000) Discourse on colonialism, *Monthly Review Press*, New York.

Chaffey, D., Hemphill, T. and Edmundson-Bird, D. (2019) *Digital Business and e-Commerce Management* (7th edn). London: Pearson.

Christensen, C., Raynor, M. and Mcdonald, R. (2015) 'What is disruptive innovation?', *Harvard Business Review*, 93: 44–53.

D'Auria, G. and De Smet, A. (2020) 'Leadership in a crisis: Responding to the coronavirus outbreak and future challenges', *McKinsy and Company*, 16 March.

Daneels, E. (2004) 'Disruptive technology reconsidered: a critique and research agenda', *Journal of Product Innovation Management*, 21 (4): 246–258.

Davenport, T. H. (2014) 'What the heck is digitization anyway', *The Wall Street Journal*, 12 November. Available at: http://blogs.wsj.com/cio/2014/11/12/what-the-heck-is-digitization-anyway/ (accessed 27 September 2022).

Davison, R. M. (2020) 'The transformative potential of disruptions: A viewpoint', *International Journal of Information Management*, 55, December. doi: https://doi. org/10.1016/j.ijinfomgt.2020.102149

De Boer, A.-L., Bothma, J. and Olwagen, J. (2012) 'Library leadership: Innovative options for designing training programmes to build leadership competencies in the digital age', *South African Journal of Libraries and Information Science*, 78 (2). Available at: https://hdl. handle.net/10520/EJC133017 (accessed 13 December 2021).

Diamandis, P. H. and Kotler, S. (2020) *The Future Is faster Than You Think – How Converging Technologies Are Transforming Business, Industries, and Our Lives*. New York: Simen and Schuster.

Hensellek S (2020) Digital leadership: A framework for successful leadership in the digital age. *Journal of Media Management and Entrepreneurship (JMME)* 2(1): 55–69.

Javidan, M., Waldmana, D. A. and Wang, D. (2021) 'How life experiences and cultural context matter: a multilevel framework of global leader effectiveness', *Journal of Management Studies*, July, 58 (5). Doi: 10.1111/joms.12662

Juneja, P. (2021) 'The 4Cs of leadership styles for leadership in the digital age', *MSC*. Available at: https://www.managementstudyguide.com/lessons-for-business-leaders-from-the-downfall-of-charles-ghosn-of-renault-nissan.htm (accessed 29 August 2021).

Jurkiewicz, C. L. (2018) 'Big data, big concerns: ethics in the digital age', *Public Integrity*, 20 (1): S46–S59. Doi: https://doi.org/10.1080/10999922.2018.1448218

Kalakota R and Robinson M (2000) *E-business*. Roadmap for Success.

Kemper, A. (2020) 'Why creating responsible leadership requires decolonization', *Global harton bility*. Available at: https://blog.grli.org/why-creating-responsible-leadership-requires-decolonization/ (accessed 29 August 2021).

Kianto, A., Vanhala, M., Ritala, P. and Hussinki, H. (2018) 'Reflections on the criteria for the sound measurement of intellectual capital: A knowledge-based perspective', *Critical Perspectives of Accounting*, 70, July. Doi: 10.1016/j.cpa.2018.05.002

Kniffin, K. M., Narayanan, J., Anseel, F., Antonakis, J., Ashford, S. P., Bakker, A. B. et al. (2021) 'COVID-19 and the workplace: Implications, issues, and insights for future research and action', *American Psychologist*, 76 (1): 63–77.

Kotler, S. and Diamandis, P. (2015) *BOLD – How to Go Big, Create Wealth and Impact the World*. New York: Simon and Schuster.

Laundon, K. C. and Laudon, J. P. (2020) *Management Informatiom Systems: Managing the Digital Firm*. London: Pearson.

Laudon, K. C. and Traver, C. G. (2021) *E-Commerce 2020–2021: Business, Technology, Society* (6th edn). Essex: Pearson Education.

Libert, B., Wind, J. and Fenley, M. B. (2015) 'is your leadership style right for the digital age?', *Knolwedge At Wharton*, 6 February. Available at: https://knowledge.wharton. upenn.edu/article/the-right-leadership-style-for-the-digital-age/ (accessed 28 August 2021).

Neubauer R, Tarling A and Wade M (2017) Redefining leadership for a digital age. *Global Centre for Digital Business Transformation*. 1–15.

Osterwalder, A. (2004) *The Business Model Ontology – A Proposition in a Design Science Approach*. Switzerland: Lausanne.

Owie, E. T. (2017) 'A review of the digital age and its implications for leadership and management', *Proceedings of the iSTEAMS Multidisciplinary Cross-Border Conference*, 211–216. Available at: https://www.researchgate.net/publication/320707278_A_Review_of_the_Digital_Age_and_Its_Implications_for_Leadership_and_Management (accessed 27 September 2022).

Saykili, A. (2019) 'Higher education in the digital age: The impact of digital connective technologies', *Journal of Educational Technology and Online Learning*, 1–15. doi: 10.31681/jetol.516971

Sedziuviene, N. and Vveinhardt, J. (2009) 'The paradigm of knowledge management in higher educational institutions', *Engineering Economics*, 5. Available at: https://www.researchgate.net/publication/228976361 (accessed 27 September 2022).

Statista (2020, October 26) 'IT skill shortages facing IT leaders worldwide 2017–2020'. *Statista*. Available at: https://www.statista.com/statistics/662423/worldwide-cio-survey-function-skill-shortages/

Steward, T. A. (1997) *Intellectual Capital: The New Wealth of Organisations*. New York: Doubleday.

Wang, B., Liu, Y., Qian, J. and Parker, S. K. (2021) 'Achieving effective remote working during the COVID-19 pandemic: A work design perspective', *Applied Psychology*, 70 (1): 16–59.

Westerman, G., Bonnet, D. and McAfee, A. (2014) *Leading Digital: Turning Technology into Business Transformation*. Boston: Harvard Business Review Press.

Wiig KM (1995) Knowledge management methods. *Arlington (TX)*.

Wilson, E. J. (2004) 'Leadership in the digital age', in G. Goethals, G. Sorenson and B. MacGregor, *Encyclopedia of Leadership*. Thousand Oaks, CA: SAGE. pp. 858–861.

WorldSkillsUK (2021) 'Disconnected: Exploring the digital skills gaps', *WorldSkillsUk*. Available at: https://www.worldskillsuk.org/insights/disconnected-exploring-the-digital-skills-gap/ (accessed 27 September 2022).

Chapter 10

Afriat, H., Dvir-Gvirsman, S., Tsuriel, K. and Ivan, L. (2021) '"This is capitalism. It is not illegal": Users' attitudes toward institutional privacy following the Cambridge Analytica scandal', *The Information Society*, 37 (2): 115–127.

Alavi S (2021) Reproductive Responsibility and the Racial Biopolitics of Choice. Available at: https://sites.brown.edu/publichealthjournal/2021/12/13/reproductive/.

Andrew, J. and Baker, M. (2021) 'The general data protection regulation in the age of surveillance capitalism', Journal of Business Ethics, 168 (3): 565–578.

BBC News (2020) 'Facebook founder sees wealth hit $100bn after TikTok rival launch', 7 August. Available at: https://www.bbc.co.uk/news/business-53689645 (accessed 22nd June).

BBC News (2022) 'Roe v Wade: What is US Supreme Court ruling on abortion?'. Available at: https://www.bbc.co.uk/news/world-us-canada-54513499 (accessed 27 June 2022).

Bakir, V. (2021) 'Freedom or security? Mass surveillance of citizens', in S. J. A. Ward (ed.) *Handbook of Global Media Ethics*. Cham: Springer International Publishing. pp. 939–959.

Bauman, Z., Bigo, D., Esteves, P., Guild, E., Jabri, V., Lyon, D. and Walker, R. B. J. (2014) 'After Snowden: Rethinking the impact of surveillance', *International Political Sociology*, 8 (2): 121–144.

Berda, Y. (2013) 'Managing dangerous populations: Colonial legacies of security and surveillance', *Sociological Forum, Wiley Online Library*, 627–630.

Boyd, D. and Crawford, K. (2012) 'Critical questions for big data: Provocations for a cultural, technological, and scholarly phenomenon', *Information, Communication and Society*, 15 (5): 662–679.

Braatvedt, K. (2020) 'The dividual interior: Surveillance and desire', *Idea Journal*, 17 (01): 13–28.

Brown, A. J. (2020) '"Should I stay or should I leave?": Exploring (dis)continued Facebook use after the Cambridge Analytica scandal', *Social Media + Society*, 6 (1): 2056305120913884.

Brunon-Ernst, A. (2013) 'Deconstructing panopticism into the plural panopticons', *Beyond Foucault: New Perspectives on Bentham's Panopticon*. Surrey: Ashgate publishing. pp.17–42.

Bushwick, S. (2022) Yes, Phones Can Reveal if Someone Gets an Abortion. Available at: https://www.scientificamerican.com/article/yes-phones-can-reveal-if-someone-gets-an-abortion/ (accessed June 30th).

Cadwalladr, C. and Glendinning, L. (2018) 'Exposing Cambridge Analytica: "It's been exhausting, exhilarating, and slightly terrifying"', *The Guardian*, 29 September. Available at: https://www.theguardian.com/membership/2018/sep/29/cambridge-analytica-cadwalladr-observer-facebook-zuckerberg-wylie (accessed 22 June 2022).

Cadwalladr, C. and Graham-Harrison, E. (2018) 'Revealed: 50 million Facebook profiles harvested for Cambridge Analytica in major data breach', *The Guardian*, 17 March. Available at: https://www.theguardian.com/news/2018/mar/17/cambridge-analytica-facebook-influence-us-election (accessed 23 June 2022).

Chowdhury, R. (2022) 'America's high-tech surveillance could track abortion-seekers, too, activists warn', *Time*, 6 June. Available at: https://time.com/6184111/abortion-surveillance-tech-tracking/ (accessed 25 June 2022).

Clarke, A., Parsell, C. and Lata, L. N. (2021) 'Surveilling the marginalised: How manual, embodied and territorialised surveillance persists in the age of "dataveillance"', *The Sociological Review*, 69 (2): 396–413.

Clifford, C. (2019) 'Aerospace engineer: Space is like the "Wild West," with trillions of dollars to be made from surveillance and communications', *CNBC*, 14 May. Available at: https://www.cnbc.com/2019/05/14/trillions-to-be-made-on-surveillance-communication-from-space.html (accessed 23 June 2022).

Cormack, D. and Kukutai, T. (2022) 'Indigenous peoples, data, and the coloniality of surveillance', in A. Hepp, J. Jarke and L. Kramp (eds) *New Perspectives in Critical Data Studies*. Cham: Palgrave Macmillan. pp.121–141.

Crist, R. (2022) Starlink Explained: Everything to Know About Elon Musk's Satellite Internet Venture. Available at: https://www.cnet.com/home/internet/starlink-satellite-internet-explained/ (accessed 28th June).

Dencik, L. (2019) 'Situating practices in datafication – from above and below', in H. C. Stephansen and E. Treré, *Citizen Media and Practice*. London: Routledge. pp. 243–255.

Dencik, L. and Cable, J. (2017) 'The advent of surveillance realism: Public opinion and activist responses to the Snowden leaks', *International Journal of Communication*, 11: 763–781.

Deleuze, G. (1992) 'What is a dispositif. Michel Foucault', *Philosopher*, 159–168.

Ed Glossary (2015) 'Aggregate data'. Available at: https://www.edglossary.org/aggregate-data/ (accessed 27 June 2022).

Faubion, J. D. (2002) *The Essential Works of Foucault 1954–1984: Power*. UK:Penguin

Fischer, D. (2019) 'Relational leadership and regional development: A case study on new agriculture ventures in Uganda', *Journal of Developmental Entrepreneurship*, 24 (02): 1950010.

Foucault, M. (2002) *Power: essential works of Foucault 1954–1984*, Vol. 3 (Ed. J.D. Faubion). London: Penguin Books.

Foucault, M. (2006) *Psychiatric Power: Lectures at the College de France, 1973–1974*. New York: Palgrave Macmillan.

Galič, M., Timan, T. and Koops, B.-J. (2017) 'Bentham, Deleuze and beyond: An overview of surveillance theories from the panopticon to participation', *Philosophy and Technology*, 30 (1): 9–37.

Garrett, P. M. (2021) 'Surveillance capitalism, COVID-19 and social work': A note on uncertain future(s)', *The British Journal of Social Work*, 52 (3): 1747–1764.

Given, L. M. (2008) *The SAGE Encyclopedia of Qualitative Research Methods*. Thousand Oaks, CA: SAGE.

Greenwald, G., (2013). NSA collecting phone records of millions of Verizon customers daily. *The Guardian*, 6(06), p.2013.

Hinds, J., Williams, E. J. and Joinson, A. N. (2020) '"It wouldn't happen to me": Privacy concerns and perspectives following the Cambridge Analytica scandal'. *International Journal of Human-Computer Studies*, 143: 102498.

Jian, G. (2022) 'From empathic leader to empathic leadership practice: An extension to relational leadership theory', *Human Relations*, 75 (5): 931–955.

Jimenez-Luque, A. (2021) 'Decolonial leadership for cultural resistance and social change: Challenging the social order through the struggle of identity', *Leadership*, 17 (2): 154–172.

Keen, S. (2007) *Empathy and the Novel*. Oxford University Press on Demand.

Kinder, T., Stenvall, J., Six F. and Memon, A. (2021) 'Relational leadership in collaborative governance ecosystems', *Public Management Review*, 23 (11): 1612–1639.

Lomborg, S., Dencik, L. and Moe, H. (2020) 'Methods for datafication, datafication of methods: Introduction to the Special Issue', *European Journal of Communication*, 35 (3): 203–212.

Lohr, S. (2012) 'The age of big data', *The New York Times*, 11 February.

Madsen, O. J. (2014) 'Governmentality', in T. Teo (ed.) *Encyclopedia of Critical Psychology*. New York, NY: Springer. pp. 814–816.

Mayer-Schonberger, V. and Cukier, K. (2013a) *Big Data: The Essential Guide to Work, Life and Learning in the Age of Insight*. Oxfordshire: Hachette UK.

Mayer-Schoenberger, V. and Cukier, K. (2013b) *Big Data. A Revolution that will transform how we live, work, and think.* London: John Murray Publishers.

Mayer-Schönberger, V. and Cukier, K. (2013) *Big Data: A Revolution that will Transform How We Live, Work, and Think.* Boston, MA: Houghton Mifflin Harcourt.

Mignolo, W. (2011) *The Darker Side of Western Modernity. Global Futures, Decolonial Options.* Durham, NC: Duke University Press

Mishra, P. and Suresh, Y. (2021) 'Datafied body projects in India: Femtech and the rise of reproductive surveillance in the digital era', *Asian Journal of Women's Studies*, 27 (4): 597–606.

Oksala, J. (2013) 'Neoliberalism and biopolitical governmentality', in S.-O. Wallenstein and J. Nilsson (eds), *Foucault, Biopolitics and Governmentality*. Sweden: Södertörns Högskola. pp. 53–72.

Owens, K. and Walker, A. (2020) 'Those designing healthcare algorithms must become actively anti-racist', *Nature Medicine*, 26 (9): 1327–1328.

Oxford English Dictionary (n.d.) 'surveillance, n', *OED Online*, Oxford University Press. Available at: www.oed.com/view/Entry/195083 (accessed 27 June 2022).

Prakasam, N. and Huxtable-Thomas, L. (2021) 'Reddit: Affordances as an enabler for shifting loyalties', *Information Systems Frontiers*, 23 (3): 723–751.

Quijano, A. (2007) 'Coloniality and modernity/rationality', *Cultural Studies*, 21 (2–3): 168–178.

Reid, A. (2013) 'Angus Reid Global Poll'. *HuffPost*, October 30. Available at https://angusreid.org/more-canadians-britons-view-edward-snowden-as-hero-than-traitor-americans-split/ (Accessed June 12, 2022.)

Rose, N. (1996) 'Governing "advanced" liberal democracies', in A. Sharma and A. Gupta (eds) *The Anthropology of the State: A Reader*. pp. 144–162.

Rose, N. (1999) *Governing the Soul: The Shaping of the Private Self* (2nd edn). London: Free Association Books

Rushe, D. and Milmo, D. (2022) 'Zuckerberg sued by DC Attorney General over Cambridge Analytica data scandal', *The Guardian*, 23 May. Available at: https://www.theguardian.com/technology/2022/may/23/mark-zuckerberg-sued-dc-attorney-general-cambridge-analytica-data-scandal (accessed 22 June 2022).

Smit, B. (2014) 'An ethnographic narrative of relational leadership', *Journal of Sociology and Social Anthropology*, 5 (2): 117–123.

Sparkes, M. (2022) 'How can we prevent AI from being racist, sexist and offensive?'. *New Scientist*, 254 (3392): 14.

Statista (2022) 'Meta (formerly Facebook Inc.) revenue and net income from 2007 to 2021', *Statista*. Available at: https://www.statista.com/statistics/277229/facebooks-annual-revenue-and-netincome/#:~:text=This%20strategic%20rebranding%20came%20as,over%20114%20billion%20U.S.%20dollars (accessed 27 June 2022).

Stavig, L. I. (2022) 'Unwittingly agreed: Fujimori, neoliberal governmentality, and the inclusive exclusion of Indigenous women', *Latin American and Caribbean Ethnic Studies*, 17 (1): 34–57.

Taipale, J. (2015) 'Empathy and the melodic unity of the other', *Human Studies*, 38 (4): 463–479.

Taiuru, K. (2022) Maori Data Sovereignty, Available at: https://www.taiuru.maori. nz/compendium-of-maori-data-sovereignty/#DEFINITIONS_OF_MAORI_DATA_ SOVERIGNTY (accessed 28 June 2022).

Te Uepū Hāpai i te Ora—Safe and Effective Justice Advisory Group. (2019). Turuki! Turuki! Move together: Transforming our Criminal Justice System. https://www. safeandeffectivejustice.govt.nz/assets/Uploads/28ce04fd87/ Turuki-Turuki-Report-Interactive.pdf

Toki, V. (2017) 'Maori seeking self-determination or Tino Rangatiratanga? A note', *Journal of Maori and Indigenous Issues*, 5: 134–144.

Van Dijck, J. (2014) 'Datafication, dataism and dataveillance: Big Data between scientific paradigm and ideology', *Surveillance and Society*, 12 (2): 197–208.

Walter, R., Buckley, H., Jacomb, C. and Matisoo-Smith, E. (2017) 'Mass migration and the Polynesian settlement of New Zealand', *Journal of World Prehistory*, 30 (4): 351–376.

Warner, R. and Sloan, R. H. (2014) 'Self, privacy, and power: Is it all over', *Tulane Journal of Technology and Intellectual Property*, 17: 61.

White, E. and Olcott, E. (2022) 'Elon Musk's Starlink aid to Ukraine triggers scrutiny in China over US military links', *Financial Times*, 30 June. Available at: https://www. ft.com/content/df032357-51e7-4635-baaa-f053dcc0c4c1#comments-anchor (accessed 27 September 2022).

Winfrey, T. (2022) 'China concerned about SpaceX Starlink's security threat, urged To monitor Elon Musk's satellite internet', *The Science Times*, 26 May. Available at: https:// www.sciencetimes.com/articles/37874/20220526/china-s-hypersonic-missiles-eyes-destroying-elon-musks-spacex-satellites.htm (accessed 27 June 2022).

Zuboff, S. (2015) 'Big other: surveillance capitalism and the prospects of an information civilization', *Journal of Information Technology*, 30 (1): 75–89.

Zuboff, S. (2019) *The Age of Surveillance Capitalism: The Fight for a Human Future at the New Frontier of Power*. London: Profile books.

Chapter 11

Acker, J. (1990) 'Hierarchies, jobs, bodies: A theory of gendered organizations', *Gender and Society*, 4 (2):139–158.

Acker, J. (1998) The future of 'gender and organizations': connections and boundaries. *Gender, Work & Organization*, 5(4):195–206.

Acker, J. (2006) 'Inequality regimes: Gender, class, and race in organizations', *Gender and Society*, 20 (4): 441–464.

Amis, J.M., Mair, J. and Munir, K.A. (2020) The organizational reproduction of inequality. *Academy of Management Annals* 14(1): 195–230.

Anonymous (2021) A Letter to the Male "Good Apples" about How You May Be Viewed by Your Female Colleagues. *Journal of Management Inquiry* 30(1): 98–101.

Arendt, H. (1958) *The Human Condition*. University of Chicago press.

Barnes, B. R. (2021) 'Reimagining African women youth climate activism: The case of Vanessa Nakate', *Sustainability*, 13 (23): 13214.

Bartol, K. M., Evans, C. L. and Stith, M. T. (1978) 'Black versus white leaders: A comparative review of the literature', *Academy of Management Review*, 3 (2): 293–304.

Bernal DD (2002) Critical race theory, Latino critical theory, and critical raced-gendered epistemologies: Recognizing students of color as holders and creators of knowledge. *Qualitative inquiry* 8(1): 105–126.

Bertrand, M., Black, S., Jensen, S. and Lleras-Muney, A. (2019) 'Breaking the glass ceiling? The effect of board quotas on female labour market outcomes in Norway', *The Review of Economic Studies*, 86 (1): 191–239.

Bhambra, G. K. (2014) 'Postcolonial and decolonial dialogues', *Postcolonial Studies*, 17 (2): 115–121.

Brescoll, V. L. (2016) 'Leading with their hearts? How gender stereotypes of emotion lead to biased evaluations of female leaders', *The Leadership Quarterly*, 27 (3): 415–428.

Burrell, G. (1992) 'The organization of pleasure', *Critical Management Studies*, 66–89.

Calás, M. B. and Smircich, L. (1992) 'Re-writing gender into organizational theorizing: Directions from feminist perspectives', in M. Reed and M. Hughes (eds.) *Rethinking Organization: New Directions in Organization Theory and Analysis*. London: SAGE.

Collins, P. H. (1990) 'Black feminist thought in the matrix of domination', in P. H. Collins, *Black Feminist Thought: Knowledge, Consciousness, and the Politics of Empowerment*. Boston: Unwin Hyman. pp. 221–238.

Combahee River Collective (1977/1995) 'A Black Feminist Statement', *Words of Fire: An Anthology of AfricanAmerican Feminist Thought*, ed. B Guy-Sheftall, pp. 232–40. New York: The New Press.

Crenshaw, K. (1991) 'Race, gender, and sexual harassment', *Southern California Law Review*, 65: 1467.

Czarniawska, B. and Sevón, G. (2008) 'The thin end of the wedge: Foreign women professors as double strangers in academia', *Gender, Work and Organization*, 15 (3): 235–287.

Davis A. (1981) *Women Race and Class*, New York: Random House

Evelyn, K. (2020) '"Like I wasn't there": Climate activist Vanessa Nakate on being erased from a movement,' *The Guardian*, 29 Jan. Available at: https://www.theguardian.com/

world/2020/jan/29/vanessa-nakate-interview-climate-activism-cropped-photo-davos (accessed 20 February 2022).

Fernando, M., Reveley, J. and Learmonth, M. (2020) 'Identity work by a non-white immigrant business scholar: Autoethnographic vignettes of covering and accenting', *Human Relations*, 73 (6): 765–788.

Ford, J. (2005) 'Examining leadership through critical feminist readings', *Journal of Health Organization and Management*, 19 (3): 236–251.

Fotaki, M., Metcalfe, B. D. and Harding, N. (2014) 'Writing materiality into management and organization studies through and with Luce Irigaray', *Human Relations*, 67 (10): 1239–1263.

Fournier, V. and Kelemen, M. (2001) 'The crafting of community: Recoupling discourses of management and womanhood', *Gender, Work and Organization*, 8 (3): 267–290.

Gallagher, S. (2012) 'What is phenomenology?', *Phenomenology*: 7–18. London: Palgrave Macmillan.

Gardiner, R. A. (2018) 'Hannah and her sisters: Theorizing gender and leadership through the lens of feminist phenomenology', *Leadership*, 14 (3): 291–306.

Gause, S. A. (2021) 'White privilege, Black resilience: Women of color leading the academy', *Leadership*, 17 (1): 74–80.

Goffman E (1963) *Stigma: Notes on the Management of Spoiled Identity: Englewood Cliffs*, NJ: Prentice-Hall.

Harding, N. (2003) 'On the manager's body as an aesthetics of control', in A. Carr and P. Hancock (eds) *Art and Aesthetics at Work*. Basingstoke: Palgrave Macmillan. pp. 115–132.

Heidegger, M. (1962). *Being and time*. Oxford, UK: Blackwell Publishers.

hooks, B. (1989) *Talking Back: Thinking Feminist, Thinking Black*. Boston, MA: South End Press.

Hwang, S. and Beauregard, T. A. (2022) 'Contextualising intersectionality: A qualitative study of East Asian female migrant workers in the UK', *Human Relations*, 75 (4): 609–634.

Irigaray, L. (1985). The power of discourse and the subordination of the feminine. In C. Porter & C. Burke (Eds.), *This sex which is not one* (pp. 795–798). New York, NY: Cornell University Press.

Jean-Marie, G., Williams, V. A. and Sherman, S. L. (2009) 'Black women's leadership experiences: Examining the intersectionality of race and gender', *Advances in Developing Human Resources*, 11 (5): 562–581.

Jimenez-Luque, A. (2021) 'Decolonial leadership for cultural resistance and social change: Challenging the social order through the struggle of identity', *Leadership*, 17 (2): 154–172.

Johansson, M. and Śliwa, M. (2014) 'Gender, foreignness and academia: An intersectional analysis of the experiences of foreign women academics in UK business schools', *Gender, Work and Organization*, 21 (1): 18–36.

Ladkin D (2013) From perception to flesh: A phenomenological account of the felt experience of leadership. *Leadership* 9(3): 320–334.

Ladkin, D. (2021) 'Problematizing authentic leadership: How the experience of minoritized people highlights the impossibility of leading from one's "true self"', *Leadership*, 17 (4): 395–400.

Liebig, T. (2021) 'Diversity policies must avoid benefiting the already privileged', *Financial Times*, 17 November. Available at: https://www.ft.com/content/5846ca73-2b77-46c3-becd-f10965fc607e (accessed 7 February 2022).

Liu, H. (2018) 'Re-radicalising intersectionality in organisation studies', *Ephemera: Theory and Politics in Organization*, 18 (1): 81–101.

Liu, H. and Baker, C. (2016) 'White knights: Leadership as the heroicisation of whiteness', *Leadership*, 12 (4): 420–448.

Liu, H., Cutcher, L. and Grant, D. (2015) 'Doing authenticity: The gendered construction of authentic leadership', *Gender, Work and Organization* 22 (3): 237–255.

Lord, R. G. and Brown, D. J. (2003) *Leadership Processes and Follower Self-identity*. London: Psychology Press.

Ludden, D. (ed.) (2002) *Reading Subaltern Studies: Critical History, Contested Meaning and the Globalization of South Asia*. London: Anthem Press.

Ma, L. and Tsui, A. S. (2015) 'Traditional Chinese philosophies and contemporary leadership', *The Leadership Quarterly*, 26 (1): 13–24.

Merleau-Ponty M (1962) *Phenomenology of perception*. London.

Morris JE (2001) Forgotten voices of Black educators: Critical race perspectives on the implementation of a desegregation plan. *Educational Policy* 15(4): 575-600.

Netto G, Noon M, Hudson M, et al. (2020) Intersectionality, identity work and migrant progression from low-paid work: *A critical realist approach. Gender, Work & Organization* 27(6): 1020–1039.

OECD (2020) *All Hands In? Making Diversity Work for All*. Paris: OECD Publishing. Available at: https://doi.org/10.1787/efb14583-en (accessed 27 September 2022).

Ospina, S. and Foldy, E. (2009) 'A critical review of race and ethnicity in the leadership literature: Surfacing context, power and the collective dimensions of leadership', *The Leadership Quarterly*, 20 (6): 876–896.

Pitts, D. W. (2005) 'Diversity, representation, and performance: Evidence about race and ethnicity in public organizations', *Journal of Public Administration Research and Theory*, 15 (4): 615–631.

Rafaely, D. and Barnes, B. (2020) 'African climate activism, media and the denial of racism: The tacit silencing of Vanessa Nakate', *Community Psychology in Global Perspective*, 6 (2/2): 71–86.

Raman, K. R. (2020) 'Can the Dalit woman speak? How "intersectionality" helps advance postcolonial organization studies', *Organization*, 27 (2): 272–290.

Ray, V. (2019) 'A theory of racialized organizations', *American Sociological Review*, 84 (1): 26–53.

Rodriguez, J. K., Holvino, E., Fletcher, J. K. and Nkomo, S. M. (2016) 'The theory and praxis of intersectionality in work and organisations: Where do we go from here?', *Gender, Work and Organization*, 23 (3): 201–222.

Rosette, AS *et al*. (2016) 'Race matters for women leaders: Intersectional effects on agentic deficiencies and penalties', *The Leadership Quarterly*, 27(3): 429–445.

Rosette, AS, Leonardelli, GJ and Phillips, KW (2008) 'The White standard: racial bias in leader categorization', *Journal of applied psychology*, 93(4):758.

Rosette AS, Koval CZ, Ma A, Livingston R (2016) Race matters for women leaders: Intersectional effects on agentic deficiencies and penalties. *The Leadership Quarterly*, 27(3):429–45.

Thomson JJ (2013) Preferential hiring. *The affirmative action debate*. Routledge, pp.51–66.

Ubaka, A., Lu, X. and Gutierrez, L. (2022) 'Testing the generalizability of the white leadership standard in the post-Obama era', *The Leadership Quarterly*: 101591.

Zheng, W., Kark, R. and Meister, A. L. (2018) 'Paradox versus dilemma mindset: A theory of how women leaders navigate the tensions between agency and communion', *The Leadership Quarterly*, 29 (5): 584–596.

Zweigenhaft, R. (2021) 'Diversity among Fortune 500 CEOs from 2000 to 2020: White women, hi-tech south asians, and economically privileged multilingual immigrants from around the world'. Available at: https://whorulesamerica.ucsc.edu/power/diversity_update_2020.html#:~:text=Moreover%2C%20since%20most%20of%20the,%2C%20and%203.4%25%20are%20Latinx (accessed, 20 February 2022).

Chapter 12

Franta, B. (2021) 'What Big Oil knew about climate change, in its own words', *The Conversation*, 28 October. Available at: https://theconversation.com/what-big-oil-knew-about-climate-change-in-its-own-words-170642 (accessed 2 July 2022).

Liu, H. (2021) *Redeeming Leadership: An Anti-Racist Feminist Intervention*. Bristol: Bristol University Press.

Smircich, L. and Morgan, G. (1982) 'Leadership: The management of meaning', *Journal of Applied Behavioural Science*, 18 (3): 257–273.

INDEX

Page numbers in italics refer to figures and tables.